CANADIAN SPORT SOCIOLOGY

Edited by
Jane Crossman
Lakehead University

THOMSON NELSON

Australia Canada Mexico Singapore Spain United Kingdom United States

THOMSON
NELSON

Canadian Sport Sociology

Edited by Jane Crossman

Editorial Director and Publisher:
Evelyn Veitch

Executive Editor:
Joanna Cotton

Acquisitions Editor:
Brad Lambertus

Marketing Manager:
Lenore Taylor

Developmental Editor:
Glen Herbert

Production Editor:
Wendy Yano

Production Coordinator:
Ferial Suleman

Copy Editor/Proofreader:
Wendy Thomas

Creative Director:
Angela Cluer

Interior Design:
Aaron Benson

Cover Design:
Angela Cluer

Cover Image:
Anne Bradley

Compositor:
Carol J. Anderson

Indexer:
Noeline Bridge

Printer:
Transcontinental

Printed and bound in Canada
2 3 4 06 05 04 03

For more information contact Nelson, 1120 Birchmount Road, Scarborough, Ontario, M1K 5G4. Or you can visit our Internet site at http://www.nelson.com

National Library of Canada Cataloguing in Publication Data

Canadian sport sociology/
Jane Crossman, editor.

Includes bibliographical reference and index.
ISBN 0-7747-3780-8

1. Sports—Social aspects—Canada. 2. Sports—Canada—Sociological aspects. I. Crossman, Jane

GV706.5.C35 2003 306.4'83'0971
C2002-905067-7

To the memory of my father,
Edward L. Crossman,
an ardent Toronto Blue Jays fan

Table of Contents

Preface

For about 20 years I have been teaching undergraduate courses in the sociology of sport, and for that time I have been using textbooks written by American authors largely for an American audience. This was due to the unavailability of a Canadian-based textbook that met my needs and, more importantly, the needs of my students. As a result, every year I have had to augment the readings with handouts and examples applicable to the Canadian experience. One day, after having made another round of apologies for including in my lecture a fair amount of American content in what was supposed to be a Canadian-based course, I decided to approach some publishers with a proposal to edit a sport sociology textbook written expressly for Canadian undergraduate students. As far as I could tell, all the ingredients were in place to produce a comprehensive textbook suitable for undergraduate sport sociology courses: the need for it; the experts willing to contribute; an editor willing to coordinate the project; and a willingness on the part of Nelson Publishing to go forward with this project. Hence, *Canadian Sport Sociology* came into being. Worthy of note was the fact that *all* the publishers I approached gave the green light to the project, verifying my belief that, indeed, a substantial market existed for this text.

This book presents the work of various authors to help the reader understand sport sociology from a Canadian perspective. I feel confident in stating that the material presented in this book is the most current available. Because the chapter sequence has been purposely coordinated, I recommend that the 13 chapters be read consecutively. However, since their content is so distinctive, it is possible to read the chapters in an altered order.

In Chapter 1, I provide a foundation for understanding the study of sport sociology from a Canadian perspective. Following the definition and differentiation of terms relevant to the study of sport sociology, various sociological theories are presented. The focus of this first chapter is how persons are socialized into, via, and out of sport. The topics of social stratification and mobility are treated in this chapter as well.

In Chapter 2, Dr. Ron Lappage does a masterful job of condensing hundreds of years of Canadian sport history into one chapter. Highlighted are the people who influenced sport history as well as the existing social conditions and developments that have had such a profound effect on shaping the development of sport in Canada.

Dr. Ralph Wheeler, in Chapter 3, outlines the current sport system in Canada for children and youth, including school, community, and private agencies.Potential reasons for the high rate of sport dropout are outlined. From a balanced perspective, Dr. Wheeler presents some of the problems associated with sport for children and youth and offers solutions to remedy these problems.

In Chapter 4, Dr. Patricia Miller considers the relationship between sport and educational institutions in Canada from public school through to university. She describes the existing situation in each of the systems and brings to the fore the difficulties inherent in each. The situation, Dr. Miller points out, is not a particularly encouraging one.

The fact that sport is replete with deviant behaviour is expounded by Dr. Robert Stebbins in Chapter 5. He discusses the varied examples of tolerable and intolerable deviance that exist today in sport. Athlete deviance both inside and outside of sport in the form of cheating, the use of performance-enhancing drugs, and eating disorders is reviewed. In addition, the deviant behaviour of fans (hooliganism) and gambling are discussed.

In the next chapter, Dr. Kevin Wamsley deals with another form of deviance in sport: violence and aggression. He describes the theories of aggression and provides a brief historical overview of how violence and aggression have grown in our society. The celebration of violence and intimidation in sport and who endorses them is explained. The impact of all of this on youth sport is brought to the fore in this chapter. Finally, theories of the cause of spectator violence are offered and examples provided.

Gender issues is a topic integral to any comprehensive treatment of social issues pertaining to sport sociology. In Chapter 7, Dr. Helen Jefferson Lenskyj helps us understand the current issues relevant to gender and sport. The differences between sexes with regard to sport-related attitudes are outlined. The author explains that simply "opening the door" to more opportunities won't necessarily solve the problems of marginalization and exclusion. Harassment, violence against women, and sexual abuse are also discussed in this chapter.

Seguing from the theme of gender discrimination in sport, Drs. Vicky Paraschak and Susan Tirone, in Chapter 8, explore discrimination in Canadian sport through race and ethnicity. They point out that sport provides opportunities to feel pride in one's own cultural heritage; unfortunately, the system is structured so that some individuals, i.e., those of white, European heritage, feel more pride than others. When this happens, state the authors, those who are discriminated against often form leagues of their own. The sport and leisure preferences of minority ethnic people are described as well as the distinctions between the theories of marginality and ethnicity. How new Canadians pursue sport and leisure is discussed with specific reference to two studies that examine the meaning of sport and leisure for South Asian women and teenagers. The need to create equal opportunities in sport for all Canadian people is a fundamental message in this chapter.

Chapter 9, "The Economics of Sport," written by Drs. Marc Lavoie and David Whitson examines the evolution in the 1990s of the four major professional sports in North America with regard to salary, revenues, profits, and performance disparities. The paradoxical relationship between club profits and team capital values is discussed, along with remedies to alleviate imbalances and salary inflation. Drawing upon specific examples, the authors describe the difficulties for Canadian-based professional teams when compared with U.S.-based teams playing in primarily large-market areas.

The triangular relationship that exists between sport, sponsors, and television is explained in Chapter 10 by Dr. Scott Martyn. He also describes the evolution and current popularity of televised sport as well as changes to sport that have occurred as a result of the advent of television. Highlighted in this chapter is a case study of the recent media sport scandal involving irregularities in the bidding for the Salt Lake City Winter Olympics. Finally, Dr. Martyn sheds light on the multitude of viewing options that are and will be available to sport enthusiasts.

In Chapter 11, Dr. Hart Cantelon tackles the theoretical relationship that exists between politics and sport by answering a series of questions, including What is the state? What role does the government play with regard to the social welfare of its citizens? What role does public policy play in the creation of a state policy on sport? How is a national sport policy implemented and what are the positive and negative consequences of doing so? The advantages and consequences of the state presence in sport is also discussed.

In the penultimate chapter, Dr. Christopher Stevenson discusses the relationships that exist between sport and religion — more specifically, sport and Christianity. He first questions the modern claim that sport is religion by outlining the similarities and differences between the two. He then provides a history of the development of the connection between the two from the late fourth century through to today's "Muscular Christianity." Contemporary topics such as superstition and sport, the dilemma that exists for professing Christians involved in competitive sport, and evangelical Christianity's use of sport are discussed.

In the final chapter, Dr. Dwight Zakus discusses current trends in Canadian sport and also what the future may hold. First, models of change are presented. Then, in order to be able to make predictions, he outlines the current trends with regard to population growth and aging, immigration, urbanization, and sport demographics. Future directions for sport through culture, government involvement, and new technologies and in a global context are discussed in-depth.

The completion of this text would not have been possible if it had not been for the efforts of the above-mentioned contributors. Their willingness to share their expertise via the written word is very much appreciated. To them I owe a great deal of gratitude.

On behalf of all the contributors, I hope you enjoy reading this book and, moreover, that it provides you with a sound basis for understanding sport sociology from a uniquely Canadian perspective.

Jane Crossman
September 2002

List of Contributors

Hart Cantelon has recently retired from the School of Physical and Health Education at Queen's University, during which time he was cross-appointed to the Department of Sociology. He has also held Visiting Professor positions at the University of Alberta and Carnegie College of Physical Education. Professor Cantelon received B.A. (1967), B.P.E. (1969), and M.A. (1972) degrees from the University of Alberta and his Ph.D. (1981) from the University of Birmingham, England. His research has addressed questions of power and how power differentials affect sport and leisure activity. He maintained a parallel interest in ideological aspects of power and how the ideology of rationalized sport affected minor sports and notions of sport work among young people. Most recently, his research has expanded these notions of ideological power to better understand sport in a globalizing market economy. Dr. Cantelon is joint editor of *Sport, Culture and the Modern State* (with Richard Gruneau, University of Toronto, 1982); *Leisure, Sports and Working Class Cultures* (with Robert Hollands, Garamond, 1988); and *Not Just a Game* (with Jean Harvey, University of Ottawa, 1987). The latter was simultaneously published in French under the title *Sport et pouvoir: Les enjeux sociaux au Canada*. He is currently the book review editor for the *Sociology of Sport Journal*.

Jane Crossman is a Professor of Kinesiology at Lakehead University in Thunder Bay, Ontario, where she teaches the sociology of sport, mental training, and research methods. She received a B.Sc. from the University of Ottawa (1975), an M.Sc. from Lakehead University (1977), and a Ph.D. from Ohio State University (1979). Her primary research interest is psychosocial dimensions of sports injuries, and in 2001, she edited a book entitled *Coping with Sports Injuries: Psychological Strategies for Rehabilitation* and contributed a chapter to *The Sport Scientist's Research Adventures*. Dr. Crossman is an Associate Editor of *The Journal of Sport Behavior* and frequently reviews texts and other academic publications. She has helped numerous elite athletes with their mental preparation and is a member of the North American Society for Sport Sociology, a Fellow of the Association for the Advancement of Applied Sport Psychology, and a member of the Canadian Mental Training Registry. During sabbatical leaves, she has been a Visiting Professor at the Universities of Exeter and Brighton (U.K.) and the University of Otago (New Zealand).

Ron Lappage is an Associate Professor in the School of Kinesiology at Lakehead University in Thunder Bay, Ontario, where he teaches sport history. He received his B.P.E. (1967), M.A. (1969), and Ph. D. (1974) degrees from the University of Alberta in Edmonton. His primary research interests lie in Canadian sport history and, more specifically, in the history of sport in Northwestern Ontario. He has written a chapter on sport between the wars in *A Concise History of Sport in Canada* and has published and/or presented papers on topics such as the history of the Kenora Thistles, the physical feats of the voyageurs, and the lumberjack as a Canadian folk hero. Dr. Lappage is a member of the North American Society for Sport History and is former chair of Judo Canada's Coaching Certification Program. In 1987, he was inducted into the Northwestern Ontario Sports Hall of Fame for his achievements in the sports of judo and wrestling.

Marc Lavoie is a Professor in the Department of Economics at the University of Ottawa, where he started teaching about 20 years ago. He offers a course on the economics of sport and is a member of the Research Centre on Sport in Canadian Society. He has published two books on the economics of ice hockey—*Avantage numérique, l'argent dans la Ligue nationale de hockey* (1997) and *Désavantage numérique, les francophones dans la LNH* (1998)—and two graduate textbooks on post-Keynesian economics, the latest being *Foundations of Post-Keynesian Economic Analysis* (1992). He was also the co-editor of a book on the works of Milton Friedman (1993) and an Associate Editor of the *Encyclopedia of Political Economy* (1999). He has published over 100 articles in refereed journals and books, mostly on monetary economics and growth theory. Dr. Lavoie has been a Visiting Professor at the Universities of Bordeaux, Nice, Rennes, Dijon, and Grenoble, and Curtin University in Perth (Australia). Previously, he was a carded athlete and a member of the fencing squad of the Canadian Olympic Team in 1976 and 1984; he was seven times Canadian senior sabre champion between 1975 and 1986.

Helen Jefferson Lenskyj is a Professor in the Department of Sociology and Equity Studies in Education, Ontario Institute for Studies in Education, University of Toronto, and has a cross-appointment to the Faculty of Physical Education and Health. A sport sociologist, she has written six books, beginning with *Out of Bounds: Women, Sport and Sexuality* (Women's Press, 1986), as well as numerous scholarly and popular articles, on women in sport, sexual and homophobic harassment, and lesbian sport alternatives. More recently, she has developed critiques of the Olympic industry from a feminist, socialist, and anti-globalization perspective. Her first Olympic book was titled *Inside the Olympic Industry: Power, Politics and Activism* (SUNY Press, 2000) and her second was *The Best Olympics Ever? Social Impacts of Sydney 2000* (SUNY Press, 2002). Identifying as an Australian living in Canada, she conducted much of the research for the last book while she was a visiting scholar at the University of New South Wales Centre for Olympic Studies in 2000. She is a recreational athlete with a particular passion for swimming.

Scott Martyn is an Assistant Professor in the Faculty of Human Kinetics at the University of Windsor in Windsor, Ontario. A former Social Sciences and Humanities Research Council of Canada Doctoral Fellow, Dr. Martyn spends much of his time investigating the historical evolution of the Olympic Games and affiliated insignia as sport marketing properties. He concluded his Ph.D. studies at the University of Western Ontario in 2000 with the completion of his dissertation, *The Struggle for Financial Autonomy: The IOC and the Historical Emergence of Corporate Sponsorship, 1896–2000*. He has served on the executive councils of the International Centre for Olympic Studies, the North American Society for Sport History, and the International Society for Comparative Physical Education and Sport. He has recently co-authored a book, *Selling the Five Rings: The IOC and the Rise of Olympic Commercialism*, and is the managing editor of *Olympika: The International Journal of Olympic Studies*.

Patricia Miller is an Assistant Professor in the Movement Studies and Exercise Science Department at East Stroudsburg University in East Stroudsburg, Pennsylvania, where she teaches psychological and sociological aspects of sport and physical activity. She received a B.A. in Psychology from McGill University in Montreal (1993), an M.A. in Human Kinetics from the University of Ottawa (1996), and a Ph.D. and post-doctorate in Exercise Science from the University of Toronto (2000). Her research interests focus on the psychosocial development of youth and young adults through participation in sport, particularly the identity formation of competitive athletes and the relationship between identity development, career planning, and life skills acquisition. Dr. Miller has written journal articles, as well as book chapters on coaching, athletic injury and coping, and initiations in sport; regularly presents at national conferences; and is an active member of the Association for the Advancement of Applied Sport Psychology. She also works as a sport psychology consultant with individual and team athletes at the developmental and elite levels.

Victoria Paraschak is an Associate Professor of Kinesiology at the University of Windsor in Windsor, Ontario, where she teaches sociology of sport, government and sport, social construction of leisure and outdoor recreation. She received a B.P.E. from McMaster University (1977), an M.H.K. from the University of Windsor (1978), and a Ph.D. from the University of Alberta (1983). The primary focus of her research is aboriginal peoples in sport and, more broadly, in physical cultural practices. An integral part of this work is her involvement in government sport and recreation policy in the Northwest Territories. In 1999, she took a year's leave to work with seven different Northwest Territories sport and recreation organizations to establish a direction for the new millennium. This was done through the creation of a joint vision, principles, priorities, and strategic plans for the sport and recreation system. Her work focuses on power relations, social construction, self-determination, and the creation, reproduction, and/or reshaping of cultural practices through the duality of structure.

Robert A. Stebbins is a Professor in the Department of Sociology at the University of Calgary. He received his Ph.D. (1964) from the University of Minnesota. He is the author of 27 books and monographs as well as numerous articles and chapters in several areas of social science; his most recent works include *Canadian Football: The View from the Helmet* (Canadian Scholars Press, 1993); *Tolerable Differences: Living with Deviance*, 2nd ed. (McGraw-Hill Ryerson, 1996); *New Directions in the Theory and Research of Serious Leisure* (Edwin Mellen, 2001); and *The Organizational Basis of Leisure Participation: A Motivational Exploration* (Venture Publications, 2002). He is currently writing a study of sport and leisure activities in the Canadian Rockies: hobbyists in kayaking, snowboarding, and mountain climbing. In 2003, he will begin to research the role of grassroots associations in the lives of their amateur, hobbyist, and volunteer members and participants. Dr. Stebbins was elected Fellow of the Academy of Leisure Sciences in 1996 and, in 1999, elected Fellow of the Royal Society of Canada.

Chris Stevenson is Professor and Dean of the Faculty of Kinesiology at the University of New Brunswick. His undergraduate degree in England was a double major in zoology and botany. Following that, he took a master's degree in exercise physiology at the University of British Columbia in Vancouver, and during that time he took a sociology course as an elective — and his eyes were opened! At Stanford University in California he did an M.A. in Sociology and got his Ph.D.; soon after he began teaching at the University of New Brunswick. His research interests have included examining the careers of athletes; the dilemmas of Christian athletes in attempting to reconcile the values of their faith with the expectations, demands, and values of elite competitive sport; and most recently, various aspects of masters swimming. Dr. Stevenson is the past editor of the *Sociology of Sport Journal*.

Susan Tirone is Associate Professor in the School of Health and Human Performance at Dalhousie University in Halifax, Nova Scotia. She completed a B.A. at the University of Waterloo, an M.A. at Dalhousie, and a Ph.D. at Waterloo; all three of her degrees are in the area of Leisure Studies. Dr. Tirone teaches students in both the leisure studies and health studies programs at Dalhousie and her research interests have taken her into the study of minority ethnic youth and youth who live in low-income families in Canada. She has completed several studies on immigrants from non-western countries and is currently involved in a longitudinal study of young Canadians who are the children of immigrants from India, Pakistan, and Bangladesh. Through her research she also explores how poverty affects the overall health and well-being of families and children in both urban and rural communities in Canada.

Kevin B. Wamsley is Associate Professor, School of Kinesiology, and director of the International Centre for Olympic Studies at the University of Western Ontario. He graduated in 1985 with an Honours B.A. and in 1987 with a Master's degree, both from the University of Western Ontario. In 1992, he received his Ph.D. from the University of Alberta. A sport historian, he has undertaken research in the organization of gender in the Olympic Games and in leisure and masculinity in 19th-century Canada. He has edited several books on the Olympic Games and one on historical methodology, and published numerous articles in international journals, including the British journal *Social History*. He has presented keynote addresses in Singapore, Salt Lake City, and Indianapolis and is an active member of the North American Society for Sport History.

Ralph Wheeler is an Associate Professor in the School of Human Kinetics and Recreation at Memorial University of Newfoundland. Dr. Wheeler, who completed his Ph.D. at the University of Alberta, has taught and coached athletes at many levels of sport from community soccer and basketball to national-level swimming for over 25 years. He continues to play a significant role in the development of many of the provincial coaches through his involvement with the National Coaching Certification Program. Dr. Wheeler teaches sport sociology and philosophy along with several curriculum and pedagogy courses for prospective physical education teachers at Memorial. He is currently developing a conceptual approach to teaching sport skills to children and is in the process of setting up a Web-based distance education course in sport sociology.

David Whitson is a Professor of Canadian Studies in the Department of Political Science, University of Alberta. He is co-author of four books, including three on politics and sport. He has also written many articles on aspects of sport and public policy, including the hosting of international games, the challenges of using "hallmark events" to create or enhance a tourism industry, and the aspirations of regional cities to re-image themselves as "world class" destinations. Some of his most recent publications in this area include "World Class Leisure and Consumption: Social Polarization and the Politics of Place" (in Caroline Andrew et al., eds., *World Class Cities: Can Canada Play?*, University of Ottawa Press, 1999); "World

Class Sport, Globalization, and Cultural Diversity," in *Australian-Canadian Studies*, 19(2), 1999; and "The Mills Report, the Manley Subsidy Proposals, and the Business of Major League Sport," in *Canadian Public Administration*, 43(2),2000.

Dwight Zakus is a Senior Lecturer in sport management in the School of Marketing and Management, Griffith University, Gold Coast, Australia. His undergraduate degree was in Physical Education at the University of British Columbia (1974). He taught for five years at the high school level in British Columbia. He completed a Master of Physical Education in Sport Management at UBC (1983) and then went on to complete a Doctorate in Sport Studies at the University of Alberta (1989). Following this he taught for seven years at the Universities of Regina and Saskatchewan, where a large portion of his teaching was in sociology, along with many courses in sport management and sport studies. In 1997 he began teaching at Griffith University. Dr. Zakus has also worked in the field as a sport manager at UBC and with the Alberta Rugby Union. He has also co-authored a book on sport ethics and several book chapters on golf management, sport futures, the Olympic movement, and professional sport organizations. These and general interests in sport sociology and history make up his main research areas of interests.

Acknowledgments

There is no possible way that this book could have come together without the support and expertise from the folks at Nelson. First, thanks go to Brad Lambertus, who ventured to Thunder Bay to meet with me to explain in person Nelson's publishing process. Thanks are also extended to Glen Herbert, who took the first draft and cut it down to a desired length with few complaints from those contributors whose hard work was relegated to the chopping block. As if passing a baton in a relay, Wendy Yano then took over as the production editor, helping us move toward a more polished product. Along the way, Vicki Gould and Johanna Reynolds helped the contributors, when needed, to find suitable pictures for each chapter and then to secure permission to use them. Many thanks are also extended to those who reviewed both the proposal and the first drafts, providing many useful ideas for improvement. Those scholars included Dr. Steve Jackson, University of Otago, New Zealand; Dr. Stephen Wenn, Wilfrid Laurier University; Dr. Richard Danielson, Laurentian University; Dr. Monika Schloder, University of Calgary, and Dr. Linda Henderson, University of Calgary.

A personal thanks to Dr. Ron Lappage and Trish McGowan, who willingly provided me with feedback on the Preface and my own chapter. Finally, special gratitude to Wendy Thomas, who did a masterful job of copyediting each chapter with precision and a cheery disposition. To each and every one of you, I extend my heartfelt appreciation.

JC
September 2002

1

Sport Sociology in the Canadian Context: An Introduction

Jane Crossman

KEVIN FRAYER/CP PICTURE ARCHIVE

The Toronto Blue Jays and the Kansas City Royals line up for the national anthems prior to their season opener at SkyDome in Toronto on Monday, April 3, 2000.

Sport is something more than a mirror of the societies in which it is played. It is not a carbon copy of their inequalities and problems. It is a world in its own right, with its own life and its own contradictions.

Jean Harvey, "What's in a Game?" p. 19

The study of sport and its meaning in Canadian society today is a complex, controversial, critical, and oftentimes disturbing pursuit. It is also fascinating—so much so that it can foster stimulating discussion on a diverse range of topics. For better or worse, sport is ubiquitous. We read about sport in newspapers; we watch sport in its varied forms on television; we hear sport reports hourly on the radio; we click to Web sites devoted to sport and sport heroes. Next to the weather, Canadians frequently use sports as a familiar and comforting "social lubricant." We discuss how our favourite National Hockey League (NHL) team is doing, curling foursome is playing, or how the local soccer league is progressing. Like it or not, sport is an integral component of the fabric of Canadian society.

DEFINITION OF SPORT SOCIOLOGY

Sport sociology uses the study of social processes and structures to focus on the sport domain. In other words, it is the study of how humans interact with social structures that are broad in scope and diverse in nature. Sport sociologists study persons involved in sport to learn more about human behaviour so that the sport experience can be improved. They use the sociological perspective to study a vast array of issues and controversies. They also attempt to understand the relationship between sport and various social systems—such as economics, mass media, religion, education, and politics—and the processes that occur in conjunction with sport, including social stratification and mobility, deviance, violence, and inequality.

The academic study of sport sociology is relatively new. Scientific research didn't exist prior to 1960. From 1965 to 1969, Gerald Kenyon of the University of Wisconsin published a series of articles devoted to the sociology of sport, positioning it "firmly within the positivistic perspective of science" (Sage, 1997, p. 326). In the late 1960s the annual meetings of the American Alliance for Health, Physical Education and Recreation (Dance was added in 1979) included a session devoted to the sociology of sport. In 1976, this same association founded the Sociology of Sport Academy with the purpose of coordinating and promoting the study of sport sociology (Sage, 1997).

A sociology of sport society (which later became the North American Society for Sport Sociology [NASSS]) came into being after a Big Ten Symposium in 1978, thanks largely to the rallying cry of Andrew Yiannakis. The first newsletter, known as *The NASSS Newsletter*, was published in that same year; in 1980 in Denver, Colorado, the first NASSS conference took place. Canada has hosted this annual conference five times (Toronto, 1982; Edmonton, 1987; Ottawa, 1993; Toronto, 1997; Montreal, 2003). (See Web links at the end of this chapter for the NASSS Web site.)

DEFINITION OF SPORT

Every person has his or her own idea of what constitutes a sport. For some, windsurfing and ultimate Frisbee are bona fide sports; for others, these are recreational pursuits. Often laypersons interchange the use of the words *play*, *games*, and *sport* as if they were the same. Social scientists have determined that they are not and for this reason, it is important to draw clear distinctions.

Play is a self-initiated, free activity with no fixed start or stop times. If there are rules, they are made up as play progresses. Play has no tangible outcomes such as prizes or ribbons, and victory and reward are not a feature in this form of activity. Five characteristics differentiate play from games and sport (Caillois, 1961). It is free; there are no limitations to space and time; the outcome cannot be determined; the purpose of the activity is intrinsic in nature; and it may contain the element of make-believe. An example of play occurs when neighbourhood children get together spontaneously after dinner to play a game of tag.

Games involve activities with agreed-upon time, space, and terrain. Rules are introduced at this level, as well as winning. Participants may be involved for both intrinsic reasons (e.g., the feel-good factor) and extrinsic reasons (e.g., prestige, recognition, and status). Playing a game of squash with a roommate is an example of a game.

A critical factor that differentiates sport from games and play is that *sport* becomes organized at some level. Coakley (2001, p. 20) initially defined sport as "institutionalized competitive activities that involve rigorous physical exertion or the use of relatively complex physical skills by participants motivated by personal enjoyment and external rewards." An examination of the components of this definition is worthwhile.

1. *Competitive activity is institutionalized.* For an activity to be institutionalized, Coakley deems that the following four criteria must be in place: (i) rules of the activity must become standardized; (ii) a regulatory body is in place to oversee rule enforcement; (iii) the organizational and technical aspects become important, including equipment and training protocol; and (iv) the learning of the game and the skills therein becomes formalized, for example, in structured coaching situations.

2. *Rigorous physical exertion or the use of relatively complex physical skills is involved.* Many people equate sport with physical exertion. But according to Coakley's widely accepted definition (above), this does not necessarily have to be the case as long as there are complex skills involved. Throwing a curling rock would not be considered a rigorous activity for most people, but it does involve fine motor coordination.

3. *Participants are motivated by personal enjoyment and external rewards.* Personal enjoyment may wane as the level of participation increases and external rewards may become increasingly important. The late Willie Stargell once dubbed the term "work ball" instead of "play ball," reflecting his perception that the game had become more a means to earn a living than a way of seeking pleasure and fulfilment.

Another Way of Looking at Sport

Coakley (2001) proposed an alternative way of looking at sport which emphasized that "sports vary over time and from one place to another" (p. 23). Put another way, sport is a social construct—that is, we invent sport for our own purposes and according to what we value in our own culture. Furthermore, a certain activity that is considered to be a sport in one culture or subculture may not be considered a sport in another. For example, in the past, the lower class, in particular, held little reverence toward animals and engaged in such "sports" as dog and cock fighting. Today, most people would be horrified at the prospect of taking part in such activity and would be equally reluctant to consider these activities as sports.

> *...there is no universal agreement about the meaning, purpose, and organization of sports; there is no universal agreement about who will participate in sports, about the circumstances under which participation will occur, or about who will sponsor sport or the reasons underlying sponsorship. All these things vary over time from group to group and society to society.* (Coakley, 2001, pp. 24–25)

Undeniably, since the advent of television, three unique forms of sport have emerged: *corporate sport*, *pseudosport*, and *mediasport*.

Corporate sport is aligned to big business, and as in big business, the primary motive is profit. Sports leagues engage in profit sharing; official sponsors of the Olympic Games are given the right to use the Olympic logo alongside their own company's logo; television networks buy the rights to broadcast a series of games and, in turn, sell advertising slots to the highest bidders. Money is the fuel that feeds corporate sport's engine and the byproduct is sometimes corruption and greed.

Pseudosports (sometimes referred to as "trash sports") are events or activities that have been invented largely for the purposes of entertainment. According to the definition of sport that has been provided, pseudosports should not be considered bona fide sports. For the most part, they have been invented for television and often incorporate people and machinery that are big, noisy, and violent. Monster trucks, roller derby, and the World Wrestling Entertainment (WWE) are examples of pseudosports.

Another category of sport that has emerged largely because of people's insatiable need for sport on television is one I refer to as *mediasport*. These are events that restructure the rules of established sports so as to maximize the drama between contestants. Often in these contests, either great amounts of money or athletic prestige are on the line; sometimes both money and prestige are involved. Examples of such sports are skins games in golf or curling, all-star games, or battle of the superstars (whereby athletes from various sports compete against one another in a variety of physical challenges).

Basketball as Play, Game, and Sport

Basketball can be used to illustrate how one activity can be play, a game, or sport depending on the structure of the activity. Father and son shooting hoops on the driveway after dinner is an example of basketball as a form of *play*. The rules (if there are any) are made up as they go and there is no predetermined start and stop time. University students playing a game of pickup basketball during free gym time is an example of a *game*. What differentiates it from play is that there are now rules in place so that the game has some sort of form and structure. What differentiates it from sport is that it is not institutionalized. In other words, the game evolved because a few people showed up and others joined in and not because there was an organizing body in place. The university intercollegiate basketball team playing a home game against another university squad is an example of *sport*. The team is now part of a league, i.e., an organizational structure, under the jurisdiction of the Canadian Interuniversity Sport (CIS).

Physical Activities

You may be asking where other forms of physical activity fit in. For example, females ages 12 and older report that the six most popular forms of physical activity are walking, home exercise, swimming, bicycling, exercise class/aerobics, jogging/running (refer to Chapter 7 for more information on this). However, although the above activities are "physical," they cannot be categorized as either play, games, or sport. They involve some physical element, don't involve competition (unless against nature or oneself), and can be done alone. Other pursuits that can be categorized as physical activities might include gardening, in-line skating, rock climbing, bungee jumping, tai chi, and line dancing.

CHARACTERISTICS OF SPORT

Now that an attempt has been made to define sport in all its varied forms, it is important to understand what features characterize sport. In other words, what qualities make up sport that differentiates it from anything else?

Involvement

1. Sport is characterized by some form of *involvement* either at the behavioural, cognitive, or affective level (Kenyon, 1969). At the *behavioural* level, we actively get involved in sport. For example, children play hockey, pretending to be Wayne Gretzky or Hayley Wickenheiser; adolescents become members of their intercollegiate or intramural volleyball teams; middle-aged adults join a local badminton club; and seniors compete in masters' games in swimming. Unfortunately, only 34.2% of Canadians over the age of 15 (males, 43.1%; females, 25.7%) report that they regularly participate in sport. The age-gender gap was even more pronounced in the 15-to-18-year category, in which 80% of males regularly participated versus 55% for females. The data for children ages 5 to 14 were far from acceptable, with only 54% active in sports (Statistics Canada, 1998). For those who participate, soccer is the most popular (31%), followed by swimming (24%), and hockey (24%).

   There were regional differences as well with regard to amateur sport participation, with Quebec (38%) and Alberta (37%) having the highest rates and Prince Edward Island (25%) and Newfoundland (27%) having the lowest. Furthermore, there appears to be an ethnic difference in involvement in competitive sport between anglophones and francophones. For both sexes, anglophones were found to be more involved in competitive sport when compared to francophones, who were less likely to report that they were involved for reasons of "challenge" and "competition" (White & Curtis, 1990). Curtis and Birch (1987) found that more professional and Olympic hockey players were from small towns than large cities.

   Canadians today are interested in sport (remember that sport is ubiquitous), but are too frequently content to let others "do" while they watch (see Table 1.1). Canadians' favourite professional sports to watch are hockey (45.4%), baseball (14.6%), football (12.3%), and basketball (9.3%). Furthermore, Canadians prefer their own brand of football over the American version (39.3% versus 22.4% respectively) (Leger Marketing Poll, February 2002). The same survey found that in the last few years, 33.8% of spectators were less interested in watching professional sport, while 47% had the same interest level and 13.5% reported that their interest had risen. The primary reason given by the third whose interest had waned was as a result of the "ridiculously high" player salaries, followed by the departure of Canadian franchises, weak performances by Canadian teams, and player strikes.

   Sport also requires involvement at the *cognitive* level. This "refers to a person's knowledge about sport" (Leonard II, 1998, p. 115). Examples include learning the rules, skills, and strategy involved in sport; knowing about a favourite athlete; or following sport via the mass media (television, radio, newspapers, or the Internet).

TABLE 1.1 Participation Rates (%) for the Canadian Population 15 Years and Older

Sport	Total	Male	Female
Golf	7.4	11.1	3.9
Ice hockey	6.2	12.0	0.5
Baseball	5.5	8.0	3.1
Swimming	4.6	3.6	5.6
Basketball	3.2	4.6	1.9
Volleyball	3.1	3.3	2.8
Soccer	3.0	4.6	1.5
Tennis	2.7	3.6	1.8
Alpine skiing	2.7	2.9	2.6
Cycling	2.5	3.0	2.0
Cross-country skiing	2.1	1.7	2.5
Weightlifting	1.8	2.5	1.1
Badminton	1.7	1.7	1.7
Football	1.6	2.9	0.3
Curling	1.3	1.5	1.1
Bowling–10 pin	1.2	1.1	1.2
Softball	0.9	1.0	0.7
Bowling–5 pin	0.8	0.7	1.0
Squash	0.7	x	x
Karate	0.5	0.7	0.4
Figure skating	0.5	0.4	0.6
Rugby	0.4	x	x
Ball hockey	0.4	x	x
Snowboarding	0.3	x	x
In-line skating	0.3	x	x
Racquetball	0.2	x	x

x Data unavailable, not applicable, or confidential

Source: Based on data from the Statistics Canada, General Social Survey, 1998.

The third type of sport involvement is *affective*. The affective domain refers to the feeling or emotive processes that a person experiences as a result of sport involvement. We might feel less stressed after we've gone for a run, or we feel elated after having skied down a hill of powdered snow.

2. The second characteristic of sport is the element of *unpredictability*. If we could always predict the outcome of a sport contest, who would bother watching or participating? Have you ever set your video recorder on your television so that you could catch a sport contest that you were unable to watch live? On the way home to watch the match that has already occurred, did you avoid listening to the radio for fear of hearing the outcome? What if, inadvertently, you found out the final score before viewing the tape? How would you feel? Would you bother watching the game on video at all once you knew what had already happened? Many people wouldn't bother because the element of unpredictability had been removed. "In any sport, the anticipation of what might happen is almost as important as what actually happens" (Costas, 2000, p. 133).

3. Sport can be a *paradox*. The American Broadcasting Corporation (ABC) television network once started its sports broadcasts with the caption: "The thrill of victory and the agony of defeat." Joy and agony are opposites invoked from the same thing—sport. Another example of this paradox is that sport is something that is supposed to promote health, but athletes sometimes play in pain or when injured.

4. The final characteristic of sport is that there is usually a *drama* unfolding. This drama could be a contest between a pitcher and the batter or the suspense of whether the offence in football will move the ball 10 yards in order to gain a first down. Spectator sports that typically have done well in North America are ones that offer lots of drama. Recently, National Basketball Association (NBA) and now Women's National Basketball Association (WNBA) basketball has increased considerably in popularity because a drama (will the team on offence score a basket or will the defence stop them?) is offered so often. Conversely, soccer has been a tough sell in North America (even though it is the most popular spectator sport in the world) because of the low-scoring games; this is perceived by some as a lack of drama. Other strikes against the establishment of soccer as a popular spectator sport in North America are that it hasn't historically been part of our culture and it must compete with at least four other team sports that are well ingrained into the fabric of our society—baseball, basketball, football, and hockey.

   Some sports have changed their rules to make them more dramatic and hence more sellable. For example, before the advent of televised golf, golfers played under the rules of match play (head-to-head play). To heighten the drama for television, they moved to stroke play, in which a cumulative score for each golfer is kept throughout the tournament so that winning (or losing) could come down to the last putt in the last round. This produces more drama and excitement, which pay dividends come television ratings time.

CULTURAL CONGRUENCY

The Oxford dictionary defines culture as "the customs and civilization of a particular people or group." Furthermore, it is a socially invented way of feeling, acting, and thinking passed down from one generation to the next through social learning. The practices of a culture reflect what is important in that culture, and the same is true for sport. Different cultures approach sport in different ways. What is valued in one culture, competition perhaps, may not be valued in another. This link between sport and culture is called *cultural congruency*. For example, most Canadians live and work in a society that reflects the western industrial culture in which competition and getting ahead of one's opponents is deemed important. That attitude is reflected in the way we play sport. In competitive sport, one of our primary goals is to overcome obstacles in order to triumph over an opponent. This same goal is reflected in many business practices in our western industrial society. However, when a culture evolves in extreme climates such as in the northern territories in Canada, then cooperation between people is necessary in order to survive. This, then, plays out in the types of physical activities that are chosen, i.e., ones that are predominantly cooperative rather than competitive in nature. Examples of this relationship can be seen in Chapter 8, Race and Ethnicity.

Sport as a Microcosm of Society

Sport sociologists have claimed for some time that sport reflects or mirrors society. They then modified their thinking on this matter by suggesting that rather than simply mirroring society, sport is a miniature version of society, or **sport is a microcosm of society**. That is, the situations and circumstances that occur in sport also occur in society. For example, how minorities such as the aboriginal peoples were treated in sport reflected the way they were treated in society at large. This relationship can also be reciprocal: how society views Aboriginal peoples was reflected in the way they were viewed when, for example, playing lacrosse.

Current thinking is that rather than being a mirror or even a miniature version of society, sport shapes how we think and what we value. Instead of standing on the sidelines waiting for society to dictate the nature of sport, the institution of sport, largely via the mass media, is proactive in shaping what we value; how we think, act, and feel; and what we believe. For example, the small percentage of print and photo space that Canadian newspapers devote to women's sport (as opposed to the large amount of coverage given to white male athletes participating in professional team sports) might influence the importance that people place on women's sport participation and to a greater extent women's role within society today. This is one of the ways that sport reflects the inequalities found in society.

REASONS CANADIANS FOLLOW SPORT

Canadians follow sport many different ways and for a variety of reasons. We watch sports live, follow the action via the mass media (television, newsprint, radio, and the Internet), see films with sport themes, and read books about our favourite players and teams. The question posed in this section is why do people follow sport in Canada.

The reasons can be divided into two categories: **personal** and **social**.

Personal

For many, sport is a primary means of entertainment or a pastime. It piques our interest and alleviates the boredom of the everyday routine. Imagine working in a mundane job every day where nothing much changes. Sport provides a stress-seeking opportunity to raise the heart rate and get excited about a team or an athlete. Remember, one characteristic that defines sport is that it is unpredictable. This element of the unpredictable is what attracts some to avidly follow sport.

Some sport enthusiasts possess a strong identity with their favourite team ("I am a Toronto Maple Leafs fan") and, in some cases, live vicariously through this identity. If the team wins, they win. If the team loses, this loss rests on their shoulders as well.

For some, sport provides an opportunity to view violence and aggression. It also provides some followers with an opportunity to have something to gamble on; one can find everything from pari-mutuel betting on horses to hockey pools at work.

Social

Watching sport contests is, for many people, a social experience. For example, family and friends gather to watch the Grey Cup, the World Series, or the Stanley Cup finals. For some people, the primary objective is to watch the game. Less enthusiastic sports fans enjoy the company of others and partake in food, fun, and festivities. Whatever the purpose in following sport, it is a popular pastime of Canadians and will likely remain so in the foreseeable future.

SOCIOLOGICAL THEORIES

As has already been stated, sociologists study a vast array of issues and controversies. Making sense of these issues is not easy and for that reason sociologists develop theories to explain how social life is organized in an effort to link observations in some meaningful way. Furthermore, theories provide a framework for understanding phenomena being studied in the varied contexts, sport being one example. "All disciplines have competing theories that attempt to explain the phenomena that are important to that discipline, and sociology is no exception" (Landis, 1983, p. 10). For example, three theories have been developed to attempt to explain why people are aggressive. Lorenz (1966) formulated the instinct theory, which proposes that aggression is innate; Dollard et al. (1939) in his frustration-aggression theory explained aggressive behaviour by stating that people become aggressive when they are put in frustrating situations; and Bandura (1973) developed the social learning theory, which is based on the idea that people learn to become aggressive vicariously and through modelling others. All three are an attempt by the theorist to explain behaviour (in this case aggressive behaviour). If one disagrees with all or part of a theory, it is refuted as was Dollard's theory by Berkowitz (1969) when he reformulated the frustration-aggression theory. (For more information on these theories and their application to sport, see Chapter 6.) The following paragraphs contain an outline of the dominant theories in the sociological literature. Their relevance to sport will also be explained.

Functionalist Theory

This theory is based on the premise that society is composed of interrelated parts in a stable and orderly fashion. That is, in order to exist, societies or groups therein need to perform certain functions with the majority of members sharing a common set of behavioural expectations, values, and beliefs. To explain this theory, the analogy that is often given relates to the body's structure and function. In order for the human body to survive, several functions must occur, such as blood flow. So the body can perform these functions, structures have been developed such as the heart, veins, and arteries. If one of these parts breaks down, the functioning of the entire body breaks down. Likewise, according to functionalist theory, social institutions such as schools, churches, and the family are developed with the purpose of insuring the smooth functioning and survival of the society. Similarly, "if anything adverse happens to one of these institutions or parts, all other parts are affected and the system no longer functions properly" (Kendall, Murray, & Linden, 2000). Proponents of this theory ask the question "What unifies groups and keeps them together?"

In sport, functionalists deem that sports contribute to the moulding of good citizens, for example, by teaching discipline, teamwork, and self-confidence. They would also see the introduction of scholarships into the CIS as a positive move toward keeping our best university-age athletes in Canada.

Opponents of this rather conservative theory suggest that functionalism tends to ignore social change and conflict, thereby reaffirming the status quo. Furthermore, the functionalist theory "underestimates the powerful divisions in society, divisions rooted in factors such as social class, race, ethnicity, and gender" (Bryant & McElroy, 1997, p. 19).

Conflict Theory

While the functionalists stress social stability and order, the conflict theorists are of the opinion that conflict and competition are common between groups in society. While the functionalists ask what unifies groups, the conflict theorists ask who benefits and who goes without. Karl Marx felt that it was the capitalists exploiting the workers that led to their uprising and the development of a classless society. In sport we often see clashes between those who benefit from the development of a new sports facility (the owners, builders, multinational food corporations) and those who don't (those whose homes are displaced, the spectators who pay increasingly higher ticket prices). These clashes between social groups are inevitable because the wealth, power, and prestige are unequally distributed, resulting in a continuous power struggle for resources. Conflict theorists regard society as hierarchal and fragmented and emphasize the importance of power and coercion in keeping social order. Whereas Marx viewed religion as "the opiate of the masses," today sport sociologists subscribing to the conflict theory might say that "sport is an opiate of the masses." In other words, sport temporarily allows its followers the opportunity to forget the negative aspects of their lives and the ills of society such as poverty and unemployment.

People in positions of authority benefit from the conformity of others; those who are forced to conform feel resentment and demonstrate resistance, much as a child may resent parental authority. The advantaged group that possesses authority attempts to preserve the status quo (i.e., the existing set of social arrangements) and may exert coercion to achieve this end (Kendall, Murray, & Linden, 2000, p. 21).

You may note that the status quo has been referred to in both functionalist and conflict theories. Functionalists view the status quo as a positive thing whereas conflict theorists see it as a way of reinforcing the inequality that exists in society with regard to power, prestige, and resources.

What sports you watch on television, how much coverage is given, and the nature of the coverage is in the hands of the power elite—a small clique of top corporate people in decision-making positions. If you examine a current list of the *Sporting News*'s 100 most powerful people in sport, you will see that several of the people either own or are in charge of the sports programming for major television networks.

In this text there are a number of examples of conflict theory in action. In Chapter 2, Dr. Lappage writes about the exclusion of the working class from amateur status during the 19th century. In Chapter 7, Dr. Lenskyj speaks of the inequalities that still exist for women in sport today. Less funding, lack of child-care facilities, unequal opportunities to pursue a chosen sport, and less newspaper coverage are some examples. In Chapter 8, Drs. Paraschak and Tirone make it clear that the power and privilege that exist in Canada when race and ethnicity are considered is held by Caucasians of European descent and not with, for example, immigrants new to the country or Aboriginal peoples.

Interactionist Theory

So far both functionalist and conflict theories have been focusing on a macro-level analysis. Macro level examines "whole societies, large-scale social structures, and social systems" (Kendall, Murray, & Linden, 2000, p. 23). However, in symbolic interactionism the focus is on small groups such as high school teams, family, a church school class, or a bridge club.

In this theory, the focus is narrowed down to person-to-person interaction and the way individuals develop viewpoints about themselves in relation to those with whom they associate. In other words, society is seen as "the sum of the interactions of individuals or groups" (Kendall, Murray, & Linden, 2000, p. 23).

Interactionists are interested in describing patterns of interaction, how parties to the interaction interpret what is going on, the use of signs, symbols, and other forms of communication, the meanings actions have for others, and the processes of socialization and development of the self (Landis, 1983, p. 13).

How a coach interacts (both verbally and nonverbally) with one of his or her players is an example of what interactionists would be interested in. The coach attempts to evaluate which type or types of feedback the athlete best responds to and then adjusts his or her mode of delivery to maximize its effect on the athlete. Another example of interactionist theory in action is the one-to-one relationship between the injured athlete and his or her physiotherapist. The physiotherapist should communicate in a clear and understandable manner the nature of the injury and the prognosis of recovery. Failing to do so may leave the athlete fearful of the injury and doubtful of his or her chances of returning to practice and competition.

Feminist Theory

Feminist theory began several decades ago, out of the realization that the vast majority of sociological theory and methodology did not include to any significant degree the experiences of women. In fact, early feminist scholars were actually critical of sociology per se because "sociological methods, concepts, and analyses were products of the 'male social universe'" (Kendall, Murray, & Linden, 2002, p. 22).

Feminist sociologists made early attempts at generating research and theory about women in an effort to address some of the problems unique to the female experience. Such problems included women's role within society, child-care issues, poverty, violence, and harassment. An understanding of the fundamental inequalities that exist between the sexes not only in the household but in the labour force are central to feminist theory. The approach that feminist scholars take is that men and women should be equal and have equal rights and should be treated as such in the eyes of the law and in the political arena. Central to feminist theory is that gender roles are created rather than biologically determined and that irrespective of gender, everyone should have the opportunity to maximize his or her potential.

Feminist theory incorporates both the macro and micro level of analysis. In the macro level, feminist theorists try to explain how the current system of sport organization favours men over women. Part of this is due to the fact that the power in sport is still in the hands of men. In the *Sporting News*'s 2002 list of the most powerful people in sport, of the top 100, only 4 are women, the first ranked number 71. Another example of a macro-level analysis is an examination of the barriers that prevent women from fully participating in sport and physical activity.

In the micro level, sociologists analyze the person-to-person interaction males and females have within the sport domain. For example, feminist theorists may try to explain whether men and women have different coaching styles and differing ways of providing feedback and reinforcement. Conversely, the attitudes athletes have toward male and female coaches may be the focus of another micro-level analysis.

SOCIALIZING INTO, VIA, AND OUT OF SPORT

Socialization into Sport

Being involved in sport is not only a physical experience but it also creates opportunities for socialization experiences to occur. Socialization is a "means by which a society preserves its norms and perpetuates itself" (Eitzen & Sage, 1997, p. 61). This process of learning a culture and becoming a contributing member of society is what Leonard II (1998) called a "social metamorphosis" (p. 106). Furthermore, socialization is a reciprocally interactive process whereby one learns attitudes, knowledge, and values and adapts to the society of which he or she is a member. In turn, the person doing the learning (and hence, being socialized) can exert influence on the social agents doing the teaching. These social agents exert varying degrees of influence (depending on the person and his or her life circumstances) and comprise a combination of family and friends, coaches and teachers working in institutions such as schools, churches, and the community at large. In the last century, the mass media have also become a socializing agent. You will be asked at the end of the chapter to describe how you were socialized into sport. Over the years I have heard many explanations, from getting involved because an older sibling was involved to avoiding having to do something less desirable. It is worth noting that children are exposed to a variety of social experiences, some of which are sport-related and many of which are not.

Certainly, parents are predominant socializing agents when it comes to sport involvement. If one (or both) parents are actively involved and enthusiastic about a particular sport or activity, this attitude will usually positively affect their children (Statistics Canada, 1998). Moreover, if the parents include their children in their sporting ventures, they learn not only how to do a particular sport, but will often develop a lifelong appreciation for it at the same time (Welk, 1999). In other words, active children generally come from supportive families. Early experiences in sport are critical in shaping future attitudes and behaviours.

Greendorfer and Lewko (1978) and McElroy (1983) found that within the family structure, fathers were the most significant socializing agents for sport and, furthermore, were the most important predictor of sport participation for both boys and girls. This finding is particularly interesting in today's society, in which a large percentage of children are raised in lone-parent families. More recently, findings from the General Social Survey (Statistics Canada, 1998) showed that being raised in a two-parent versus single-parent family did not affect the children's participation rates (54% versus 53% respectively).

Kenyon and McPherson (1973) believe that the process of being socialized into sport was more complicated than just making a positive connection with influential social agents. They contend that personal attributes and socializing situations also play an important role in determining an individual's likelihood of participating in sport.

Personal attributes are the characteristics that make up the individual; they can be either *physical*—height, weight, and age—or *psychological*—mental toughness, determination—or *social-psychological*—the ability to work as part of a team. Despite having the physical attributes necessary to play a sport, a child may be hesitant to participate if he or she does not possess the preferred mental requisites, such as aggressiveness or determination. However, if a child possesses all the desired personal attributes and experiences repeated success, he or she will likely be more than willing to continue participating.

Socializing situations consist "of the individual's unique blend of opportunities and life experiences" (Bryant & McElroy, 1997, p. 33). For example, Canadian children from homes with household incomes under $40 000 were more likely to be involved in inexpensive sports such as baseball and basketball than children from families with household incomes of more than $80 000 (Statistics Canada, 1998). Certainly, one's social class and environment influence the opportunity to participate in certain sports. This topic will be dealt with in greater detail in the section in this chapter entitled "Social Stratification."

Socialization via Sport

It has long been the mantra of sport enthusiasts that sport provides a forum through which we learn "life's lessons." Discipline, hard work, dedication to a common cause, and other laudable personal qualities are supposed to be the outcome of having been involved in sport. In some circumstances, this may very well be the case, but in others, regrettably, this is not so. Sport is inherently a teacher neither of what is good nor of what is bad. Rather, it is the nature of the experiences in sport that may provide opportunities for socialization. While one coach may model and expound the virtues of sportsmanship and fair play to his or her athletes, another may be teaching and condoning illegal field tactics and modelling unsportsman-like conduct.

It is particularly important for children to have positive experiences in sport because these early experiences (both positive and negative) will shape the attitudes they have to sport and physical activity in their later years. It is imperative that coaches of young children make the children's growth and development needs paramount in importance. Children's sports should not be a scaled-down version of how older people play. For example, playing the best players at the expense of the lesser skilled players should not happen in children's organized sport. Every child should ideally walk away from the experience having felt that he or she had fun and experienced an equal opportunity to play, wanting to return again. More discussion regarding this issue can be found in Chapter 3, which deals with children in sport.

Socializing out of Sport

While some people are socialized into sport, others are socialized out of it. For a variety of reasons, people cease doing a particular sport or all sports for a period of time or permanently. For children it may be the demands of the activity that demotivate them or the feeling that they aren't contributing members of the team; for adolescents it may be the ability to drive a car or an interest in dating and other social activities; for young adults it may be that other roles demand their time and money, e.g., work or family; and for adults it may be not being particularly skilled or competent. We might reason that one drops out of sport because something negative has happened to the participant that deterred him or her from continuing—perhaps lack of time, money, or opportunity. This is not necessarily the case. As was pointed out above, sometimes other life choices at a particular point in a person's life need to be made, and for a time, sport isn't a primary pursuit.

Research has shown that one does not simply drop out of sport; that is, one day you're in and the next, you're out (Koukouris, 1994). In fact, leaving sport completely or for just a period of time frequently coincides with other life-changing events. A new job or the arrival of a baby may mean the other things that were part of a person's life, including sport participation, have to, for the time being, take a back seat. This does not mean that the person will never return to sport. If a return does occur, it may be to a different sport and perhaps at a different level. When children and adolescents drop out of sport, it is of concern to those who believe that regular sport participation has many benefits. As has already been discussed, only about half (54%) of Canadian children aged 5 to 14 regularly take part in organized sport (Statistics Canada, 1998). For female adolescents aged 15 to 18, the dropout rate was particularly apparent and troubling (boys participation rate = 80%, girls = 55%) (www.pch.gc.ca/sportcanada). Gould (1984, p. 87) found that the primary reasons for dropping out included an overemphasis on winning, lack of success, not playing, other conflicting activities, boredom, little improvement, and too much pressure. Furthermore, Anshel (1997) categorized children's reasons for dropping out of sport into three areas: *comparative appraisal* (children are constantly comparing their own motor abilities with the abilities of others their own age, often resulting in a feeling of inferiority); *perceived lack of ability* (how children often attribute a failed performance); *low intrinsic motivation* (instead of wanting to do the sport for its own sake or for the simple joy and fun of participation which is motivational, children who participate primarily for the tangible rewards and prestige associated with it frequently find themselves demotivated and contemplate quitting).

Numerous strategies exist to combat the dropout phenomenon, and many of them come down to the fact that participants need to feel a sense of accomplishment. Consequently, improvement should be based on self-improvement rather than a comparison to others. Children who drop out will be discussed in greater depth in Chapter 3.

Retirement Retirement is another form of dropping out of sport. The word *retirement* can be a misnomer because, for many athletes, retirement is more a transition than the connotation we have traditionally given it, i.e., giving up one's regular occupation, in this case, sport. Furthermore, research shows that the career transition in sport is best described as a process rather than a single event (Danish, Owens, Green, & Brunelle, 1997; Greendorfer & Blinde, 1985). An athlete doesn't usually wake up one morning deciding to retire that day from sport. Rather, he or she prepares for it by planning how to end that phase of his or her competitive career and move on to other forms of activities and other life goals. Often, high-performance athletes put other life processes—education, career, family—on hold so that they can train for a specific event such as the Olympics or the World Championships.

As is the case with others who drop out of sport, this career transitional process often occurs in conjunction with other changes in an athlete's life. Some doors in the person's life are shut, while others are opened. In other words, as old sport identities are dropped, new ones are picked up. "The process of leaving a role means that one also is being socialized into a new role" (Drahota & Eitzen, 1998, p. 266). For example, one moves from being a competitive swimmer to a competitive rower, or a professional football player to a recreational squash player, or from direct-primary involvement (a participant) to indirect-primary (a coach or administrator).

Athletes make a career transition for a number of reasons. Some athletes retire involuntarily, for reasons such as injury or not being selected for a team. Research shows that those who left sport because of injury had the most difficulty adjusting (Webb, Nasco, Riley, & Headrick, 1998). Others left voluntarily—for example, due to conflicting family responsibilities or for other personal reasons. These personal reasons may include factors such as not enjoying the pressures of competing or travel; lack of commitment or interest; dissatisfaction with the organization, coach, or administrators; not enjoying the self-sacrifice needed to succeed; financial considerations; and the preoccupation with training and diet. Kerr and Dacyshyn (2000) point out that the distinction between voluntary and involuntary retirement is unclear and, furthermore, voluntary retirement does not necessarily mean that the athlete won't experience adjustment difficulties.

Those who find the process difficult report missing the close friendships with teammates and fearing the uncertainty of what's ahead. They also report feeling incompetent outside of sport and indicate that simply keeping busy was not an effective coping strategy (Sinclair & Orlick, 1993). Furthermore, those who had a strong athletic identity have more difficulty than others with a less pronounced athletic identity (Webb et al., 1998). The Canadian Olympic Career Centre reports that on average, ex-Olympians take 18 months to fully adjust to their new identities.

Many athletic careers are relatively short when compared to the duration of other careers (four to seven years for baseball, football, basketball, and hockey [Leonard II, 1996] versus 30 to 40 years for other careers). However, in the case of gymnasts (and other sports where athletes peak earlier than most), unique challenges present themselves upon retirement as a result of the young age gymnasts typically begin and end their careers (Kerr & Dacyshyn, 2000).

Blinde and Stratta (1992) found that college athletes who left athletics found the experience traumatic and, in some cases, equated it with the feelings associated with death and dying as outlined by Kübler-Ross (shock, denial, anger, bargaining, depression, and acceptance). What might have contributed to such a negative response was that, in every case, the departures from sport were involuntary and unanticipated. Had they been voluntary and anticipated, the reactions could very well have been different.

Swain (1991) argues that transitions are very individual and cannot be generalized into patterns and stages. However, Ebaugh (1988) did feel that generalization was possible and developed a stage model approach to leaving. The four stages in his model include first doubts, seeking alternatives, the turning point, and creating the ex-role. Drahota and Eitzen (1998) modified this model so that it can be applied to the ex-professional athlete.

The questions that retired athletes are often faced with when making this transition in their late twenties or early thirties are "What now? How will I make a living?" and, in some cases, "How will I dig myself out of the debt that has mounted up while I was in training?" Those who make a reasonably successful transition to life beyond sport do so because they have prepared (Baillie & Danish, 1992; Schlossberg, 1981). They have obtained post-secondary education and obtained qualifications; they have networked with people who can make the right connections for them; they have been exposed to positive role models who have taught them social skills; and, more often than not, they have the support of their family and friends who provide not only monetary assistance but also social support. McGowan and Rail (1996) found that, of the women canoeists who made successful transitions (73% involuntarily), 61% felt that education and friends assisted in making it possible. Another study that investigated the coping strategies used by athletes during the career transitional process found that acceptance, positive reinterpretation, planning, active coping, mental disengagement, and seeking social support were the most effective strategies (Grove, Lavallee, & Gordon, 1997).

What is certain is that athletes need to be prepared for this transition and frequently are not (Baillie & Danish, 1992). Fortunately, professional players' associations now have an increasing awareness that they must assist their athletes in making a successful transition. Some facilitate the process of having their athletes return to formal education, while others provide incentives to branch out into different careers.

A system to support ex-Olympians in making a smooth and successful transition has evolved in Canada. Originally developed in 1985 by the Canadian Olympic Association, Olympic Athlete Career Centres in Toronto, Calgary, Montreal, and Vancouver provide career counselling to former Olympians, including training in job-search techniques and assistance in résumé preparation. In 1994, the National Sports Centres, in eight units across Canada (Victoria, Vancouver, Calgary, Saskatchewan, Manitoba, Toronto, Montreal, Atlantic Canada), partnered in the delivery of these services to help athletes (both retired and active) become the best persons they could be. This holistic approach, which is used by both active and ex-Olympians, attempts to help athletes balance all aspects of their lives (J. Goss, personal communication, February 11, 2002; S. Holloway, personal communication, February 7, 2002).

SOCIAL STRATIFICATION

> *"[S]port has historically provided a medium for displaying status, learning new tastes, and acquiring social distinctiveness"* (Booth & Loy, 1999, p. 3).

The term "stratified" refers to how something is graded or layered and "stratification" is the process through which this happens. Most societies (Canada included) are divided into social strata or social classes; one's class determines one's rank within society. This rank can be inherited or earned. One is born into a certain social class, and the level of social status that one inherits influences, to varying degrees, one's life chances. Karl Marx felt that money wasn't the factor that divided social classes; rather, it was the control of people (the more control, the higher the social class) and the access to means of production through knowledge and specialized skills. People are stratified according to a number of criteria including age, sex, race and ethnicity, socioeconomic status, and power.

Historically, the opportunity to play or hold interest in a specific sport was class-dependent. "All the evidence suggests that, irrespective of culture or historical period, people use sport to distinguish themselves and to reflect their status and prestige" (Booth & Loy, 1999, p. 1). After all, sport requires "management of the body" and this management is "central to the acquisition of status and distinction" (Shilling, 1993, p. 127). That is, the upper class participates in certain sports, such as polo, while the lower class participates in others, such as wrestling. The mixing of classes for the purposes of participating in sport was seen as negative, and when the lower class started to play a sport that was traditionally reserved for the upper class, the upper class would abandon that sport. Today, there is more mixing of classes with regard to sport participation. However, there are still variables that influence the probability of a member of a certain class playing a sport. These will be discussed later in this section.

Class Inequalities

A discussion of social stratification necessitates a discussion of the inequalities that exist between classes. A discussion of Bourdieu's (1984) distinctions (as cited by Booth & Loy, 1999) between upper, middle, and lower class follows.

Upper Class The upper classes are characterized by "inherited wealth, reverence for tradition, alliance to family, and political and economic conservatism" (Booth & Loy, 1999, p. 8). They play sport with the utmost dignity and abide by principles of fair play. After all, for the upper class it is "only a game." Popular sports engaged in by the upper class are golf, tennis, sailing, riding, skiing, and fencing. These are sports that can be "performed ... at times and in places beyond the reach of many" (Bourdieu, 1984, p. 218). In addition, the upper class used *status sticks* such as cues in billiards and foils in fencing; *status spheres*, which are small balls such as tennis and squash balls; *sporting servants*, such as caddies in golf; and *sporting animals*, such as horses and dogs in hunting (Booth & Loy, 1999).

Middle Class This class is characterized as having "self-restraint, discipline, sobriety, frugality, and piety" (Booth & Loy, 1999, p. 13). Members are concerned with health, evident in their attention to diet and appearance (men's, in particular), and play predominantly team games (contrary to the upper class, which does not). They have enough economic capital to be preoccupied with the future and "show a blind faith in inevitability of progress" (Booth & Loy, 1999, p. 15). Interestingly, they use bigger balls than the upper class in sports such as baseball, basketball, football, and soccer.

Lower Class This group has little capital and little chance of acquiring any. They are, as Kahl points out, "spectators in recreation as ... in work" (1959, p. 210). Members of the lower class are preoccupied with just getting by, and for that reason they are concerned predominantly with the present. Local neighbourhoods tend to define the boundaries of social intercourse and suspect anyone from outside this jurisdiction. When the lower class does play sport, it tends to play with balls that are low to the ground and close to the body such as bowling balls.

Determinants of the Social Status of Sports

Today, the issue of what social class participates in which sports is a complex one, confounded by a number of factors. The most obvious determinant of the social status of a sport is *cost*, which is sport- and situation-specific. For some families, the cost of putting a child into an organized sports program is prohibitive. Barriers to physical activity in relation to income have been found to include the costs of equipment and user fees (American College of Sports Medicine, 1994). People with lower incomes have been found to be less physically active than those with higher incomes (MacDougall, Cooke, Owen, Willson & Bauman, 1997).

My sport sociology students have estimated the following costs for participating in certain sports in Thunder Bay (see Table 1.2). These costs include equipment, registration, travel, test fees, and other incidentals. You can see from Table 1.2 that there is a huge difference in cost between participating in, for example, basketball and alpine ski racing. Hence, without outside funding, families with modest household incomes couldn't afford a child in high-cost sports.

TABLE 1.2 The Cost of Participating in Organized Sport in Thunder Bay

Sport	Cost
Basketball	$80
Soccer	$222
Baseball	$350
Karate	$740
Golfing (municipal)	$1520
Ice hockey (not goalie)	$1570
Figure skating	$3400
Alpine ski racing	$6000

The *structure* of the sport is also a determining factor of its status. Generally, the upper class prefers individual sports, while the middle and lower classes predominantly play team sports. The upper class consists largely of persons in professional positions who require flexibility in their schedules in order to fit in a round of golf or a squash game. In many cases they might have difficulty fitting in the practice and competition time required by a team sport. The exception to this is rugby, which is played around the world by many people in professional occupations. This may be attributed to the fact that historically, rugby has been a popular sport in the privileged boys' schools in England.

Physical contact is also a determinant of the status of a sport. Generally, the upper class prefers little or no physical contact, while the lower class prefers physical toughness and hitting. Again, rugby may be the exception to the rule. Members of the upper class also situate themselves in sports that are cognitively demanding such as billiards and tennis.

Advertisements The next time you watch sports on television, note what kinds of commercials are being shown. Chances are the commercials reflect the social stratum that is watching the contest. For example, in many team sports, such as football and baseball, beer is being advertised as well as trucks, mid-range cars, and soft drinks. On the other hand, commercials played during golf tournaments appeal to the upper social stratum that is watching and feature investment firms and luxury cars.

Stadium Seating Between 1991 and 2000, the average ticket price increased 93% for major league baseball, 81% for the NBA, and 90% for the NHL—more than three times the rate of inflation (Coakley, 2001). As ticket prices increase, spectators become increasingly segregated, and social class becomes more evident in the stands. The cost of tickets is the primary consideration that delimits sectors of the population from attending games, providing one doesn't wish to eat anything during the game and doesn't require a means of transportation to the venue (including parking), or wish to buy a program or a souvenir. Increasingly, the ability to attend a professional sport contest is only for those with a sizable disposable income and certainly not for a family just trying to make ends meet.

The irony of this situation is that those from the lower class and even the middle class who might have helped pay for the stadium and subsidize the team through their taxes never get to see the inside of the stadium. On the other hand, corporate boxes lining the insides of arenas and stadiums are tax write-offs for the corporations that rent them. Furthermore, new stadiums are often built on inexpensive land, which can result in the dismantling of poor neighbourhoods, and subsequently, the displacement of the lower-class people who lived in them (Eitzen, 1996).

Also relevant to a discussion of social stratification in sport is the fact that the control of sport is largely in the hands of white American males, according to a poll taken by *Sporting News* (2002). Heading the list is perhaps one of the few exceptions, Tiger Woods. Included on the top 10 list as well are commissioners (National Football League [NFL], National Basketball Association [NBA], Major League Baseball [MLB]), media moguls, a sporting goods company chairman and CEO, an MLB team owner, an owner of a sports marketing company, and two beer company executives. Three Canadians made the top 100 most powerful and include at 39, Richard Pound (IOC); at 78, John Manley (deputy prime minister and Industry minister); and at 97, William Kitchen (B.C. provincial court judge).

SOCIAL MOBILITY

Social mobility in sport is movement up or down the social ladder as a result of sport participation. *Upward social mobility* is achieved through an increase in income, education, or occupational prestige, or a combination, such as getting drafted into the pros. Conversely, *downward social mobility* is a significant decrease in income or prestige (or both) due to, in the case of sport, the loss of a job, off-field behaviour, not getting selected for the team, retirement, or injury.

Upward social mobility occurs when an athlete is recruited into the pros or receives an athletic scholarship, thereby opening the door for further *education* to occur, which is one of the most important predictors of occupational mobility. For both boys and girls, the class positions of both the father and mother influenced educational attainment, but that has decreased in influence since the post-1960 period.

When someone from a lower social stratum goes to university, primarily with the intention of playing a sport, a number of things happen that can propel him or her into a higher social class. First of all, he or she may obtain a degree that could qualify him or her for a better paying position following the varsity career. (Research shows that Canadians with more education get better paying jobs [Statistics Canada].) While pursuing an education, an athlete may also learn new social skills (attitudes and behaviours) aligned to persons from higher social strata. These new social skills, in turn, may allow him or her to network more readily with people of influence who can help the athlete make connections that will pay dividends when it comes time for job placement.

On the other hand, if the athlete fails to obtain an education and qualifications that will translate into a job or career, and assuming he or she doesn't make it to the pros (and the chances of making it are slight [Coakley, 2001]), the result is often downward social mobility. A myth is that sport provides a means of experiencing upward social mobility and, even when it is true, it is for only the very gifted (Eitzen, 1996). Researchers have also studied the relationship between ethnicity and social mobility and have found that ethnicity is "as much a resource as a drawback to social mobility" (Isajiw, Sev'er & Driedger, 1993, p. 177).

CONCLUSIONS

Sport sociology provides an interesting, vibrant, and ever-changing context in which to study Canadian society. If you were to determine all the ways that sport, in its varied forms, has affected your life, that effect might be a sizable one.

Sport and many of the social processes that you will read about in this text have a reciprocal relationship. For example, in the case of the mass media, sport sells newspapers; in turn, newspapers help sell sport, thereby assisting one another achieve their goals and objectives.

While sport involvement can provide a potentially healthy, invigorating, exhilarating, and rewarding way of spending time, a critical examination of the institution we call sport reveals that all is not well. Inequalities still exist in how minorities, such as women and Aboriginal peoples, are treated. This inequality exists because some groups, i.e., members of the upper class, have the power and resources with which to manipulate others who are, more often than not, the consumers. Undoubtedly sport is shaped to a large extent by economic factors that, in turn, help shape the stratification patterns that exist within the system.

Other problems, such as drug use and cheating in sport, are now eroding the fabric of all that is sport in its purest sense. It is the task of sport sociologists not only to uncover the problems that exist in sport today, but also to offer solutions to mend what is becoming a splintered and fragmented institution.

Critical Thinking Questions

1. Discuss how sociology differs from psychology. Using retirement from sport as an example, differentiate what a sociologist would study versus a psychologist.
2. Provide three examples of cultural congruency in sport today.
3. List and briefly explain who the various agents were that socialized you into sport.
4. Why do you think sport is so popular in Canadian society today?
5. Do you think sports today are still stratified? If so, in what way(s)?
6. Why do you think pseudosports are popular among the lower class?
7. Watch the commercials from five different sports noting which social stratum the commercial is being geared toward.

Suggested Readings

Donnelly, P. (Ed.). (2000). *Taking sport seriously: Social issues in Canadian sport.* Toronto: Thompson.

Eitzen, D.S. (1996). Classism in sport: The powerless bear the burden. *Journal of Sport & Social Issues*, 20, 95–105.

Gruneau, R. (1999). *Class, sports, and social development.* Champaign, Ill.: Human Kinetics.

Web Links

North American Society for the Sociology of Sport (NASSS)
http://www.nasss.org
NASSS's Web site with information on conferences, members, the history of the organization, etc.

North American Sport Library Network (NASLIN)
http://www.sportquest.com/naslin
Communication and resource sharing.

Sport Canada
http://www.pch.gc.ca/sportcanada
Home page of Sport Canada.

SPORTDiscus
http://www.sportdiscus.com
Sports, fitness, and sports medicine database.

2

A Brief History of the Rise of a Canadian Sport Culture

Ronald S. Lappage

NORTHWESTERN ONTARIO SPORTS HALL OF FAME

Port Arthur Ski Club members at a ski meet hosted by the Fort William Ski Club at Mount McKay in the 1930s.

Sport is not peripheral to society; indeed it is central to life and reflects the dominant social and political concerns.

A. Metcalfe, *"Working Class Physical Recreation in Montreal, 1860–1895"*

WHY HISTORY?

Why does a chapter on the history of sport in Canadian society appear in a Canadian sport sociology textbook? Simply put, in order to understand the present, one needs a knowledge of the past. Sport sociologists have used historical methods to study the social, political, economic, and ideological factors that have influenced sport in all historical eras in order to study sport in contemporary society. As an example, gender issues related to Canadian sport are discussed in this textbook (Chapter 12). To better understand the contemporary issues related to this topic, one needs to be aware of how women's involvement in sport in Canada evolved from adoring spectators of male-dominated sports around the mid-1800s to active participants today. There have been many hurdles along the way, and women still face obstacles in achieving equity with men in the sports world. It is important for the reader to be familiar with the obstacles women have encountered in the past to comprehend the gender issues in sport today.

To provide a historical framework for the themes discussed in this chapter, four time periods in Canadian history have been selected: pre-1840, 1840 to 1918, 1918 to 1961, and 1961 to the present. The early development of organized sport in Canada prior to 1840 will be examined first. Although sports clubs developed in Canada as early as 1789 (N. Howell & M. Howell, 1969), they began to proliferate in central Canada by the 1840s. Therefore 1840 has been chosen as the starting date for the next era, which carries through to the end of the First World War in 1918. Significant developments occurred in sport in Canada during the next period up to the passage of the Fitness and Amateur Sport Act in 1961. This Act signified the beginning of the modern era in Canadian sport, which has been characterized by the growth of government involvement in fitness and amateur sport and the rapid expansion of professional sport.

SPORT BEFORE 1840

The physical activities of the Inuit, Native Indians, voyageurs, and the early French and English settlers were usually utilitarian, impromptu, and spontaneous. It was not until the early 19th century that organized sports began to develop in the urban areas, especially in the garrison towns where British soldiers and their officers were stationed to protect British interests in Upper and Lower Canada. Since at that time commissions in the army were purchased, the British officers came from the aristocracy or upper middle class and hence were wealthy, well educated, and inbred with the English public school's sports and games tradition and the concept of Muscular Christianity. The officers were regarded as desirable escorts by young ladies and inspired female participation in riding, sleighing, skating, and dancing.

By the end of the Napoleonic Wars in 1814, there were approximately 30 000 British troops in British North America. Although many of these were withdrawn or disbanded shortly after, those who remained played an important role in the early development of sports and recreational activity in Canada. Not only did they contribute funds for trophies and awards in many different sports, but they also provided the necessary organization and leadership. It was only natural that the officers sought to establish sports and games common in their homeland. Therefore cricket, rowing, track and field, horse racing, and fox hunting were promoted by the garrisons. Prior to Confederation, cricket had become a major sport in Canada, and horse racing in the early decades of the 19th century depended almost entirely on support from garrison officers. By 1840, clubs called Tandem clubs formed in centres such as Toronto, Montreal, Halifax, Niagara, and Quebec. These clubs, with a large proportion of their membership composed of military officers, catered to the socially elite as did most other sports clubs that were formed before 1840.

Sports clubs provided the foundation for the early development of organized sport in Canada. Typically, the members of sports clubs formed before 1840 were upper- or middle-class British males who resided in one of the larger urban centres such as Montreal, Toronto, or Halifax. Initially the clubs focused more on socializing and excluding natives and the working class than they did on playing procedures and the organization of competitions. The Montreal Curling Club (MCC) is a good example. The club's earliest (1807) rules reflected social concerns and exclusivity rather than playing procedures. Fraternizing and dining were emphasized, and it is believed that only two or three of the original 21 members even knew how to curl. However, as the MCC developed, while maintaining its social and ethnic exclusivity, it played an important role in the development of curling in Montreal during the 1820s and in southern Ontario during the 1830s. This was a pattern followed by other sports clubs that developed at later dates in Montreal, Toronto, and other urban centres.

While the socially elite were forming exclusive sports clubs, the urban working classes were socializing and pursuing some of their sporting interests in taverns, saloons, and drinking shanties, which provided not only liquor but also places to sing sporting songs, play billiards, and partake in other forms of sporting activity such as wrestling matches, prize fights, contests of strength, and blood sports. The latter included inhumane activities such as bear and bull baiting, dog fights, and cockfighting, which persisted well into the 20th century even though governments at all levels passed laws against them (C. Howell, 2001).

Up to about 1840, there was very little mingling of the upper and lower classes in sport. The upper classes, who were predominantly white, Anglo-Saxon, and Protestant (WASP), referred to themselves as "gentlemen amateurs." They excluded from their competitions anyone who was or had been by trade or employment for wages a mechanic, artisan, or labourer (McIntosh, 1968), for it was felt that a person who was involved in work as a regular routine was bound to be stronger and fitter than those engaged in sedentary activities. The fact that they also frequently excluded other non-WASP groups such as the Negro, native Indian, Irish, and to a lesser extent, the Scot under the pretence that they were professionals clearly indicates their desire to maintain the established social order (Cosentino, 1975).

Prior to 1840, little inter-city competition took place because primitive means of transportation made travel long and uncomfortable. The first steamboat appeared in 1809, making the journey from Montreal to Quebec in 36 hours, but until 1842 when canals between Kingston and Montreal were completed, the trip from Montreal to Toronto entirely by water was not possible. Some of the journey between these two major centres had to be made by stage coach, which was a very slow and tedious trip. Although steamboat travel was faster and more convenient than road, inter-town journeys for match play often necessitated several days being spent away from home. Only the wealthy upper or middle classes could afford to be away from work for extended periods of time, and consequently most inter-community competition was restricted to the socially elite (Lindsay, 1985).

1840 TO 1918

After 1840, Canada gradually evolved from a colony dependent upon the fur trade to a nation with new industries based in urban areas. The 1851 census indicated that, for the first time, Upper Canada had a larger population than Lower Canada. The largest cities at that time were Montreal (57 715), Quebec (42 052), Toronto (30 775), and Hamilton (14 112). In 1867, the population of the new Dominion of Canada was approximately 3.5 million of which, by 1871, about 20% lived in towns or cities. This percentage of urban dwellers rose to 35 by 1901, and by 1921 half of Canada's citizens lived in urban centres. Along with this trend to urbanization there also was a growth of industrialization in Canada. At the time of Confederation most manufacturing in Canada was of a local handicraft nature requiring very little capital, and most of the country's trade was based on farm, fishing, and timber products. However, by the end of the century the factory system, based on both heavy and light industries, was well established in urban areas. Rapid technological developments paralleled the growth of urbanization and industrialization in Canada (Jobling, 1970). It should not be surprising that many changes in sport occurred in Canada during the period from 1840 to 1918.

Improvements in transportation significantly influenced the development of sport in Canada. Inter-community competition in many sports increased significantly with the laying of the railroads. Cheaper and special excursion rates were introduced, enabling working-class athletes as well as their fans to travel more frequently (Jobling, 1970). As soon as railway connections between several towns were established, irregular challenges in sports often gave way to regular league play. This increased interaction in sports led to a need for the codification of rules in games such as lacrosse and hockey, which were indigenous to North America. A Montreal dentist, Dr. W.G. Beers, can be given credit for developing a set of rules for lacrosse around the time of Confederation while a McGill University student, J.G.A. Creighton, did the same thing for ice hockey during the 1870s (Cox, 1985). With the completion of the Canadian Pacific Railway (CPR) in 1885, it was possible to travel across the entire country by rail. Although the trip from Vancouver to Toronto or Montreal was long and tedious, athletes from the east and west were able to compete against each other, setting the stage for the formation of national sports organizations as well as national championships.

Railway expansion also opened the door for more sporting interaction to take place between teams in Canada and the United States. This was particularly evident in baseball, which by the 1870s started to replace cricket as Canada's most popular summer sport. Baseball flourished in the smaller towns and cities of southern Ontario within the London–Guelph–Hamilton triangle, which had convenient railway connections with areas in the United States, the home of baseball (R. Howell & M. Howell, 1985). By the beginning of the First World War, baseball undoubtedly was the most popular summer sport played and watched in Canada, and its American ties were readily evident (Metcalfe, 1987).

A national communication system permitting rapid transmission of information from coast to coast was also developed during the latter half of the 19th century. Before Samuel Morse invented the telegraph in 1842, information about sports results often took weeks to travel from the competition site to towns across the country; consequently, there was little interest generated. This changed, however, when the telegraph system was fully in place; results were sent across the country right after the competition, stimulating public interest and fan support (Keyes, 1989b). For example, when the Kenora Thistles won the Stanley Cup in 1907, fans congregated in the local arena to eagerly await the play-by-play account of the final game as it came over the wire (Lappage, 1988). The completion of the Atlantic cable in 1866 brought British and European sports results to Canada almost simultaneously with the end of the competition, and when the famous Paris crew, the foursome from Saint John, New Brunswick, won the world rowing championship in 1867, there was a tremendous public interest in the event across Canada (Fisher & Wise, 1974). The telephone, invented by Alexander Graham Bell in 1874, further enhanced communications and supplemented or replaced the reporting of sports results by telegraph toward the end of the 19th century.

Another form of communication, the newspaper, also promoted greater public interest in sport as the 19th century progressed. The steam-powered printing press and faster and more efficient typesetting methods enabled the mass production of newspapers and consequently the development of the sports page. Aided by the rapid availability of sports results from telegraph, and later telephone transmission, sports writers reported daily on sports events in the major newspapers. With constant attention from the press, Canadian sports heroes such as Ned Hanlan, the world champion sculler from Toronto (1880s), and Tommy Burns, Canada's only heavyweight boxing champion (1906), emerged as national celebrities.

The trend to urbanization and the progress in technology facilitated the development of organized sport in Canada. During the 1840s the British officers in garrison towns and cities continued to play a leadership role in sport, and by this time, more inter-community competition was occurring. As well, an emerging commercial middle class dominated by young native-born Canadian private-school graduates was starting to play an important role in the organization of sport. As the 19th century progressed, this group gradually replaced the British officers in providing leadership in sport in Canada (Metcalfe, 1987). During the 1850s, the withdrawal of most of the British troops left a noticeable void in sports activity in the communities in which they were located. In 1861, following the outbreak of the Civil War in the United States, about 11 000 troops were rushed back to British North America. Although these numbers were not as high as in 1814, their impact on sport was considerably greater because a different Canada received them. The country had developed to a stage where many more people were interested in pursuing recreational activities (Lindsay, 1970). By the early 1870s, most British officers and soldiers had left Canada or had been absorbed into civilian life leaving the organization of sport to the emerging commercial middle class.

Don Morrow (1989) has described Montreal as the cradle of organized sport in Canada and for good reason. After 1814, Montreal became the headquarters for the British imperial forces in Canada, and consequently the influence of the British officers upon the development of sport was strongly felt in this city. The Hunt Club (1829), Cricket Club (1829), Tandem Club (1837), and Racquet Club (1839) were all formed by the officers of the Montreal garrison, along with like-minded members of the social elite. In 1842, Canada's earliest track and field organization, the Montreal Olympic Club (MOC), was founded by the 93rd Highland Regiment, and the following year the Montreal Snow Shoe Club (MSSC) was established. This club organized snowshoe tramps, races, and social events and served as the prototype for other snowshoe clubs such as the Beaver, the Alexandria, and the St. George's, which were formed in Montreal during the 1860s and 1870s. By the later 1870s, there were 20 thriving snowshoe clubs in the city, and the many snowshoeing events set an example for the organization of Montreal sport. Organized lacrosse was also initiated in Montreal with the formation of the Montreal Lacrosse Club (MLC) in 1856. Lacrosse grew slowly in Montreal until the 1860s when Dr. W. G. Beers actively promoted the game and through the MLC established the first set of rules. By the end of Confederation year, there were 80 clubs in Quebec and Ontario and lacrosse went on to flourish as one of the most widespread and popular sports in Canada. Montreal was also the home of North America's first golf club, the Montreal Golf Club (1873), which set the pattern for the development of clubs in Quebec, Toronto, Hamilton, and other areas (Morrow, 1989).

Probably the most significant development in establishing Montreal as the cradle of organized sport in Canada was the formation of Canada's first multi-sport club, the Montreal Amateur Athletic Association (MAAA). It resulted from the amalgamation of the MSSC, the MLC, and the Montreal Bicycle Club (MBC) in 1881. Its members were instrumental in the formation and administration of at least 10 national governing bodies in rugby-football, hockey, cycling, baseball, figure skating, bowling, and water polo between 1882 and 1906. Numerous Canadian titles were won by MAAA athletes (including four Stanley Cup titles between 1886 and 1902), and even Canada's first Olympic gold medal was won by a club member, Etienne Desmarteau (Morrow, 1989).

By the time the MAAA was formed, the differentiation between an amateur and a professional had changed from one of class distinction to one based on the earning of money through sport (Cosentino, 1975). Amateur purists saw money as the root of all evil in sport, and professionalism was considered the prostitution of sport. To combat the increasing trend toward professionalism, the MAAA followed the lead of the British and Americans by organizing the Canadian Amateur Athletic Association (CAAA) in 1884.

MAAA executives dominated the affairs of the CAAA during its early years and became embroiled in what has been called the "athletic war" in 1906. The Canadian Amateur Athletic Union (CAAU), formerly the CAAA, would not allow amateur athletes to compete with or against professionals. To avoid the hypocrisy of "shamateurism," whereby athletes were receiving money "under the table" in order to retain their amateur status and that of their teammates, the MAAA advocated that the amateur code be liberalized to permit freedom of play between amateurs and professionals. This proposal was staunchly opposed by the conservative elements of the CAAU, based primarily in Toronto, and resulted in the MAAA-led members forming the Amateur Athletic Federation (AAF of C) in 1907 (Morrow, 1989). However, over the next few years, the CAAU continued to gain in strength as clubs, sport governing bodies, and amateur athletic associations from across the country hastened to join so that by 1909, the CAAU claimed 900 clubs and associations with over 60 000 additional members, a far cry from the 36 clubs of 1906. Finally, in 1909, the newly formed AAF of C, based in Montreal, succumbed to the will of the powerful CAAU and re-joined the organization, which modified its name slightly to the Amateur Athletic Union of Canada (AAU of C), hence temporarily laying to rest the issue of amateurs and professionals being allowed to compete freely with and against each other.

In the years preceding the Great War, the AAU of C moved to consolidate its position as the sole authority in matters pertaining to amateur athletics (Metcalfe, 1987), and, by 1914, boasted a membership of 1300 clubs and 100 000 registered athletes (Kidd, 1996).

With the onset of the Great War in 1914, many sports leagues ceased operation, and in the few leagues that continued, only those where it was advertised that the gate receipts were turned over to war charities were well attended. While civilian activities were severely curtailed, sports thrived in the military, and the AAU of C gave its blessing to the mixing of amateurs and professionals as long as they were in uniform. The war may well have strengthened the hold of sports on many Canadians as the army gave more men opportunities to participate than the amateur clubs had ever done. Other changes brought about by the war also improved conditions for sports. For example, mobilization accelerated the movement of young men and women to the cities and towns and hence increased the membership base for clubs of all kinds. Furthermore, the greatly increased participation of women in the wartime labour force validated feminist demands for access to traditionally male-exclusive spheres, including sports (Kidd, 1996).

The preceding discussion of the development of organized sport in Canada has focused on men's sport but little has been said about women's involvement in sport or recreational activity. The accepted leisure activities—for example, fishing, hunting, horse racing, canoeing, snowshoeing, lacrosse, and cricket—of the frontier settlers and military personnel were pursued only by males while women sat as adoring spectators and participated in the post-event social festivities. Although many female settlers were forced by circumstances to engage in strenuous physical activity, only leisure pastimes such as croquet and dancing, which required little physical exertion, were thought to be acceptable for them. The medical opinion of the day was that the physical demands of sport could be harmful to the female reproductive organs. Furthermore, women were restricted by their clothing—long skirts, crinolines, tight corsets, hats, and gloves—all of which hampered their movement. In the late 1850s, when American feminist Amelia Bloomer popularized the bifurcated pants known as "bloomers," women began to experience freedom of movement without loss of dignity. By the time of Confederation, horseback riding and snowshoeing became acceptable leisure pursuits for women, and when the safety bicycle came on the market in 1885 women took to bicycling as an enjoyable outdoor pastime. By the late 1800s, tennis, curling, golf, basketball, baseball, and even hockey were added to the list of sports that women played. Nevertheless, many men were still strongly opposed to women participating in vigorous physical activity, partially to preserve what had traditionally been a male domain and partially from a genuine concern that women could not withstand the physical and emotional stresses of competitive sport. Such concerns were shared by many American female physical educators who were against aggressive competition for women in their schools and universities. They established policies and procedures that limited the physical demands of competition and set standards (such as girls' rules in basketball) that protected female participants. These American attitudes toward women in sport played a significant role in central Canada as Canadian women sought advanced degrees in American universities, and female sport leaders in Canada looked for guidance from American professional organizations. Therefore, after the turn of the century, a chasm began to develop between educational and community sport for women; that is, between what was practised in physical education classes and in community sports leagues (Keyes, 1989c).

Just as women had limited opportunities to participate in sport prior to 1918, so too did Canada's Aboriginal people, but for different reasons. Early in the 19th century "gentlemen amateurs" categorized Aboriginal people as "professionals" in sports such as lacrosse and snowshoeing where they clearly were superior competitors. The reality was that the upper class did not want to be humiliated by being defeated by socially inferior native Indians. When the Amateur Lacrosse Association was formed in 1880, all Aboriginal people, by virtue of their race, were automatically ranked as professionals and were allowed to play with whites only in exhibition matches or to act as trainers. It wasn't until the rival, skill-oriented Canadian Lacrosse Association (CLA) was formed in 1887 that Aboriginal people were allowed to play lacrosse as amateurs. In snowshoeing races there was a special category for native Indians (Cosentino, 1975). Because it was a crowd-drawing feature, the Indian race, varying in distance from two to four miles, was usually the first event on the racing card. Incentives were offered to native Indians competitors to perform at near-maximum speed early in the race so that spectators could sadistically witness their agony in the last stages of the contest. Often clubs would offer novelty events for native Indians that had as their objective ridicule and entertainment for the white spectators. Such degrading practices were also prevalent in track and field and lacrosse (Morrow, 1989). Throughout the press of the day and into the early years of the 20th century when a native Indian's Christian name appeared, the enjoinder "(Indian)" was attached so as to put their achievements into perspective and to distinguish them from other segments of society (Cosentino, 1975). Even Tom Longboat, the famous Onondaga Indian from the Caledonia Reserve near Hamilton who dominated distance running around 1908, was subject to racial discrimination. In the press he was usually identified as a native, "a designation which implied distinction from and inferiority to whites. Many treated him no better than a racehorse" (Kidd, 1983, p. 48). Such racial discrimination against Canada's Aboriginal people can still be observed today, but it tends to be less conspicuous and more subtle.

1918 TO 1961

Many major events took place in Canada and the world from 1918 to 1961. The "roaring twenties," the Depression, the Second World War, and the early stages of the Cold War all fall within this time frame. Within this historical context, the face of sport changed significantly. The trend to urbanization noted earlier continued so that by 1921 approximately 50% of Canadians were urban dwellers (Lappage, 1974). This expansion of urban centres coupled with a growing American influence and technological developments in transportation and communication led to the proliferation of professional sport.

During the 1920s, the AAU of C managed to maintain its stranglehold on amateur sport, but "shamateurism" persisted and became more of a problem during the Depression as athletes found it hard to resist under-the-table-payments or reimbursement for time away from work ("broken time payments"). Equally attractive were the jobs that were sometimes offered in return for playing for a company team (C. Howell, 2001). The AAU of C suffered a severe blow in 1937 when two major affiliated sports withdrew from the union—ice hockey because it could no longer abide by the restrictive policy that prohibited "broken time payments," and basketball because it wanted its independence and was frustrated by the domination of the union. If it were not for the Second World War, it is likely that other sports would have left the AAU of C within the next few years. The COA, having increased its self-determination with each passing Olympic festival, finally declared its autonomy in

1948. "This was a serious blow to the power and prestige of the AAU, which was now relegated to subordinate status as a mere member of the Olympic Association" (Schrodt, 1983, p. 5). After 1948, the AAU of C's hegemony in amateur sports gradually diminished, and the union finally dissolved in 1970. By the 1950s, most sports had formed international federations, each determining its own eligibility for world championships. When the AAU of C lost its sanctioning powers for international athletes, it also ceased to exert any serious influence over amateurism in Canada (Schrodt, 1983).

While the AAU of C was experiencing its difficulties in controlling amateur sport, professional sport was gaining in prestige in Canadian society. As early as the beginning of the 20th century, the concept had been taking hold that "professional" meant not only one who competed for money but also one with a high degree of skill. With the rise of professional leagues such as the National Hockey League (NHL) and the influence of the radio, the notion was nurtured that the more money an athlete received the more skilled he was. Thus the amateur athlete started to be thought of as someone who wasn't good enough to be a professional (Cosentino, 1975).

Professional sport experienced a tremendous boom in the United States after the First World War, and American sports heroes such as pitcher-slugger Babe Ruth, boxer Jack Dempsey, running back Red Grange, and golfer Bobby Jones, promoted through the press and radio, became as popular in Canada as they were south of the border. As well, Foster Hewitt's "Hockey Night in Canada" radio broadcast from the gondola in Toronto's Maple Leaf Gardens elevated professional hockey players, especially the Maple Leafs, in the eyes of Canadians (Kidd, 1996). Canadians' love affair with Saturday night hockey broadcasts—although transmitted by television today—has continued into the 21st century.

During the inter-war years, expanded newspaper and magazine coverage of sporting events along with radio broadcasting extended the boundaries of the sporting audience (C. Howell, 2001). By the early 1950s television started to capture the attention of sports enthusiasts. In 1952, hockey was first seen on Canadian television, and within a few months baseball and intercollegiate and professional football games were also broadcast. By 1954, sporting events like the Grey Cup, the World Series, Davis Cup Tennis, and the perennial *Hockey Night in Canada* attracted enthusiastic television audiences (R. Howell & M. Howell, 1985). However, many Canadians who did not own television sets or were plagued with poor reception still experienced professional hockey, football, boxing, and baseball by listening rather than watching (C. Howell, 2001). Television had its greatest influence on sport in the post-1961 era.

Improvements in transportation enhanced the development of sport both at the amateur and professional levels in Canada after the Great War. The number of automobiles on the road tripled between 1920 and 1930, providing greater opportunities for inter-community and regional competition while faster and more comfortable rail travel led to increased inter-provincial and national competitions (Lappage, 1974). In the early 1920s national finals between eastern and western representatives began to emerge rapidly. The first Canadian championship automobile races were held in 1920, while both the Dominion ski championships and the annual East versus West football game for the Grey Cup started in 1921. In 1922, the national finals for badminton commenced, and in 1924, the first sanctioned national basketball championships for both men and women were held. As a result of this increased East–West competition, a stronger rivalry between eastern and western Canada arose in the early 1920s (Lappage, 1977). Commercial air travel, although in existence since the chartering of Trans-Canada Air Lines in 1937, did not start to influence sport in Canada until toward the end of the 1918–1961 period. By the 1950s, athletes could travel across the country or overseas by air, hence furthering the opportunities for national and international competition.

Indeed, during the 1918–1961 period, Canada's participation in international competition increased significantly. Canada has entered all the Summer Olympics since 1904 and has also been a participant in the Winter Olympics since their inauguration in 1924. Furthermore, Canada hosted the first British Empire Games held in Hamilton in 1930 and was host again in 1954 in Vancouver. In addition to being a regular participant in the British Empire (Commonwealth) Games, Canada has also been actively involved in the Pan American Games since 1955 (N. Howell & M. Howell, 1969). Numerous world championships including the World Hockey Championships can also be added to Canada's involvement in international sport prior to 1961. Although Canadian athletes such as Percy Williams, Ethel Catherwood, Duncan McNaughton, and Barbara Ann Scott were recognized for their gold medal performances at the Olympics, it was probably Canada's hockey teams that drew the greatest attention in the sports world. Canada dominated international hockey up to the end of the Second World War, losing the title only two times (1933 and 1936). However, between 1947 and 1961, other rising hockey powers (Czechoslovakia, Russia, Sweden, and the United States) collectively won the championship seven times (N. Howell & M. Howell, 1969).

Canadian pride was at stake. The national concern about our loss of hockey prominence opened the door for the federal government to get more actively involved in sport and fitness. The result was the passage of the Fitness and Amateur Sport Act (Bill C-131) in 1961. Before the significance of this Act is discussed, some background information regarding the federal government's involvement in sport and fitness should be given.

As early as 1909, the federal government promoted military drill in Canadian schools through the Strathcona Trust Fund (Gear, 1973). During the Depression, through various programs the federal government provided money to the provinces on a cost-sharing basis to fund physical training projects designed to maintain the health and morale of the young unemployed. Several provinces drew on these funds to implement programs similar to the Provincial-Recreation (Pro-Rec) Program that British Columbia had started in 1934 to provide recreational opportunities for its youth (Lappage, 1978). These programs provided the basis for the National Physical Fitness Act of 1943 which was intended to promote the physical fitness of the people of Canada (West, 1973). Many problems, too detailed to recount in this brief history, were encountered, and the Act was repealed in 1954. The federal government claimed that the Act had become ineffective, that the programs were more the responsibility of the provinces and municipalities, and that it was too costly to administer (Cosentino, 1988).

It is readily apparent that all the aforementioned programs related to physical education, fitness, and recreation rather than competitive sport. Up to the 1950s, the federal government generally steered clear of involvement in sport, but a growing concern about Canada's poor performances in recent international competition, especially with its drop from prominence in world championship hockey, stimulated the federal government to take action. Even as the National Physical Fitness Act of 1943 was being repealed in 1954, the Canadian Sports Advisory Council, which represented the various sports governing bodies, was lobbying the federal government to become more actively involved in amateur sport and the fitness of Canadians. In 1958, this council circulated a brief that focused on sport and fitness issues such as national prestige, defence, production, health status, culture, fitness as a benefit to the economy, and evidence of physical-fitness deficiencies. The next year, in an address to the Canadian Medical Association (CMA), the Duke of Edinburgh, drawing on information from this brief, challenged the CMA to deal with the poor fitness level of Canadians. As a result, the CMA and the Canadian Association for Health, Physical Education and Recreation (CAHPER) combined their efforts to lobby the government to deal with this issue (Keyes, 1989a). Some members of parliament also spoke about how the Union of Soviet Socialist Republics (U.S.S.R.) and other Communist countries were promoting mass participation to increase the health of their nations and hence their performance in international sport. This indicated another reason why the government should be concerned about physical fitness—to advance sport as a tool in the fight for democracy (Gear, 1973).

The Fitness and Amateur Sport Act (Bill C-131), whose purpose was to provide access to sport and fitness for all Canadians, was adopted unanimously by the House of Commons on September 25, 1961. The ten provisions of the Act were expressed in vague, general terms, leaving latitude for interpretation of the government's intentions during the early years of its implementation. It marked the beginning of a new era in the development of Canadian sport—the age of government involvement.

Before moving on to this modern age of sport development in Canada, we should briefly examine women's involvement in sport from 1918 to 1961. After the First World War, women's participation in sport increased rapidly. Indeed, the 1920s and 1930s became known as the Golden Age of Sport for Canadian women. By the early 1920s, participation had grown to the point that girls and young women of all classes engaged in sports through universities, schools, leagues, clubs, and church groups. More permissive dress codes allowed women to discard bulky dresses and bloomers for shorts and T-shirts, greatly increasing their mobility and their enjoyment of physical activity. Moreover, as women took part in a wider range of sports and adopted a tougher, more aggressive style of play, newspaper and radio coverage of women's sport increased. Several women such as Fanny Rosenfeld, Alexandrine Gibb, and Myrtle Cook-McGowan wrote women's sport columns in major Canadian newspapers during the inter-war period (C. Howell, 2001). To encourage Canadian women's participation in international competition, Alexandrine Gibb proposed that a women's organization be formed in affiliation with the AAU of C. This new Women's Amateur Athletic Federation (WAAF), founded in 1926, operated for more than a decade until it was disbanded with the outbreak of the Second World War (Kidd, 1996).

During the 1920s, a number of women sporting heroes emerged, elevating the image of female athletes. In 1928, at the Amsterdam Olympics six Canadian female track and field athletes, affectionately known as the "matchless six," won two gold medals and one silver plus a fourth and fifth placing, earning more points than any other women's track and field contingent. When they returned to Toronto they were welcomed by 300 000 people lining the streets from Union Station to Sunnyside Stadium (Kidd, 1996). Equally popular were the famous Edmonton Grads, who dominated women's basketball in Canada, winning every

Canadian championship from 1923 to 1940, all 27 games that coincided with the Olympic Games, and the Underwood Typewriter North American Championships for 17 consecutive years (C. Howell, 2001). Their coach, Percy Page, insisted that the Grads behave as ladies both on and off the court. They portrayed an image of wholesome Canadian girls who played the game (according to men's rules) skilfully and aggressively and yet retained their femininity. The Grads helped destroy the perception that some males had of female athletes as "leathery faced Amazons with flat chests and bony limbs and a walk like a knock-kneed penguin" (C. Howell, 2001, p. 118). Starting in the 1920s, innuendos, such as the one above, concerning lesbianism were often directed at women who participated in traditionally masculine sports and at women who failed to meet the feminine stereotype because of size, body type, or muscular development (Lenskyj, 1988). These homophobic attitudes have been a persistent problem for girls and women and still exist today (Keyes, 1989c).

During the Second World War, women's participation in sports declined as young women entered the labour force to replace the men fighting overseas. Work and the increased burdens at home left little time or energy for sports. After the war, renewed gender stereotyping discouraged women from participating in sports other than those that portrayed a feminine image such as diving, synchronized swimming, golf, tennis, and figure skating. Barbara Ann Scott, who won a gold medal in figure skating at the 1948 Winter Olympics, was the ideal female athlete. She was Canada's sweetheart—a petite blond doll on ice—whose appearance rather than athletic talent was emphasized by the press (Morrow, 1987). Doubts that female athletes could withstand the physical demands of strenuous sport persisted into the 1950s. In 1954, 16-year-old Marilyn Bell helped shatter the myth of the fragile female by swimming across Lake Ontario, demonstrating the physical capacity of a well-conditioned female athlete (Keyes, 1989c). Fortunately, attitudes toward women's participation in sport were beginning to change. "With the emergence of second-wave feminism in the 1960s and 1970s, more and more Canadian women began challenging the boundaries of what was considered acceptable physical activity for women" (C. Howell, 2001, p. 121).

1961 TO 2002

Remarkable changes have occurred in the world during the last four decades. Man has walked on the moon and now commutes regularly to a space station circling the earth; the Cold War has ended and several former Communist countries have dissipated; the War on Terrorism has begun; air travel has become commonplace; and computers and the Internet are important parts of our daily lives. Amidst all this change it should come as no surprise that sport has also quickly transformed.

Rapid technological progress, especially in communication and transportation, has influenced sport in many ways. Television has had a profound effect on sport in Canada since the early 1960s. Generally television has popularized elite-level sport but has detracted from community-based sport. Why should one go to the local arena to watch a senior hockey team in its quest for the Allan Cup when one can watch, from the comfort of one's living room, the best hockey players in the world compete for the Stanley Cup or an Olympic gold medal?

Sports have been important in moulding Canadian nationalism, and it has been television that has brought these events into Canadian homes. *Hockey Night in Canada*, originally broadcast over the radio, continued its popularity on television, and in 1957 the Canadian Broadcasting

Corporation (CBC) televised the Grey Cup Game for the first time. In 1972, the Canada–U.S.S.R. hockey series, broadcast from Canadian cities and Moscow, captured the interest of the nation, and in 1976 and 1988 Canadians watched the Olympic Games hosted by Montreal and Calgary with great pride. The attention given to Canadian sport on television in the 1960s and 1970s created national heroes at a time when in the United States the cult of the hero was rapidly disintegrating. Colin Howell (2001) suggests that somehow Canadians seem less willing to politicize their sporting heroes, perhaps because our successes in elite-level international competition are relatively rare and our heroes tend to be understood not as representatives of particular interest groups, but rather as affirmations of our nationhood.

Paradoxically, although television has helped establish a Canadian identity through sport, it has also facilitated and accelerated the Americanization of Canadian sport. As we have become increasingly exposed to American television, Canadians have developed a stronger interest in American professional sports. The National Football League (NFL) and Superbowl Game now attract a large Canadian following and the National Basketball Association (NBA), with only one Canadian franchise, is ardently watched by Canadian basketball fans. Even the highest level of our national game, the National Hockey League (NHL), which is brought to most Canadians by television, has shifted south of the border with the majority of the franchises located in larger American cities.

The airplane has also greatly influenced the transformation of sport in Canada since 1961. Today an athlete or coach can travel by air from Vancouver to Toronto in less time than it took to go from Toronto to Montreal by rail during the inter-war period. Air travel is regularly used by inter-university teams in the western provinces, by amateur athletes travelling to national and international meets, by professional athletes commuting throughout North America for league play, and by coaches, officials, and sports administrators attending meetings and clinics. Air travel has also opened the door for the average working person to become more involved in amateur sport as an official, coach, or volunteer and, along with the implementation of government travel assistance, has facilitated the democratization of the operation of national sports organizations (Keyes, 1989a).

As previously mentioned, the Fitness and Amateur Sport Act of 1961 marked a turning point in the involvement of the federal government in fitness and amateur sport in Canada. The immediate effect was felt in the form of unprecedented stimulus to the agencies active in the fields of fitness, recreation, and sport across the nation. Volunteers, who for years had paid all their own expenses to promote their sport, suddenly found government willing to reimburse them for attending meetings, coaching clinics, or accompanying their teams to national competitions. The Act, through its ten provisions, promoted fitness and amateur sport at all levels and allowed the government to fund research, bursaries and fellowships, conferences, coaching, national and international competitions, as well as to provide practically any other support required. In 1962, the Fitness and Amateur Sport Directorate, which employed full-time civil servants, was created to carry out the day-to-day administration of the Act. It was originally envisaged that cost-sharing agreements between the federal and provincial governments to distribute the maximum of $5 million per year available through the Act would be effective in developing mass-sport and physical fitness programs across the country and thus establishing a base from which elite athletes would rise. However, during the 1960s, many problems were encountered in the administration of the federal–provincial agreements and Canada continued to perform poorly in international sport. Although the federal government did assist with the funding of the Pan American Games in Winnipeg and the first Canada Winter Games in Quebec City, both held during the nation's centennial year, its role was predominantly indirect and passive (Keyes, 1989a). This changed dramatically at the end of the decade.

Overt political use of sport had its origin in a 1969 campaign speech when Prime Minister Pierre Trudeau linked sport with culture in promoting national unity, a major issue of the day. By this time, sport was taking up an important part of television programming and thus was being introduced to millions of Canadians. This made it attractive as a device that could be used as a national unity symbol, one that could counterbalance the divisive cultural and political forces that existed in the late 1960s. Trudeau's election promise to establish a task force on sport was fulfilled in 1969, and the following year John Munro, the Minister of Health and Welfare, announced his "Proposed Sports Policy for Canadians," which implemented many of the task force's recommendations (Macintosh, 1985). He established a larger and more influential Directorate for Fitness and Amateur Sport, overseen by bureaucrats with expertise in sport and fitness who would assume a more direct control over sports organizations. As well, four important arm's-length agencies to be funded by the federal government but controlled by independent boards of directors were created—the National Sport and Recreation Centre, Hockey Canada, Sport Participation Canada (Participaction), and the Coaching Association of Canada (CAC).

The National Sport and Recreation Centre was organized in Ottawa to provide office space and support services to the national sport organizations, thereby transferring their administration from the kitchen tables of volunteers to the offices of professional executive directors. Hockey Canada was formed to deal primarily with Canada's poor showing in international competitions (the U.S.S.R. dominated international hockey during the 1960s) and was intended to organize national teams. Participaction was created to encourage Canadians to improve their physical fitness, and the CAC was formed to develop better coaches at all levels in Canada.

In 1971, the federal government's fiscal commitment to fitness and amateur sport was about $6 million, but by the next year following the implementation of many of the task force's recommendations, this figure jumped to approximately $11 million, with two-thirds going to amateur sports. In 1978–79 the funding more than tripled to $35 million with as much as three-quarters being allotted to the development of high-performance sport. Noteworthy among the programs developed during the 1970s were Game Plan (1973), which provided extra funding to prepare Canada's elite athletes for the 1976 Olympic Games held in Montreal, and the Athlete Assistance Program, which funded carded athletes to enable them to dedicate more of their time to training (Keyes, 1989a).

Clearly, during the 1970s, the federal government embarked on a course of direct aggressive promotion of the development of high-performance athletes at the expense of mass sport and fitness. Success in high-performance sport could be attained through a substantially smaller outlay of money and could be easily verified in quantitative terms. Because of its visibility, high-performance sport also had the potential for a much more attractive political payoff than did mass sport and fitness programs. Federal government efforts in improving the performance of Canadian athletes paid off in the late 1970s and early 1980s. At the 1976

Montreal Olympics, although they did not win any gold medals, Canadian athletes had a respectable showing, and at the 1978 Commonwealth Games in Edmonton, Canada staged a spectacular sport triumph by placing first ahead of England and Australia. At the 1984 Olympics in Los Angeles, Canada had its best ever performance—although it could be argued that this was because most of the Communist countries boycotted these Games.

The federal government's efforts to promote high-performance sport have also served to maintain and develop a Canadian sport identity. As previously discussed, the attractiveness of sport on television and the use of sport to sell commodities and services has resulted in a North American professional sport image dominated by American telecasts, business, and sport enterprises. The expansion of professional hockey into the United States and the introduction of Major League Baseball (MLB) and NBA basketball into Canada have given additional momentum to this trend. However, the improved performance of Canadian athletes in international competitions provides Canadians with sports heroes who are not part of the North American professional sport package, thus countering the threat to Canadian identity of the all-pervasive mass culture of the United States (Macintosh, 1985).

This positive image of Canada's elite international athletes was tarnished by Ben Johnson, whose gold medal for his record-breaking 100-metre sprint at the 1988 Seoul Olympics was stripped from him when drug testing showed that he had used steroids. The Dubin Inquiry, which resulted from this scandal, revealed that banned substances were well known and used in Canada's community of athletes, coaches, and officials. The response of the federal government, which itself contributed to the problem by emphasizing the importance of high-performance athletics, was to establish a new Canadian anti-doping organization that coordinates and administers anti-doping initiatives. It is not surprising that after the Dubin Report was released the federal government's support for elite amateur sport changed drastically. Sport budgets were cut and more responsibility for raising their own funds was placed on the national sporting organizations. In recent years, this has meant a new emphasis on the corporate sponsorship of athletics and on fundraising in the private sector (C. Howell, 2001). With stricter anti-doping controls in place, a rejuvenation of the wholesome image of Canada's elite amateur athletes, and the recent success of Canadian athletes at the Winter Olympics in Salt Lake City, it will be interesting to see if the federal government restores some of the funding that previously was available to high-performance sport.

This chapter would not be complete without a quick discussion of women's participation in sport during the modern era. In 1970, the Report of the Royal Commission on the Status of Women made a number of recommendations relating to sport for women and identified inequalities that needed to be addressed. Women's sports in Canada were underfunded, and in addition to women's lower level of participation, they were underrepresented in coaching and sports administration and at the executive levels of sport (C. Howell, 2001). During the 1970s, Fitness and Amateur Sport launched a number of initiatives to address some of the inequalities that existed. One of the most significant projects was a planning workshop that resulted in the formation of the Canadian Association for the Advancement of Women and Sport, which has acted as a catalyst for women's rights in sports.

Nancy Greene, Canada's tiger of the ski slopes, advanced the prestige of women in sports during the sixties and seventies. She captured the World Cup in downhill skiing twice (1967, 1968) and won a gold and a silver medal at the 1968 Winter Olympics. With her aggressive skiing style and fresh-faced appearance, she became a favourite of the press and was recognized as a valuable ambassador for Canada throughout the world (Fisher & Wise, 1974). Greene was the first Canadian female athlete to benefit commercially from her athletic success and later became a successful entrepreneur. Since her retirement in 1968, she has played an influential role in the development of sport both as a member of the Task Force on Sport and as a promoter of downhill skiing through the Nancy Greene Ski League (Keyes, 1989c). At the turn of the century, she was honoured as Canada's female athlete-of-the-century.

Another female athlete who did much to advance the cause of women in sport was Abby Hoffman. She represented Canada in track at four Olympics, four Pan American Games, two Commonwealth Games, three World University Games, and at the Maccabiah Games. She has been a strong advocate for women's rights in sport and has been a popular speaker on this issue at conferences, clinics, workshops, and seminars throughout the country. While serving as director general of Sport Canada, she supported a women's program that has been innovative and far-reaching (Keyes, 1989c).

Many other Canadian female athletes, too numerous to mention here, have recently achieved at the highest levels of sport and advanced the cause for the equality of the sexes in sport. No longer are women regarded as fragile human beings who cannot withstand the physical and emotional stresses of competitive sport. They have now run marathons and competed in hockey at the Olympic Games. There are still barriers to be lowered before true equality in women's sport is achieved, but women have made many advances since the days when they were adoring spectators restricted in movement by long skirts, crinolines, and tight corsets.

CONCLUSIONS

In this chapter you have learned how physical activity in Canada has evolved from the informal, spontaneous, unstructured play of the Aboriginal peoples, coureurs de bois, voyageurs, and early French Canadian and British settlers to the more formal games played by the British garrisons and urban upper class. With the development of sports clubs and national organizations, games became institutionalized and consequently evolved into sports as defined in Chapter 1. Initially, sports were played and controlled by the wealthy upper and middle classes, but with shorter working hours and improved transportation and communication systems, sports gradually opened up to all classes. With the growth of government involvement in sport and fitness after 1961 and post-World War II technological progress, the opportunities for all Canadians to participate in sports as athletes, coaches, officials, or administrators have increased significantly.

You have also read about the development of the amateur-professional dichotomy in Canadian sport, the influence of technology upon sport, and the evolution of women's involvement in sport. With this historical background, you should now have a better understanding of the issues related to contemporary sport that are discussed in this textbook.

Critical Thinking Questions

1. Which technological development do you think has had the greatest impact upon sport in Canada?

2. Why has Montreal been called "the cradle of organized sport in Canada"?
3. Why did the Amateur Athletic Union of Canada start to lose its control of amateur sport?
4. What is the significance of the Fitness and Amateur Sport Act of 1961?
5. How did "broken time payment" affect Canadian sport history?
6. How did the Ben Johnson drug scandal at the 1988 Seoul Olympics affect government involvement in Canadian sport?

Suggested Readings

Fisher S.F., & Wise, D. (1974). *Canada's sporting heroes: Their lives and times.* Don Mills, Ont.: General Publishing Company Limited.

Howell, C. (2001). *Blood, sweat, and cheers: Sport and the making of modern Canada.* Toronto: University of Toronto Press.

Howell, R.A., & Howell, M.L. (Eds.). (1985). *History of sport in Canada.* Champaign, Ill.: Stipes Publishing Company.

Howell, N., & Howell, M.L. (1969). *Sports and games in Canadian life: 1700 to the present.* Toronto: Macmillan of Canada.

Kidd, B. (1996). *The struggle for Canadian sport.* Toronto: University of Toronto Press.

Metcalfe, A. (1987). *Canada learns to play: The emergence of organized sport, 1807–1914.* Toronto: McClelland and Stewart Limited.

Morrow, D., Keyes, M., Simpson, W., Cosentino, F., & Lappage, R. (1989). *A concise history of sport in Canada.* Toronto: Oxford University Press.

Web Links

International Centre for Olympic Studies (ICOS)
http://www.uwo.ca/olympic/
Includes facilities, Olympic fellows, publications, conferences, lecture series, and related sites.

International Society for the History of Physical Education and Sport (ISHPES)
http://www.umist.ac.uk/sport/ishpes.html
Includes conferences, members, history, conference proceedings, awards, links to sport history sites.

North American Society for Sport History (NASSH)
http://www.nassh.org/
Includes newsletters, members, history, conferences, publications, links to related sites.

Sport Information Resource Centre
www.sirc.ca
A subscription site containing a wide variety of literature and statistical databases.

3

Children, Youth, and Parental Involvement in Organized Sport

Ralph E. Wheeler

RALPH WHEELER

Youth sports programs should focus on what is best for the athletes.

Play is basic to all normal, healthy children. It provides pleasure and learning and a minimum of risks and penalties for mistakes.

C. Schaefler and H. Kaduson, *The Quotable Play Therapist*

The rise in popularity of organized sports programs for children is still a relatively new phenomenon in comparison to the history of organized sports for adult populations. The focus on formal games for children may have had its earliest beginnings in North America with the founding of Little League Baseball in the United States in 1939. In the decades since, sports programs for children have grown at a phenomenal rate.

Today, nearly three million Canadian children and youths between the ages of five and eighteen participate regularly in organized sports programs. These programs are offered by a number of organizations and groups that serve to govern and control these activities in order to ensure children receive the positive benefits from their experiences. Critics would argue that many of the initial objectives of organized sport for children have been lost in the highly institutionalized sport models that have emerged. This chapter will review the organizational structure of children's sport in Canada; examine some of the reasons why children participate in youth sport and the benefits gained from this involvement; and finally, explore a number of issues and concerns related to organized sport programs. These areas include

- dropout and burnout in organized sport,
- overemphasis on performance, winning, and specialization,
- limiting children's choices in organized sport,
- parental involvement in kids' sports, and
- coaches' influence in children's sport.

In order to examine these issues, this chapter will employ a number of theoretical perspectives introduced in Chapter 1. These theories provide contrasting views of organized sport for children. It is only by seeing sport from a number of alternative perspectives that we can make informed decisions about the overall merits of sport for children and youths.

THE ORGANIZATION OF MINOR SPORT

In Canada, organized sport for children and youths now begins in the pre-school years and is delivered through four main separate agencies or institutions. These include school-based sports, publicly funded community sport and recreation organizations, private sport clubs, and service agencies and special interest groups. These groups offer a plethora of sport programs and provide diverse experiences through various levels of training and competitive activities. Many of these programs, while they may have different rules for participation than adult programs, typically include many of the characteristics of adult-based sport, complete with training schedules, elimination competitions, and championships.

School Sport

Sport at the high school level has long been an element of the Canadian sport scene. Organized sport at the elementary school level, however, is a relatively new phenomenon encouraged initially by physical educators concerned about the low activity levels among children in this age group. School sports programs were an attempt to address this concern and originally involved inter-school sport activities on a somewhat informal basis. Today, these programs may involve scheduled games and can run from several weekends to a two-to three-month season. Coaches and officials are usually volunteers from the school staff or from within the community.

Because of a number of obstacles, elementary school sport has not achieved the potential outcomes envisioned by its early proponents. The absence of adequate resources such as facilities, qualified coaches, and funding have continued to prevent sport at the elementary school level from having any significant impact on overall student activity levels. Coupled with this is the fact that many of the schools that do sponsor sports programs tend to mirror a high school model, which caters to a minority of students. As well, even though costs associated with school sports programs are usually minimal, student participation is limited based on the number of teams sponsored by a particular school. This has caused many physical educators to seek alternative activities and strategies to encourage kids to become active.

Community-Based Sport

Community-based sport and recreation programs have become extremely popular activities for children in all parts of Canada. It is not unusual, for example, to find both boys and girls playing a wide variety of sports such as hockey, soccer, baseball, basketball, and tennis as part of a community-organized league. These programs are publicly subsidized and offer sport opportunities within a range of competitive levels. Coaches, officials, and league organizers, who are responsible for setting up and running all aspects of the program, include both paid staff and volunteers. Programs are usually organized around "house leagues," which may loosely represent local neighbourhood boundaries. Registration fees are fairly modest, and children are assigned to teams more or less on a random basis, the emphasis being on fun and participation. House league participants may practise and play one or two times per week. In addition, most programs support an "all-star" league selected from among a pool of talented players in a particular age group or division. At this level, competition takes on a more serious focus, with teams conducting tryouts, running regular training sessions, and competing in both league and tournament competitions. Teams from a community all-star league may also compete for the right to represent their respective communities in regional, provincial, and inter-provincial championships. Unlike house leagues, which usually play during the weekdays, all-star competitions are generally held on weekends. In this organizational structure, it is not unusual to find children participating simultaneously in both house league and all-star levels.

Private Sports Clubs

While community-based sports programs encourage wide participation and are relatively inexpensive, more and more children are opting to take part in privately organized sports clubs. One reason for the emergence of private sports clubs is to provide a higher level of training and competition not usually available through school and community-based sport. While these two programs may serve to identify talented youngsters, private clubs are perceived as having the potential to develop that talent into the elite level. Programs operating under this model tend to be sport specific, require far greater time commitment from the participant, and can be much more costly.

Many of these programs are highly structured with scheduled daily training programs. Emphasis is on the development of athletic talent and the promotion of competitive prowess. Children are carefully groomed for success at each of the various levels of competition.

Private sport clubs operate in both public and privately owned facilities and offer training and competition in such popular individual sports as swimming, gymnastics, figure skating, martial arts, tennis, track and field, cycling, wrestling, and rowing. Various team sports such as hockey, basketball, and soccer are also organized by private sport clubs. These sport clubs may operate with annual budgets that range from several thousand dollars to hundreds of thousands and employ both full- and part-time coaches, instructors, and administrators. Club membership fees can range from a modest hundred dollars annually to several thousand dollars, in addition to travel costs to competitions.

Service Agencies and Special Interest Groups

Co-existing and often sharing the same facilities with these three organizations are a number of other groups that also promote and deliver sport programs for children. These include YM/YWCAs, church groups, boys' and girls' clubs, and independent groups of like-minded individuals. As in other organizations which offer sport programs, a wide variety of activities exists for the participant. The main purpose of sport programs among these groups is to use sport as a vehicle to promote their particular set of values and beliefs.

In Canada, organized sport associations for children exist for a number of reasons. At the school level, sport is tied to educational objectives and is seen as a way to get and keep children active. Community programs attempt to promote sport opportunities for children through a variety of activities at a reasonable cost to the participant. Increasingly, however, there is a growing trend for children who aspire to become successful athletes to join private sports clubs. These clubs generally specialize in a particular sport and provide opportunities for children to excel at a high level within that sport. As many of these clubs must operate on income generated through membership fees and corporate sponsors, they resemble in many ways the practices and structures found in adult sport organizations.

Clearly, minor sports organizations have become an integral part of the social structure of most communities. With few exceptions, almost every province that has a sport association responsible for governing and promoting that particular sport will likely have youth programs in place, often starting as early as age five for many children. As Leonard (1998) notes, "What is remarkable and unprecedented is that there are sport leagues for children who have not even entered the primary grades" (p. 123). The significance of these programs with respect to the psychological, social, and physical effects on the participants will be discussed in another section of this chapter.

FACTORS DETERMINING CHILDREN'S INVOLVEMENT IN SPORT

While children still gather in community playgrounds and neighbourhood parks to enjoy spontaneous, informal games, an increasing number of boys and girls are now engaged in adult-controlled sport-related activities. A 1998 Statistics Canada Survey found that more than half of all Canadian children aged five to fourteen (almost 2.2 million) reported that they regularly took part in some kind of organized sport activity. Table 3.1 shows the 10 most popular sport activities for children in this age category.

The survey also examined some of the underlying reasons for the increase in the participation rates of children in organized sport. Of the 2220 families surveyed, the majority of children involved in sport were from middle-class to upper-class households. The study

TABLE 3.1 Top 10 Sports Among Canadian Children Aged 5 to 14

Sport	Percentage of Active Children in the Sport
Soccer	31
Swimming	24
Hockey	24
Baseball	22
Basketball	13
Downhill Skiing	7
Figure Skating	6
Karate	6
Volleyball	5
Cycling	3

Source: Based on data from the Statistics Canada, General Social Survey, 1998

found that 73% of children from families with annual incomes over $80 000 were enrolled in organized sports programs; this dropped to 49% when the family income was below $40 000. Nevertheless, results revealed that in households where parents were involved in sport activities, children were four to eight times more likely to participate in sport than in families where parents had no athletic involvement, regardless of income levels.

The literature related to participation in minor sport programs offers many reasons for the increased involvement of children in organized sport. Welk (1999), in a review of recent studies in this area, identified five categories or determinants of physical activity for children. These included personal, biological, psychological, social, and environmental. Welk concluded that "the most commonly identified determinants were self-efficacy/perceived competence, enjoyment, some degree of parental influence and access to programs and equipment" (p. 11).

Coakley (2001) suggests that changes associated with family structure and the perception parents have about the role sport can play in their children's development has had a major impact on participation levels in organized sport. Perhaps one of the biggest changes, he contends, is the increase in the number of families with both parents working. For working parents, after-school and summer sport programs offer a safe, adult-supervised environment where children may acquire valuable social and athletic skills. Coakley also suggests that parenting ideology has changed related to the perception of what it means to be a "good parent." Parents are now expected to be more accountable for the behaviour and whereabouts of their children. This makes sport a highly attractive alternative to "hanging out" at the mall or the video arcade.

Several other factors also play a role in determining involvement for children in organized sport. Nixon and Frey (1996) identify both social background and status factors such as social class, gender, race, and ethnicity as influential in determining participation. They also point out that regional considerations such as where one lives, whether in an urban or rural area, may also affect sport involvement based on available opportunities (p. 82).

Perhaps the single biggest factor for an increase in sport participation for children is the growing concern among the public that many children are engaged in inactive, unhealthy lifestyles. Coupled with this is the perception that physical education programs across the country have had little or no influence in changing fitness levels of children. Particularly disturbing is the trend for schools, once seen as the focal point for the total health of the child, to reduce physical education opportunities for students. It is not surprising that many parents, in attempting to address this issue, look for opportunities to enroll their children in organized sport programs.

Motivating Factors for Participation

It is clear from the literature that most playful activities, including sports, are appealing to children for a number of reasons. Children find that many elements of sport are both intrinsically and extrinsically rewarding. Participants at all levels of sport are guided in their involvement by a combination of these two motivating forces. Siedentop (1994) concluded that perceptions related to "competence, affiliation, and fun were more important to children than the reward of winning" (p. 137). A study by Klint and Weiss (as cited in LeClair, 1992) reported that the top 10 motives for participating in youth sport were

1. learning new skills,
2. getting in shape or getting stronger,
3. improving skills,
4. having fun,
5. staying in shape,
6. being challenged,
7. using the equipment,
8. competing at higher levels,
9. being physically active, and
10. the teamwork (p. 94).

The National Coaching Certification Program, an educational program for coaches in Canada, also suggests that participants in sport are motivated by both intrinsic and extrinsic considerations, such as

1. a desire for achievement—a wish to improve, master new skills, and pursue excellence,
2. a need for affiliation—a desire to have positive and friendly relations with others,
3. a desire for sensation—a desire to experience the sights, sounds, and physical feelings surrounding a sport or the excitement in a sport, and
4. a desire for self-direction—a wish to feel a sense of control, to feel in charge (NCCP, Theory Level I Manual, pp. 2–9).

BENEFITS OF ORGANIZED SPORT FOR CHILDREN

Today, children are being encouraged to become involved in organized sport activities at an early age. Youth sport has come to occupy an important place in the amateur sports system in Canada along with community, school, and intercollegiate sport. The existence of a number of organizations offering a wide selection of programs provides boys and girls with opportunities to participate at many different levels. As long as government funding and public and private sector support continue, we will very likely see an expansion of these programs in the future. The proponents of early and continued participation in sport point to a number of benefits to be gained through this involvement.

Many of the benefits of participation in sport programs are similar to those credited to quality physical education programs. Supporters of minor sports programs emphasize the unique role these programs play in the overall growth and development of children. The health benefits of activities, which improve physical fitness, are thoroughly documented in both the medical and physical education fields. Greenberg and Pargman (1986) summarize the importance of participation in physical activities during a person's formative years:

> *Much of what occurs in adult life is influenced by childhood experiences. An appreciation for physical activity, sport, and exercise (or for that matter, aversions toward these experiences) is particularly implanted in us when we are very young. And as children grow and develop, their values are further shaped and modified.* (p. 131)

The health-related outcomes from vigorous sport activities include improvement in muscular strength, flexibility and endurance, regulation of body weight, decrease in the risk of heart disease, and the release of tension and anxiety. Some of the social and psychological benefits of sport include the promotion of a positive attitude toward physical activity, the improvement of self-confidence, increasing self-esteem and self-control, and an avenue for fostering social competence.

Sport may also be used as a setting to learn important transferable life skills, which enable us to succeed in the environments in which we live (Danish & Nellen, 1997). Such life skills become important for children as they learn to deal with family, school, and neighbourhood environments.

Despite the overwhelming evidence supporting the benefits of sport and physical activity for youths, numerous studies have been published that show alarmingly low fitness levels among young people. Siedentop (1994) contends that this is not a recent concern and suggests that "the general picture of a nation of unfit children and youth has been consistent in both professional and popular literature of the past quarter century" (p. 180).

CONTROVERSIES AND ISSUES IN CHILDREN'S SPORT

As the popularity of children's sport has grown, so too have the scrutiny and the criticism of these programs. Critics have come to question the merits of organized sport participation for children as young as four or five years of age with respect to a number of areas of concern. Many of the professionals involved in physical education and sport remain convinced of the need for changes to be made in minor sport if children are to reap the benefits that sport has to offer. This section will review a number of the interrelated issues associated with children and youths in minor sport. These include ethics in youth sport, withdrawal from sport, overemphasis on performance and winning, sport specialization, dropout and burnout, parental interference, and the role coaches play in youth sport.

Ethics in Youth Sport

The often highly competitive and achievement-oriented nature of organized sport for children can create many dilemmas for participants, coaches, administrators, spectators, and officials who make decisions that can affect the outcome of a competition. In many of these instances, emotions such as resentment, anger, fear, and frustration are likely to play a role in the decision-making behaviour of an individual. Examples abound in sport where one's moral values and ethics are put to the test. "Ethics is concerned with issues of right and wrong in human conduct. It is concerned with what is good and bad; what is authentic and not authentic. Ethics is also concerned with the notions of duty, obligation, and moral responsibility" (Malloy, Ross, & Zakus, 2000, p. 46). One of the most obvious examples where ethical values are tested in children's sport is the relative importance placed on winning. For a coach or player, after countless hours of practice in preparation for a competition, to suggest that winning isn't important is both naive and unrealistic. On the other hand, if winning is important, what lengths does one go to in order to win? Is winning more important than acting within the rules of the game or treating your opponents fairly? If winning is important, how does this affect our definitions of strategy, rule bending, and cheating? Can we remain honest, fair, respectful, and unselfish if the ultimate goal is to win? These and other questions call for us to consider the ethical dimension of our behaviour. The ethical behaviour of those involved in sport is perhaps the overarching concern with respect to many of the current issues facing youth sport today.

Sport organizations throughout the country have taken steps aimed at improving or maintaining ethical standards of fair play, sportsmanship, and the conduct of individuals involved in their programs. Numerous documents, codes of conduct, fair play rules, and coaches' and players' creeds exist and attempt to prescribe guidelines to serve as the basis for making reasoned judgments related to sport activities. While these efforts reflect a legitimate concern for the general well-being of the participants, in the final analysis, responsibility for ethical behaviour is still very much an individual choice.

Why Children Quit Youth Sports

Even though many children enjoy their participation in sport and continue this participation well into adulthood, a large percentage discontinues their involvement at an early age. According to Martens (1980), in a paper entitled *The Uniqueness of the Youth Athlete: Psychological Considerations*, the most commonly reported causes for withdrawal from minor sport are

1. not getting to play,
2. negative reinforcement,
3. mismatching,
4. psychological stress,
5. failure, and
6. over-organization (reported in Leonard, 1998, p. 126).

Similar reasons were reported by children in a study carried out by the Youth Institute at Michigan State University. Summarizing the results of this research project, Eitzen and Sage

(2003) found that the major reasons given by children for leaving sport included loss of interest, not having fun, too time consuming, poor coaching, and too much pressure. It would appear that while children participate in sports for a number of reasons, it also remains clear that when their motivations for participating in sport are not met, they are likely to lose interest and discontinue their involvement.

Overemphasis on Performance and Winning

One of the most controversial areas of organized sport for children is the highly competitive nature of some programs and the overemphasis on performance and winning. It is not unusual for sport clubs, and in some cases community-based sport programs, to promote the programs they offer. In order to recruit new members and boost registration numbers, they highlight their dedication to excellence and showcase the previous competitive successes of their athletes and teams. Parents regard this as an attractive feature of a program as it is perceived to develop values and norms that are important for real-life competitive situations. Many sport professionals and physical educators feel that the emphasis in youth sport should not be one of a highly competitive nature but rather the enhancement of physical, cognitive, and affective development of the participants. Wuest and Bucher (1995), in a criticism of youth sport as it currently exists, surmise that "this development is particularly critical during the child's younger years. The fun of playing (rather than the beating of an opponent) should be stressed, participation opportunities for many children of all abilities should be provided (rather than limiting participation to the gifted few), and the development of skills within the sport and in other sports should be stressed" (p. 274).

Sport Specialization

Directly linked to the emphasis on the competitive aspects of sport for children is the emphasis on developing highly skilled athletes. The process for identifying athletic talent in Canada is based on a feeder system that is designed to progressively target and train athletes for the elite levels. Table 3.2 shows the typical age for beginning to train in the 10 most popular sports in Canada. Children who show promise are systematically moved through a series of skill development stages and engage in longer, more intense training sessions and competitions. Because of the amount of effort, time, and resources involved in this development phase, successful athletes are inevitably urged by a coach or club official to choose one sport in which to participate. Parents are persuaded that their child's progress and chances for success at the elite level of the sport will be enhanced if there is year-round commitment to the sport. The prospect of becoming an age-group champion, or the dream of making a national team, becomes a powerful motivation for both parents and children.

Critics claim, however, that programs that revolve around elitism and specialization undermine many of the positive aspects of sport. Regimentation, routine, and adherence to a long-term training program increasingly influence and shape the experiences of children in organized sports programs. The values, which emerge from programs based on competitive success, can be in conflict with, and in some case act to subvert, the avowed ideals of children's sports.

TABLE 3.2 Typical Age Range for Starting to Play Top 10 Sports

Sport	Age
Soccer	7–8
Swimming	5–6
Hockey	9–10
Baseball	8–9
Basketball	7–8
Downhill skiing	6–7
Figure skating	5–6
Karate	5–6
Volleyball	10–12
Cycling	12–13

Source: Local Sports Programs

Specialization Within a Sport

While some parents want to give their kids the advantage of an early start by choosing to specialize in a particular sport, there is another interrelated dimension to this trend that sees children taking on specialized roles. Some programs are so highly structured that emphasis is placed on choosing to specialize in a particular position within that sport. For example, it not unusual for children to refer to themselves by their playing position: a soccer player is now a "striker" or a "fullback," and the age group swimmer is a "butterflyer" or a "freestyler." The athlete comes to view his or her role in the sport from the perspective of the relative status of the position, thus further limiting and detracting from the fundamental purpose of sport for children.

Limiting Children's Choices in Organized Sport

A further consequence with respect to specialization in organized sport is that it limits children's opportunities in other sports and non-sport activities. Exclusive participation in one sport activity at an early age can have physical and emotional implications for a child. Physiologically, injuries associated with over-training or improper technique or conditioning are far more frequent when a child engages in a single sport over a long period. Repetitive movements that cause impact or strain to the joints can lead to damage in the fragile growth area of the bone and can result in permanent disability or can impair normal growth patterns. Limiting intensive involvement in sports that are physically demanding and providing children with a choice of less strenuous or more skill-oriented activities may help prevent these overuse injuries from occurring.

Sport medicine professionals have also begun to raise a concern related to the likelihood of head injuries occurring in contact sports. Until recently, severe contact resulting in head injuries during sporting events were classified as concussions only when a player exhibited typical symptoms, such as disorientation or loss of consciousness. Doctors are now suggesting that any blow to the head, even if it does not appear severe enough to cause the classic symptoms of a concussion, can still have long-term health consequences. What this suggests is that young athletes in such sports as hockey, football, rugby, or soccer where contact is permitted may be more susceptible to head injuries than was previously thought.

Dropout and Burnout

Another concern that continues to be of major significance in children's sport is the high percentage of children who leave sport at an early age. A number of negative consequences arise from this trend. As children advance from one level of sport to the next, participation becomes progressively more selective for those who remain in the programs. The most promising players are often children who physically mature earlier than their peers and consequently have a greater chance for athletic success in their age group. Under this system the so-called late bloomers soon become discouraged, as limited playing time and fewer opportunities are made available to them. Related to this is the fear some children may have of physical injuries, particularly in such sports as soccer, hockey, and football when greater physical contact is introduced and permitted. This exclusionary model serves to make sport less attractive to children as they get older. Minor hockey in Canada serves as a prime example of a sport based on a system that promotes and caters to the talented as they move through the various levels. Statistics show that registration for minor hockey programs has remained steady, with hockey continuing to be one of the most popular sports for Canadian children. However, the age at which children leave minor hockey has fallen from 15 or 16 years of age to 13, and in some cases 12 (Adams, 1993). While such reasons as the desire to pursue other interests, a lack of facilities, and rising costs may be contributing factors in the drop in age for leaving hockey, an equally significant factor appears to be related to who gets to play. Children who show promise in the sport are being selected at an earlier age for specialized treatment. Kids who fail to make travel teams or who aren't selected to play in an all-star league simply drop out. This system of screening out the less talented is not limited to team sports, as is evidenced by the high numbers of children who quit or drop out in such individual sports as swimming, gymnastics, and figure skating.

The process of dropping out of sport was examined as early as 1976 by Donald Bell, who found that athletes, apart from not getting to play, may be "induced" to quit because of a continuing series of degrading or humiliating experiences. For example, "being yelled at, criticized, or ridiculed by coaches, parents, or teammates" are frequently reported as negative experiences that serve to drive children from a particular sport (cited in Nixon & Frey, 1996, p. 91). Other factors causing children to leave a sport may be related to performance anxiety, forming new friendships outside the sport, or simply losing interest in the sport. It is not unusual for children who drop out of one sport activity to take up another sport that might offer a more enjoyable and satisfying experience.

Another negative consequence associated with an emphasis on specialization and the demands placed on young athletes to succeed is the possibility of burnout. Coakley (2001) reports that this condition occurs when "age-group champions with the potential to succeed in their sport felt they had lost control over their lives and were unable to explore and develop their identities apart from sports. As stress increased and fun decreased, they burned out" (p. 89). Figler and Whitaker (1991) further explain the phenomenon as being the result of "too much participation, success, and pressure at too early an age. The causes may be physical, psychological, or a combination of elements" (p. 122). Lumpkin, Stoll, and Beller (1994) cite over 35 reasons why athletes burn out in sport. In youth sport, they report the 10 most common burnout factors are

1. overuse and fatigue,
2. overtraining,
3. recurrent injuries,
4. over-specialization,
5. poorly trained coaches,
6. demand for improved performances,
7. overemphasis on winning,
8. loss of intrinsic motivation,
9. changing interests,
10. conflict of values (p. 61).

Research has shown that children who leave sport at an early age because of burnout and the unrealistic pressure from coaches, parents, or peers are unlikely to become participants in any other sport activity in the future. Many burnout situations can be avoided, however; coaches and parents need to recognize burnout symptoms and provide programs that protect young athletes from having excessive demands placed on them at such an early age.

Parental Involvement in Children's Sport

For the majority of parents who enroll their children in organized sport, their participation is limited to driving the kids to and from practices or games. In between, they are content to sit in the bleachers or along the sidelines and play the role of fan, encouraging and enthusiastically cheering their kids along. On other occasions, they may volunteer in a coaching or officiating capacity. This scene is played out in hundreds of communities across the country each day. These parents are more concerned with supporting their children and making the sport experience fun than in keeping track of their child's playing time or scoring statistics. Most parents who are involved at this level are interested in the redeeming benefits sport has to offer their children. Recently, however, a negative element of this involvement has emerged that is a major concern for both critics and supporters of minor sport.

The issue appears to be the sometimes over-zealous nature of a minority of parents who engage in displays of unacceptable behaviour before, during, and after their children's sport events. These go beyond well-intentioned parents cheering and rooting for a team or player to include verbal and even physical abuse against opponents. In some cases these abusive behaviours are even directed toward their own children. James Deacon, in a recent article for *Maclean's* magazine, noted that the bad behaviour of some parents in hockey "is so common it even has its own name—rink rage" (Deacon, 2001). He goes on to suggest that "hostile behavior at youth games is far more pervasive and sometimes violent than it was a generation ago" (p. 22). A survey of recent newspaper articles seems to support this view as reported incidents of abusive parents threatening coaches, assaulting opposing players, and taunting officials appear to have reached epidemic proportions.

In what is perhaps one of the most abhorrent and blatant examples of a parent's involvement having dire consequences, a hockey father attacked another parent after becoming incensed over rough play during a kids' summer recreational hockey game. As the children watched, Thomas Junta from Reading, Massachusetts, attacked and fatally injured Michael Costin, who had been supervising games between two groups of children. Junta was charged with manslaughter, subsequently found guilty, and sentenced to a six- to ten-year prison term.

Other incidents of a far less serious nature than this terrible tragedy occur on a daily basis in children's sport. While parents involved in team sports appear to be the most culpable, individual sports are not immune from abusive parental behaviour. Incidents of a pushy parent who attempts to influence the judges in gymnastics or a father who becomes enraged when his child is disqualified at a swim meet seem to be occurring more frequently. Regardless of the sport, evidence strongly supports the charge that parents are taking their kids' sport involvement more seriously than ever before. There are a number of reasons for this rise in parental interference in sport.

For the parent with aspirations for or dreams of their child becoming a top-level athlete or making a national team, sport is not about playing games or having fun. These parents willingly make sacrifices in order to give their youngster every chance to succeed. The possibility of having their child "make it to the top" despite the odds is an underlying motive for many parents involved in minor sport. Parents with this goal in mind are often prepared to do whatever it takes. This ranges from buying the most expensive equipment and paying exorbitant club fees, to relocating the entire family closer to a training facility or sending a young child to live and train elsewhere in the country. Parents are also often expected to commit a great deal of their own time to club-sponsored activities such as fundraising projects or serving on committees. It comes as no surprise, therefore, when parents feel they have a stake in what happens and attempt to exert undue influence over their child's sport experience.

A second reason for increased interference by parents in children's sport may be an implicit desire to experience sport vicariously through their children. Parents who have had unsuccessful athletic experiences in their youth sometimes unwittingly pressure their children to succeed in an effort to make up for their own lost opportunities. Even the most restrained parent can lose perspective when faced with the dilemma of giving a child "the chance I never had."

A third reason for parents becoming overly involved in their kid's games is the prospect of future financial rewards. The tantalizing possibility of a college scholarship, endorsements, or a professional contract can become more than just wishful thinking for some parents. It is not unusual to see parents with inflated hopes registering their children in gymnastics, track and field, or figure skating immediately following an Olympic Games. The publicity surrounding these events and the million-dollar contracts for medal winners can become a powerful, if unrealistic, motivator for some parents.

While much of the literature on parental involvement focuses on the overly involved or "pushy" parent, there are a number of dangers associated with parental under-involvement. Children may be more likely to quit sport when parents fail to take an active interest in their child's sport involvement. The support and encouragement are needed most at the initial stage of participation. Children need to feel their efforts are appreciated, which is implicit through their parents sharing the sport experience with them. A lack of parental participation may inadvertently open the door for the development of an unhealthy coach–athlete relationship. "Where the athlete is distanced from the parent(s), either emotionally or because of family conflict, she may turn to her coach or other authority figure to take on the role of substitute or surrogate parent. She may even fantasize that this person is, in fact, her substitute father or mother" (Brackenbridge, 2001, p. 72).

Influence of Youth Sport Coaches

While parental involvement in sport has come under heavy criticism for the negative consequences this involvement may produce, it is the coach who has perhaps the greatest potential to influence children in minor sport. The youth sport coach is in a position to provide an atmosphere in which children can realize the many positive benefits of sports participation. Whether these benefits exist for the participant depends to a large extent on a coach's understanding of the purposes and goals of youth sport. One program that has played a significant role in providing education for coaches in this area is the National Coaching Certification Program (NCCP). Since 1975, coaches in Canada have had the opportunity to receive formal training in coaching through the National Coaching Certification Program. This five-level program is a cooperative venture between the provinces and the federal government and is designed to provide fundamental coaching principles and skills, in addition to the particular techniques of each sport. To date, thousands of volunteer coaches from every level of sport in Canada have taken advantage of this program. In fact, many local sport organizations now have requirements in place that specify only certified coaches are permitted to coach in their league or program.

However, despite the best efforts of these and other educational programs to ensure qualified coaches, a number of issues and concerns related to coaches continues to plague youth sport. Nixon and Frey (1996), in discussing the aversive effects of sport programs for children, reported that while children lose interest and drop out of sport for a number of reasons, problems related to coaches were major factors in their decision to quit. These problems were often associated with "punitive activities by coaches, unrealistic expectations, and harsh and unfair treatment of players" (p. 91). In the past several years, there have been numerous incidents of youth sport coaches who have resorted to unethical, exploitative, and oppressive practices in order to produce a winning team or an elite athlete. Reports of falsifying birth certificates, using ineligible athletes, tampering with equipment, and flirting with starvation diets are just some of the disturbing stories that have made their way into the headlines in recent times.

Perhaps the most frightening and abhorrent phenomenon related to organized youth sport to emerge in the past decade has been that of sexual harassment and exploitation of young athletes. In a 1999 *Sports Illustrated* special report entitled "Who's Coaching Your Kid?" William Nack and Don Yaeger point out that "after decades of being ignored, minimized, or hidden away, the molestation of athletes by their coaches is no longer the sporting culture's dirty little secret" (p. 43). The report reveals that "although child molestation is by no means confined to sports, the playing field represents an obvious opportunity for sexual predators." With few background checks carried out and little supervision of coaches, "youth sports are a ready-made resource pool for pedophiles." In an exposé in *Maclean's*,

James Deacon (1997) reveals the true extent of this behaviour. Quoting from a Canadian study undertaken by Kirby (1996) that examined incidents of sexual harassment and abuse among national team athletes, he reported that Kirby had found some disturbing results. She found that nearly 9% of the athletes who responded to the survey reported having been previously subjected to a sexual assault by a coach or team authority figure and most went unreported. Of the athletes who reported assaults, one in five were under 16 of years of age (p. 54). Nack and Yaeger (1999), in an 18-month review of newspaper stories, found "more than thirty cases of coaches in the U.S. who had been arrested or convicted of sexually abusing children engaged in nine sports from baseball to wrestling" (p. 43). In the wake of new revelations of sexual improprieties involving minor-sport coaches, sport organizations at all levels have come under increasing pressure to take measures to ensure the safety of young athletes. Consequently, a number of sports have developed national guidelines for dealing with sexual assault and harassment incidents. On the local level, many sport organizations have now enacted policies, which require all coaches to submit to a background check.

Unfortunately, these measures may not be enough to keep sexual predators out of sport, particularly in the larger centres where thousands of volunteer coaches would need to undergo screening. It could be argued that police departments who would normally be responsible for reviewing the backgrounds of these coaches simply would not have the time or the resources to do so. Regardless, several precautions need to be taken on behalf of children in organized sport programs to help safeguard them against sexual exploitation. First, where it is feasible, organizers should insist on a background check by police. Where this is not practical, volunteer coaches should, as a condition to coach in a league, be required to submit to a check of their conduct, either through an employer or from previous coaching positions. Second, parents need to be aware of the danger signs that might suggest a sexually abusive or a harassing relationship and to take steps to protect their children. As Nack and Yaeger (2001) point out, parents should be concerned when a child's interest in a sport suddenly diminishes. Parents should try to be present at their children's practices and games as unattended children are seen as easy targets. Parents also need to be wary of coaches who lavish expensive gifts on players or spend an unusual amount of time with a child. Perhaps most importantly, parents need to talk to and inform their children about what is considered inappropriate behaviour by a coach and to reassure them about reporting any improprieties that may occur between athletes and coaches.

CONCLUSIONS

The original objectives of organized sport for children have become obscured or replaced in many programs with an overemphasis on elitism, performance, and the pursuit of athletic glory. The current sport system in Canada comprises school, community, and private agencies. These serve to promote and maintain an exclusionary model in which young athletes are often pressured to succeed by overzealous parents and domineering coaches. As a result of this inappropriate pressure and interference, more and more children are expressing the view that sports are no longer fun. This is reflected in the research that shows nearly three-quarters of all children in organized sport drop out before they reach the age of 15. While it can be argued that parents and coaches have the most influence on a child's sports experience, all too often this influence has taken on negative overtones. The consequences of this shift in the attitude about the objectives of youth sport in recent years has led to a much less harmonious environment than ever before.

Critical Thinking Questions

1. What has led to the increase in the popularity of organized sport for children over the past several decades?
2. What are some of the benefits and problems of early specialization for children in organized sport?
3. Parents and coaches appear to be mainly responsible for putting unrealistic expectations on children who are involved in organized sport. Is this an accurate statement? Are there other people and/or factors involved that contribute to the pressure felt by these children?
4. Studies have shown that more than 75% of all children who participate in organized sport drop out by the time they reach the age of 15. What suggestions and changes would you make to the structure of youth sport in Canada to encourage children to remain in sport?
5. As a parent of a child involved in organized sport, what precautions would you take to ensure that children remain safe from coaches who might seek to exploit them?
6. Assuming that you are in charge of organizing a new sports program for children in your community, what steps would you take to ensure all children in the program receive equal participation opportunities?

Suggested Readings

Coakley, J.J. (2001). Sports and children: Are organized programs worth the effort? In *Sport in society: Issues and controversies* (7th ed.). Boston: McGraw-Hill.

Donnelly, P. (1997). Youth. In *Taking sport seriously: Social issues in Canadian sport*. Toronto: Thompson Educational Publishing, Inc.

Eitzen, D.S., & Sage, G.H. (2003). Children and sport. In *Sociology of North American sport* (7th ed.). Toronto: McGraw-Hill.

Hall, A., Slack, T., Smith, G., & Whitson, D. (1991). Youth and education. In *Sport in Canadian society*. Toronto: McClelland and Stewart Inc.

LeClair, J. (1992). How children become athletes. In *Winners and losers: Sport and physical activity in the '90s*. Toronto: Thompson Educational Publishing, Inc.

Malloy, D.C., Ross, S., & Zakus, D. H. (2000). *Sport ethics: Concepts and cases in sport and recreation*. Toronto: Thompson Educational Publishing, Inc.

Web Links

The Center for Sports Parenting (CSP)
http://www.sportsparenting.org
Provides practical advice for coaches, parents, educators, and others involved in youth sports.

National Alliance for Youth Sports
http://www.nays.org
Contains information related to children and youth in organized sport.

Sport Information Resource Centre
http://www.sportquest.com
A search engine and directory providing a wide variety of sport and fitness information.

4

Sport in Canadian Educational Institutions

Patricia S. Miller

Women's varsity volleyball in the CIS.

My university sport has been a main part in shaping who I am today, how I see things, how I work, my priorities. My sport experience has been amazing. I would not trade it for anything in the world.

Fourth-year university track and field athlete

The opening quote from a fourth-year university track and field athlete captures the sentiments of thousands of student-athletes across the country. For many Canadian youth, sport plays a central and defining role in their lives. One of the most common ways they access sport and physical activity is through their schools, colleges, and universities.

Sport and movement programs exist at all levels of the educational system in Canada, yet in slightly different forms in the various educational settings. We will see, for example, that sport and physical activity are promoted through physical educational classes, intramural opportunities, and inter-school competition in most public schools across the country. Similarly, many Canadian colleges and universities offer a program of study in physical education or a closely related academic discipline and provide participant opportunities through recreational, intramural, and intercollegiate programs.

Consistent with the functionalist perspective, one view maintains that the mission of Canadian educational institutions is to socialize children and youth into the dominant social values and goals. The objective is to ensure youth and young adults learn and internalize social and vocational skills that will allow them to become productive members of society. According to this perspective, the role of sport in educational institutions is to contribute to this mission. Sport is seen as a tool to transmit cultural values and teach individual strengths such as leadership, self-discipline, self-determination, and mental and physical fitness.

An alternative perspective, however, is that sport detracts from the educational mission of our schools. That is, as opposed to producing critical, independent thinkers who excel academically, sport distracts students from academic activities and perpetuates dependence and immaturity. Conflict theorists may adopt this position, arguing that sport within the education system encourages apathy and acquiescence among youth and young adults who, as adults, fail to question the status quo. We will consider this theme of education through sport in the public school system and later at the university and college level.

PUBLIC SCHOOL SYSTEM

The British North America Act of 1867 granted provinces individual jurisdiction over the direction and operation of their schools (Anderson et al., 1989). As a result, there are numerous organizational and curricular differences across the country. However, sport is almost always incorporated in school curriculums under physical education, and in co-instructional activities in the form of intramural and inter-school sport programs.

Physical Education

We will begin by considering physical education in Canadian schools, starting with a brief history and moving forward to examine the current status of school physical education.

History of Physical Education Physical education programs in Canadian schools date back to the middle of the 18th century, at which time they were heavily focused on drills and gymnastics (Anderson et al., 1989; Morrow et al., 1989). Militaristic interests dominated physical education for decades, due in large part to the influence of Lord Strathcona, who developed a trust fund to support the formation of cadet corps and teacher training in physical education (Anderson et al., 1989; Morrow et al., 1989), and later by a government at war and in need of a healthy, young population. Repetitious, rigorous calisthenics characterized physical education programs in Canada until the middle of the 20th century.

The concern for fitness persisted, but progressive steps were taken to incorporate sports and games into physical education programs in the 1940s and 1950s, particularly with the advent and explosion of physical education programs of study in Canadian universities (Anderson et al., 1989; Morrow et al., 1989). Until then, sports such as football, lacrosse, and baseball had been promoted outside the education system by regional, provincial, and national groups. Instruction in a broad range of activities such as those listed above, as well as dance and movement, eventually became the primary focus of physical education classes across the country.

Yet physical education was a low priority within the education system (Anderson et al., 1989). A national conference of health professionals held in 1972 drew attention to the position of physical education, and a recommendation was made to devote 30 minutes a day to physical education (Anderson et al., 1989). A major trend in elementary and secondary school physical education programs of the 1970s and 1980s was the promotion of Quality Daily Physical Education (QDPE) (Canadian Association for Health, Physical Education, Recreation, and Dance, 1989). Schools across the country began to introduce mandatory physical education throughout their regular curriculum, requiring students to complete a physical education course in each year of study. The status of physical education changed dramatically in the ensuing years.

Current Status of Physical Education Today, curriculums nationwide advocate a philosophy of promoting personal and social responsibility among Canadian youth (Marcotte, 1997). This philosophy is embodied in physical education, where personal and social responsibility is enhanced through the development of respect for self, respect for others, leadership, and a healthy lifestyle (Chad, Humbert & Jackson, 1999). Despite this goal of promoting personal and social responsibility and the continued national support for QDPE (Chad, Humbert & Jackson, 1999), school physical education is being devalued in the new curriculums across the country (Kidd, 1999; Lathrop & Murray, 1998). Elementary schools providing daily physical education are in the minority (Chad, Humbert & Jackson, 1999). Indeed, only one in four children enjoys daily physical education classes (Canadian Fitness and Lifestyle Research Institute, 2000). At the secondary level, only Quebec and Nova Scotia require students to take physical education beyond the 10th grade (Spence, Mandigo, Poon & Mummery, 2001). Educational reform in the other provinces has significantly reduced the number of physical education credits students must fulfil before graduation, and in many cases, even these abridged requirements are not met (Hardman & Marshall, 2000). This displacement of physical education is occurring at the same time obesity among Canadian children is on the rise (Kidd, 1999; Limbert et al., 1994) and more Canadian youth are leading inactive lifestyles than ever before (Cragg, Cameron, Craig & Russell, 1999).

Barriers to Quality, Daily Physical Education A number of systematic barriers make it difficult for schools to provide quality, regular physical education (Humbert & Chad, 1998). First, parents and teachers place greater emphasis on academic subjects, as a result of increasingly competitive university entrance requirements and an ever more uncertain job market. Second, the preferential scheduling of academic subjects discourages students from selecting physical education options. Third, schools lack facilities and resources, both financial and human, and while many collaborate with local agencies in the use of public facilities, serious limitations exist. Finally, there is a need for teachers trained specifically in the principles of physical education and opportunities for their professional development. Providing quality physical education is difficult without adequately prepared teachers.

Decline in Physical Education Enrolment The outcome, of course, has been a drastic decline in the number of students enrolled in physical education across the country. In a study of the secondary school physical education enrolment in Alberta, for example, Spence and his colleagues (Spence et al., 2001), found a significant decline in enrolment beyond Grade 10 when physical education was no longer compulsory. Enrolment records indicate this decline is more pronounced among females (Gibbons & Van Gyn, 1996; Gibbons, Van Gyn, Wharf-Higgins, & Gaul, 2000; Humbert, 1995; Spence et al., 2001). For example, only 10% of British Columbia female high school students take physical education when it becomes an option in Grades 11 and 12, compared to 25% of their male peers (Gibbons et al., 2000). Females have been discouraged from pursuing physical education by verbal, physical, and sexual harassment from male classmates, the lack of female role models, and their dissatisfaction with curriculum content and delivery (Gibbons, Wharf-Higgins, Gaul & Van Gyn, 1999; Humbert, 1995). Some educators have recommended co-educational physical education be eliminated altogether, and "females only" physical education classes have been piloted in several settings (Gibbons et al., 2000). These innovative programs have enjoyed initial successes, yet it is clear elementary and secondary school physical education must address the needs and interests of both male and female students if the current trend is to be reversed.

Healthy Active Living Some educators are trying to reverse this trend by introducing curriculum reform that integrates a healthy active living philosophy into physical education classes. Healthy active living favours active participation over competition and accents physical activity across the lifespan for everyone connected to schools, including students, teachers, school staff, family, and official, government, and community members (Luke, 2000; Mandigo, 2001). Healthy active living has been incorporated into the physical education curriculum in several provinces, including Ontario (Mandigo, 2001) and Alberta under the Ever Active Program (Mandigo, 2001; Schwartz, 2000; Spence et al., 2001). It is hoped this approach will encourage children and young adults to live healthy active lifestyles well into adulthood.

Intramural Sport

In addition to physical education, sport and physical activity are delivered in elementary and secondary schools through intramural programs. Intramural programs are voluntary and offer structured games such as volleyball, basketball, and hockey, as well as unstructured movement opportunities such as walking, cooperative games, and playground activities. Intramural programs are typically offered before and after school and at lunch-time, although they must often compete for limited space and facilities.

Intramural programs are usually organized by students and supervised by teachers and/or volunteers. A membership-based, not-for-profit national organization, the Canadian Intramural Recreation Association (CIRA), supports intramural and recreation programming in the education system. Founded in 1977, CIRA and its 10 provincial and territorial affiliated associations provide projects, programs, and resources, including volunteer and paid staff, to help teachers and student leaders plan, organize, and operate intramural and recreation programs.

CIRA currently operates three national programs, including the Student Leadership Development Program (SLDP), an initiative designed to empower students through the development of organizational and interpersonal skills. In the past five years, over 1700 elementary and secondary schools have participated in the SLDP, which means that over 17 000 students have delivered their own intramural and recreation programs and improved their own leadership and organizational skills (CIRA, 2002). The two remaining programs are the Playground Leadership Program designed to teach students how to create and maintain safe spaces for play, and Health in Perspective, a peer mentoring smoking prevention and cessation program targeted specifically at girls aged 10 to 15 years.

Inter-School Sport

Inter-school sport programs operate in much the same manner as physical education programs in Canada, that is, on a province-by-province basis. Even more so, however, inter-school sport programs also share the philosophy of education through sport that characterizes elementary and secondary physical education and intramurals in Canada.

History of Inter-School Sport Historically, sports and games were promoted outside the school context by local, regional, and provincial enthusiasts (Morrow et al., 1989). As noted earlier, popular sports such as football, lacrosse, baseball, and ice hockey were incorporated into physical education curriculums in the 1940s and 1950s. Inter-school sport programs followed shortly thereafter, due in large part to the efforts of interested teachers. Inter-school sport programs continued to expand in the following years, and sports such as track and field, volleyball, and rugby grew in popularity among boys and gymnastics and field hockey among girls (Anderson et al., 1989; Morrow et al., 1989).

In the late 1970s and into the 1980s, several forces hampered the progress of inter-school sport programs (Macintosh, 1990). First, Canada experienced a recession, and provincial transfer payments for education were cut. School board funding for co-instructional activities, including inter-school sport programs, were affected. Second, the aging teaching population lost enthusiasm for volunteering in extracurricular activities. Traditionally, teachers volunteered an average of 10 years to coaching, after which they were replaced by new, eager teachers. However, the climate of financial restraint that existed in the 1970s and 1980s meant new teachers were not being hired and there was a shortage of teachers interested in coaching inter-school sport programs. Third, teachers who did continue to contribute to after-school activities became more aggressive in their efforts to secure compensation, and when it was not forthcoming, some withdrew their input. Finally, liability issues reduced participation in traditional, yet high-risk inter-school sports such as football and gymnastics. In some provinces, Alberta and Nova Scotia, for example, gymnastics was eliminated altogether from inter-school sport programs.

One more event occurred during this time that changed school sport programs. Several highly publicized court cases challenged policies that prohibited girls from participating on boys' teams (Macintosh, 1990). The incidents drew attention to the inequity of opportunities for male and female athletes across sport. Schools recognized that greater opportunities for female students had to be created, a considerable task given the declining financial and human resources of the period.

Current Status of Inter-School Sport Today, each province has a secondary school athletic association (for example, the Ontario Federation of School Athletic Association and the British Columbia School Sports Federation) that outlines eligibility and playing rules and organizes provincial playoffs. Sports are divided by gender, age, and level of competition. Seasons are purposely kept short, about six to ten weeks, to allow students to participate in multiple activities, the most popular of which have become soccer, rugby, and volleyball. Unlike the United States, which holds national championships in partnership with major corporate sponsors like McDonald's and Dr. Pepper (Eitzen & Sage, 2003), there are no national championships in Canadian high school sports, nor is there yet a strong push for them.

Outcomes of Inter-School Sport Research from the United States indicates that participation in high school sports is positively associated with a range of academic and developmental benefits. Athletic participation tends to contribute to increased academic achievement for both boys and girls (Fejgin, 1994; Kerr, 1996). Athletic participation also seems to be related to higher educational aspirations and higher post-secondary obtainment (Fejgin, 1994; Kerr, 1996; Melnick, Sabo & Vanfossen, 1992a).

Researchers in the United States have also found high school athletes, particularly boys, enjoy higher self-esteem (Holland & Andre, 1994) and greater popularity among peers (McNeal, 1995; Melnick, Sabo & Vanfossen, 1992a). Boys and girls who participate in high school sports drop out (Kerr, 1996; McNeal, 1995; Melnick, Sabo & Vanfossen, 1992b) and engage in delinquent behaviour less often than non-athlete peers (Kerr, 1996; Landers & Landers, 1978; Spreitzer, 1994).

The literature on U.S. high school sport has not been entirely positive. Melnick and his colleagues cautioned that many of the advantages noted above are mediated by gender and race. For example, Sabo, Melnick, and Vanfossen (1993) reported participation in high school athletics had little effect on the educational expectations or later attainment of black males and females. Some critics argue the reason there is higher academic achievement and less delinquency among athletes is because they conform to strict, oppressive sport norms. Further, there is growing concern in the United States that high school sport is approaching intercollegiate athletics and will succumb, if it has not already, to the same excesses seen at the university level, including the recruitment of under-prepared students, poor academic performance and low graduation rates, and the exploitation, both physical and psychological, of student-athletes (see, for example, Adler & Adler, 1991; Blinde, 1989).

Similar concerns are not widespread in the Canadian setting. In fact, the limited available research suggests Canadian high school athletes experience the same benefits, but not necessarily the same risks. There appears to be either no relationship (Tremblay, Inman & Willms, 2000) or a positive one (Anderson et al, 1989; Okihiro, 1984) between school sports and academic achievement among Canadian students. Student-athletes from the province of Ontario, for example, performed better academically than their non-athlete peers (Anderson et al., 1989).

Several theoretical perspectives are available to explain the relationship between academic achievement and sport participation. First, increased self-esteem stemming from involvement in inter-school sport programs may translate to the academic setting and facilitate academic success. Second, participation in inter-school sport programs may engender a commitment to one's school. Improved academic performance may be an ancillary outcome of fulfilling or maintaining this commitment. Third, student-athletes may encounter a support network their non-athlete peers do not experience. This support network may include teachers who grade student-athletes more leniently or give them extra tutoring, a school system that provides more scholastic or career guidance to student-athletes, and athletic figures such as coaches and teammates who reinforce academic achievement. James (1995), for example, found that male and female African Canadian high school athletes who found their classrooms alienating were able to develop meaningful connections to peers and teachers through their sport involvement.

In addition, many schools insist student-athletes achieve a certain academic standard in order to participate in inter-school sport programs. There is the possibility student-athletes invest in academic matters simply to remain eligible to play.

Finally, there is a strong belief in the ability of sport to promote the acquisition of a host of developmental skills, including leadership, communication, interpersonal, decision-making, and problem-solving skills. The acquisition of these skills in the sport setting and their subsequent application in the academic setting may encourage academic achievement.

In addition, there has been some indication that those who participate in high school sport not only perform better academically while in high school, but also develop higher educational aspirations, that is, they aspire to attend college and university in greater numbers than their non-athlete peers. The relationship seems to be stronger for males from lower social classes. By extension, there is a suggestion higher educational aspirations lead to greater education attainment, career mobility, and later life earnings. However, sport sociologists have begun to question these long-term benefits of sport participation, and convincing evidence has not been forthcoming to support these theories.

There does appear to be a strong relationship between high school sport and adult participation in sport and physical activity. Researchers have found participation in high school sport is a valuable predictor of sport participation among adult males and females, even for those more than 20 years beyond high school (Curtis, McTeer & White, 1999).

Despite the benefits of inter-school sport programs, many of the barriers that emerged in the 1970s and 1980s have not yet been fully removed. In fact, in many provinces, they have been exacerbated by further financial constraints and educational reforms. One of the major problems facing inter-school sport programs today is the escalating workload of teachers. Increasing teaching and supervision responsibilities and changing curriculums have reduced the time teachers have to contribute to co-instructional programs. Quebec and Manitoba have experimented with different incentives to encourage teachers' continued investment in extra-curricular activities including time off, reduced workloads, and financial remuneration. However, most provinces continue to rely on teachers to volunteer and many have been pressed to increase the involvement of community volunteers, despite concerns about liability and educational integrity. For example, in Ontario, where the future of inter-school sport programs is in jeopardy following recent educational reforms, approximately 10% of coaches are students and 15% community volunteers (Ministry of Education, 2001). Some school boards have been forced to introduce user fees for co-instructional programs, a serious hardship keeping many children from lower socioeconomic classes from inter-school sport programs. The future of inter-school sport programs will depend heavily on the willingness of teachers to invest their time, in many cases without compensation, and the openness of the provinces, school boards, trustees, and parents to consider creative alternatives.

INTER-UNIVERSITY SPORT

Athletics have a long history in Canadian universities. Inter-university competition dates back to before the turn of the 20th century, although it was quite different from the highly centralized bureaucratic organization that exists today (Moriarty & Holman-Prpich, 1987). Then, student leaders put together teams, challenged other universities to games, and, in the 1890s, formed inaugural leagues (Morrow et al., 1989). Football and hockey games and track and field events were held between a handful of Canada's older universities: McGill, Toronto, and Queen's. As interest in inter-university sport grew, universities assumed a leadership role and subsumed inter-university competition within their educational agendas. In so doing, inter-university sport was infused with the same philosophy of education through sport that we have seen in physical education and inter-school sport programs at the elementary and secondary levels.

History of Inter-University Sport

The Canadian Intercollegiate Athletic Union (CIAU) was formed in 1906 to oversee athletics in Ontario and Quebec universities (Canadian Interuniversity Sport [CIS], 2002; Morrow et al., 1989). The primary function of the CIAU then was to determine and maintain consistent rules and regulations for inter-university competition in the two provinces. The CIAU, or Central Division as it was known, grew to 19 institutions by the middle of the 20th century. The CIAU was dissolved in 1955 as members opted for two regional conferences: the Ontario Quebec University Athletic Association (OQUAA) and the Ottawa-St. Lawrence Athletic Association (OSLAA). Additional universities joined over the years, for example, Waterloo joined the OQUAA in 1961 and Ottawa and Carleton both in 1968.

In 1971, the OQUAA and OSLAA were reorganized into the Ontario Universities Athletic Association (OUAA) and the Quebec Universities Athletic Association (QUAA) for members in Ontario and Quebec, respectively (Ontario University Athletics, 2002). The QUAA later became the Quebec Student Sports Federation (QSSF), which provides sport opportunities for universities, as well as colleges and high schools in Quebec. Notably, inter-university sport in most Quebec institutions continues to be closely associated with or a distinct part of student services. Ouellet (1986) stressed that this approach respects the right of students to participate in the governance of athletics.

There were intercollegiate athletic associations other than the CIAU in Canada in the early part of the century. Universities in eastern Canada operated sport programs within the Maritime Inter-Collegiate Athletic Association, which revised its name to the Atlantic Intercollegiate Athletic Association (AIAA) in 1969 with the inclusion of Memorial University from Newfoundland (Atlantic University Athletic Association, 2002). In western Canada, the Western Intercollegiate Athletic Association (WIAA) was founded in 1920 with members from British Columbia, Alberta, Saskatchewan, and Manitoba (CIS, 2002). The

WIAA split in 1971 into the Canada West Universities Athletic Association (CWUAA) and the Great Plains Athletic Conference (GPAC), with one noticeable member from Ontario, Lakehead University. Lakehead University left GPAC in 1988 to join the OUAA as a full member.

Universities in the early part of the century focused primarily on competition within their respective conferences and were not keenly interested in national level competition (Anderson et al., 1989). By the late 1950s, it was apparent athletic associations across the country were grappling with parallel issues and that national collaboration would be beneficial. A national organization could help universities across Canada develop consistent and appropriate sport rules and regulations, coordinated agreements with national sport organizations, and improved national and potentially international competition. Furthermore, national championships could augment the profile of inter-university athletics and bolster student interest and support. The CIAU was reconstituted in 1961 as the governing body of inter-university sport for all provinces and operated as an autonomous organization for 10 years.

The CIAU experienced significant changes in the 1970s, transformations brought about by several simultaneous forces (Anderson et al., 1989; Hall, Slack, Smith & Whitson, 1991; Morrow et al., 1989). First, inter-university sport continued to expand across the country and administrative and organizational demands escalated. It was necessary to establish a permanent office and board of directors.

More importantly, the status of sport within the larger social context in Canada was changing. Greater numbers of sporting events were being televised and, as a result, sport became an attractive vehicle to sell goods and services, including political ideologies and platforms (Schneider, 1997; Taylor, 1986). The government saw the potential of sport to promote the Canadian culture on the international scene and national unity on the domestic scene. The Ministry of Fitness and Amateur Sport developed an agenda of high-performance sport and looked to universities to develop high-performance training centres (Department of National Health and Welfare, 1969). Initially, federal support for inter-university sport was limited, as was the overall budget for sport in Canada. But during the 1970s, federal funding was earmarked for travel equalizations, national championship travel, and involvement in international competition.

Federal government involvement in inter-university sport was received with mixed feelings (Schneider, 1997; Taylor, 1986). A focus on high-performance sport meant direct and indirect costs of supporting national teams, practical constraints over access to and use of space and facilities, and philosophical conflicts over high-performance sport versus broad-based programming for the general student body (Jackson, 1986; Semotiuk, 1986). However, support of high-performance sport within institutions of higher education also meant more qualified and experienced coaches for intercollegiate programs, improved competition, new revenue through renting of facilities and services to national teams, and research and athlete testing opportunities for sport science labs (Hall et al., 1991; Jackson, 1986).

One of the steps universities took to promote high-performance sport in the ensuing years was to create full-time coaching positions and hire male and female coaches on non-academic routes, ending a long tradition of faculty-coaches (Schneider, 1997; Taylor, 1986). In addition, universities increasingly favoured separate athletic and academic units (Schneider, 1997), despite earlier recommendations to establish and/or maintain integrated athletic and physical education departments (the Association of Universities and Colleges of Canada, 1966; Mathews, 1974). These changes led some to argue inter-university sport was jeopardizing educational integrity in favour of athletic excellence.

The recession of the early 1980s reverberated throughout Canadian inter-university athletics. Federal funding declined and funds allocated for university sport were no longer available, triggering more than a decade of fiscal restraint (Anderson et al., 1989). Athletic departments struggled to stretch existing resources and find new sources of funding, including camps and corporate sponsorship. Universities in western Canada and Memorial University in the east were particularly hard hit by escalating travel costs, and several were forced to drop varsity programs. Between 1972–73 and 1977–78, 36 programs were cut from the universities in Canada West (Anderson et al., 1989). While under serious financial limitations, athletic departments also wrestled with providing opportunities for female athletes (see Box 4.1) and operating competitive inter-university sport programs for a small population of student-athletes concurrently with broad-based sport and recreation opportunities for the wider student and local communities (Schneider, 1997; Taylor, 1986).

In June 2001, members of the CIAU agreed the new name Canadian Interuniversity Sport (CIS) would more accurately reflect its mission, function, and breadth. Today, CIS includes all 49 major degree-granting institutions, save one, in four regional conferences: Atlantic University Sport (AUS), QSSF, OUA, and Canada West. Notably, Simon Fraser University does not compete in the CIS, due to its recruitment and scholarship policies and is instead a member of the U.S. National Association of Intercollegiate Athletics (NAIA). The CIS is a single-tiered system that offers national championships in 9 sports for men and 10 for women, a collective of over 10 200 student-athletes and 550 coaches.

In addition to CIS, a national body governs athletic competition between colleges across Canada. The Canadian Colleges Athletic Association (CCAA) actually outnumbers the CIS with 95 member institutions representing five regional conferences. Historically, colleges in one province competed against each other in a small and variable number of sports. In 1971, the provinces of British Columbia, Alberta, Saskatchewan, and Manitoba formed the Four-West Championship for interprovincial competition in seven sports. Four-West merged with the Ontario Colleges Athletic Association and the Quebec Colleges Athletic Association to form the CCAA. Today, the CCAA holds national championships in eight events—men's and women's badminton, soccer, volleyball, and basketball—and holds open championships in golf and cross-country running.

Current Status of Inter-University Sport

A number of challenges face Canadian inter-university sport today. Among the most pressing is the role and governance of intercollegiate athletics in institutions of higher education, followed by concerns about gender equity, athletic scholarships, and sport initiations and hazings on Canadian campuses (see Box 4.1). Let us consider each in turn.

The Role and Governance of Canadian Intercollegiate Athletics

There is considerable debate about the role of inter-university athletic programs in Canadian universities. There are those who support inter-university programs because they contribute to Canada's high-performance sport system. The use of educational institutions to develop high-performance athletes does raise some questions about who actually governs and controls university athletics (Armstrong-Doherty, 1995; Inglis, 1991). Others oppose spending for inter-university programs and feel the limited resources should be directed to recreational and instructional programs for the wider student and local communities. The majority endorses inter-university athletic programs and feels they are a fundamental component of students' overall development. The dominant ideology is that sport contributes to students' overall development in two ways. First, university sport promotes the academic achievement of student-athletes. Second, it encourages the acquisition of valuable life skills and the successful negotiation of age-appropriate developmental tasks, notably identity formation. Research suggests these ideals, although closely held, are not always met.

Academic Achievement of Student-Athletes As noted earlier, the escalating emphasis on high-performance sport, growing autonomy of athletic departments, and increasing number of coaches accountable to athletic and not academic mandates caused concern that the integrity of educational institutions was being compromised. Similar criticisms have been lobbied against intercollegiate athletics in the United States, where significant research has considered the academic performance of university student-athletes, particularly those in high-profile sports such as football and men's basketball (see, for example, Adler & Adler, 1991; Thelin, 1994). Prompted by the changes taking place in Canadian university sport, and in part by the research trends in the United States, several Canadian researchers examined the academic performance of Canadian student-athletes (Curtis & McTeer, 1990; Danylchuk, 1995; Martens, 1985; McTeer & Curtis, 1999). Early studies suggested participation in university athletics contributed to greater academic achievement among Canadian student-athletes as evidenced by higher GPA and graduation rates. Later studies, however, cautioned that Canadian student-athletes were not faring as well as their non-athlete peers and earlier advantages were waning.

Martens (1985) compared the annual and overall university GPA, graduation rate, and time needed to graduate of 91 male and 121 female intercollegiate athletes from 10 sports with non-athletes matched on gender and high school GPA. The participants were enrolled in the Physical Education Department at the University of Victoria between 1970 and 1980. Non-athletes' annual and overall university GPA significantly surpassed the annual and overall university GPA of athletes, although this relationship held only for those enrolled from 1970 to 1974. The annual and overall GPA of student-athletes enrolled from 1975 to 1980 did not significantly differ from non-athletes. Athletes graduated significantly more often than their non-athlete peers, although the athletes did take longer to graduate.

Several years later, Curtis and McTeer (1990) compared the cumulative GPA, graduation rate, and graduation status (with class versus late) of athletes and non-athletes enrolled between the late 1970s and early 1980s in a small and a large Canadian university, University A and University B, respectively. The athlete sample included male football, hockey, and basketball players. Comparisons found athletes tended to do as well as their non-athlete peers and, in some cases, even better. Athletes were equally likely to graduate, with the exception of those in honours programs at University B who were more likely to graduate. Athletes and non-athletes took about the same amount of time to graduate, with the exception of athletes in general programs at University A who took longer but graduated as often as non-athlete peers. Athletes achieved GPAs equivalent to their non-athlete peers, and athletes in honours programs at University A achieved significantly higher cumulative GPAs.

BOX 4.1 INITIATION AND HAZING IN CANADIAN INTER-UNIVERSITY SPORT

Recent hazing incidents at the University of Guelph, McMaster University, and the University of Western Ontario triggered alarm over sport initiations on Canadian campuses. A hazing activity involving a first-year wide receiver with the University of Western Ontario and two male engineering students from the same university left one student injured, another charged with criminal negligence causing bodily harm, and a university community reeling.

Despite anti-hazing laws, surveys of U.S. high school and university students revealed both groups were subjected to sport-related initiations in overwhelming numbers (Hoover, 1999; Hoover & Pollard, 2000). Hazing incidents included forced drinking, physical humiliation, public nudity, sexual games, being exposed to physical danger, and even performing criminal acts. Some student-athletes reported initiations were fun and exciting, made them feel closer as a group, or gave them an opportunity to prove themselves. Others, however, said they just went along with it, were scared to say no, or did not know what was happening.

A Canadian study on sport initiations warrants special mention. Johnson (2000) conducted in-depth interviews with current and former male and female student-athletes from a Canadian university with a large athletics program about the incidence, significance, and consequences of sport-related hazing practices. All the athletes interviewed had been hazed during high school and all had been involved in some initiation activity upon arrival at university. Many later organized initiation events for incoming student-athletes, despite unpleasant and lasting memories of their own experiences. Johnson characterized initiations as acts that articulate the masculine ideals of power and hegemony, reinforce the patriarchal structure, and marginalize homosexuals and women through humiliation and objectification.

Johnson (2000) did sense student-athletes were increasingly willing to question abusive hazing practices and described them as poised for change. In collaboration with a colleague, Johnson developed a handbook for coaches and student leaders outlining alternative, welcoming orientation activities (Miller & Johnson, 1998). One of these activities, a weekend retreat at a ropes and challenge camp, was organized for athletic teams at the University of Toronto in the fall of 2000. Student-athletes from six athletic teams and their coaches participated in a low ropes course, rock climbing and belaying, canoeing, kayaking, and cooperative games. Initial feedback from first-year players, team leaders, and coaches was positive, and organizers believe such alternative activities will help break the cycle of initiations.

The other available Canadian study compared the academic performance of athletes from 22 men's and 19 women's sports enrolled at a large Ontario university over a two-year period (Danylchuk, 1995). In contrast to the earlier findings, Danylchuk found student-athletes were struggling academically. The high school grades of the athletes and non-athletes did not significantly differ, yet non-athletes consistently outperformed both male and female athletes while at university. In comparison to their male peers, female student-athletes had higher entrance averages and achieved significantly higher GPAs during the two years of university study, although this advantage disappeared when compared to female non-athletes.

Recall, Curtis and McTeer (1990) found male hockey, football, and basketball players performed as well as, if not better than, their non-athlete peers. However, in an investigation of the academic performance of both male and female student-athletes from the same university for a more recent period, 1988 to 1993, athletes appeared to be doing worse than non-athletes (McTeer & Curtis, 1999). Athletes achieved lower GPAs and were less likely to graduate than their non-athlete peers, despite being enrolled in less demanding majors. These findings are sobering. Less than a decade after student-athletes achieved grades and graduation rates equivalent to, if not better than, non-athletes, they were earning lower grades and graduating less often.

McTeer and Curtis (1999) suggested a number of factors may be to blame. The demands placed on student-athletes by coaches and administrators may be on the rise across Canada as universities use inter-university sport to increase student and community interest. Student-athletes' time may be stretched even thinner than in the past as greater emphasis is placed on academic performance and graduate studies. Finally, tuition increases mean most students must now work throughout the school year and may have less time and energy to devote to academics. Further research is needed to determine why the academic performance of student-athletes has declined in recent years.

Acquisition of Life Skills In 1984, Chelladurai and Danylchuk surveyed athletic administrators across the country about the goals of intercollegiate athletics (Chelladurai & Danylchuk, 1984). In addition to athletes' physical growth, intercollegiate athletics were intended to promote psychological and emotional development. The athletic administrators believed the acquisition of skills relevant to future employment, including leadership, responsibility, and respect for authority, and increasing student-athletes' future career opportunities were fundamental goals of Canadian inter-university sport. Indeed, when athletic departments are criticized for placing too much emphasis on sport or for expecting too much from student-athletes, they often assert that inter-university sport encourages not only physical but overall development, and not only for those students directly involved, but for those who act as coaches, team managers, officials, sports information officers, and even fans.

Despite the developmental goals of sport programs in Canadian universities, there is little empirical evidence Canadian university students benefit directly from participation in university sport. For the most part, the acquisition of skills such as those listed above is assumed or inferred. Furthermore, there is little proof that skills learned in sport are transferred to and facilitate success in other settings, particularly the classroom.

One of the major problems with examining the developmental outcomes of involvement in university sport is the difficulty separating benefits related specifically to sport from general maturation effects. Miller and Kerr (2002) attempted to address this issue by asking male and female student-athletes from a large Canadian university what developmental benefits, if any, they experienced as a result of participating in university athletics. The researchers also asked student-athletes to what degree they were able to transfer skills learned in university sport to other settings. The student-athletes asserted they acquired valuable life skills through sport, including leadership, communication, independence, and self-confidence. However, the student-athletes had difficulty recalling how and in what context they had acquired these strengths, as well as how they might be useful in future pursuits, conditions that developmental theorists argue are necessary for successful skills transfer (Danish & Nellen, 1997). Research documenting the developmental outcomes of participating in Canadian inter-university sport is needed if we are to advocate these as educational experiences of life-long value.

Identity Formation Identity formation is of particular significance to our discussion of the overall development of university student-athletes. It is during the college and university years that we wrestle with such questions as "Who am I?", "What do I want to do with the rest of my life?", and "Where am I going?"

Many students enter college and university in a state of identity foreclosure. Identity foreclosure occurs when an individual prematurely commits himself or herself to a particular role, often a socially prescribed or accepted role, without adequate exploration of the role and his or her likes and dislikes, ambitions, and goals (Marcia, 1993).

Student-athletes may be particularly at risk of developing identity foreclosure because the demands of being both a student and an athlete prohibit the exploration of self within a broad range of roles. Indeed, Murphy, Petitpas, and Brewer (1996) found both male and female student-athletes had higher identity foreclosure scores than non-athletes. Moreover, sport scientists have discovered that identity foreclosure may result in a range of difficulties, including emotional and psychological trauma when the sport role is interrupted (Brewer, 1993; Chartrand & Lent, 1987; Grant & Darley, 1993; Pearson & Petitpas, 1990), a willingness to engage in risk behaviour (Brewer et al., 1993), and poor career and future planning (Grant & Darley, 1993; Murphy et al., 1993; Pearson & Petitpas, 1990).

The bulk of the research summarized above examined identity foreclosure among U.S. collegiate athletes. Miller and Kerr (in press) investigated the identity formation of Canadian male and female athletes from volleyball, basketball, track and field, and swimming. The researchers found the participants over-identified with the athlete role during their early university careers at the expense of meaningful investment in their academic and social selves, consistent with the experiences of their U.S. peers. However, the Canadian student-athletes shifted their investment from athletics to academics as they progressed through university and demonstrated deferred role experimentation in their academic and social lives in their upper years. These findings suggest that Canadian student-athletes may over-identify with the athlete role in their early university careers, yet that they are able to avoid identity foreclosure through the exploration of other roles during their senior years. It may be that Canadian student-athletes falter initially, but eventually recover and successfully progress through the developmental task of identity formation.

Gender Equity Numerous factors have influenced women's intercollegiate sport in Canada and the United States (Hums, MacLean, Richman & Pastore, 1994). The United States has been largely affected by Title IX, a key provision of the Education Amendments Act of 1972, stipulating funding would be withheld from any institution that failed to provide equal access and quality of services based on gender. Universities contested Title IX for almost 10 years on the basis that no federal funding went directly to athletic departments, and as such, they were exempt from equity requirements. A Supreme Court decision in 1984 supported this argument, and within a year, the Office of Civil Rights suspended ongoing investigations involving university athletics. The Civil Rights Restoration Act of 1988 restored Title IX and charged that all athletic departments were required to provide equal access and opportunities for female students or risk losing federal support (Sage, 1990). Women in the United States have secured greater opportunities as universities work to meet Title IX, although there is still a long way to go before female student-athletes there enjoy true equity.

Canada does not have similar legislation. Instead, under the general principles of the Charter of Rights and Freedoms, universities are compelled to provide equity with regard to athletics. It is unclear to what degree gender equity in Canadian university athletics has been reached.

The CIAU, now CIS, conducted gender equity studies in 1992–93 and again in 1998–99 (Haines, 1999). The data showed Canadian universities have made notable advances toward gender equity during the last decade but, like their U.S. counterparts, still have progress to make. The number of women participating in inter-university sport has climbed over the last few decades, yet there is still a slight gap in athletic opportunities for male and female student-athletes in Canadian institutions. In 2000–01, of the 10 200 student-athletes participating in CIS sports, approximately 5600 were men and 4600 women.

In addition, the data also reveal that there remains a visible difference in the opportunities for women in coaching and administrative positions within the CIS, as well as in the resources and funding invested in women's programs (see Box 4.2).

Athletic Scholarships Financial aid for student-athletes was sanctioned by the CIAU in 1981 provided the value of the scholarship did not exceed $1500 and the recipient met certain criteria. The conditions and value of athletic scholarships have been heavily debated over the years, at times threatening to divide the CIAU (Hall et al., 1991). Frustrated by losing talented athletes to U.S. colleges, some universities, notably those in western Canada, contested CIAU scholarship regulations. They argued larger athletic scholarships would entice Canadian student-athletes to stay at home and enrich Canadian inter-university competition. Other schools, however, were philosophically opposed to scholarships based on athletic ability. Many of the Ontario universities argued athletic scholarships would threaten the academic integrity of educational institutions and lead to exploitation and corruption similar to that seen on U.S. campuses.

The issue of athletic scholarships was revisited at the CIS annual meeting in June 2000. Ontario universities, who make up two-thirds of available votes, were expected to block-vote against proposed changes, including a revision allowing scholarships for entering student-athletes. In spite of anticipated and, indeed, initial disagreements, member institutions agreed to a number of changes. The CIS moved to allow athletic scholarships equivalent to tuition and compulsory fees for entering students provided they had a minimum average of 80% and for continuing students provided they had completed two semesters of full-time study in the preceding academic year and achieved a 70% average.

While the CIS provides overriding principles, individual institutions can agree within their conference to operate under different policies provided they fulfil the CIS minimum requirements. OUA member institutions voted not to provide athletic scholarships to entering student-athletes (OUA, 2001). This decision reflected their continued concern that athletic scholarships for incoming student-athletes would show preference for athletic over academic performance, as well as questions about the impact of CIS policy changes on recruiting practices and the policing thereof. Some observers predicted the OUA's position would eventually make it difficult for Ontario universities to recruit talented athletes and result in a two-tiered system in Canadian inter-university

BOX 4.2 HISTORY OF WOMEN IN INTER-UNIVERSITY SPORT

The Women's Intercollegiate Athletic Union (WIAU) was founded in 1923 to provide opportunities for female university student-athletes in Ontario. The Ontario-Quebec Women's Intercollegiate Athletics (O-QWICA) governed athletic competition for women enrolled at both Ontario and Quebec universities, and the Atlantic Women's Intercollegiate Athletic Association (AWIAA) for female student-athletes in the Maritimes. WIAU and O-QWICA merged in 1971 to form the Ontario Women's Interuniversity Athletic Association (OWIAA). In 1969, a proposal to develop a national organization was endorsed by each of the conferences, and in 1970 the Canadian Women's Intercollegiate Athletic Union (CWIUA) sanctioned the first women's national championship in volleyball.

Notably, many of the women's regional conferences merged with the men's during the following decades. The AIAA and AWICAA merged to form the AUAA in 1974. The CWIAU itself converged with the CIAU in 1978. The last major merger took place only very recently. The OWIAA, after 60 years of providing competitive athletic opportunities for female students in Ontario universities, joined the OUAA in 1997 to become Ontario University Athletics (OUA).

The number of part-time head coaching positions for women in both women's and men's programs, and full-time head coaching positions for women in men's programs, increased from 1992–93 to 1998–99 (Haines, 1999). Yet there have been no new full-time head coaching positions for women in women's programs, while 14 such positions opened up for men (Haines, 1999). This data reflects a trend that has been taking place in Canadian universities over the last two decades (Hall, Slack, Smith, & Whitson, 1991). Records also reveal that both women and men coaching women's programs earn less than men coaching men's programs, and that significantly fewer dollars are spent on recruiting, marketing, and promotion of women's programs (Haines, 1999).

sport, reminiscent of the NCAA (Rayner, 1998). The impact of these developments remains to be seen.

Members also agreed to a new gender-equity policy mandating that financial support for male and female student-athletes must be proportional to the number of CIS male and female student-athletes at the issuing institution (CIS, 2000a). Scholarship data from 2000–01 revealed male athletes, who make up 53% of CIS student-athletes, received an unequal 66% of athletic scholarships (CIS, 2000b). CIS expects universities to eliminate this discrepancy and will assess their progress in 2003 and their compliance by 2005–06 (Charbonneau, 2002).

CONCLUSIONS

At the university level, inter-university programs continue to enjoy support among sport enthusiasts and those who believe in the philosophy of education through sport. Yet diverse interest groups, including Canada's high-performance contingent, the general student population, and the broader communities in which universities exist, are challenging varsity programs for increasingly limited space and resources. Further, research suggests university student-athletes' education, both academic and personal, may not be directly enhanced as a result of participation in inter-university athletics.

These trends should not be disheartening. The value of sport as an educational tool is enduring. Sport has the potential to contribute to the development of our youth, and our education system is the best way to help children and youth develop healthy, active lifestyles. The challenge is to provide sport opportunities that truly embody the philosophy of education through sport.

Critical Thinking Questions

1. Why are physical education programs being devalued across the nation? What efforts are being made to reverse this trend?
2. Identify the challenges that confront inter-school sport programs. If you were a member of a local school board and supporter of the inclusion of sport within educational institutions, how would you address these challenges?
3. Research suggests the academic achievement of Canadian student-athletes has changed over the last three decades. Describe these changes and explain why they have taken place.
4. Why are athletes at risk of experiencing role engulfment? What are the consequences of role engulfment?
5. Summarize the arguments for and against athletic scholarships and predict the impact of recent CIS policy changes on inter-university sport in Canada.

Suggested Readings

Adler, P., & Adler, P. (1991). *Backboards and blackboards: College athletes and role engulfment*. New York: Columbia University Press.

Kerr, G. (1996). The role of sport in preparing youth for adulthood. In B. Galway and J. Hudson (Eds.), *Youth in transition: Perspectives on research and policy.* Toronto: Thompson Educational Publishing, 293–301.

McTeer, W., & Curtis, J. (1999). Intercollegiate sport involvement and academic achievement: A follow-up study. *Avante, 5*, 39–55.

Miller, P.S., & Kerr, G.A. (in press). The role experimentation of intercollegiate student-athletes. *The Sport Psychologist*.

Thelin, J.R. (1994). *Games colleges play: Scandal and reform in intercollegiate athletics.* Baltimore: Johns Hopkins Press.

Web Links

Canada West Universities Athletic Association
http://www.universitysport.ca/cwuaa
Information about inter-university sport in British Columbia, Alberta, Saskatchewan, and Manitoba.

Canadian Colleges Athletic Association
http://www.ccaa.ca
Information about intercollegiate competition across Canada.

Canadian Interuniversity Sport
http://www.universitysport.ca
Information about inter-university sport programs in Canada, including media and corporate information about the CIS.

Canadian Intramural Recreation Association
http://www.intramurals.ca
Information about intramural and recreation programming for elementary and secondary schools nationwide.

The Ontario Federation of School Athletic Associations
http://www.ofsaa.on.ca
Information about inter-school sport programs in Ontario.

Ontario Physical and Health Education Association
http://www.ophea.net
Online community of organizations and individuals committed to promoting physical activity among children and youth.

Ontario University Athletics
http://www.oua.org
Information about inter-university sport in Ontario.

5

Deviance and Sport

Robert A. Stebbins

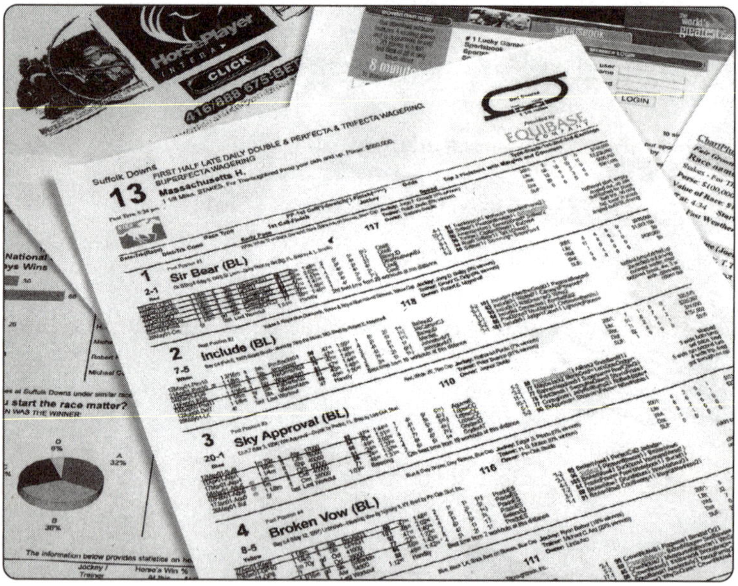

BOB STEBBINS

Internet gambling on sports can reach deviant levels.

It was a flash of sporting brilliance. The muscle-bound, shaven-headed sprinter, born in Jamaica but wearing the colours of Canada, rose explosively from the starting blocks; 100 metres and 9.79 seconds later he raised his index finger in arrogant triumph. Ben Johnson, competing at the 1988 Seoul Olympics, had become the world's fastest man.

Within hours he had also become, for many, its most reviled. Mr. Johnson, the doctors reported, had failed a drugs test. As he slunk from the Olympic village in disgrace, the second-placed Carl Lewis, from America, stepped forward to take the gold medal. Mr. Johnson's humiliation, said the sporting authorities, was proof that sport will not tolerate performance-enhancing drugs.

The Economist, Superhuman heroes, June 6, 1998

Sport is not generally the scene of serious player deviance, such as crime of the mugging, murder, and mayhem variety. To be sure, deviance can be found in sport, as in every other walk of life, but in this sphere it tends, with some notable exceptions, to be regarded with tolerance. Even bench-clearing brawls in baseball and football and man-to-man punch-ups in ice hockey fail, at bottom, to qualify as anything other than minor infractions of society's moral norms.

In this chapter we look first at the general idea of tolerable deviance and then at three different ways it manifests itself among athletes and, more selectively, among fans: deviance for sport, deviance for fun and need, and deviance with sport. Not included in this review, simply because of insufficient space or because the subject is covered elsewhere in this volume, is broad coverage of deviance by nonplayers, such as coaches, team owners, sports administrators, parents, and spectators, which can be considerable and at times most intolerable.

TOLERABLE DEVIANCE

Deviance is behaviour judged as violating the community's moral norms. This judgment is collective, a result of many people having sufficient power or influence to make the judgment stick. Moral norms are the broad directives by which community members implement their institutionalized solutions to problems significantly affecting their valued way of life. These norms indicate in a general way what the community expects of its members in particular areas of social life and what it considers rejections of those expectations. Thus moral norms stand apart from other kinds of expectations such as ordinances, regulations, customs, and folkways.

Moreover, some deviant acts, despite their moral overtones, are tolerated by most members of the community. **Tolerance** is an attitude or orientation that individuals hold toward certain activities or thoughts of others that differ substantially from their own (Stebbins, 1996, p. 3). It is a relatively passive disposition, falling roughly midway between scorn or disdain toward an activity or thought pattern on the one hand, and embracement or acceptance of it on the other. Both scorn and embracement, in contrast to tolerance, are active approaches to the behaviour in question. When something is tolerated it is accorded legitimacy, though perhaps grudgingly. At the same time, because tolerated thought and behaviour are nonetheless mildly threatening, people have little interest in actually adopting tolerated behaviours or thought patterns as their own, or even accepting them as alternatives they might conceivably adopt in the future.

The presence of tolerance in society gives **tolerable deviance** its special status. With such deviance, the welfare of the community is still believed to be preserved. But this outlook holds true just so long as such behaviour is enacted by only a small proportion of members in a way that is only mildly threatening to the community's majority. Tolerable deviance stands in contrast to **intolerable deviance**, which greatly threatens the established order, causing the community to scorn it and therefore to try to eliminate it. Hagan (1991, pp. 11–12) developed three measures for empirically distinguishing mildly threatening tolerable deviance from the highly threatening intolerable variety. Intolerable deviance is likely to be accompanied by the following: considerable agreement about its wrongfulness; a harsh community reaction; and a judgment that it is especially harmful. With tolerable deviance there is a significantly lower level of agreement about its wrongfulness; a significantly more lenient community reaction; and a belief that only the deviant is harmed, and then not seriously.

Many Canadians are ambivalent about one or more of the activities falling under the heading of tolerable deviance. They know they ought to refrain from engaging in them, yet they find it difficult to escape their magnetic pull. This is the type of deviance Becker (1963, p. 26) had in mind when he observed that "it is much more likely that most people experience deviant impulses frequently. At least in fantasy, people are much more deviant than they appear." Little wonder that tolerable deviance is the classificatory home of most forms of deviant leisure.

TYPES OF TOLERABLE AND INTOLERABLE DEVIANCE

The relationship between tolerable and intolerable deviance is, however, more complicated than the preceding pages suggest. In this regard, note that tolerable deviance may be classed as criminal, noncriminal, or legitimate. *Criminal tolerable deviance*, though actually illegal according to criminal law, is generally treated by police and the wider community alike as having minor importance compared with mainstream intolerable deviance. That is, criminal tolerable deviance is seldom officially challenged. Several conditions explain this response. The laws in question may be vague, exemplified well by those pertaining to the production and sale of pornography. Or they may be difficult to enforce, as are those pertaining to group sex, cheating at gambling, and player violence in sport. And some laws have, at certain points in history, low police priority. Those dealing with disorderliness, marijuana consumption, and recreational use of prescription drugs are three examples. In short, those who tolerate a form of deviance fail to see it as inherently evil.

Noncriminal tolerable deviance lies outside the jurisdiction of law. In Canada at present no laws exist prohibiting adultery (when morals of minor children are not endangered) or striptease work (when done within legal limits of undress). Nudism practised in private resorts is frequently not illegal, nor are heavy drinking and nonpublic drunkenness. The Criminal Code of Canada defines as illegal only certain forms of gambling, while saying nothing about others. In the realm of sport, cheating appears to be the most widespread form of noncriminal tolerable deviance.

Legitimate tolerable deviance is actually guaranteed by law. Canadians have the legal right to think as they wish, and so some hold religious and political beliefs that deviate significantly from those of the majority in the community. They may also embrace beliefs about the supernatural, thus rejecting scientific explanations of physical and psychological reality. Certain minor forms of mental disorder are also tolerable and quite within the law. Serious or mild mental disorder is a guaranteed right if, according to the general public, it amounts to no more than a "warped" set of beliefs. Neuroses, as opposed to psychoses, which must be classified as intolerable deviance, include such reactions as phobias, neurotic anxiety, partial personality impairment, and obsessive-compulsive acts. The eating disorders of anorexia and bulimia discussed later in this chapter exemplify this kind of deviance in sport.

The relationship between tolerable and intolerable deviance is portrayed in Table 5.1. Note the overlap in the criminal deviance–criminal laws cell. We shall see that athletes, if they deviate at all, are most likely to engage in some form of noncriminal tolerable deviance, less likely to engage in either criminal or legitimate tolerable deviance, and least likely to engage in intolerable deviance (considered shortly).

TABLE 5.1 Tolerable and Intolerable Deviance

Threat Scale	Norms	Criminal Deviance	Noncriminal Deviance	Legitimate Deviance
Great	Mores	ID	ID	–
	Criminal Laws	ID/TD	–	–
Mild	Other Moral Norms	–	TD	TD

ID = Intolerable deviance; TD = Tolerable deviance; – = Logically impossible cross-classification

Source: Reprinted with permission of McGraw-Hill Ryerson Ltd. Robert A. Stebbins. (1996). *Tolerable Differences: Living with Deviance*, 2nd ed. Toronto: McGraw-Hill Ryerson, 5.

Of course, much more of a case must be made for classifying a type of deviance as tolerable or intolerable than has been made so far. This is done, in part, in Stebbins (1996, Chapters 3 to 10) as well as in the sample of works cited later in this chapter. In the meantime, it should be understood that the types of tolerable and intolerable deviance in a community extant at a particular time in history reflect the current values of people collectively powerful enough to influence public opinion and shape legislative, enforcement, and judicial practice. In other words, their definition of threat is the one by which some forms of deviance are officially treated as intolerable, while other forms are unofficially treated as tolerable. Groups lacking such power may look askance on some of these generally tolerated forms of deviance, as do, for example, many smokers when reflecting on today's restrictive laws governing smoking in public places.

The foregoing three types of tolerable deviance constitute an incomplete list. Moreover, because the distribution of power changes, the list tends to change as well. Some forms of intolerable deviance may gradually become tolerable, as is currently evident to a greater or lesser extent for abortion, use of heroin, and production and consumption of obscenity (Winick, 1991). Meanwhile, tolerable forms may drift toward intolerability, which appears to be happening today for smoking and has already happened, in a way, for use of performance-enhancing drugs in sport.

By contrast, intolerable deviance is behaviour in violation of powerful criminal and noncriminal moral norms. Its core forms are illegal—what Glaser (1974, p. 60) calls "crimes of predation." These acts include theft, rape, burglary, murder, forgery, and assault as well as swindling, embezzlement, and other types of fraud. Bribery falls in this category, too, and appears most commonly in sport in the form of surreptitiously paying athletes to underplay a match so that their team loses (and the one betted on by the briber wins). Noncriminal forms of intolerable deviance are seen as bizarre mental aberrations or severe, destructive addictions; they include suicide, alcoholism, drug addiction, compulsive gambling, and severe mental disorder (e.g., psychosis). They violate the moral precept that people be in control of their thoughts, behaviour, and emotions. Clearly, some forms of deviance are tolerated when carried out at a certain level, for example, heavy drinking or habitual gambling, but become ever more scorned as they become addictive. Because intolerable deviance compared with the other types is least common among athletes and because space is limited, it will not be covered in this chapter.

Why Engage in Tolerable Deviance?

Further, the tolerable deviance perspective offers three broad reasons that help explain why people, athletes among them, engage in such behaviour. One, sometimes people turn to such deviance because it is interesting or pleasurable to do as *leisure* during free time. The section of this chapter on deviance for fun provides a number of examples. Two, in general terms, people sometimes engage in tolerable deviance as a livelihood or as an aid to a livelihood or a serious amateur pursuit. In sport, it appears that this *work-related* tolerable deviance is limited primarily, if not exclusively, to the role of helping athletes attain their goals. The next section on deviance for sport shows how this reason for tolerable deviance is expressed.

Three, some tolerable deviance serves as a mode of *adjustment*, as a way of arriving at a behavioural balance between personal needs and goals, on the one hand, and the demands of other people and society, on the other. This is ordinarily a long-term process taking several years. While most, if not all, tolerable deviance can be seen as a form of adjustment, much of it can also be identified and justified as leisure or work or both. Still, a residual category of deviant adjustment exists for which, in our culture, there is no explicit term. Residual adjustments, known in sociology as "residual rule breaking" (Scheff, 1984, p. 38), are sometimes lumped by professionals and the general public under the heading of mental illness or mental disorder. We consider some instances of this in the section on deviance in sport undertaken out of need.

While theories of crime and deviance abound, only the foregoing perspective bears directly on tolerable deviance, the principal form found in sport. Certain of the other theories, though they never directly refer to such deviance, do nonetheless help explain indirectly its emergence, persistence, decline, and place in the larger society. Although these theories—they are anomie-strain, labelling, value-conflict, functionalism, and medicalization—cannot be adequately covered here, interested readers can find elsewhere a detailed review of them (Stebbins, 1996, Chapter 2).

DEVIANCE FOR SPORT

Athletes may deviate from the moral norms of their society or their sport for two reasons, both justified in the name of the sport they are playing. One, they may hope to gain a particular advantage while competing against other athletes, be they people on their own team or competitors in a match. Two, athletes may deviate as a way of expressing negative emotions, usually anger, but more rarely hate. Sometimes deviance for sport occurs as cheating, sometimes as use of performance-enhancing drugs. Eating disorders and violence have also been justified in the name of sport. With partial exception of the second, all seem best classified as either noncriminal or legitimate tolerable deviance.

Cheating

When athletes cheat, they intentionally violate one or more rules of the game, the object being to gain momentary advantage in the unfolding contest. According to this definition, judgments by officials, however accurate, fail to identify cheating, if athletes implicated in them had no intention of breaking rules. For example, players explained in a study of amateur and professional football (Stebbins, 1993) that "face-masking" calls by referees can be of this sort; they are not evidence of cheating, because a man's hand can accidentally slip around the mask of a player on the other team in the course of intense and rapidly moving action. Still, academic cheating by student athletes whose grades determine whether they play school-sponsored sports does, according to this definition, qualify as cheating. It will not be covered here, however, because little scientific literature exists on the matter (Coakley, 2001, p. 156).

Delattre (1975, p. 136) writes that, logically, a person must either cheat at a game or compete in it; it is logically impossible to do both, for competition is the very essence of games. Moreover,

> *when a person violates the rules which govern competition, he treats his opponents as means merely to his end of victory. The symbols of victory have status or meaningfulness only because they stand for triumph in competition; without the opposition, they are worthless. Attainment of these symbols by cheating is therefore the exploitation of those who competed in good faith. Competitors are equally reduced to means merely in cases where the end of the cheater is prize money or gambling profit. Without the competition there can be neither prize nor wager, and the cheater simply uses the bona fide competitors solely for his own gain. Cheating is thus a paradigm case of failure to act with respect for the moral status of persons as ends. (Delattre, 1975, p. 136)*

Fraleigh (1982) observes further, following the same logic, that the "good foul"—when player A knows that the penalty for fouling B is less inimical for A's competitive interest than letting B continue to play—is also a failure to compete on the part of A.

Performance-Enhancing Drugs

To use performance-enhancing drugs—known in both sport and scientific circles as "doping"—is to take or have administered to humans or animals a substance designed to elevate athletic output. Some of these substances have been demonstrated to change the body more or less permanently, as do anabolic steroids, whose principal effect is to strengthen muscle. Others have been demonstrated to momentarily aid endurance and help overcome fatigue, notably amphetamines and, in large doses, caffeine. Barbiturates and benzodiazepines work momentarily to control tremors. Finally, still other drugs have been claimed to have one or more of these effects as well as others, even though not unequivocally shown in carefully controlled tests to do this; they include cocaine, ephedrine, and phenyl.

Except for cocaine, these substances are not illegal, even if some are available only by prescription in some countries. But apart from caffeine, they are scorned by all official sports organizations, which nowadays go to great lengths to ensure that only drug-free athletes compete at events within their jurisdiction. Hence, taking them is a special kind of cheating. How effective this control is is unclear, however. On the one hand, very few contemporary athletes are apprehended for use of performance-enhancing drugs, as carried out through extensive random and announced testing. On the other hand, an unknown but probably large number of athletes, aided by some doctors and pharmacists, outsmart the tests. There is evidence demonstrating that many athletes would use some of the aforementioned drugs if they knew that taking them would ensure they would win but not be caught (*The Economist*, 1998, p. 12).

There is also the question of which drug is being tested for. It is far more difficult to disguise use of amphetamine, for instance, a drug that to be effective must be consumed at the sport event itself, than use of steroids. The latter may have been used much earlier in the athlete's life and, at the time of the contest, is no longer detectable. So the modern doping situation in sport remains clouded in ambiguity and inconclusiveness:

> *The period of high and increased usage among athletes in the Olympic Games, so typical of the period from 1972 to 1988, appears to be over. Whether the Atlanta Games of 1996, supposed to be "the cleanest ever," were indeed so clean remains an open question. Biomedical testing was certainly at an all-time high and yet produced only few positive tests. Suspicion abounds, however, whether individual athletes were able to conceal their involvement with drugs or got away with it for reasons having to do with the inconsistency, reliability, and validity of testing methods and procedures.* (Lüschen, 2000, p. 473)

All this adds up to a textbook case of noncriminal tolerable deviance.

Perhaps, then, this special form of "cheating," as it is sometimes referred to, should simply be made legal within sport so that everyone could have equal access in safe doses to the drugs in question. After all, argue proponents of this policy, sport is already inherently unequal, in that contestants are born with different abilities, have access to different facilities, are trained by coaches with different abilities and approaches, and so on.

This was decidedly not the position taken by the federal Dubin Commission of Inquiry (Dubin, 1990), established in 1988 in wake of the Johnson scandal and headed by Charles Dubin, then Associate Chief Justice of Ontario. The commission produced 70 recommendations pertaining to the use and abuse of drugs and banned practices in sport. Among the recommendations was its position that individual cheaters must be stopped, without however, questioning in any important way the conditions encouraging such deviance, among them financial rewards, media pressure, and a win-at-all-costs attitude (Hall, Slack, Smith, & Whitson, 1991, p. 225).

> *In events such as weight lifting and in many of the power events in track and field, it was [in the 1988 Olympic Games] difficult to meet these [A-card level] standards without using anabolic steroids. The athlete was placed in a Catch-22 position, in which fame and rewards were promised to the winners, while the alternatives were mediocrity and/or retirement.* (Macintosh & Whitson, 1990, p. 136)

At present it is difficult to tell how the drug issue will be resolved in the coming decades.

Eating Disorders

Anorexia nervosa and bulimia nervosa, the two eating disorders most commonly found in sport circles, are classified by the American Psychiatric Association (2000, pp. 583–595) as mental disorders, albeit mild and tolerable ones compared with schizophrenia, paranoia, and similar afflictions. A mental disorder

> *is conceptualized as a clinically significant behavior or psychological syndrome or pattern that occurs in an individual and that is associated with present distress (e.g., painful symptoms) or disability (i.e., impairment in one or more important areas of functioning), or with a significantly increased risk of suffering death, pain, disability, or an important loss of freedom.* (American Psychiatric Association, 2000, p. xxxi)

Such a pattern is more enduring than a one-time reaction to a particular event. Nor is it normal behaviour for a subgroup whose values conflict with those of the larger society.

Weight control is the syndrome at issue in sport. As deviance, it is effected in unusual ways, such as by use of laxatives, induced vomiting, and recourse to fasting and diet aids. These practices raise the question of the nutritional status of athletes engaged in them. One study of female athletes (Beals & Manore, 1998) found that they had significantly lower intakes of energy, protein, and fat than control groups, while vitamin and mineral intake was about the same, possibly because the athletes took supplements.

Certain people in certain sports are more at risk of developing eating disorders than other people in other sports. Female athletes are at greater risk than male athletes (also true for eating disorders in general), and risk is greatest in gymnastics, field hockey, long-distance running, and to a lesser extent, figure skating and dancing (Yates, Shisslak, & Crago, 1994, p. 41). Risk increases in sports stressing bodily leanness and body image coupled with public display of scantily clad athletes.

And speaking of body image, Davis (1999, pp. 87–89) describes how its ideal form for North American females in general (not only those in sport) has over the past century come to be seen by both sexes in ever diminutive terms. Thinness is the watchword of today. Being anorexic in appearance is desirable, even if having anorexia nervosa is not. Being thin is not a universal value, however, for in many developing countries plumpness or moderate fatness are prized, if not idealized (Davis, 1999, p. 89).

In turns out that overcommitment can lead to eating disorders, with persistent, perfectionist high achievers being at greatest risk (Yates, Shisslak, & Crago, 1994, p. 43). When they are sensitive to cultural values of thinness or fitness or both, their level of risk rises still higher. And they are at even greater risk if they pursue a diet or exercise program (and some do both). Finally, risk mounts again if the body is severely stressed through strenuous exertion, sustained calorie deficit, and the like. Still, not all compulsive, or overcommitted, athletes develop eating disorders. But with or without such symptoms, these athletes do tend to remove themselves from family, friends, and other free-time activities, occasionally exerting themselves despite pain and exhaustion and possibly winding up with a case of chronic depression or chronic fatigue. Hughes and Coakley (1991) have dubbed this "positive deviance," so-called because these athletes are excelling along socially valued lines rather than violating moral norms.

Violence

Violence, the subject of the next chapter, is examined here strictly for its deviant qualities, which perhaps surprisingly, are not found in all types. Smith (1983, pp. 8–21) identified four: brutal body contact, borderline violence, quasi-criminal violence, and criminal violence. Presented here along a continuum of increasing seriousness and disapproval, the first two can be said to be tolerable and the second two intolerable. All can also be conceived of as special forms of cheating.

Smith observes that brutal body contact conforms to official rules of the sport in question and is more or less accepted by players. It includes such bone-jarring incidents as tackles, blocks, body checks, and collisions. Some of these, it turns out, can be delivered with such enthusiasm as to be considered excessively brutal; more force is used than necessary to do the job. Thus body contact shades into borderline violence. The latter, though prohibited by official rules, is still more or less accepted by all concerned. The celebrated hockey fistfight, late hit in football, high tackle in soccer, and knock-down pitch in baseball exemplify well this type.

Quasi-criminal violence, according to Smith, violates official rules, to a significant degree player expectations, and even criminal law. It is more or less unacceptable (i.e., intolerable), primarily because it is, in legal terms, a form of assault resulting in serious injury. Criminal violence is so serious (often there is death) that the matter falls entirely within the jurisdiction of law. Most of the time it occurs just before or after a contest, rather than during it.

DEVIANCE FOR FUN AND NEED

Most of the time when athletes engage in deviance outside sport they do so for fun or to meet a need. Three deviant leisure activities are considered in this section: juvenile delinquency, recreational drug use, and deviance out of need.

Juvenile Delinquency

The common-sense idea that regular participation in organized sport insulates many adolescents against organizing their leisure lifestyles around delinquent activities enjoys a significant measure of scientific support. We are speaking here of a special kind of teenage excitement referred to by Katz (1988, Chapter 2) as "sneaky thrills"; theft, break and enter, shoplifting, and joyriding are the main types. Miracle and Rees (1994) note that

> *in summary, there is some support for the idea that high school athletics can provide a deterrent and even a reform function to counteract juvenile delinquency, although it is not clear why this might occur. High school athletes may be forced to conform to school norms by the threat of losing a valued activity, or they may want to conform because sport confirms the value of school culture. Interpersonal networks formed through athletics are less likely to be delinquent, and in this way athletes are protected from involvement in groups where committing delinquent acts may be given high status.* (Miracle & Rees, p. 108)

This is not to say, however, that busy, committed high school athletes are absolutely clean in this regard, only that they are not generally inclined toward these activities.

In fact, adolescent athletes conforming in this manner are at risk of engaging in sporadic positive deviance, in good part because they identify strongly with their team or sport group. When this crowd decides to vandalize something, shoplift a few articles, or even gang-rape a girl, they may be drawn in significant part to the activity through powerful attachment to these friends.

Recreational Drug Use

The fact of positive deviance also helps explain the use of recreational drugs among adolescent athletes, the drugs in question being primarily alcohol and marijuana. From time to time, individuals join their friends in sport to smoke dope or get drunk. But other forces are also at work.

Thus Iso-Ahola and Crowley (1991) found that leisure boredom is associated with drug abuse, although the causal relationship between these two variables still remains to be established. Surprisingly, the bored male adolescent drug abusers they examined turned out to be more active than the control group of nonabusers in such sports as football, baseball, gymnastics, skateboarding, and rollerskating. That the first were still bored even though they participated in active serious leisure lifestyles led the authors to suggest that therapists could possibly discourage further recreational drug use by providing abusers "with copious opportunities to experience leisure activities that potentially meet the same needs that were formerly met through substance abuse" (Iso-Ahola & Crowley, 1991, p. 269). The authors neglected to identify these leisure activities, though they did cite research indicating that substance abusers are more likely than nonabusers to seek thrilling and adventurous pursuits, while showing little taste for repetitious and constant experiences. In other words, these youth were looking for leisure that could give them optimal arousal, that was nevertheless a regular rather than an infrequent activity, such as bungee jumping or roller-coaster riding, but that did not however require long periods of monotonous preparation. The routine drills of, say, hockey or football practice and the slow rates at which skills are perfected in these sports hold little appeal for these adolescents.

Because athletes are often in the public spotlight, there is a certain curiosity in the wider community about their use of alcohol and drugs. The press, in many instances, is all too ready to cater to these interests by carrying detailed accounts of the latest episodes of abuse of these substances by professionals and high-profile amateurs. Given that such coverage tends to suggest that use of drugs and alcohol is rampant among athletes, sociologists have been at work trying to determine if rates of use in sport are different from rates of comparable age and sex categories in the general population.

Alas, research in this area is equivocal for both alcohol and marijuana use. Naughton (1996) and Wechsler et al. (1997), for example, found that both male and female intercollegiate athletes in the United States drink more often and more excessively than other students. Still, Carr, Kennedy, and Dimick (1996) found in a study of white, middle-class high school students that male athletes had both higher rates of regular alcohol use and higher rates of abstinence from alcohol, while female athletes had rates similar to students outside sport. Clearly, much research remains to be done in this area.

The picture is much the same for marijuana use. Ewing's (1998) study of high school athletes revealed that males were more likely to have tried marijuana and to have used it more often than comparable nonathletes. He also found that male athletes were more likely than nonathletes to first experiment with marijuana while still in high school. As for female athletes they use marijuana less often than males, generally preferring to wait until after high school before trying this drug for the first time. By contrast, a study of Alberta university athletes showed that drug (including marijuana) and alcohol abuse paralleled that of other Canadian university students (Spence & Gauvin, 1996). Baumert, Henderson, and Thompson (1998) came to the same conclusion in their extensive investigation of American high school students. Still another study, this time of adolescents (Stuck, 1988), revealed a bimodal distribution similar to that of Carr et al. on alcohol use: some athletes go in for alcohol (mainly beer) and marijuana, while others abstain altogether from these substances. Here, too, more data are needed before definitive generalizations can be made.

Alcohol and marijuana are by far the most popular with athletes who find pleasure in drug consumption. Tricker and Connolly (1997), for example, found in their study of American athletes that 32% of their sample had used marijuana at least once during their lifetime, compared with 5% who had used amphetamine or cocaine. Rates of alcohol use are generally somewhat higher than those of marijuana, while there are male–female differences in that women prefer wine and men prefer beer (Issari & Coombs, 1998). Other drugs used, albeit comparatively infrequently, are heroin, cocaine, and LSD or ecstasy (Pan & Baker, 1998).

Deviance out of Need

For want of a better word, "need" refers here to deviance enacted in response to some kind of inner force, as expressed in assault (anger), hard drug use (addiction), and drug trafficking (need for money). All qualify as intolerable deviance. For reasons similar to those given for alcohol and marijuana use, the public is highly curious about these forms of deviance among high-profile athletes. Their interest is well served by a press equally eager to report instances of it. So, again, given that such coverage tends to suggest that use of drugs and alcohol is rampant among athletes, sociologists have been trying to determine if rates of such criminality in sport differ from rates of comparable age and sex categories in the general population.

Unfortunately, in this instance, systematic research is in extremely short supply, with nothing whatsoever available on drug trafficking among athletes. Crossett (1999) has taken up the issue of assault on women by male athletes, a hot media topic as anyone who followed, for instance, the Mike Tyson (boxing) and O.J. Simpson (football) stories can attest. Still, no one has conducted a study conclusively showing that athletes are more inclined than others of same sex and similar age to commit assaults, whether against men or women (Lapchick, 2000, p. 18). In face of this lack, the stereotype prevails that they are more inclined to do just that.

Crossett (1999, p. 254) views male athletes' assaults on women either as structurally encouraged or as situationally appropriate for constructing and maintaining one's place in the masculine hierarchy. Viewing athletes' violence against women this way directs attention to the social circumstances in which such crime is committed. He says some athletes may lack certain social constraints that other men feel. At the same time the former may be further encouraged to perpetrate violence against women by their power in the masculine hierarchy, the way their masculinity is constructed, and the extent of support given by other men. Additionally, some behaviours and conditions associated with athletics and masculinity (e.g., drinking, head injury) may have physiological consequences that further increase the likelihood an athlete will treat women violently.

Lapchick (2000) says that media stories about drug use among high-profile athletes are and surely should be disturbing. But, he continues:

> *Those stories are rarely, if ever, put in the context of the 1.9 million Americans who use cocaine each month or the 2.1 million who use heroin throughout their lives. A total of 13 million people (for a staggering 6 percent of the American population) use some illicit drug each month! When you look at the 18–25 male age group in general, the percentage leaps to 17 percent. Twenty-two athletes [the number discussed in a preceding newspaper article] represent a small fraction of a single percent of the more than 400,000 who play college and professional sports in America.* (Lapchick, 2000, p. 17)

Data of this sort are even rarer in Canada. Box 5.1 examines a case of this kind of deviance in Europe.

DEVIANCE WITH SPORT

This section examines three of the many ways that people use sport to engage in their own peculiar forms of deviance. The first of these is excessive gambling. Hooliganism and ticket scalping are also covered.

BOX 5.1 RACING DEMONS

Use of performance-enhancing drugs may grab sporting headlines, but the real tragedy is what happens later

by Bruce Crumley, Paris

His career in cycling propelled him from the anonymity of local races to the glitter of European and World Championship events as a member of the French national team. The rider, who asks to be identified only as Michel, says his fondest memories are of the "incomparable euphoria of strength and power I'd get finding myself at the head of a tired and flagging pack, knowing I was about to pull away and ride to victory." But like a growing number of athletes, Michel attained such elation the wrong way. He eventually realized that performance-enhancing substances had ensnared him in the trap of addiction to even worse drugs. Last year Michel, who is 25, underwent several weeks of specialized detoxification treatment for cocaine and heroin addiction developed during his racing career. "I didn't realize just how big it had become," he says, "until a doctor warned me if I didn't get help soon, I'd be dead within months."

Once the worst-kept secret in sport, doping has become so common that many fans now see it as inevitable. But behind the casual use of drugs designed to improve athletic performance is a tragedy carefully hidden from view: the transformation of many athletes into drug addicts. Nobody knows how many develop dependencies that continue after their careers end. But the numbers at risk are probably larger than fans or even athletes realize.

In France, studies have indicated the scale of the problem. A 1999 report by experts at Paris's Monte Cristo drug treatment center found 18% of the 5000 high-level athletes surveyed reporting drug dependency—most consequent to sports doping. That inquiry was launched after the discovery that 20% of the clinic's patients seeking methadone treatment for heroin addiction had backgrounds in elite sports. Generally, French sports medicine experts believe around 10% of the nation's 13 million registered athletes have used performance-enhancing substances—a practice that will ultimately lead to addiction in 300 000–350 000 athletes, according to some estimates. And that's just in France. Says Charles Mercier-Guyon, one of a handful of French doctors authorized to conduct drug tests at sports events: "No country or sport has a monopoly on doping, and all will be affected by the problem of addict-athletes as doping spreads."

Although full-blown addiction among active athletes remains rare, experts say use of drugs for improving performance vastly increases the threat of substance abuse and dependency when a doping athlete is sidelined by injury or forced to retire from sports. "Doping requires athletes to defy social aversions for using drugs and syringes for nonmedical purposes," notes Patrick Magaloff, director of the French Olympic Committee's anti-doping mission. "Because that taboo has been broken during their careers, athletes who have doped are often less inhibited about using drugs in normal life than clean athletes or nonathletes." That risk is confirmed by officials at the Monte Cristo Clinic, where 20% of patients seeking methadone treatment for heroin addiction report a background in high-level sports.

Even when clean, many athletes suffer a heavy psychological blow when forced to leave the athletic elite. "When you remove an athlete from that obsessive, glorified lifestyle and place him in the larger, more diffuse 'real world,' he's going to feel lost, anonymous and often severely depressed," says Gérard Cagni, director of the sedap drug clinic—one of two in France with in-patient programs tailored for athletes. When such a competitor also has a history of doping and drug use, the risk of addiction—and an unwillingness to recognize it as a severe problem—can complicate matters. "The continued use of drugs can, in the athlete's mind, constitute a link to the sporting past," says Cagni, himself a former French track champion. "Even after abuse is recognized as destructive, the psychological associations remain very hard to break down."

Also difficult to undermine is the fan-assisted denial that doping is somehow different from drug abuse; that it involves only euphoria-free, high-tech products like muscle-building steroids and blood oxidizing agents administered by attentive medical experts. "Sports fans protect the heroic image of athletes by using the term doping rather than taking drugs in sports," Michel points out. In reality, the drugs of choice for athletes today are amphetamines, cocaine, heroin and huge doses of caffeine-substances experts say often escape detection through a combination of masking agents, passage of time and connivance by officials. A popular injectable cocktail of those substances—known as a *pot belge*—contains drugs that are purer and far more addictive than those sold on the streets.

"Only the very top athletes are supplied and administered by doping experts," says Pierre Dolivet, director of the Chalet du Thianty, France's other in-patient drug center catering to athletes. "The non-stars usually improvise with drugs and doses—often even sharing syringes, despite the AIDS threat. When you see what these people are doing to themselves you understand the darker meaning of winning at any cost."

Because the biggest stars-turned-addicts can afford the luxury and privacy of exclusive detox clinics in Switzerland, the public rarely learns the risk of dependency posed by doping. Dolivet's Thianty clinic costs $130 a day for its five- to seven-month courses. It receives some outside funding to help less well-off athletes, but dozens of others cannot afford the treatment. Sports clubs and federations could help but don't. "They don't want to be associated with the problem," Dolivet laments. "If you admit your athletes have become addicts from doping, you admit doping is a real problem. No one will do that."

Given the refusal of sports authorities to effectively tackle drug use—and consequent addiction—there's little hope the tide will turn any time soon. Indeed, health-care professionals helping pick up the pieces of lives shattered by doping dependency say the only real hope is that fans stage a revolt—not out of love for the game or the players, but from fear that their children, intent on attaining sporting glory, may wind up with the booby prize of addiction.

TIME Europe (2001). 12 March (Vol. 157 No.10).

Deviant Gambling

The deviant aspects of gambling, since they are considered elsewhere (Stebbins, 1996, pp. 9–10), will not be treated again here. Of interest in this chapter is gambling that occurs on the outcomes of games and competitions in a wide range of sports. Chief among these in Canada are football, hockey, soccer, and baseball as well as basketball, horse racing, and auto racing. With off-track betting being illegal in Canada (and most American states), bettors are limited to parimutuel systems, wherein players wager against each other rather than against a bookmaker. Roughly 80 to 90% of the betting pool, to which the gamblers contribute directly, is returned to them. Horse racing is by far the most popular form of parimutuel gambling in North America (Stebbins, 1996, p. 151). In addition, Canadians bet illegally with bookies on horse races and games in team sport, primarily in football, hockey, basketball, and baseball, an "extremely popular" form of leisure, according to Gomme (1998, p. 392).

Sports events offer an interesting and socially acceptable way to enjoy free time by wagering, as long as wagers are, according to local standards, moderate and infrequent. But people push the moral limit when they gamble regularly with large sums two to three times a week, thereby turning acceptable behaviour into a form of tolerable deviance (Dickerson, 1984, p. 38; Joyce, 1979, p. 155). The public attitude at this point is that the money lost could be better spent on family needs. This, in Walker's (1992, p. 153) view, constitutes "heavy gambling"; it is deviant though not substantially problematic. Accompanying the relative tolerance of heavy gambling is a lingering allegiance to the Protestant work ethic and the principle that people should earn their livelihood through conventional means. Gambling as tolerable deviance, whatever its legal status, becomes intolerable deviance to the extent that it is either compulsive, or pathological, or shows close connections with the criminal underworld.

The Internet has greatly expanded opportunities for and ease of sport gambling. Nonetheless, the odds and point spreads are established here, as in the media, by bookies, whose first interest is to ensure that they profit sufficiently from particular games and matches. Still, since ease of access to gaming has always helped explain its elevated rates in society, it is likely that sports gambling of all kinds will increase in Canada, where online participation is still a "relatively new recreation" (*Journal of Addiction and Mental Health*, 1999, p. 5).

Hooliganism

Because hooligans and hooliganism are covered in the next chapter, all that need be said in the present one relates to its fit in the tolerable deviance framework. To the extent that hooliganism is about violence, it can be classified as intolerable, criminal activity. But it is not wholly that, even if inter-fan fighting, which is part of it, is what the press and the general public seize on. Rather, as Richard Guilianotti (1999, p. 49) observes: "Football hooliganism in its contemporary sense refers not to 'traditional' outbreaks of disorder, but instead to the social genesis of distinctive fan sub-cultures and their engagement in regular and collective violence, primarily with rival peers [who support the other team]."

Moreover, hooliganism is intolerably deviant leisure. Guilianotti (1999, pp. 52–53) points out that participants get an "emotional buzz" when fighting with opponents. The hooligan's goal is to enter and leave the fray with body and mind intact, a sign of skill and competence in such circumstances that gains high respect with peers. Says Guilianotti, hooliganism holds for the hooligan the same appeal as "high-risk" sport holds for its enthusiasts. Both types are voluntarily experienced.

Ticket Scalping

Atkinson (2000) studied ticket scalping leading to entry to professional sports matches in an Ontario city. In Ontario "ticket speculation" (ticket scalping) occurs when someone sells or attempts to sell a ticket to someone else for more than its face value. If convicted, the speculator could be fined as much as $5000. Atkinson learned that this work-based form of criminal tolerable deviance, unlike ordinary ticket sales, is a "negotiated economic exchange." Scalpers, who possess tickets that, to make a living, they must nevertheless sell in a limited time frame, meet customers who, though they want those tickets, also know that they can bargain for a favourable price. Negotiation on both sides proceeds by typifications of the other as, for example, easy marks, hard bargainers, and scalpers desperate to make sales.

CONCLUSIONS

Will we eventually be able to rid sport of the kinds of deviance considered here? Not likely. As noted in Stebbins (1996, pp. 1–2) deviance from or nonconformity with the norms of the group that bear on morality is one of human kind's oldest concerns. Collective life is possible only when certain crucial rules of behaviour are observed by all or a large majority of members of the community. These rules are an important part of the complicated, standardized solutions that evolve in response to the problems people encounter while living in proximity to one another. They are nothing less than strategies for personal and social survival (Martindale, 1962, p. 39). Such solutions take years to develop and crystallize. They are seen by most community members, especially those having greatest power and interest in preserving the status quo, as indispensable to the quality of community life.

Standardized solutions to similar problems eventually coalesce into social institutions that, in turn, become the backbone of all societies and their constituent communities. Some problems solved in this fashion are basic to social and physical life; they deal with how to secure food and shelter, how to transform biological individuals into social persons, how to ensure that members of the community conform to the rules considered necessary to its welfare. These are the institutions of economy, polity, family, and education. Other problems and their solutions, though perhaps not quite so basic to human survival, are nevertheless very seriously regarded in many societies. They include the problems and solutions associated with engaging in sex, using power, dealing with the supernatural, exposing the human body, owning property, dealing with other people, using mind- and mood-altering substances, and pursuing leisure (when it is proper not to work, and what is done at this time). Here we find the aforementioned institutions, as well as those of religion, work, leisure, and culture (e.g., art, science, popular culture). Sport is a notable part of the last three of these.

At bottom, many of these solutions are arbitrary. Objectively speaking, other strategies are possible. That different solutions to the same problems are often found in different societies, and occasionally in different communities within the same society, substantiates this observation. The possibility of adopting a different solution to a given problem is soon recognized by those in the community least committed to the prevailing solution. The next logical step for them, using surplus energy left over from meeting life's obligations (Rojek, 2000, pp. 158–161), is to seize the initiative to explore an option more compatible with their interests. Thus, there is always a sociological side to morality: exploration, or straying from accepted ways of meeting a major institutional problem, is "deviance" or "wrong," while abiding by those ways is "conformity" or "right." Sport-related deviance can be understood in this light.

Critical Thinking Questions

1. Should athletes be permitted to take performance-enhancing drugs?
2. Is it right for athletes to use alcohol or marijuana for pleasure when at their leisure (not participating in their sport or working at a job)?
3. Should athletes caught engaging in deviance for fun be given exceptional press coverage, as seems to be the practice nowadays?
4. Should Canada legalize betting on sport, such as by allowing betting shops or legal bookmakers?
5. Should Canada try harder to eliminate violence in hockey, including even the borderline variety?

Suggested Readings

Eitzen, D.S. (2000). Social control and sport. In J. Coakley and E. Dunning (Eds.), *Handbook of sports studies* (pp. 370–381). London: Sage.

Fraleigh, W. (1982). Why the good foul is not good. *Journal of Physical Education, Recreation, and Dance,* 52(January), 41–42.

Hughes, R., and Coakley, J. (1991). Positive deviance among athletes: The implications of overconformity to the Sport Ethic. *Sociology of Sport Journal*, 8, 307–325.

Lüschen, G. (2000). Doping in sport as deviant behavior and its social control. In J. Coakley and E. Dunning (Eds.), *Handbook of sports studies* (pp. 461–476). London: Sage.

Stuck, M.F. (1988). Beliefs and behaviors—Sport and clean living. *Arena Review*, 12(1 May), 13–24.

Web Links

The Anorexia On-line Support Group Network
http://www.angelfire.com/amiga/anorexiasupport/egroup.html
A large collection of personal testimonials about being anorexic and dealing with this disorder.

Australian Sports Drug Agency
http://www.asda.org.au
Supplies information on drug testing, anti-doping policy, various drugs used in sport, and related issues.

The Sports Ethics Institute
http://www.sportsethicsinstitute.org
Addresses the ethical issues flowing from answering the question "What standards of conduct should govern in the complex world of sports?"

About Steroids.com (StoneCo)
http://www.aboutsteroids.com
A frank discussion about the use, effect, history, and long-term consequences of regular steroid consumption.

6

Violence and Aggression in Sport

Kevin B. Wamsley

Violence, for some, is part of the game.

The game is so fast, so exciting, so much fun to watch, why do we have to turn the ice red so often?

Wayne Gretzky, quoted in Fischler, 1991

> *They forced the Canadiens to relinquish their beachhead, and fighting commenced in earnest as it spilled back onto the ice... Moe decked Durnan with a roundhouse right. Laycoe and Lamoureux slugged toe-to-toe until arm weariness forced them to quit. Meanwhile, Richard had slammed Juzda so hard over the head that his stick snapped, but 'the Beast,' as the Ranger defenseman was known, rose like a stegosaurus from some primeval ooze and slammed Richard to the ice. Bouchard succeeded in wrenching Hextall's stick from him and then floored him with one punch. Moe came to the rescue and broke a stick on Bouchard's skull. Butch acted as if nothing had happened. Another Ranger defenseman, Joe Cooper, ducked a dangerous Murph Chamberlain haymaker and countered with a stiff right hand that deposited the Montrealer in a side promenade seat. Juzda left Richard, picked up a loose stick, and broke Buddy O'Connor's cheekbone. (Stan Fischler [1991], popular hockey writer, describes what he calls "Hockey's Single Greatest Fight," between the New York Rangers and Montreal Canadiens, March 16, 1947)*

Some people might be repulsed by the above description of a hockey fight while others may find it interesting or even stimulating, and hockey fans may agree or disagree with superstar Wayne Gretzky's sentiments about the state of the game. Indeed, there are divergent popular opinions about the place of rough play, violence, and aggression in sport. This chapter focuses specifically on these issues, offering descriptions and discussion of some of the theories that have been posited to explain why sport has been or can be so violent both on and off the field. It raises questions about the scholarly focus on exclusively structural or functional explanations about violent play and about violent crowd behaviour, while considering the approach of other academics who have taken aspects of specific subcultures or other social variables into account in their studies.

In July 2001, when Thomas Junta, a hockey parent, beat coach Michael Costin to death in a rink in Massachusetts, people took notice; in January 2002 he was sentenced to a prison term to extend from six to ten years. Once again, the issue of violence in sport was inscribed across the news and sports pages in North America. For more than one hundred years, a period coined the "modern age" of sport (Guttman, 1978), participants, coaches, and spectators have been killed, maimed, and injured in rings, arenas, fields, and bleachers. In most instances of significant harm, whether one player sustains a catastrophic injury or several hundred fans are crushed or engaged in a brawl, journalists, academics, judicial critics, and average citizens ask the question: Why did this happen, or perhaps implicitly, why is there violence in sport? Then, it seems, the question is muted until the next incident. Further, the average sports fan is likely to defend fighting in hockey, the crunching tackle in football, or the sport of boxing itself. For the entire 20th century, now into the 21st century, we have always accepted that in sports where space is contested, where bodies are used as weapons (Messner, 1990) to gain ground or maintain control of a ball or puck, athletes can be hurt or injured (Young, White, & McTeer, 1994) and that such physical confrontations are a necessary and exciting feature of sports. Athletes enjoy the physical contact, the violent hits and tackles; spectators seem to enjoy the body checks and fights; and television networks sometimes focus in on the best hits of the week, regardless of, or even particular to, the physical harm experienced by the player.

With this and the historical tradition of rough sport in mind, the legitimizing functions of legal procedure, generally, and the intellectual analysis of human behaviour in sport have dichotomized such actions as violent or aggressive, unacceptable or acceptable, part of the game or not part of the game, and consensual or not consensual. As such there are different accepted norms for different sports, degrees of harm and assertiveness, a blurring of the distinction between a measure of physical intimidation and an act of violence. Through sport, violence has been contextualized. How can we explain why violence and aggression are considered important parts of sport, often celebrated, often respected?

DEFINING TERMS

Aggression

The popular use of "aggression" in sport suggests that it is a positive channelling of emotional and physical energy or intensity toward a legitimate goal. However, Smith (1983) and Coakley (2001) use the term "aggression" in reference to behaviour designed to cause physical or psychological harm.

Violence

Smith (1983) and Coakley (2001) categorize violence as all types of physical aggression, intended to harm or injure others. It follows, then, that all violence is aggressive but some forms of aggression are used to intimidate opponents and not to cause harm.

THEORIES OF AGGRESSION

Instinct

A popular view, held by athletes and spectators alike, is that violence can be attributed strictly to human biology or instinct. It is argued that humans respond violently when they are confronted by particular situations, and that this type of response is programmed by evolution and the need to survive as a species. Often such a response can be labelled the "fight or flight" reaction to confrontation. Ethologists or scientists who justify human behaviour using purely biological explanations have forwarded these hypotheses, used to explain why people behave violently on or off the field. It is instinctual, they argue, for people to react violently during confrontations, such as those created through sport between opponents or between fans in the stadium and arena. Supposedly, sport provides an outlet or release for these natural tendencies toward aggression, a *catharsis* effect. In support of this theory, one would argue that tensions naturally build between two hockey players or two fans that confront one another during a game. Finally, tensions run so high that the two players or spectators decide to fight, thereby releasing these energies "safely" (Lorenz, 1966). These models purport, then, that sport becomes a *safety valve* for unhealthy aggression (Pearton, 1986). It is easy for individuals with an interest in sustaining levels of violence in sport to ensure popularity and profit, for example, to justify fighting and rough play by calling it a basic human instinct. However, there is no evidence to support this theory of aggression in human beings. Indeed, and as Dunning (1999) has argued, sport provides the conditions for such outbursts, and, further, sports create tensions.

Frustration

A second theory often employed to explain violent confrontations in sport or even to provide solutions to broader social problems is the frustration–aggression hypothesis. It is argued that frustration in particular circumstances causes aggression. Once again, according to this model, players or fans supposedly release pent-up frustration through participation in sport or through vicarious consumption from the bleachers. Sport, this theory suggests, is *cathartic* for spectators, channelling frustrations from their daily lives into harmless aggression toward opposing teams or other spectators (Dollard et al., 1939). Pearton (1986) argues that the frustration–aggression hypothesis loses much of its explanatory power because frustration is but one of a long list of factors that can lead to aggression. Sometimes aggression occurs without frustration, and sport can cause frustration for participants, particularly if winning is equated to self-esteem or proving oneself (Coakley, 2001). Consequently, sport is not necessarily or simply an appropriate tool of emotional control, particularly when some groups and individuals find it fun and exciting (Dunning, 1999).

SOCIAL LEARNING

Advocates of the social learning theory (Bandura & Walters, 1963) argue that violence and aggression are behaviours that people have come to understand through social relationships with others, by imitation, or are learned from cultural exemplars, sport heroes for example, or significant others. It follows, then, according to this model, that violence has a cultural history, that certain values are passed down through generations, and that various institutions, symbols, and structures of meaning reproduce or endorse aggression or aggressive tactics to achieve goals. Violence and aggression become means to attain certain ends. In some sports, according to this theory, rule-bound aggression is built in to the common cultural understandings of how they should be played and, historically, these sports leagues have been able to operate outside of the law, to police themselves (Young & Wamsley, 1996). Frustration over the outcomes of games, the calls of officials, or the tactics of opposing players may lead to forms of aggression, some of which have been normalized as reasonable if not desirable behaviours—in other words, the actions of passionate athletes who care intensely about sport, the outcome of a significant championship, or standing up for a teammate. As such, the channelling of anger into ritualized confrontations, such as berating an official, has come to be naturalized within a sporting context, whereas this behaviour might not be tolerated outside of the sporting context. It is commonly asserted that certain forms of aggression on the playing field would bring criminal charges on the street.

SPORTING CULTURE

From the earliest eras of Aboriginal games, to the colonial period in North America, to the emerging sports of the period of the Industrial Revolution in the 19th century, violence and aggressive behaviours have always been present in various cultural forms. Physical capacity and competition were fundamental aspects of the fur trade and early agrarian economies, when men routinely tested one another for fun but more seriously while competing for labour opportunities (Wamsley, 1999). Prior to the 1840s, in Canada, a violent code of honour was meted out in the relationships between the self-fashioned male gentry (Morgan, 1995), and men of all classes routinely fought in the rural and urban taverns and public stockades, and whipping posts was reshaped in pre-Confederation Canada into institutional houses (Wamsley & Kossuth, 2001). The violence of the duel and of the public hangings,

BOX 6.1 VIOLENCE IN SPORT OR VIOLENCE AS SPORT?

An alternative approach or quite different point of departure with respect to the issue of violence, distinguishing between the instrumental or goal-oriented violence commonly associated with the middle classes and their rationalized sports of the mid-19th century and expressive violence or violence for pleasure, is discussed by Elias and Dunning (1986) among others (Dunning, 1999). Conley's (1999) research on fighting in 19th-century Ireland supports such a distinction, as does recent work on tavern culture in 19th-century Canada (Wamsley & Kossuth, 2001). The historical evidence in these studies suggests that understanding *violence as sport* is as important as the more frequently employed paradigm of *violence in sport*. Indeed, Conley's (1999, p. 57) citation of 19th-century author William Carleton (1867) is quite similar to the context invoked in the citation of 20th-century hockey writer Stan Fischler (1991) above:

> *I know not however whether it was fair to expect them to give up at once the agreeable recreation of fighting. It's not easy to abolish old customs, particularly diversions; and everyone knows that this is the national amusement of the finest peasantry on the face of the earth. To be sure skulls and bones are broken, and lives lost; but they are lost in pleasant fighting–they are the consequences of the sport, the beauty of which consists in breaking as many heads and necks as you can.*

punishments and fines, and controlled, ritualized aggression became ensconced in organized sports by moderate political reformers who saw themselves as more civilized and rational than their predecessors in government office. In this social environment, the boys of elites were taught to be the leaders of the empire through rites of passage that often entailed measures of hardship, endurance, and violent contests (Brown, 1986). Middle-class men celebrated a public profile of physical empowerment through club sports such as lacrosse and snowshoeing, and later hockey and other sports. Through sport, masculinity was tested through an on-field, rule-bound aggression where participants and spectators came to associate the male body with power and authority, tempered by the values of Christianity and a code of fair play. Sports were viewed as rough and vigorous, a place for men.

Spectator interest in baseball and hockey piqued the interest of commercial entrepreneurs who sought gate receipts and captivating local interest in sport for profit. Moral entrepreneurs, including instructors at YMCAs, were interested in using sport to shape the character of young Christian men; the sports promoter looked for ways to bring "respectable" citizens out to watch what were formally considered to be "rough" sports. Promoters and participants tended to create narratives about the modern, scientific, and highly technical aspects of their sports, boxing in particular, to attract a broader base of spectatorship (Wamsley & Whitson, 1998). By the turn of the century, organized sports such as hockey had been imbued with unique social trajectories, creating a self-contained sport subculture with norms, values, and rules that became relatively insular from legal and moral challenges registered from the "outside." Aggression and violence were accepted as being an important part of manly sports. Commenting on the issue of violence in boxing, and sport more broadly, Judge Snider in 1911 argued:

> *It will be a long time before Parliament will think it wise to so hedge in young men and boys by legislation that all sports that are rough and strenuous or even dangerous must be given up. Virility in young men would soon be lessened and self-reliant manliness a thing of the past.* (Wamsley & Whitson, 1998, p. 426)

Communities supported town teams and the character and tactics employed to gain victory; in order to compete with other towns, team owners and town boosters attempted to build local support by hiring the best players available from outside of the community. The enthusiasm and rivalries promoted through hockey and other sports sometimes led to fan aggression and incidents of violence during the early 20th century (Gruneau & Whitson, 1993; Young & Wamsley, 1996).

Following both World Wars I and II, thousands of men returned home after witnessing and surviving the horrors of war violence, killing other human beings, and trying to rationalize why people were dying painful deaths around them; it was no coincidence that the sports of boxing and wrestling were very popular in these eras, and that rough versions of masculinity were celebrated through rugby football and ice hockey.

During the 1930s, 1940s, and 1950s, radio broadcasts brought sanitized but exciting commentaries to living rooms. However, the popularization of television in the 1960s brought clear visions of aggressive and exciting play to most households in Canada. And town boosterism, capitalizing on performance and local spirit with respect to all levels of sport, was well entrenched. On the margins of amateur and professional sports, professional wrestling and roller derby, theatres of violence and hyper-masculinity, complete with villains and heroes, began to grow in popularity as well. After *Hockey Night in Canada* on Saturday nights, parents and children could tune in to *All Star Wrestling* to watch former Canadian Football League player and self-professed "Canada's Greatest Athlete" Gene Kiniski as he battled make-believe villains such as "The Sheik" or "Abdullah the Butcher" supposedly from the Middle East or "Sigfried Schteinky" who sported German officer's boots and a Nazi flag. On Saturday afternoons, children could watch Paul "The Bear" Rupert and "Skinny Minny" Miller deliver punches and elbows and mock violence on the roller rink.

When second-wave feminism had made some social and political gains by the early 1970s, argues Nelson (1994), men sought solidarity and assurance through watching and admiring violent sports. Leagues such as the National Football League (NFL) and National Hockey League (NHL) did little to curtail aggression and violence. Indeed, the expansion hockey teams of the late 1960s and early 1970s used physical intimidation and violent tactics to offset the skill imbalance created among NHL teams as a result of league expansion. Further, this type of intimidation and frequent fisticuffs during games marked an era in professional hockey during which certain teams, such as the Philadelphia Flyers or "Broad Street Bullies" and "Big Bad Bruins" capitalized on the media reputations created by them, for them, to gain respect on the ice. Specialized sport television, such as the American Broadcasting Corporation's *Wide World of Sports*, capitalized on exciting highlight packages, violent tackles, body checks, dramatizing rough play and reinforcing the dangers and excitement of sports for men. Historical traditions, tactics, techniques, and long-accepted codes of physical manhood were punctuated in elaborate and systematic fashion by sport television. Such media representations of violent but revered masculinities were powerful endorsements of appropriate manhood. And owners, league administrators, coaches, and players were all too willing to capitalize on the popularity of aggressive sports, in spite of any risks of injury, pain, or physical and psychological impairment of the athletes involved. The athletes had to embrace these values wholeheartedly, lest they be left in the minor leagues or forced into another line of work.

The celebration of violence and intimidation in sport, endorsed through media representations and league administration, had deep ramifications for all levels of sport, from early children's participation through the junior ranks. Codes of conduct for all participants were well understood, from the "good" penalty to the "necessary" fight to stand up for a teammate or just to inspire play to gain team momentum. However, a fundamental corollary to these extensive and rather complex codes of masculine conduct has been the tendency to endure and even celebrate pain and injury as a rite of passage and part of being a man in a men's sport. Men who have grown up playing sport in the 1970s and 1980s have been told to "suck it up," to "be a man," or have been accused of playing like girls or old women. The bipolar association of male weakness or frailty with femininity has been a feature of organized sport for more than a century. As a consequence, participants in sport have tended toward positioning bodily injuries as badges of male courage at all levels. Being tough and being tolerant or resistant to pain have been normalized in most sports. However, research suggests that female athletes view the pain and sport injury nexus in a similar light. Young & White (1995) found similarities in the attitudes of male and female athletes with respect to physical danger, aggression, and injury.

At the elite levels, Young (1993, p. 390) argues that sports have become hazardous workplaces, where profit, socially recognized and celebrated, comes at significant cost, "in the form of compromised health and safety standards, or, in other words, injury, disablement, and human loss." Day-to-day pain and injury, disabled lists, injury-reserve lists, team doctors and physiotherapists, drugs, therapeutic medicines and techniques, massage tables, hot tubs, and ice packs are all part of the emotional or technical inventories of most sport teams. More broadly, falls, hits, and catastrophic injuries are the mainstays of highlight packages for specialized sport channels and even "news" stories on network television. Scenes of broken legs in football, such as Joe Theismann's; knockout punches at the hands of Mike Tyson or even ring deaths in boxing; hard slides and bean balls in baseball; blood-letting, lost teeth, broken bones, and concussion-causing body checks, such as those on Eric Lindros in hockey; cart-wheeling, rag-doll spills in alpine skiing, such as Todd Brooker's end-over-end; wall-smashing car crashes and deaths, such as Dale Earnhardt's in auto-racing; jockey and horse spills in horse racing; stomping and raking in rugby; torn muscles in sprinting and weightlifting; severe crashes in cycling; or mishaps such as heads hitting diving boards, as did Greg Louganis in diving, all are replayed over and over again for popular consumption. Often the catastrophic damage done to human bodies is presented as news; recently, however, a market has developed for the sports "blooper," where suffering is often invoked as having comedic value, or entire videotaped volumes are dedicated to violent highlights in the context of a comedy of physical wonders, such as Don Cherry's *Rock 'Em Sock 'Em Hockey*, now beyond ten editions.

In this era of widespread, edited, graphically represented violence, professional wrestling and other forms of sport entertainment, such as ultimate fighting, have captured significant market followings. Sports entertainment entrepreneur Vince McMahon has parlayed his father's business into the multimillion-dollar World Wrestling Entertainment extravaganza, which reaches from weekly television, to pay-per-view events, to music recordings, wrestler fashions, movie character spin-offs, magazines, product lines, video games, and children's clubs and cartoons. Professional wrestling sells violent sport theatre to millions of viewers.

Older gimmicks of staged, severe facial bleeding, chair throwing, and "foreign object" wielding have given way to more complex plot lines, steroid-induced hyper-muscular figures, "giants" and "little people," and elaborate technical displays of lighting and fireworks in staged matches—often with real consequences, as seen recently in the death of Calgary wrestler Owen Hart, who fell 50 feet before a match when a poorly choreographed stunt went sour.

Professional wrestling remains an extant caricature of many of the worst qualities of sport, bodybuilding, Hollywood acting, and beauty pageantry. Yet such caricatures are a chilling reminder of some of the common features of modern sport: violent plot lines, overtraining and hyper-muscularity, anger and suffering, drug taking, and the reproduction of gender stereotypes (Atkinson, 2002). It could be easily dismissed as pure entertainment, if not for its significant place in popular culture as part of a much broader constellation of actively created social meanings about human bodies that are reproduced day to day for both spectators and participants through sport and sport theatre.

YOUTH SPORT

Violent and aggressive altercations at children's sporting events are all too common. While coaching education programs deal explicitly with the issue of winning and the use of aggressive play and tactics of intimidation, there are few programs that deal with issues of parent aggression against officials and against one another. This ranges from berating a referee for a particular call to committing violent acts over game outcomes. The incidents of assault on referees have become so common that the National Association of Sports Officials now provides "assault insurance" for officials (Albom, 2000). On the heels of the Junta–Costin incident, numerous examples have been recounted of violence and aggressive acts by parents and coaches in North America. Fathers have struck other fathers during baseball games; full-scale brawls involving both players and parents have ensued during youth football games; Little League managers have been beaten up by irate parents; young players and young referees have been assaulted during and after baseball, hockey, football, and soccer games. The consequences of such assaults have ranged from punch abrasions to facial lacerations to broken jaws.

SPECTATOR VIOLENCE AND AGGRESSION

Canadians are familiar with the famous Rocket Richard riots of 1955 during which significant property was destroyed, looting occurred, and many were arrested in the streets of Montreal. Rioting and property destruction were similar in 1994 in Vancouver after the Stanley Cup playoffs. Although these and most of the above examples are particular to the United States and Canada, sports fan violence is considered to be an international phenomenon. Young (1991) has analyzed several explanations for collective violence, including British soccer hooliganism. He offers examples (p. 540) of crowd violence, including

- a soccer riot in Peru, where 300 died and 500 were injured following a disallowed goal;
- "Nickle Beer Night" in Cleveland, Ohio, when fans fired objects at players and umpires;
- a World Cup cricket match in Sydney, Australia, when 80 fans were arrested and jailed;

- fans from Liverpool, England, charged the seating area of Juventus, Italy, crushing 39 soccer fans to death; and
- significant property destruction in Hamilton, Ontario, after a Grey Cup victory when 3000 fans celebrated riotously.

Several theoretical explanations have been posited to determine why crowd violence occurs. Contagion, Convergence, Crowd Decision, Emergent Norm, Value-Added, and Catharsis theories (Young, 1991) are often used to explain collective behaviour or crowd aggression. Contagion theory suggests that a crowd mentality exists, one that is influenced by a few leaders, with the consequence of the crowd acting in concert as one unit. Young (1991) argues that this fails to explain why some crowds are passive or why some crowd behaviours are rational and systematic. Convergence theory proposes that individuals with common interests or goals come together as a crowd and use the formation for protection to engage in aggressive behaviours. This fails to explain, Young (1991) argues, why like-minded individuals behave differently in crowd situations. The Crowd Decision model suggests that there is a rational decision-making process by which members of the crowd weigh the rewards of aggressive action versus the costs and conclude that there is more safety in numbers. This, Young (1991) says, assumes that all crowd behaviour is rational and negates the possibility that crowd actions may be spontaneous or reactive. Conversely, Emergent Norm theory suggests that crowd uniformity is just an illusion, that behaviour results from a series of messages or cues that individuals receive from one another in particular situations. A weakness of this theory, then, is that it does not explain crowd behaviour that is systematic or ordered (Young, 1991). The Value-Added theory points to many factors that may lead incrementally to collective aggression, including ethnic, religious, or regional differences between fans, structural strains, dissonance between outcome and expected outcomes, media-induced hostilities, referees' decisions, violence by players, and opportunities for fan violence. In this model, it is difficult to discern what determinants are necessary to precipitate crowd action (Young, 1991). Finally, Catharsis theory, discussed above, suggests that sporting events serve as a "safety valve" for fans to vent their daily frustrations vicariously, through the action on the field, or by behaving aggressively in the stands. But, as both Young (1991) and Dunning (1999) argue, sport can create frustration and participating in violence can be pleasurable for some people. These theories do not adequately explain crowd violence, as Young (1991, p. 542) suggests:

> *Collective crowd disorders at sports events are extremely complex, varied, and often highly organized rather than spontaneous phenomena, and attempts to explain their occurrence must be based on historically-grounded interpretations of, among other factors, social structure, class, politics, and gender.*

Both Young (1991) and Dunning (1999) point to unique historical circumstances and political contexts and explicit political reactions to hooliganism and crowd violence, whether in Europe or North America, as being vital considerations to any understanding of collective behaviour, or fan aggression more specifically. The social origins of spectator violence, Dunning (1999, p. 158) argues, are to be found in what he refers to as the social, political, and economic "fault-lines" of each country, be they religious, ethnic, or related to social class or language. Young's call for historically grounded interpretations is particularly important. The Richard riots, for example, cannot be explained merely in relation to specific crowd behaviour. They were deeply rooted in extant historical tensions between French and English communities, manifested through political, economic, and religious relations between diverse populations. Some determinants such as long-standing political policies of assimilation were clearly evident, while the response of individuals during the riots was significantly different.

As Murphy et al. (1990) have suggested, many factors may come to bear on spectator behaviour during sporting events, including alcohol consumption, the social significance of the event, the historical importance of rivalry between teams or towns, the type of crowd management techniques and infrastructure employed by stadium organizers, and the type of sport being played. As Coakley (2001) has argued, crowd behaviour tends to be sport specific with respect to disruptions and emotional eruption, but watching contact sports does not necessarily lead to violent actions by spectators. North American hockey is far more violent than soccer in Europe, but this is not a good indicator of the potential for crowd violence. Indeed, the subcultural organization of soccer fans is significantly different than for hockey or American football. The outcome of important games or championships is also not a good indicator or predicting factor. Rioting or crowd violence may occur during the celebration of victory, during losses, or without respect to outcome. In this sense, sport managers and promoters must be aware of the historical and social specificity of each event, the meanings attached to the sport itself, the extant rivalries between teams, and the potential for violence when emotionally charged spectators congregate in significant numbers.

CONCLUSIONS

It is evident that biologically based theories do not adequately explain the problem of violence in modern sport. To suggest that human instinct is the primary factor in determining behavioural outcomes in volatile social situations is to ignore the historical context of aggression and the culturally approved and endorsed methods of dealing with confrontation both on and off the field. Research suggests that complex social and historical factors intertwine to produce a sporting culture through which ritualized aggression is normalized and psychological and physical intimidation is wielded as a strategy to achieve desired goals in sport, sometimes with violent outcomes. As a result, during the 20th century, some professional sports arenas have become dangerous workplaces where pain, chronic and catastrophic injuries, and unhealthy training patterns are not only commonplace but also routinely celebrated as being appropriately masculine and team-oriented environments. A significant and disturbing corollary to the widespread spectatorship and conspicuous consumption of violence-oriented sports and sport spectacle entertainment is the prevalence of violent incidents involving youth sport in North America.

Research that explores collective violence suggests that most current theories about crowd behaviour do not adequately address the nuances of the specific events in question. Specific historic, political, and cultural circumstances must be considered in each case to explain the phenomenon of spectator violence.

Critical Thinking Questions

1. If violence is fun for some people, what ramification does that have for the organization or understanding of sport?
2. When should violence in sport be a concern?
3. Is there such a thing as *positive aggression?*
4. How does aggression in player or fan behaviour affect life outside of sport?
5. If two people consent to participate in a sport where one or both of them could become seriously injured or killed, are we obligated to provide a ring for this sport or to prevent it?

Suggested Readings

Coakley, J. (2001). *Sport in society: Issues and controversies* (7th Ed.). St. Louis, Mo.: Mosby.

Dunning, E., & Sheard, K. (1979). *Barbarians, gentlemen and players: A sociological study of the development of rugby football.* Oxford: Martin Robertson.

Dunning, E. (1999). *Sport matters: Sociological studies of sport, violence and civilization.* London: Routledge.

Gruneau, R., & Whitson, D. (1993). *Hockey Night in Canada: Sport, identities and cultural politics.* Toronto: Garamond Press.

Smith, M. (1983). *Violence and sport.* Toronto: Butterworth.

Young, K. (1991). Sport and collective violence. *Exercise and Sport Science Review,* 19, 539–87.

Young, K., White, P., &. McTeer, W. (1994). Body talk: Male athletes reflect on sport, injury, and pain. *Sociology of Sport Journal,* 11, 175–94.

Young, K. (2000). Sport and violence. In J. Coakley & E. Dunning (Eds.), *Handbook of sport studies* (pp. 382–409). London: Sage.

Web Links

BBC Sport Forum
http://news.bbc.co.uk/sport1/hi/sports_talk/forum/1495029.stm
Contains stories of football (soccer) violence and links to other sites.

Joseph Matteucci Foundation
http://www.jmf4peace.org
Provides school training programs to reduce youth violence.

Mentors in Violence Prevention program
http://www.sportinsociety.org/mvp.html
A gender violence prevention and education program based at Northeastern University's Center for the Study of Sport in Society.

Playlab, University of Connecticut
http://playlab.uconn.edu/frl.htm
Includes a lengthy list of references on violence and aggression in sport.

Scholarly Sport Sites, University of Calgary
http://www.ucalgary.ca/library/ssportsite/biblio.html
Contains a comprehensive listing of coaching-related articles.

Sport Safe—"Anti-Violence Policy for Recreation Facilities"
http://www.sport.gov.bc.ca/ssafe.htm
A downloadable document with extensive suggestions on how to keep recreation facilities violence free.

7

Gender Issues in Sport

Helen Jefferson Lenskyj

FRANK RAYMOND/COURTESY OF I.D.E.A.S. PHOTOGRAPHY

Stacey Mortimer, defence, senior AAA, OWHA

You can't be a female athlete without addressing questions of femininity, sexuality, fear, power, freedom, and just how good you are compared with men.

M.B. Nelson, *Are We Winning Yet? How Women Are Changing Sports and Sports Are Changing Women*

As we enter the 21st century, more Canadian girls and women than ever before are enjoying the benefits of sport and physical activity. At the same time, there remain significant barriers to full female participation. This chapter begins with an analysis of various theoretical and political approaches to understanding gender inequality in sport and physical activity, with an emphasis on the impact of harassment and violence on girls and women. Feminist and anti-racist initiatives that address inequalities based on gender, ethnicity, social class, sexuality, and ability are explored. Finally, recommendations based on human rights and health rationales are evaluated. (A discussion of the important ways in which boys and men are affected by gender ideologies and stereotypes of "masculinity" in Canadian sport is beyond the scope of this chapter; for an analysis of these issues, see, for example, White & Young, 1999.)

WAYS OF UNDERSTANDING WOMEN, SPORT, AND THE "ISMS"

A critical sociological approach to understanding women's issues in the context of Canadian sport and physical activity aims at identifying the ways in which sexism interacts with other *systemic* barriers, including racism, classism, heterosexism, motor elitism, and ableism, to prevent full female participation, and to perpetuate longstanding male-dominated sporting practices. A critical approach goes beyond simply describing current trends; it also seeks to *explain* why these conditions prevail, and to *interpret* the meanings behind the social relations of sport and physical activity (White & Young, 1999). Finally, this kind of research often includes recommendations for educational interventions and policy innovations, with the goal of addressing social injustice and promoting social change. In other words, critical sociological research has an overt political agenda and offers a serious challenge to the status quo.

Sexism refers to discrimination based on biological sex, that is, maleness or femaleness; racism is discrimination based on ethnic identity and/or skin colour; classism refers to discrimination against people of low socioeconomic status. Heterosexism is discrimination based on the presumption that heterosexuality is the only acceptable expression of sexuality; the irrational fear and hatred of lesbians, gay men, and other sexual minorities is termed homophobia. Motor elitism refers to the practice of privileging and rewarding those who are athletically gifted, to the detriment of children and adults whose body types, fitness levels, muscular strength, eye-hand coordination, and other physical traits prevent them from participating successfully in mainstream sport. People with physical or other disabilities are in this category, and the term "ableism" refers to exclusionary practices that fail to take disability into account, particularly the failure to make sport and recreation programs and facilities fully accessible. The targets of these various "isms" are girls and women; Black people, people of colour, and ethnic minorities; working-class and poor people; gays, lesbians, and other sexual minorities; and people with disabilities or limited physical capacities.

It is important to recognize that significant numbers of Canadian girls and women are doubly or triply disadvantaged; in addition to sexism, they experience discrimination as a result of their ethnic backgrounds, sexual identities, socioeconomic status, and/or disabilities. A recent study of Indo-Canadian females (Vertinsky, Batth, & Naidu, 1996) identified how sweeping generalizations and racist stereotyping of South Asian females as weak, passive, and uninterested in physical activity falsely implied that they were a homogeneous group and that they should adjust in order to fit into existing sport or educational systems. While recognizing that traditionally "feminine" physical activities were promoted over more demanding contact sports in some Indo-Canadian communities, the authors emphasized the need for systemic change, as well as for alternative, culturally appropriate programming strategies to enable young Indo-Canadian women to enjoy their physicality and participate in sporting activities of their choice.

Discrimination experienced by women and members of disadvantaged minority groups ranges from exclusion and marginalization, to verbal and physical harassment, and even to violence. Such discrimination can be challenged under Canadian law; for example, courts have established that it is the responsibility of the employer or the educational institution to ensure discrimination- and harassment-free conditions. Unfortunately, this does not mean that discrimination and harassment have been eliminated from Canadian sport and physical activity contexts. In many situations, the process is complaint-driven and therefore is reactive rather than proactive; the burden falls on those who experience the problem to lodge complaints or lawsuits, often a costly and time-consuming process. Moreover, from their already disadvantaged position, many women may correctly believe that it is futile to complain. In a recent example, women at an Ontario university were sexually harassed by professional football players who were using university facilities for training; the women were reluctant to pursue any formal complaint procedure for fear of reprisals from these men and from football fans on the campus.

LIMITATIONS OF LIBERAL APPROACHES

The more common liberal approaches, which rely on psychological rather than critical sociological theories, tend to conceptualize a universal or generic Canadian girl or woman who, according to this line of thinking, simply needs opportunity and encouragement in order to become physically active. This approach is in evidence whenever sport administrators ask, "What can we do to get more girls and women involved in sport?" rather than asking, "What are the systemic barriers that keep certain groups of girls and women out?"

This generic female is generally assumed to be able-bodied, white, heterosexual, young to middle-aged, and middle-class. More specifically, it is assumed that she

- has sufficient discretionary income to purchase clothing and equipment, and to pay registration fees and travel costs;
- has family members who will support and not undermine or prevent her efforts to become physically active;
- will not be harassed because of her gender, skin colour, ethnicity, body size, sexual orientation, disability, age, or any other characteristic;
- has ready access to transport and facilities that are safe and barrier-free;
- will enjoy Canada's mainstream sport and recreational activities and embrace their underlying value systems.

In reality, there are still significant systemic barriers to full female sporting participation in Canada. The values and practices in men's professional team sports—most notably ice hockey, football, and basketball—dominate most Canadians' understanding of the term "sport." To the limited extent that amateur sport is recognized, the "faster, higher, stronger"

Olympic model privileges male athletes, who, as a gender group, are likely to be faster, higher, and stronger than females as a group (although it is important to acknowledge that there is significant overlap in the performance of males and females at all levels). Flawed assumptions about the actual context of Canadian sport and physical activity include the following:

- that it is a safe and welcoming place for all girls and women, regardless of their ethnic and social class backgrounds, sexual orientations, or abilities;
- that comprehensive anti-harassment policies and effective complaints procedures are in place, in order to address sexual, racist, homophobic, and all other forms of harassment;
- that existing physical activities reflect a wide range of human values and priorities, including enjoyment, cooperation, and camaraderie, as well as winning and improving one's performance;
- that sport as currently constituted will not need to be changed; it is assumed that girls and women will have to change to fit into existing patterns and practices.

Liberal approaches have dominated women's sport advocacy and research in most western countries, including Canada, since the 1960s' wave of the women's movement. This approach defined formal equality primarily in relation to girls' and women's access to the same or equivalent sport and recreational opportunities as boys and men. The liberal agenda focused on removing policy and legislative barriers that prevented girls and women (mostly white and middle-class) from enjoying the same opportunities as their male counterparts. In addition to increasing female participation at the club and community levels, this approach called for more Olympic sports and events for women, more balanced media coverage of female athletes, and more women in coaching, officiating, administration, and the sport media.

These are all strategies that critics have characterized as the "add women and stir" approach. In other words, although the resulting mix was quantitatively different—there was in fact more female involvement at all levels—it was not qualitatively different from the original. The shortcomings of traditional male-dominated models of sport and physical activity were perpetuated, rather than challenged, by these initiatives, with the result that women's competitive sport was often indistinguishable from men's. For example, the 1997 National Film Board documentary, *The Game of Her Life*, which followed the Canadian women's national ice hockey team as it trained for the 1998 Winter Olympics, revealed the same mainstream approaches to coaching, training, and winning that characterized men's competitive sport.

There was little recognition in liberal feminist discourse that the male-defined model of sport might need reforming—or, indeed, transforming—to reflect the priorities of women and men who valued enjoyment, health, and social relationships over corporatized sporting spectacles and winning at all costs. Despite their goal of promoting opportunities for girls and women of all ability levels, liberal sport advocacy organizations routinely highlighted the credentials and achievements of Olympic sportswomen, while failing to recognize the chilling effect that this kind of preoccupation with high-performance sport might have on girls and women whose abilities and aspirations were "average" rather than "Olympian"—in other words, the vast majority of the female population.

SHORTCOMINGS OF THE "ROLE MODEL" MODEL

Although liberal initiatives produced important gains in policy and legislative changes, assumptions about a universal Canadian female resulted in insufficient attention being paid to the impacts of systemic racism, classism, ageism, ableism, and homophobia on girls' and women's lives. As a result, gains were not evenly distributed across the boundaries of race and ethnicity, social class, age, ability, and sexuality. Often relying on a few high-profile female athletes to serve as "role models," liberal approaches largely ignored interlocking systems of discrimination and oppression that made it impossible for the majority of girls and women to emulate the few who were successful when judged by mainstream standards of competitive sporting achievement. The "role model" approach rested on the assumption that a major barrier to female sporting participation was lack of imagination, inspiration, and aspirations: in other words, "it's all in our heads."

According to this way of thinking, girls and women simply needed to see real evidence—a successful high-performance athlete who, as a "role model," would inspire them to great sporting heights. Nowhere was it acknowledged that the role model's international success in a narrow range of physical activities that were classified as sport in contemporary western society was largely dependent on her body type, socioeconomic status, geographic location, family activity patterns, and other interacting individual and sociocultural variables. Biological inheritance, for example, plays a major role in determining physical activity behaviours, while children with active parents and higher family incomes have significantly greater sport participation rates than those with inactive parents and lower incomes (CFLRI, 2000; Physical activity promotion, 1999).

This is not to suggest that positive examples of female athleticism in girls' and women's everyday lives (as opposed to sporting celebrities giving motivational talks) are unimportant. As discussed later in this chapter, girls and women enjoy the social side of sport and physical activity, and the presence of exercise partners or friends who share an interest in a particular sporting activity is highly valued.

In relation to the effectiveness of the "role model" approach, although it is valid to assume that very young children may have difficulty thinking in abstract terms and may need concrete evidence in order to understand some concepts—for example, the idea of a female athlete succeeding in a male-dominated sport—this is not the case from preadolescence on. Indeed, in 1985, 12-year-old Justine Blainey was quite capable of understanding injustice and sex discrimination and equally capable of imagining herself playing at the top level of ice hockey competition—at that time, on a boys' team. Justine was barred from playing on the Etobicoke (Toronto) Canucks "A" team, despite her success at the tryouts, because she was a girl; at this time, sex discrimination in sport was specifically excluded from the provisions of the Ontario Human Rights Code. (Ironically, around the same time, the Ontario Ministry of Tourism and Recreation had established its own "role model" program, with Olympic sportswomen visiting schools to give inspirational talks to girls.)

The (male) Ontario Hockey Association fought all the way to the Supreme Court of Canada to keep players like Justine out of their leagues, but in the end, the court ruled that sex discrimination in sport contravened the provisions of the Canadian Charter of Rights and Freedoms. The struggle for equality, unfortunately, did not end with this decision; accounts of qualified girls who were excluded from boys' teams regularly appeared in the Canadian media throughout the 1990s.

SOCIAL CHANGE, RADICAL ALTERNATIVES

Radical and socialist feminists recognized that the roots of women's oppression needed to be addressed. Lobbying for increased female access to existing male-defined sporting activities would not be successful if other, more deeply-rooted social problems remained unaddressed: for example, the impact of male violence on girls and women's lives, the links between the subculture of men's team sports and violence against women, and the economic disadvantages experienced by women as a gender group.

Drawing on the concepts of accommodation and resistance, radical feminists examined not only the impact of male power and privilege on women's lives, but also women's capacity to resist discrimination and oppression. Hence, women were not portrayed as helpless victims, but rather as active agents who have developed a range of resistance strategies as well as creative woman-centred sporting alternatives, such as community softball leagues organized on feminist principles (see, for example, Birrell & Richter, 1987; Lenskyj, 1994a).

Sexuality issues were central to these kinds of analyses. Radical feminists examined the ways in which heterosexist assumptions, rigid definitions of feminine (that is, heterosexual) behaviour, and the chilly climate created by sexual and homophobic harassment discouraged female sporting participation. As was the pattern in other traditionally male-dominated domains, the sexual identities of female athletes and women in sport leadership routinely came under suspicion. Characterized as "intruders" in a male domain, they were accused of being "unfeminine," man-hating, and/or lesbian. "Feminine" girls and women, according to this line of thought, played gender-appropriate sports that enhanced their heterosexual attractiveness, and at the same time posed no threat to the myth of male athletic superiority. Although women's international profile in competitive sports like soccer and basketball has recently challenged some of this thinking, the popularity of long hair and jewellery still suggests adherence to conventional femininity.

These ideological arguments had particular power over adolescent girls and young women who were experiencing family, peer, and media pressure to establish their heterosexual credentials. In other words, to pursue sport, particularly traditionally male sport, through one's adolescence was to risk being labelled lesbian (Lenskyj, 1997). Needless to say, many women in sport, as in every other area of human activity, are in fact lesbian. With increasing acceptance of sexual diversity and the human rights of sexual minorities in other sectors of Canadian society, it is to be hoped that the longstanding issue of homophobic harassment in female sport will eventually be resolved.

VALUES AND PRIORITIES: GENDER-RELATED DIFFERENCES

Extensive research evidence shows how girls and women tend to value the social side of sport—especially the fun and friendship—more than their male counterparts, who are more likely to name winning and beating their opponents as their top priorities. This does not mean that female athletes don't want to win, or that male athletes don't enjoy the camaraderie of sport. Rather, these findings indicate that there are gender-related patterns of values, interests, and priorities (Lenskyj, 1994b). It is important to remember, too, that the significance of winning is learned—it is not an innate characteristic of all women or all men—and it cannot be assumed that all participants, regardless of their ethnocultural backgrounds, attach the same value to this component of sport.

It is important to recognize that these so-called female values are socially constructed and transmitted, and are not a necessary outcome of biological femaleness. In men's sport, there is historical evidence from Canada, the United States, Europe, Australia, and elsewhere to show that existing sporting systems and practices have long been compatible with socially constructed and biologically based notions of what it means to be male. In these countries, sport has been treated as an essential component of boys' physical development and socialization into manhood, but, until the last decades of the 20th century, it was seen as largely irrelevant for female socialization and development.

Social and biological factors interact in the sporting context to contribute to the construction of gender identity. For example, physical training, in combination with male hormonal changes in adolescence, promote muscular development, which is both an indicator of physical maturation in the young male, and an important asset for the aspiring athlete. In contrast, physical training may slow down the onset of puberty in girls, and it may delay the development of girls' breasts and hips, which are indicators of female maturation; furthermore, girls' normal hormonal changes at puberty lead to increased body fat, which is a liability rather than an asset in most sports. Hence, sport fits neatly into both biological and societal definitions of desirable masculinity but is incompatible with most definitions of femininity.

HUMAN RIGHTS RATIONALES

The two related rationales—human rights and health—are used by women's sport advocates to support arguments for equality in sport and physical activity. The human rights approach argues that discrimination against girls and women, and against ethnocultural or other minorities, contravenes the Canadian Charter of Rights and Freedoms, as well as most provincial human rights codes.

Because boards of education, municipal recreation programs, provincial sports organizations, and colleges and universities are subsidized either fully or partially with public money, they are required to operate on equitable principles. It is unfair, for example, for a disproportionate amount of university students' compulsory athletic fees to be spent maintaining the men's football team; in this common scenario on Canadian university campuses, female students are in effect forced to subsidize sports in which they themselves are ineligible to participate. Similarly, since property tax revenues support the building and maintenance of municipal ice rinks and baseball diamonds, it is unfair to girls and women if boys' and men's leagues receive the best time slots and the bulk of the playing time. With allocation policies often giving priority to longstanding users, women trying to establish new leagues are at a distinct disadvantage under this system.

As noted above in relation to the Blainey case, human rights strategies have achieved some noteworthy successes. It could also be argued that it is preferable to base a complaint on justice and human rights rather than on health or other utilitarian arguments: in other words, discrimination and injustice have no place in a democratic society.

HEALTH RATIONALES: PROS AND CONS

The health approach emphasizes the benefits of regular physical activity on population health and the negative impacts of inactivity: chronic health problems, increased burden on health care, absenteeism, and decreased workplace productivity. Since there is ample evidence to show that Canadian girls' and women's physical activity participation rates are below those recommended for optimal health (to be discussed in a later section), the health argument is particularly relevant for women.

There are both strengths and weaknesses to this approach. Pragmatically, it is clear that, in these times of drastic cutbacks to health, education, and social service budgets, as well as the generally right-wing political climate across Canada, provincial and federal governments are more likely to be persuaded by health arguments than by appeals to human rights, equity, and social justice in relation to female exclusion from the full range of sporting and physical activity opportunities.

However, if the emphasis is solely on the economic costs of inactivity, there is the danger of reducing the full humanity of women and men, so that they become cogs in an economic machine rather than citizens in a democratic country with well-founded expectations that social justice and equity, as well as health and economic security, should prevail.

The 1998 Canadian Heritage subcommittee's report (Mills, 1998), titled, appropriately, "Sport in Canada: Everybody's Business," provided a good example of the dangers of economic reductionism. Mass participation in sport was identified as "one of the best ways to achieve our social and economic objectives"; a 10% decrease in the numbers of inactive Canadians, the report claimed, would produce a $5-billion saving in health care costs. Increased youth participation, particularly among "at risk" youths, would "develop better potential for this growing human resource"; reduced rates of unwanted pregnancies, drug use, and crime were also listed among the benefits. Low female participation rates were treated not only as a health issue—because inactive females, the report claimed, were at higher risk of cardiovascular disease, osteoporosis, breast cancer, colon cancer, adult-onset diabetes, and hypertension—but also as a problem for "the vitality of the sport sector in Canada"—that is, "sporting goods manufacturers and the overall sport services sector" (Mills, 1998).

With regard to the question of research evidence to support its rather sweeping health-related claims, the subcommittee generally relied on reports or briefs submitted by sport organizations, including Sport Nova Scotia, the Canadian Association for the Advancement of Women and Sport (CAAWS), and the Canadian Association for Health, Physical Education and Recreation (CAHPER). For example, while Sport Nova Scotia was cited as the source for the reference to reduction in unwanted pregnancies among young women who are active in sport, this was in fact an American research finding popularized by Nike advertisements and probably attributable to self-esteem rather than sport itself.

It is possible, however, to examine the health benefits of physical activity from an equity and social justice perspective without reducing women or men to mere economic assets. There is no doubt that regular physical activity is essential for girls' and women's physical and psychological health and well-being, and that in a democratic society every effort should be made to ensure that barriers to full participation are removed. Conversely, since it is widely known that there is a strong correlation between physical exercise and the prevention of many chronic diseases, there is an obvious injustice at work when diseases related to inactivity produce or exacerbate health problems, pain, and suffering in the female population. Black women and Native women, for example, are particularly vulnerable to certain chronic, and ultimately life-threatening, conditions, with a sedentary lifestyle constituting a significant risk factor for heart disease, stroke, and diabetes (Wells, 1996).

Girls as well as boys require regular physical activity to ensure cardiovascular benefits, good bone development, healthy weights, and long-term health promotion. Childhood activity is a key element in the prevention of chronic disease and obesity in adulthood, and regular activity patterns established in childhood are likely to be maintained in adulthood (Ganley & Sherman, 2000; Summerfield, 1990). Psychological benefits for children include overall emotional well-being, positive self-concept, and lower levels of tension, anxiety, and depression (Psycho-physiological contributions, 1998).

It is important to recognize that female preoccupation with weight loss through exercise and/or dieting is, in most instances, an unhealthy result of societal, family, peer, and media pressure on girls and women to achieve an ultrathin body in order to be seen as heterosexually attractive. Although exercising is a healthier strategy than dieting, the emphasis on weight loss often leads to dangerous eating behaviours. About 25% of women who suffer from anorexia nervosa (self-starvation) engage in high levels of physical training, and about 50% use exercise for weight-loss purposes. Indeed, surveys have shown that more than 50% of the general Canadian female population (aged 10 and over) exercise in order to lose weight; since only about 30% of Canadian females are at risk due to obesity, these figures demonstrate that significant numbers of girls and women of average or below-average weight are trying to lose weight (Moriarty & Moriarty, 1986; Stephens & Craig, 1990).

Formerly a health concern only among young, middle-class, white females, eating disorders are prevalent among ethnic minority females as well, and effective interventions are urgently needed. The "body equity" workshops described by Toronto educators Carla Rice and Vanessa Russell (1995) are an excellent example of a feminist and antiracist initiative that addressed the ways in which oppressions are embodied and interconnected. By politicizing weight prejudice and connecting it to other systems of oppression, the workshops provided a much-needed alternative to the more common, individualistic "body-image" approach.

HEALTH AND FITNESS INITIATIVES: IMPACTS ON GIRLS AND WOMEN

Various provincial and national initiatives of the 1970s and 1980s—the Canada-wide ParticipAction campaign and CAHPER's Quality Daily Physical Education (QDPE), for example—aimed at increasing Canadians' regular participation in sport and recreational activities. With girls and women having lower participation rates at the outset, physical educators and sport leaders anticipated that these programs would prove particularly beneficial for females. Despite some initial successes, however, gains were not sustained, and the inactivity levels of Canadian adults have not dropped since the mid-1990s (CFRLI, 1999). The QDPE program, which required 30 minutes of daily physical education, was followed in only 10% of Canadian schools. Equally disturbing, recent figures from British Columbia for enrolment in year 11 and year 12 physical education courses show a generally steady decline for both male and female students since 1992, a growing gender gap, and an unprecedented low rate of approximately 10% female enrolment in 1999–2000 (Deacon, 2001).

Statistics Canada's 1998 report, "Sport Participation in Canada," showed that, between 1992 and 1998, adult (aged 15+) sport participation rates declined by almost 11%, and the gender gap widened by 3%. The 1992 figure of 38% regular female involvement in sport dropped to 26%, compared to 43% of men. Some of the general decline, according to the Statistics Canada report, could be attributed to the rising popularity of "Internet surfing" as a "relatively inexpensive" leisure activity, when compared to the increasing cost of transportation, sporting equipment, and registration fees.

This explanation failed to take into account the economic disadvantage experienced by women as a gender group in the current Canadian context of an economic recession and a national housing crisis, and the limited likelihood that women with minimal discretionary income would consider the purchase of computers and monthly charges for Internet servers even "relatively" cheap.

Socioeconomic disadvantage interacts with race and gender discrimination in limiting female access to sport and recreation. Activities such as tennis, golf, figure skating, gymnastics, and skiing are frequently organized and practised in expensive and elitist ways—in private clubs, for example—with the result that working-class and minority girls and women are often excluded. With the growing trend toward charging user fees for admission to community recreation centre facilities and for basic instructional programs, even activities like swimming and fitness classes, which used to be free, and hence, accessible to low-income women and their children, are now beyond the reach of many. Similarly, a recent Ontario survey showed that 43% of publicly funded high schools charged a fee for instructional physical education, and 61% had an athletic fee ranging from $5 to $90; in the majority of schools, subsidies were available for students unable to pay, but it is likely that the fee requirement would be a deterrent for many students (People for Education, 2001).

Age is another significant factor for both male and female participation rates, with a clear decrease for both sexes over the life span. The age group 15 to 18 years participated in sport at twice the national rate: 68% were involved in sport at least once per week, compared to the overall rate of 34%. For adults 55 and over, the rate dropped to about 20%. Female rates were lower than male rates in every age category, with the most dramatic gap in the 15 to 18 age group, where 80% of males and only 55% of females reported regular participation. Although the gender gap decreased as age increased, some of this trend was attributable to men's more dramatic drop in participation over the life span. However, even in the 55 and over age group, male rates were 10% higher than female (Sport Participation in Canada, 1998; CFLRI, 1999).

With women having longer life expectancy than men, they are more likely to experience both health problems and economic deprivation in old age, and hence they face additional barriers in accessing affordable recreational activities. A physical recreation program for seniors—mostly women—sponsored by the University of Alberta and featured in the 1991 National Film Board documentary "Age Is No Barrier," demonstrated an effective alternative approach to promoting physical activity among older women. Fun, friendship, and collaboration were emphasized over competition and achievement of external standards of success. The program showed, too, how personal relationships were central to women's learning and enjoyment.

The CFLRI and Statistics Canada findings demonstrate the importance of introducing regular and enjoyable physical activity into girls' lives from a young age. The barriers to starting a new sport or recreational pursuit increase with age, particularly for those who cannot build on a foundation of basic skills, physical competence, and confidence that they have developed in their youth. Research indicates that inactivity poses a widespread threat to children's health, with two-thirds of Canadian children not sufficiently physically active for optimal growth and development. The 1999 Canadian Lifestyle and Fitness Research Institute (CFLRI) Physical Activity Monitor found that girls continued to be less active than boys; only 39% of girls, compared to 52% of boys, met the required level, and the figure for girls aged 13 to 17 dropped to 32%. With regard to regular sporting participation, the figures were 61% for boys aged 5 to 14 years, and only 48% for girls (CFLRI, 1999). Two earlier Canadian surveys also indicated the risks for girls and young women: their self-image and confidence declined during adolescence (Canadian Teachers' Federation, 1990; Holmes & Silverman, 1992), and there was a corresponding drop in their physical activity levels (Stephens & Craig, 1990).

BEHIND THE STATISTICS: CAUSES AND EFFECTS

Three related variables—education level, family income, and labour force participation—all had clear impacts on female participation. Female students (high school, college, or university) and women with part-time or full-time employment were more likely to be active in sport than women who were not in the labour force, with the latter group including women doing unpaid housework and child care in the home. Women with family incomes of $80 000 or more had almost double the participation rates of those with incomes under $20 000 (Sport Participation, 1999).

Lack of time for physical activity was identified in earlier surveys as a major barrier for women (see, for example, Stephens & Craig, 1990), and the 1998 survey confirmed this finding, with both lack of time and lack of interest cited as equally important reasons for women's low participation. (Men, particularly those in the 20 to 24 and 25 to 34 age groups, also reported lack of time as the major barrier.) This is an interesting finding in light of the female labour force participation figures noted earlier. Many women who work full time experience a double workday; that is, if they have traditional male partners, and/or if they are mothers of young children, they probably complete several hours of domestic and child-care work at the end of each workday. It might be assumed these women would have less time for sport or physical activity than their unemployed counterparts. However, given the correlation between educational attainment, earning capacity, and sporting participation, it appears that, for many fully employed women, their (relative) financial independence enhances their leisure choices. In other words, they do not have to use family finances to pay for recreation-related expenses.

Power relations in traditional families give men ultimate authority over women and children, especially daughters, and men's controlling of women's time and activities extends to their leisure pursuits. The prospect of women engaging in sport and recreation purely for their own enjoyment is antithetical to traditional expectations that women should put others' needs before their own. As a result, women may arrange their leisure activities to fit with family expectations, or they may try to combine child care with a physical activity such as walking or swimming. These kinds of creative individual solutions do not address systemic problems such as power relations and the sexual division of labour in the family, or the absence of affordable child care in the community.

The survey findings also reflected girls' and women's tendency to value the social interaction that accompanies physical activity and to view competition as a lower priority. For example, among active Canadians, 40% of males took part in competitions or tournaments,

BOX 7.1 HIGHLIGHTS FROM THE CANADIAN ECONOMIC GENDER EQUALITY INDICATORS, 2000

- Women aged 15 to 24, when compared to their male counterparts, work 18% more; although the share of paid work done by young women is high, their share of unpaid work is even higher.
- Income imbalances between women and men are declining, but women's after-tax income is only 63% of men's.
- Women work an additional 15 minutes a day or the equivalent of more than two additional weeks per year.
- Women are making slow, steady progress into fields that have been heavily male-dominated.
- Yet women are also increasing their share in female-dominated fields and men are staying away from these areas.

Source: Adapted from the Canadian Advisory Council on the Status of Women

Despite these obstacles, there is some evidence that Canadian girls and women engage in physical activities that are not usually defined as sport. When questioned about their exercise frequency in Statistics Canada surveys (1994–95), females aged 12 years and older reported much higher participation rates in the categories of walking for exercise, home exercise, and aerobics or fitness classes than males, and slightly higher rates for swimming. Similarly, the 1998 Statistics Canada survey showed that men and women preferred different sports: swimming, baseball, and volleyball were women's top choices, while hockey, golf, baseball, and basketball were men's.

TABLE 7.1 Female Participation in Physical Activities: Eight Most Popular Choices

Walking	69.7% of all females*
Home exercise	29.6
Swimming	23.3
Cycling	22.1
Exercise class or aerobics	10.5
Jogging or running	10.1
Bowling	9.5
No activity	8.7

* respondents 12 years of age and older; respondents could participate in more than one activity; participation rates by activity

Source: Based on Statistics Canada, National Population Health Survey, 1994–95

The survey findings also reflected girls' and women's tendency to value the social interaction that accompanies physical activity and to view competition as a lower priority. For example, among active Canadians, 40% of males took part in competitions or tournaments, compared to 29% of females, although the latter figure represented an increase of 5 percentage points over the 1992 findings. With regard to the sport preferences of children aged 5 to 14, however, some new trends were identified: although hockey was the favourite for boys and swimming was girls' top choice, both boys and girls put soccer in second place, followed by baseball and basketball.

Surveys that examined physical activities rather than sports produced somewhat different results. A fitness survey conducted in 1988 reported that walking was the top physical recreation choice for both males and females aged 10 years and older, while gardening was the second (Stephens & Craig, 1990). The 1999 CFLRI report found that 81% of adult Canadians listed walking as the most popular activity, 70% gave yard work and gardening as second choice, and 54% listed swimming. Women are more likely than men to take part in yoga, tai chi, exercise classes, and walking for exercise, while adolescent girls are more likely than boys to list walking, social dancing, ballet, exercise, and dance classes.

Although the sex differences in the 1998 survey might well reflect discriminatory practices in access to facilities and programs, it is important to avoid using the male yardstick to judge female sporting achievement, preferences, and practices. This "female deficit" model upholds traditional male values and attitudes in sport as the ideal. Female perspectives are judged by the male standard and found lacking, and girls and women are then blamed for having an "attitude" problem—for example, they don't understand that winning is all that matters!

SYSTEMIC BARRIERS: VIOLENCE AGAINST WOMEN

The threat of harassment and violence poses a serious obstacle to women's sport and recreational choices. Minority women experience additional problems of harassment or discrimination on the basis of their race or ethnicity, social class, or sexuality. Women as a group, and adults over 65, are more likely than men and younger adults to avoid walking or cycling for exercise because of safety concerns (CFLRI, 1999). Working class and/or minority women may live in areas of the city where personal safety is a particularly serious concern, and parents of young women may justly fear for their daughters' welfare when walking or travelling on public transit to community recreational programs. Expectations in some traditional families—where domestic and child-care chores are expected to take priority over recreation—may further constrain girls' and women's options (see, for example, Borowy & Little, 1991).

There was growing recognition in the 1990s that many male sporting practices actively promoted woman-hating attitudes and violence against women (Lenskyj, 1992a, 1992b). Football coaches, players, and fans, for example, use misogynist and homophobic insults and obscenities to motivate the home team and to put down their opponents (Pronger, 1993). Such practices served as powerful symbols of the marginalization and brutalization of women. Statistics from American university campuses showed that male intercollegiate athletes were overrepresented among students convicted of sexual assault, including date rape and gang rape (Bausell, Bausell, & Siegel, 1991; Warshaw, 1988). Similarly, some prominent professional athletes were accused and, in some cases, convicted of sexually assaulting female spectators, sports journalists, and cheerleaders. The mythology surrounding male sporting heroes and the sense of entitlement that comes with their status make it difficult for victims of sexual assault to report to police and to testify in court, particularly when the perpetrator is a millionaire sports figure (Benedict, 1998; Robinson, 1998).

The connection between wife assault and major male sporting events like the Super Bowl began to receive public attention in the early 1990s. The numbers of women who were victims of sexual assault, date and acquaintance rape, or wife assault escalated significantly at the time of any major North American sporting event. In 1993, NBC-TV, the network that broadcast the Super Bowl, agreed to air a free public service announcement during the pregame program, and American and Canadian television stations and newspapers also carried announcements and reports on the links between domestic violence and major sporting events in an attempt to raise public awareness.

THE "CHILLY CLIMATE" PROBLEM

Analyses of gender-equity issues in education and employment recognize the problem of the "chilly climate" or "poisoned environment" and its role in deterring female participation, and there are clear parallels in the sport and physical activity context. An unwelcome, unsafe, or even threatening environment can be created by men's verbal or physical harassment, by non-verbal behaviour, and by the physical surroundings. It is important to note that concepts such as chilly climate and poisoned environment are recognized in legal contexts as forms of sexual harassment. For example, the first sexual harassment complaint lodged at the University of Toronto in the 1980s involved a male professor who was alleged to have persistently leered at women using the swimming pool. A current problem involves men "surfing" pornography sites on computers in the athletic centre. Although these practices are permitted under the university's computer policies (in the interests of freedom of sexual expression), the location of the terminals in a public area near the women's locker room is a cause for concern.

The "dripping tap" experience—sexual innuendoes, intrusive touching, unwanted and persistent requests for dates or sex, and displays of offensive images of women—erodes the morale and resistance of many women who work, study, or train in these settings (Dagg & Thompson, 1987). Alternatively, they may develop a high level of tolerance for sexual harassment in order to survive. If a woman experiences sexually harassing behaviour at the hands of a male coach, or is threatened with reprisals if she does not have sex with him, she may be forced to give up her sport. Even the less serious forms of harassment, including coaches' inappropriate criticism of girls' or young women's body size and shape, may contribute to dangerous eating patterns such as self-starvation, bingeing and purging, with sometimes fatal consequences (Davis, 1999; Lenskyj, 1993). In most situations, the coach has significantly more institutional power and privilege than the athlete, by virtue of his status as coach, his gender, race, age, social class, and sexual orientation, and so the odds are stacked against the female target of harassment.

THE SEXUAL ABUSE PROBLEM

In 1993, CBC television aired a ground-breaking public affairs program called "Crossing the Line," which examined the problem of sexual harassment and sexual assault of girls and young women at the hands of male coaches. Many of the men whom they named as harassers were pursuing successful careers as coaches of female athletes, in some cases, with the complete approval of the athletes' parents and the university administrations, while their female victims had abandoned their sporting careers and were hurt and disillusioned by the experience. The fact that two of the documented cases involved university sport was particularly disturbing, since at that time most Canadian universities and colleges, unlike community sports clubs and organizations, had harassment policies in place. Psychological abuse was clearly illustrated in the CBC documentary. The young women's perceptions of the coaches' complete control over their lives were both illuminating and disturbing:

"He owned your body and he owned your mind."
"He could have asked us to do almost anything."
"He was always in your head."

Coaches achieved this psychological control through some clichéed, but effective messages:

"No one remembers who comes second."
"I can replace you—I made you and I can break you."

It was clear that the powerful "win at all costs" mentality and the young athletes' overwhelming dedication to training made it even more difficult for them to report the abuse. Time after time, a powerful, charismatic male coach would persuade a young woman that his abusive actions were "for her own good" and that reporting the harassment would cause him to lose his job and thereby ruin her chances, and the team's chances, of winning. CBC reporter Hana Gartner's response was illuminating: she had difficulty believing that these girls had remained silent when their silence served to protect the men who were abusing them. Like many viewers unfamiliar with the everyday world of high-performance sport, Gartner seemed baffled that a young woman would tolerate this kind of abuse, just because of a game. What was missing from the documentary was an analysis of the subculture of competitive sport—women's as well as men's—where the drive to win at all costs transcends other considerations. The CBC documentary succeeded, however, in raising public awareness, and some national sports organizations subsequently took action and formulated harassment policies and procedures (see Donnelly, 1999, p. 119). Ironically, it was a crisis in boys' hockey—when news of sexual-abuse cases involving male coaches became front-page stories in 1997—that prompted Canadian sport administrators to take the most dramatic and far-reaching policy initiatives to address the problem of sexual harassment and abuse in youth sport (Donnelly, 1999).

CONCLUSIONS

The preceding analysis examined the roots of existing inequalities experienced by Canadian girls and women both inside and outside the context of sport and physical activity. Strategies for change must take into account the broader social context, most notably the powerful impacts of interlocking systems of oppression. Liberal strategies that simply "open the door" by introducing more programs, classes, or teams for girls and women rarely address the problems of marginalization and exclusion experienced by specific groups of girls and women, particularly those who suffer the effects of racism, classism, homophobia, ableism, and violence. Feminist and anti-racist initiatives hold more promise of empowering minority females through challenging systemic barriers.

Critical Thinking Questions

1. What changes could be made to high school physical education programs to make them more welcoming (a) to girls and (b) to students from ethnic minority backgrounds?
2. Debate the following statement: "Violence is an essential component of contact sports." Discuss the implications for female participation in contact sports.

3. What are the pros and cons of sex-integrated sport (a) for children under 12, (b) for adolescents, and (c) for adults?

4. Select a particular government sport department, sport organization, or recreation centre, and discuss the following questions with regard to gender, ethnicity, and social class:
   Who allocates the resources?
   Who makes decisions?
   Who operates the programs?
   Who has access to power?
   Who participates in the programs?
   Who works in the office?
   Who cleans and maintains facilities?

5. Debate the following statement: "People who enjoy sport and value democracy would be ill-advised to support any aspect of the Olympics.... Their energies would be better directed towards other regional, national and international sporting competitions that are currently conducted in more ethical and less exploitative ways" (Lenskyj, 2000, p. 195).

Suggested Readings

Brackenridge, C. (2001). *Spoilsports: Understanding and preventing sexual exploitation in sport*. London: Routledge.

Griffin, P. (1998). *Strong women, deep closets: Lesbians and homophobia in sport*. Champaign, Ill.: Human Kinetics.

Lenskyj, H. (1986). *Out of bounds: Women, sport and sexuality*. Toronto: Women's Press.

White, P., & Young, K. (Eds.). *Sport and gender in Canada*. Don Mills, Ont.: Oxford University Press, 1999.

Women in Sport and Physical Activity Journal. From 1992 to the present, two issues per year: An interdisciplinary, international forum for women-centred issues and approaches to sport and physical activity.

Web Links

Canadian Fitness and Lifestyle Research Institute, Ottawa
http://www.cflri.ca
Annual statistics on Canadians' participation in sport and physical activity, and other research findings, with breakdowns by gender, age, income levels, education, etc.

Sport Information Resource Centre, Ottawa
http://www.sportquest.com
Leading bibliographic database producer of sport, fitness, and sports medicine information.

Status of Women Canada, Ottawa
http://www.swc-cfc.gc.ca/direct.html
A national organization committed to improving women's economic autonomy and well-being, eliminating systemic violence against women and children, and advancing women's human rights; information on gender-based analysis, and other research tools.

Tucker Center for Research on Girls and Women in Sport, University of Minnesota
http://www.education.umn.edu/tuckercenter
Follow links to "Resources" for excellent bibliographies on specific topics—a valuable research tool.

University of Toronto, Graduate Collaborative Program in Women's Studies
http://www.utoronto.ca/womens/resrces.htm
"Collection of Women's Resources on the Net": links to dozens of feminist Web sites in Canada and internationally.

8

Race and Ethnicity in Canadian Sport

Victoria Paraschak and Susan Tirone

Katie Illnik, an Inuk from Yellowknife, Northwest Territories, moved to Edmonton, Alberta, to pursue more competitive soccer opportunities as part of her high school experience.

Pride in one's roots is essential to finding one's voice.

C. Spence, *The skin I'm in: Racism, sports and education*

We shall not cease from exploration
And the end of all our exploring
Will be to arrive where we started
And know the place for the first time.

T.S. Eliot, "Little Gidding," *Four Quartets*, 1943

We all have individual characteristics that differentiate us from or connect us to others. Hair colour, gender, height, skin colour, ethnicity, and eye colour are a few examples of such characteristics. Think of how you would describe yourself for a minute. When we thought about this question, Vicky described herself as female, brown haired, hazel eyed, 5'4", urban Canadian, and white. Susan described her physical attributes in a similar way but she lives in a rural community. Yet as each of us lives out or "does" our lives, those individual characteristics are continually reshaped by our experiences. For example, Vicky recollects how some children have considered her tall, while adults often claim that she is short. Her eye colour varies with what she wears, and her ethnicity has been shaped by years in the Canadian north, and the specific cultural practices she learned there and continues to do. She is also often quizzed on her race, because of her research on First Nations peoples. Susan notes that her studies of Canadian immigrants and children in those immigrant families help her to reflect on what is meaningful in her own life, having been raised within a large extended Italian Canadian family. So while, when asked, we can each describe our individual characteristics, that description changes over time and from the perspectives of others. We continuously construct the ways we see ourselves, and that involves the social world in which we live. Our individual characteristics are much less definitive than we might, at first, think.

Some of these characteristics take on a particular social significance in our society. While eye colour remains unimportant at a social level, characteristics such as ethnicity and skin colour—or race—have become socially constructed markers of difference. In North American society broadly and in sport, persistent patterns of unequal treatment have developed around these markers. Individuals assigned those characteristics get identified as part of a group who share traits differentiating them from others. Our sense of ourselves is thus constructed in relation to groups we believe are similar to or different from us.

We know ourselves, and our culture, in part through our bodies. For example, as we "do" physical activities, such as sports, we shape, reinforce, or challenge the understanding we—and others—hold about our racial and ethnic identities. Students in a physical education class learning basketball all perform the same activities, but the ways those movements reinforce or challenge each individual's sense of his or her own race and ethnicity influence the meaning assigned to those movements, and the enjoyment felt or not felt within the class. After school, an Asian youth may head to a program where she participates with others from her ethnic background in activities tied to her cultural roots. Through this process, she reinforces the importance of her ethnic identity in a manner not possible in her earlier gym class on basketball. A Black male student, practising with the school basketball team at the end of the day, feels confirmed as a talented athlete as he emulates the playing styles of his favourite NBA players. Another student heads home to spend time with her family, having no interest in after-school athletics. Day after day, these students continue to know themselves and to represent themselves to others through their involvement—or non-involvement—in physical activities.

This chapter explores the relationship between movement, race, and ethnicity in Canada. It builds on two assumptions, which are captured in the quotes at the start of the chapter. First, we believe that movement opportunities in Canada—such as sport—potentially provide the opportunity for all individuals to generate a feeling of pride in their cultural heritage. However, the sport system has been structured so that some individuals—specifically Caucasians of European descent—are privileged to feel racial and ethnic pride more so than others. Second, we encourage our readers to enter into a reflective process through which they can better understand how race and ethnicity are constructed in our society and in sport. By doing so, they can more knowledgeably shape their own identities while honouring the individual identities desired by others, prerequisites for creating an inclusive sport system in Canada.

RACE, RACISM, AND SPORT IN CANADA

Canada has an early history, in amateur sport, of discrimination by race. Cosentino (1998) argues that while "class" formed the basis of amateurism in England, in Canada "race" became the definer of who could compete. This was evident as early as 1835, when Black jockeys were banned from competing at the Niagara Turf Club. In 1880, Aboriginal players were excluded, by race, from competing in amateur competitions for lacrosse—a game that had originated in Aboriginal culture! As late as 1913, the Amateur Athletic Association of Canada opted to ban Blacks, by race, from competing in Canadian amateur boxing championships, since "competition of whites and coloured men is not working out to the increased growth of sport" (Amateur Athletic Union of Canada, quoted in Cosentino, 1998, p. 13). Even the first definition of an amateur in Canada, created by the Montreal Pedestrian Club in 1873, noted that no "labourer or Indian" could be given that designation.

Yet Canada is also a country where Blacks have, at times, found acceptance as athletes more readily than in the United States. Jackie Robinson broke the colour barrier in Major League Baseball playing for the Brooklyn Dodgers in 1947. However, the president of the Dodgers, Branch Rickey, actually signed Robinson in October 1945 to play professionally for the minor league Montreal Royals. While Robinson played that first year, he experienced intense racism during games in the United States. In Montreal, however, he had great fan support. Scott (1987, p. 37) writes:

> *Robinson's play made him a beloved sports figure in Montreal. Children hounded him for autographs, while adults poured into the ballpark to see him steal bases and score runs. As a Montreal sportswriter noted, "For Jackie Robinson and the city of Montreal, it was love at first sight."*

Three decades later, Warren Moon was able to play professional football as a Black quarterback in Canada when that opportunity was not available in the United States. After being selected as the 1978 Rose Bowl Most Valuable Player, Moon was completely overlooked by the National Football League in its 1978 U.S. college draft. As a result, he came to play with the Edmonton Eskimos in the Canadian Football League and won five Grey Cup titles with them. In 1984, he became the highest paid player in football when he joined the Houston Oilers of the National Football League (Mullick, 2002).

These examples demonstrate different ways that "race" has been given social meaning in Canadian sport. Such meanings are indicative of broader societal race relations. Frideres (1988), writing on racism in Canadian society, noted that "racism in Canada from 1800 to 1945 was reflected in restrictive immigration policies and practices regarding non-white immigrants, particularly the Chinese, Blacks and Jews, and by the treatment of native peoples" (p. 1816). Racist sport practices during this period would thus have reinforced, and been shaped by, broader understandings of race. Canadian attempts to address racial inequity through legislation coalesced in the 1982 Canadian Charter of Rights and Freedoms (CCRF), where equality rights in the public domain were entrenched. Section 15 stated:

> Equality Rights
>
> 15. (1) Every individual is equal before and under the law and has the right to the equal protection and equal benefit of the law without discrimination and, in particular, without discrimination based on race, national or ethnic origin, colour, religion, sex, age or mental or physical disability.
> (2) Subsection (1) does not preclude any law, program or activity that has as its object the amelioration of conditions of disadvantaged individuals or groups including those that are disadvantaged because of race, national or ethnic origin, colour, religion, sex, age or mental or physical disability. (CCRF, 1982)

Human Rights Commissions have also provided a legal avenue for addressing racial inequities in Canada. Participants and administrators who wish to make sport a more welcoming—and legislatively aligned—place for all can benefit by understanding the social construction of race and racism in sport. This section explores some of the ways that race has become, and remains, an indicator or "marker" that provides meaning in our everyday sporting practices.

The Concept of Race

"Race" is a term used to establish socially constructed distinctions between groups of people based on their genetic heritage. These distinctions, marked by skin colour, take on social significance because of differences assigned to members of these groups. For example, we could look at a group of people and assume that some are Caucasian, Black, Aboriginal, or Asian. It is, however, our belief that the colour of their skin indicates immutable differences between them that makes race a socially significant category in our society. We might look to Caucasians for leadership, Blacks for athletic talent, Aboriginal peoples for environmental guidance, and Asians for academic excellence. By assuming that race automatically gave individuals an advantage in some areas more so than others, we would be reproducing race-based understandings of human behaviour.

Skin colour has taken on social meanings in North America that privilege Caucasians over others. A hierarchy of privilege and discrimination has thus been created, commonly referred to as racism. Spence (1999, p.15), quoting Carl James (1995, p. 37) explains it this way:

> *Racism... is the uncritical acceptance of a negative social definition of a colonized or subordinate group typically identified by physical features.... These racialized groups are believed to lack certain abilities or characteristics, which in turn characterizes them as culturally and biologically inferior.*

Racial classification systems and ideas about race emerged in the 16th and 17th centuries, while Europeans were exploring and claiming dominion over different parts of the world. As they encountered people who appeared and acted different, these strangers were placed in an evolutionary hierarchy. Those most similar to Caucasians were judged to be the most evolved and civilized. Whiteness became the norm by which others were judged. The exploitation of people from other "races" thus became justified on the basis of their presumed inferiority relative to Europeans.

Social Darwinism extended Charles Darwin's theory of natural selection into the social realm. This theory provided British and American social theorists with a scientific tool for determining the superiority of some races over others, and thus with a justification for endorsing racial inequality (Coakley, 2001). The presence of slavery in Canada, beginning in 1628 (Spence, 1999), and the colonization and legislative regulation of First Nations within North America reinforced in similar ways the subservient position of Blacks and Aboriginal peoples relative to Canadians of European descent. This race logic eventually became institutionalized as a racial ideology involving "skin color, intelligence, character, and physical characteristics and skills" (Coakley, 2001, p. 247).

Identification by race is not, however, a straightforward process. What did it take, for example, for someone to be considered Caucasian, or Black, or Aboriginal, or Asian, and what were the consequences? The social constructedness of this process can be seen in the ways that race was defined for, and applied to, different groups in Canada. For example, historically, just "one drop of black blood" identified individuals as Black, even though they may have had white ancestors (Coakley, 2001).

In contrast to this, the British North America Act, which constituted Canada as a country in 1867, identified "Indians" as a race apart from other Canadians and placed them under federal jurisdiction. The Indian Act of 1876, which controlled almost every feature of Aboriginal social life, served to separate them further from other Canadians on the basis of race. Treaties were the third factor regulating native life. Here again, the underlying premise was that Aboriginal peoples had an "uncivilized nature" that must be altered before they could enjoy full civil rights. Everyday practices, such as performing traditional dances, were outlawed. It was not until 1960 that First Nations, as a race, could vote federally in Canada (Paraschak, 1997).

Chinese migrants were treated differently yet again. They were forced to pay a head tax to enter Canada beginning in 1885, and in 1902, the Royal Commission on Chinese and Japanese Immigration concluded that Asians were "unfit for full citizenship...obnoxious to a free community and dangerous to the state" (Wickberg, 1988, p. 416). Chinese and East Indian Canadians were not given the right to vote until 1947.

In contrast to these examples, being Caucasian in North American society has remained unmarked. White people have thus not needed to think of themselves in racial terms. They are privileged by race. They have access to opportunities in society without having to worry that their race will be a barrier.

Tiger Woods, a prominent professional golfer of mixed Black, Asian, Aboriginal, and White heritage, brought the complexity of defining individuals by race to public notice in 1997. After his successful first year on the tour, and his win at the Masters specifically, the press heralded him as a successful Black golfer. Woods, however, eventually clarified publicly that he had developed a different racial description for himself as a youth, based on his background. He called himself a CABLINASIAN, to reflect his CAusasian, BLack, INdian, and ASIAN genetic heritage. In this way, he highlighted two important points: racial labels can be assigned to people without those labels being accurate, and the way individuals view themselves may be quite different from the racial category assigned to them by others.

Doing Race, Doing Racism

Race as a socially constructed idea becomes naturalized (i.e., accepted as "truth") as individuals, on a daily basis, behave as if it were true. West and Zimmerman (1991), in their discussion on "doing gender," point out that this process involves individuals behaving in appropriately masculine or feminine ways, "but it is a situated doing, carried out in the virtual or real presence of others who are presumed to be oriented to its production" (p. 14). Applying this to race, "doing race" means that individuals act in relation to each other in ways that confirm their socially constructed beliefs about race. It is through the acting out, the "doing" of race on a day-by-day basis, both with regard to our own race and the race we assign to others, that we maintain a society where race has social meaning and consequences.

Stereotypes—rigid beliefs about the characteristics of a racial group—take on importance as we live or "do" them into existence by operating as if they were true. Spence (1999), in his study of Black male athletes in a Canadian high school, heard from these youths that their teachers encouraged them athletically, but not academically. This treatment fit with the stereotype that Blacks as a race are athletically more and academically less gifted than Whites. As these athletes worked hard on athletic competence and gained status through their success, they had less time to give to academics, and thus their actions, in the end, reinforced the stereotype. All the while, they and their teachers were "doing racism."

"Doing race" can also be carried out in ways that offer positive race-connected meanings to members of a group, providing them with a form of cultural expression that is uniquely their own. Majors (1990), for example, identified "cool pose" as a creative way that Black men express their masculinity in a society where opportunities are limited and racism is institutionalized. Wilson (1999, p. 232) describes the expression of cool pose in sport this way:

> *Sport, particularly basketball, are sites where young Black males symbolically oppose the dominant White group and create [a positive race-connected] identity by developing both a flamboyant on-court language (now popularly known as "trash talking") and a repertoire of spectacular "playground" moves and high-flying dunks.*

While this way of "doing race" was initially generated by Black male youth, Wilson (1999) also discusses ways that this style has been incorporated by sport marketers to sell to a mass audience, and in particular to sell the National Basketball Association Toronto Raptors. These advertising messages, he argues, undercut the resistant symbolic message that cool pose provides Black males, while potentially reinforcing stereotypic Black male images to Canadian audiences. Sport marketers were "doing racism."

Race Relations

In society, individuals always act in relation to others. The possibilities within which we live are thus formed through the "social relations" that exist between individuals and groups. Through social relations, rules are created concerning how things work and how resources can be distributed. They thus become "power relations" because those rules always provide for or privilege some people over others. Race relations are a particular type of power relations—they privilege individuals on the basis of race. Gruneau (1988, p. 22) defines power as "the capacity of a person or group of persons to employ resources of different types in order to secure outcomes." He then identifies three measures of power in sport: the ability to structure sport, to establish sport traditions, and to define legitimate meanings and practices associated with dominant sport practices. These measures of power, differently shaped by race, can be seen when looking at mainstream sport, and at race-structured sporting opportunities such as all-Aboriginal sport competitions.

Whitestream Sport

Claude Denis (1997) uses the term "whitestream society" "to indicate that Canadian society, while principally structured on the basis of the European, 'white', experience, is far from being simply 'white' in socio-demographic, economic and cultural terms" (p. 13). Extending his term, the rules of mainstream or "whitestream" sport have been primarily shaped by individuals of White, European heritage, in ways that privilege their traditions, practices, meanings, and sport structures. This is an example of "institutionalized racism," since the structure of the system, if followed, will always produce outcomes that discriminate against those who are not White—it will privilege Caucasians over others.

Differential treatment of individuals, by race, occurred in whitestream sport in various ways. For example, the ability of George Beers, in 1860, to create and then institutionalize lacrosse rules in a manner that he found meaningful, as opposed to the ways the game was played by Aboriginal Canadians, demonstrates his privilege by race over the originators of the game of lacrosse (Cosentino, 1998, p. 15). As well, during this period Black and Aboriginal athletes were banned, by race, from competing against White Canadians in a wide variety of sports. If they did compete, descriptors such as "Indian" or "coloured" were added after their name, to indicate that they were different from, and subservient to, White competitors.

When overt discrimination was eliminated in sport, other more subtle forms of racism remained. The organization of sport privileged those activities that were played in international competitions, including the Olympics and World Championships. The federal government criteria for funding sports reflected this; physical activities that fell outside the whitestream model were not seen as legitimate and were denied federal funding. For example, the Northern Games Association, which organized yearly Inuit and Dene traditional games festivals in the Northwest Territories beginning in 1970, was informed by letter in 1977 that their federal sport funding would be stopped. The letter pointed out that the Games activities, which had their origin in Aboriginal cultures, were not deemed to be "legitimate sport" according to the parameters of the funding agency. Aboriginal organizers argued that their traditional activities were also "sports," but they had less power over defining "legitimate" sports, and thus lost their funding (Paraschak, 1997).

A third drawback to whitestream sport in Canada is the discomfort experienced by marginalized peoples in mainstream sport experiences. In a 1991 TSN documentary, titled "Hockey, A White Man's Game?", both individual and institutionalized racism in hockey was detailed. Ted Nolan, an Aboriginal NHL player, spoke of the racism he faced from his teammates as a teenager, and the isolation he felt as a result. Other Aboriginal players spoke about the racial slurs they endured while playing. And they spoke about the structure of hockey in Canada, which took them far away from their families and support systems, and how that structure in hockey made it more difficult for them to succeed in light of their cultural practices. Since Aboriginal players were not able to structure sport in preferred ways, they found it difficult to feel part of, or to succeed in, professional hockey (TSN, 1991).

Patterns of differential treatment based on race have been documented in various professional sports. The Centre for the Study of Sport at Northeastern University, for example, has provided a racial report card for several years on discrimination within the various professional sports leagues operating in North America. They report on progress in the elimination of

BOX 8.1 FEDERAL GOVERNMENT APPROACHES TOWARDS NATIVE SPORT IN CANADA: CONTINUITIES AND CHANGES, 1972–2002

The federal government rationale for funding Aboriginal sport has remained consistent throughout the past 30 years, since Sport Canada first funded the Native Sport and Recreation Program in 1972. Their hope is to prepare native peoples for success in mainstream sporting opportunities. The government identified Aboriginal sport in Canada as a concern because of the marginalized status of First Nations athletes within the Canadian sport system. They have also been prompted to act when the success of prominent aboriginal athletes, such as Sharon and Shirley Firth, Alwyn Morris, and Angela Chalmers, fostered an interest in the potential of Aboriginal sport talent more generally. Recently, potential benefits through health care savings, reduced numbers of youth at risk, and economic benefits from international competitions such as the North American Indigenous Games (NAIG) have also been cited as a rationale for their involvement in, and funding of, Aboriginal sport.

Aboriginal sport organizations have likewise remained consistent in their rationale. They wish to create a system more aligned with Aboriginal values, as seen by the recent creation of National Coaching Certification Program (NCCP) coaching units on racism, holistic approaches to sport, and traditional foods. They are fostering all-Aboriginal teams and competitions that remain under Aboriginal control and represent Aboriginal peoples in their preferred manner, such as the Iroquois Nationals in lacrosse and Team Indigenous in hockey. They have thus increasingly developed Aboriginal sport based on a belief in their separate nationhood. However, there has been an increased willingness by Aboriginal sport volunteers to work within the mainstream sport system. Examples include joint involvement in the NCCP and in elite athlete development, and the administration of the NAIG in conjunction with provincial and territorial sport departments.

The federal government and Aboriginal sport organizations continue, however, to struggle over differing perspectives on some fundamental issues. For example, should aboriginal sporting events, such as the NAIG, be organized by nation or by province and territory? Can Aboriginal values, such as a holistic approach toward life, be incorporated into elite sport opportunities? What activities (i.e., traditional or mainstream) should be promoted by Aboriginal sport organizations? How much interplay should there be between the Aboriginal and mainstream sport systems, and what forms should it take (e.g., the placement of Team Indigenous with the Assembly of First Nations versus the Aboriginal Sport Circle, the relative value of segregated versus mainstream approaches toward Aboriginal sport)? These and other contentious questions continue to illustrate the difficulties faced by Aboriginal sport organizers as they try to carve out a unique approach toward sport within a set of structures that some have termed a global sport monoculture. Governments—federal, provincial, and territorial—likewise struggle with these questions, as they become more intertwined with the Aboriginal sport system. Clearly, Aboriginal participants are "getting into the mainstream just like everyone else," but they continue to try to do this on their own terms.

discrimination, both among the players and in the administration of sport. In Canada, research has focused more on ethnicity than race. The discriminatory treatment of French Canadians in the National Hockey League (NHL) has been explored in the areas of salary discrimination, entry discrimination, underrepresentation at certain positions or "stacking," and underrepresentation on certain teams (Longley, 2000). For example, Longley (2000) completed a study that looked at all French Canadians playing in English Canada or the United States on NHL teams from 1943 to 1998. His analysis identified an underrepresentation of French Canadian players on English Canadian versus U.S. teams. After discounting many other explanations, Longley provides support for the thesis that French–English tensions may lead English Canadian teams to discriminate against French Canadian players. This explanation was strengthened when the degree of underrepresentation in English Canadian teams was shown to be greater during seasons when sovereignist political threats in Quebec were highest.

Lavoie (1989), researching player positions in the NHL, highlighted how francophones were more numerous in the goalie and forward positions, while rarely playing as defencemen. He argued that discrimination against francophone defencemen stems from the more subjective nature of that position. He pointed to the primarily anglophone club management, who would prefer anglophone players when other talents were equal, and argued the Quebec-based teams likewise prefer francophone players (Hall et al., 1991). Lavoie has also documented entry discrimination against francophone players, as evidenced by their underestimation in draft position relative to their future offensive performance. In an examination of veteran players during the 1993–94 season, for example, he found the French Canadian players suffered from entry discrimination at the time of the draft. Although the two teams within Quebec did not discriminate against English Canadian players, the American teams did discriminate against French Canadians (Lavoie, 2003). All these studies point to the possibility of systemic discrimination, based on ethnicity, in the NHL.

Claims of discrimination in the Canadian Football League have focused on a different factor: nationality. As early as 1973, research suggested that Canadians in the CFL were stacked primarily on defence, and in supporting and reactive positions (Ball, 1973, cited in Hall et al., 1991). Meanwhile, American imports were placed in the more desirable positions, such as quarterback. In 1979, Jamie Bone, a former Canadian university quarterback, unsuccessfully tried out for the Hamilton Tiger-Cats. He subsequently complained to the Human Rights Commission that the CFL's designated import rule discriminated against him on the grounds of national or ethnic origin because it prevented Canadians from being hired to play quarterback. The Commission concluded

> *that it was always in a team's best interest to select the most talented quarterback regardless of his national origin, and that although a particular CFL coach may mistakenly perceive the designated import rule to favour hiring imports to play that position, the rule itself does not.* (Hall et al., 1991, p. 178)

Whitestream sport, then, provides varying opportunities for athletes depending on their race. This differential treatment can be overt, such as racial slurs that make participation uncomfortable for those groups. Discriminatory treatment is also, at times, built into the existing system of sport. In Canada, for example, francophones experience various types of discrimination in professional hockey, demonstrating that ethnicity, as well as race, has an impact on sporting opportunities. Marginalized groups have thus had to look elsewhere for alternative sport opportunities—or to create some themselves.

Race-Structured Sport Systems

Opportunities for sport, created by and for racial groups outside mainstream society, have a long history in Canada. When Aboriginal or Black athletes were banned from whitestream sport, they often countered with the creation of their own leagues and competitions, limited to participants from a specified racial background. This provided organizers with the opportunity to assign their own meaning to sport and to develop traditions in keeping with Aboriginal, or Black, or Asian cultural understandings. And it created opportunities for marginalized groups to play sport when they did not have that chance in the mainstream sport system.

An example of a race-structured sporting event would be the North American Indigenous Games, first held in 1990 in Edmonton. These international Games, restricted to those of verifiable Aboriginal ancestry, "stress fun and participation while encouraging our youth to strive for excellence" (AS/RA of British Columbia, 1995). The Games comprised solely mainstream sports, because the intent was to provide a stepping-stone to national and international level sport competitions; however, the cultural program showcased various traditional games and dances. The 2002 Games, held in Winnipeg, had over 6000 participants celebrating Aboriginal culture, as well as competing in sporting events organized by Aboriginal sports organizations.

Through this event, people involved in Aboriginal sports such as athletes, coaches, and organizers experience more "power" in sport than is found in the whitestream system—they are in charge of its structure, its practices and meanings, and the traditions they will continue into the future. Unfortunately, these race-structured opportunities rarely qualify for the kinds of financial and material rewards given to "legitimate," whitestream sport, although the Canadian government has recently acknowledged the presence of the all-Aboriginal sport system in Canada through federal policy and funding (see Box 8.1).

People sometimes attach the term "reverse racism" to situations where normally privileged individuals—usually Caucasians—are excluded from opportunities on the basis of race. For example, non-Aboriginal people cannot compete in the North American Indigenous Games, even though Aboriginal athletes can theoretically compete in mainstream sporting events. As the Charter of Rights and Freedoms, section 15(2) directs, however, efforts to address "the conditions of disadvantaged individuals or groups including those that are disadvantaged because of race" are seen as a necessary part of providing equality rights, because such efforts are required to help right the imbalance created by unequal privilege in the first instance. This section on racism in sport has documented the individual and institutionalized racism present in whitestream sport in Canada. In order to ensure that all Canadians, regardless of race, have opportunities to find meaningful participation in sport, race-structured sporting opportunities are currently needed to ensure that the sport system, broadly, in Canada provides for the needs of all Canadians. Until whitestream sport broadens and becomes truly inclusive, alternative race-structured opportunities should be celebrated and supported as part of the Canadian sport system. In this way, the institution of sport becomes a more welcoming practice reflective of the cultural meanings and traditions of all Canadians, regardless of race.

ETHNICITY, SPORT, AND LEISURE IN CANADA

The Way We Think about Leisure and Sport

Sport participation and the enjoyment of spectator sports are some of the most popular leisure activities for Canadians. Researchers who study the concept of leisure activity have contributed a great deal to our understanding of the ways in which people spend their free time and about the aspects of life that provide people with a sense of enjoyment, fulfilment, relaxation, and fun. These concepts characterize what leisure means to North Americans and to people throughout the western world. For example, their work helps us understand aspects of family leisure such as how motherhood and family responsibilities affect women's ability to structure leisure and how women's leisure is different from men's leisure (Bialeschki & Michener, 1994; Hunter & Whitson, 1992; Shaw, 1992, 1997; Wearing, 1998). Social psychologists have explored what motivates our choice of leisure pursuits and the notion of leisure constraints, a literature that helps us understand that leisure choice is not universal and overcoming the barriers one faces in attaining leisure may be quite difficult but not impossible (Iso-Ahola, 1999; Jackson, Crawford, & Godbey, 1993; Mannell, 1999). Researchers have also looked at the work–leisure dichotomy and have tried to make sense of why some people forgo leisure for workaholic lifestyles while others, who experience unemployment or underemployment, crave the structure, routine, and economic stability of a regular job that provides them with the financial freedom to pursue leisure even though they have less time (Reid, 1995; Schor, 1992). By focusing on developmental phases in the life cycle, other researchers have explored how, with each stage of life from childhood through retirement, we experience both challenges and opportunities for leisure that change with our responsibilities, economic situation, and social relationships (Freysinger, 1995; Kelly, 1993). Through this work we have developed a rather comprehensive understanding of leisure, which from the perspective of many North Americans means the way we spend our free time and the activity we do that contributes to our sense of fulfilment, relaxation, and enjoyment. But most of the research was developed from studies of people who are white and whose ancestors originated in western European countries and, as such, might not accurately reflect the ways in which leisure is meaningful for people who identify with minority ethnic cultures in this country.

If we are to understand leisure preferences of minority ethnic people it is important that we understand what ethnicity is and how it affects the choices one makes and what a person values in life. When we think about ethnicity, we are referring not just to the physical characteristics that are immediately evident when we look at someone, like their skin and eye colour, but also to their behavioural characteristics that make them who they are. Ethnicity takes into account a person's religious practices, their clothing, their language or accented English, the food they eat, and other behaviours they value as a result of their cultural heritage. In the same way that race has social significance in our society, so does ethnicity. People who identify with others who share their same ethnicity often encounter unequal treatment or unequal access to resources that are taken for granted by dominant-group Canadians. Some minority ethnic people assume the behaviours and values of the dominant groups as they become accustomed to life in Canada. This process is referred to as assimilation (Li, 1990). Others sustain some and at times most of their traditional cultural practices. The degree to which people assimilate into the dominant or host society contributes to how they identify themselves and to how they are identified by others. Understanding how ethnicity influences leisure choices and leisure preferences is essential if we are to understand the meaning of sport for ethnic minority people in Canada.

In focusing their attention on issues of race, ethnicity, and leisure of minorities, researchers have determined that leisure has different meanings for some minority ethnic groups in North America (Allison, 1988; Floyd, 1998; Gramann & Allison, 1999; Stodolska and Jackson, 1998; Washburn, 1978). In trying to explain the differences between the leisure of minority people and those who identify with dominant groups, they have relied primarily on two theoretical perspectives: marginality theory and ethnicity theory. Marginality theory suggests that the differences in participation are due to the poverty experienced by many minority racial and ethnic people, a function of the discrimination they face in accessing training and education, as well as jobs. Therefore, under-participation in activities like sport is due to their marginalization in society. This perspective might explain why some Canadians do not choose the same opportunities for leisure as the majority white population but it falls short when applied to the vast majority of immigrants who are not marginalized by poverty. In fact, a recent study indicates that almost one-third of immigrant families arriving in Canada start their lives in poverty compared to 13.2% of Canadian families, but once they adapt to their new lives incomes for the average immigrant family exceed that of the average Canadian-born family (Beiser, Hou, Hyman, & Tousingant, 1998). Newly arrived immigrant families may not have access to the same opportunities for leisure as the Canadian norm but once settled, marginality as a result of poverty is not necessarily a factor preventing their participation in leisure activity.

Ethnicity theory is based on Washburn's (1978) thesis that differences in leisure between dominant and minority populations are the result of variations in the value systems and social norms of the minority groups. This approach suggests that ethnic subgroups interact with dominant cultural groups for school, jobs, and commerce and when needs cannot be met within the subgroup. However, many minorities maintain their distinct cultural identity through family and community ties, both of which are central to leisure. Using this approach, theorists compare the ways in which the leisure of minority people is like the leisure experience of dominant groups. Problematic here is that the leisure of the white, Eurocentric majority is held as the norm and minority people are considered as "others" for the sake of comparisons. This approach fails to explore the unique opportunities for leisure evident in minority cultural groups as a result of their cultural heritage.

With the passing of the Multiculturalism Act of 1988, Canada officially declared its support for cultural freedom of minority people. The term "cultural pluralism," first introduced in 1915 by Kallen, refers to the approach our country takes with regard to receiving and welcoming immigrants. It means that in Canada, we as hosts support newcomers to preserve their cultural identity if they choose to do so (Glazer, 1970). Our approach differs from that of our neighbours to the south. In the United States, immigrants are expected to shed their unique cultural practices and adopt new ones based on the values and beliefs of the host country, and as a result of this process of assimilation they will contribute to building a better nation. This second approach is commonly referred to as the "melting pot" perspective (Glazer, 1970). Cultural pluralism, on the other hand, recognizes that for many newcomers, meaningful experience incorporates "stubborn chunks" of cultural practice and preference and is "more like a chowder than a melting pot" (Bhabha, 1994, p. 219). Some aspects of life do change with immersion in the host culture. But other "chunks" remain intact and provide the basis on which some minority people create cultures "in-between" that of the dominant majority and the cultures known to the migrant in their own homeland (Bhabha, 1994; Hollingshead, 1998). As a result of our legislation, Canadians officially support physical cultural practices like sport, dance, music, and religious expressions that are meaningful to people of all minority cultural groups and are meaningful to the experience of leisure. However, we are only beginning to understand the meaning of leisure from the perspective of immigrant groups and the challenges they face related to discrimination, racism, and the indifference of many dominant-group Canadians toward their physical cultural practices.

New Canadians and Leisure

Many languages have no words for the concept of leisure, so it is reasonable to expect that some newcomers to Canada, whose first language is not English or French, will not understand what we mean when we talk about leisure. As well, the value often associated with free time and private time to do the things we like, such as sports, is not universally understood or valued. Evident in a 1991–92 study that explored the meaning of leisure in the lives of a group of women who were immigrants from India and Pakistan was the sense that North American leisure means something different to minority people (Tirone & Shaw, 1997). The women described how for them family was central to their happiness and their ability to relax and enjoy life. While the same is true for many North American women, it is as common in North America for women to want a break from the demands of their families and to value the time they have for their own experience or what they know as leisure. For example, Canadian women with young children may not have a great deal of time to themselves to pursue their own activity and for relaxation, but they do attempt to structure their lives in ways that allow some time for themselves. If they fail to achieve that time, they miss it (Wearing, 1998). The South Asian women saw life differently. For them, the aspects of life that we in North America associate with leisure, such as gaining a sense of satisfaction, enjoyment, and fulfilment, are evident when they are involved with their husbands, children, and even their extended family in their homes. The women were reluctant to go to adult-only social gatherings because they resented North American traditions that place priority on privacy, and they perceived North Americans as selfish for wanting leisure time to be alone or with friends outside the family (Tirone & Shaw, 1997). Canadians may find it difficult to understand how anyone could interpret their desire for free time at the end of a day as selfish. As well, it is difficult for most Canadians to comprehend that someone would not value or actively pursue opportunities to develop skills that will afford them opportunities for personal fulfilment. But the women placed their families first and foremost in their lives, and family was their leisure.

The South Asian women structured their lives around their families and hoped their children would do the same when they grow up. They were particularly concerned that by raising their children in Canada, where children have tremendous freedom to pursue activities outside the home and where people value time away from the family, their children would learn to be selfish. Their concerns had a great deal to do with the importance of sport in Canadian society and how within the context of dominant cultural groups in Canada, it is quite normal for young people to spend a great deal of time away from their family homes because of their involvement in sport. In Canada, leisure is defined as the opportunity to be free to do what one wants and is valued for how it contributes to personal fulfilment and personal goal attainment. In much of our social interactions, Canadians put a high priority on individualism, autonomy, and independence and tend to favour the protection of individual rights over the rights of the collective (Pedlar, 1996). On the other hand, many minority ethnic people identify with cultures that place priority on the collective family and community, as is evident in the lives of the South Asian participants in the two studies described here. For them, leisure is often meaningful when it involves interactions with family members and possibly with members of the minority community. That is why leisure, such as sport participation, that takes the young people away from their families, is considered to be self-serving and is unacceptable to those who value the group more than the individual. In order for dominant-group Canadians to understand the place and meaning of leisure for new Canadians, it is important to gain an appreciation for the value individuals and groups associate with sustaining their cultural traditions and ensuring the maintenance of the collective culture.

The Children of Immigrants

A second study focused on the leisure of 15 teenagers and young adults who are the children of immigrants from India, Pakistan, and Bangladesh and who lived in several cities and small towns in Ontario (Tirone, 1999–2000; Tirone & Pedlar, 2000). These Hindu, Sikh, Muslim, and Christian young people attended Canadian high schools where they became well acquainted with friends who had a great deal of freedom to pursue leisure. The South Asian teens were attracted to the activities most Canadians consider to be normal teenage activity: taking part in sports, community recreation, school band practice and dances, and just hanging out with friends. But their parents preferred that they be involved in activity with the family and with friends who were also South Asian, so they experienced much of their involvement in sports through the South Asian social and athletic clubs to which they and their parents belonged. As well, it was common for them to attend sports night with their parents and with families of other South Asian teens who frequently rented gym space at schools and recreation facilities. Several of the participants reflected back on their early school years with some regret that they had little autonomy in their lives and consequently little opportunity to join activities like sports and recreational activities with their friends, because these occurred outside the home and beyond the control of their parents. Their parents, who were concerned that sports and recreation would take them away from their studies, often prohibited their athletically inclined children from participating in sport and physical activity unless it was for fun. In spite of their regrets and sadness over their restricted leisure, the young people had a deep-rooted respect and genuine appreciation for their families and for their rich traditional cultures. Their commitment to sustaining traditional cultural practices had much to do with how traditions enriched their leisure.

All the participants in the second study were involved in their churches or cultural associations and treasured their traditional roots, which included learning traditional languages, cooking and eating traditional foods, wearing traditional clothing, and practising minority religions. In comparing themselves to some of their peers who did not know about their family's roots and cultural heritage, they felt privileged. They also explained the difficulties they encountered when peers, teachers, and coaches had little understanding of or appreciation for their desire to adhere to their traditions. For example, one male is a member of the Sikh religion and has worn a turban since he was in Grade 4. While it was not a problem for him, he was aware of other Sikh teens who stopped wearing turbans as a result of the teasing they experienced and the potential for racially motivated conflicts they preferred to avoid.

The women participants in the study were interested in sport participation, but for the Muslim women who wore traditional clothing, it was problematic if they were required to wear shorts or tight-fitting clothing. Rather than compromise their commitment to religions that stipulate they wear loose-fitting clothing and a head scarf (*hijab*) they preferred to not participate. Also problematic for the women is that some sports facilities do not provide the privacy they require for their activity. For example, Muslim women who adhere to traditional cultural practices require complete seclusion from being observed by anyone outside their group for swimming. In recognizing their need for privacy, several recreation facilities in the country provide window shades and close the galleries in order for the women to have the opportunity to swim.

Racism and Indifference

Several of the participants in the studies described in this section wore traditional clothing; some of the young men wore turbans, and the women wore *lengas* and a *salwar camise*, a long tunic worn over loose-fitting pants. That means they were identifiable as minorities by their skin colour and by the way they dress. As well, many were differentiated from their dominant-group peers by their adherence to religious traditions, such as the observance of Ramadan, which occurs for a period of one month each year in the ninth month of the Muslim calendar. During the month of Ramadan, Muslims fast from sunup until sundown and participate with family and friends in prayer. For the young people who were devoted to Islam, it was essential that they observed the fasting, and consequently during Ramadan it was very difficult for those who were athletes to continue to train or to participate in competitions. For example, one young male participant described how as a wrestler competing for a provincial championship, he was not given an opportunity for a break between matches. Since he was fasting and had not eaten any food that day, he was weak and tired and did not win the meet, but placed second in the competition. This young Muslim student faced considerable health risks by not letting his coaches know that he was fasting. Had he disclosed to his coaches his situation with regard to the Ramadan fasting, he would most likely have found the organizers and coaches willing to accommodate his needs somehow. However this participant, and many others in the study, were reluctant to discuss their specific religious requirements because of the discrimination and racism they often faced.

The most unsettling finding of the study of minority ethnic youth was that all the participants had at one time or another encountered overt acts of racism that hindered participation in activities such as sports, physical activity, and recreation. Name-calling was the most frequent form of racism they encountered and it was most evident during early school years. The young people described incidents at summer camp, during school sports, and as part of competitive teams. Equally disconcerting was the fact that when asked how the organizers, coaches, and leaders of the activities responded when name-calling occurred, no participants could recall a single intervention made on their behalf by a teacher or a leader. The young people were on their own to handle the racist remarks without the assistance or intervention of an adult. One participant described how he was expelled from school as a result of a physical fight he had after being called a racist name, while the other participant in the fight did not suffer the same consequences.

People of Many Cultures: What It Means for Sport

Our understanding of leisure for minority ethnic people in Canada may be enhanced if we reflect on how minority people in Canada are like the "stubborn chunks" of the chowder pot

BOX 8.2 INDO-CANADIAN TEENS, SPORT, AND LEISURE

The following quotes were provided by the participants in two studies of Canadians who identify with the cultures of India, Pakistan, and Bangladesh as they described their experience of sport and other leisure activities:

Re: Persuading parents to let her "hang out with friends":

I would try to find a Gujarati word that would fit. And I could never find one.... They have a word, "Rakhardvu," and that kind of means to hang out.... Now my parents understand. (laughs). "Where you going?" Rakhardvu. Yeah, I'm going to hang out. Yeah, even my mother didn't know what it meant. When I first started saying it she said, "What does it mean?" It means hanging out. So she said, "Oh okay."

Re: Parents are reluctant to attend social functions without their children:

I hate to leave the kids behind but we have to because a lot of the times they don't include kids. The Christmas dances are the same thing. We go to the Christmas dances and kids are left behind.

Re: Restricting participation in sports:

Say you are a really good athlete, like my brother. Actually myself too when I was younger. We had the chance of going on and becoming [skilled]. And our parents said, "No." Once they found out we were good at something, they took us out of it right away. They didn't want us [in it], and they still say this. They don't want us to put our mind to sports and not to school. They wanted 90% school and 10% sports.

Re: Traditional clothing:

When we were really young it was hard for a lot of kids in elementary school. Because that is when you really get picked on, if you do [wear a turban]. I know some kids who have had a real problem with it and they have cut their hair because they can't take the teasing.

Re: Discrimination and indifference:

I remember being called all the racial things you can ever imagine....

See I have been lucky. Whenever I have played, whether it was soccer or baseball, I guess a lot of it is, you have to prove yourself. Once you prove yourself, you are fine. If you don't prove yourself—if she is playing tennis and she is really just learning for the first time, and she can't even hit the ball—well that is like a double whammy for her. But if she can smash that ball down the end line, they will look at her in a different light.

Question: But does she have to be even better than normal, because she is not White?

Answer: Yes. So that is where the racism comes in. So I have been lucky because when people have seen me play, I guess I'm pretty quick. And I guess that would be a big point of it.... But I have been lucky. Like I said, I have been able to hold my end.... I think the only part now, is because I feel at times that I can't hold my end with the [name of province] team, that I feel a little less... [pause]

Question: Is it because they are so much better than you are?

Answer: I think a bit of it does. But a bit of it is because I am the only brown person there too.

Re: Pride in one's heritage:

There is a difference. A lot of Caucasians who are born here don't even know what their background is, their heritage. They don't know if they are German or Italian. And I think a lot of them do regret that. Because what they have is the Canadian culture. They don't have a culture. All it is is hockey games and beer. Hockey is the religion.

Well, I don't want to be like everyone else. I am glad that I have another language besides French and English that I can communicate to people in. I am proud of that. And I am also glad that I have another religion other than Christianity, or whatever. Which is the norm in Canada. It puts me apart from everyone else.

in Bhabha's metaphor. Rather than assimilating in their leisure, minority Canadians will quite likely continue to celebrate the cultural practices that are meaningful to them, and they will also adopt some practices from the culture of the dominant groups around them. Our understanding of what is meaningful in the practices that people choose as part of their leisure is further complicated because many Canadians identify with several minority cultures as well as with the dominant majority culture. This is evident in the 1996 Census, in which more than 35% of Canadians indicated that their ancestors belonged to more than one ethnic or cultural group. Of those reporting that their ancestors were of a single origin, 29% said their ancestors originated in countries outside of Britain, France, and Europe (Statistics Canada, 1998).

Many ethnic minority families are adamant that their children should pursue an advanced education well beyond high school. They also have a tendency to restrict activities that they perceive to be in conflict with this goal. So, like the young people in the study described here, other immigrant children may not be allowed to participate in extracurricular sports or on teams even if they are promising athletes. In communities that have attracted many minority families, this trend will have serious implications for the development of competitive sports in the future.

Immigrant families today tend to be more secure economically than were immigrant families in years gone by. The relative affluence of immigrants who are established in Canada and the collective nature of many immigrant groups affords them the ability to create social clubs, which sponsor recreation and sports activities. We will likely see tremendous growth in these clubs, which are especially important venues for participation and which shield the participant from the discrimination and racism they may encounter in mainstream activities (Stodolska & Jackson, 1998).

When people who identify with the dominant white majority in Canada try to make sense of leisure for those who identify with minority cultures, they do so from their own value perspective. Canadians value leisure time and spaces for achieving personal goals. We value the time we have for ourselves and our independence, which often takes us away from our immediate families and away from those we grew up with. We also value that distance as a sign of personal autonomy, often associated with maturity and leadership. So it is no wonder we find it difficult to understand the desire of the people in the studies mentioned earlier to maintain close ties with their immediate and extended families. We also question the young people in their teens who choose to wear traditional clothing that sets them apart from other Canadian teens, because it not only demonstrates their connection and membership with a minority cultural group but it is also an overt symbol of their religion. Few white Canadians, other than clergy members, intentionally distinguish themselves through their clothing as members of religious groups. Once Canadians gain an understanding of the meaning and importance of collective well-being for ethnic minorities, we will be able to understand a bit better that what is meaningful in leisure for minority people is different from that of dominant-group Canadians. As minority people grow in number and as people from more diverse cultures migrate to Canada, we will hopefully see leisure and sport opportunities develop in ways that allow minority youth an opportunity to enjoy the activity but also to include family members in the experience. For example, more sport associations are likely to develop within minority communities as a way to promote activity and to sustain cultural involvement in that activity. The new way of doing sport, for these Canadians, will benefit the collective well-being of the group, and thus ultimately the well-being offered by sport to all Canadians.

CONCLUSIONS

Race and ethnicity are aspects of our heritage that take on social meaning in Canadian society. These constructed meanings become naturalized each time we "do" them in accordance with the dominant beliefs around us. Caucasians of European descent in Canada have been the most privileged in sport, with those from other racial backgrounds often discriminated against both overtly and through systemic racism. Whitestream sport has emerged, legitimizing select activities such as Olympic sports, and marginalizing other activities that do not fit within such understandings. Segregated sporting opportunities have likewise emerged, enabling organizers and participants from marginalized groups to structure their own experiences in sport in ways that foster pride in their cultural heritage, while giving them opportunities to play that are not available otherwise. Legitimizing these sporting opportunities, and the alternative ethnic practices preferred by immigrants and their descendants, takes us one step further toward creating a sport system that is representative of all individuals in Canada.

Critical Thinking Questions

1. If you encounter children from a minority ethnic family—identifiable from their distinct clothing and accents—what are some of the questions you might ask them to determine if there are factors that may prevent or restrict their participation in sport or physical activity? If you determine that they do indeed have special needs, how might you facilitate their involvement in sports or physical activity?
2. What are two ways that a coach, teacher, or sports administrator might respond to an incident of overt racism such as name-calling, directed at a teenager in a basketball program?
3. How do you "do race" in your life? In sport?
4. Write about an incident where the social meanings attached to race influenced your life, by either privileging you or providing a barrier to opportunities you wished to experience.

5. Write a code of conduct for sport that would align it with the Canadian Charter of Rights and Freedoms.
6. How do race-structured sporting events address discrimination in mainstream sport?
7. Outline examples of how sporting performances can provide opportunities for decreasing racial distinctions and for increasing racial distinctions.

Suggested Readings

Cosentino, F. (1998). *Afros, Aboriginals and amateur sport in pre World War One Canada*. Canada's Ethnic Group Series, Booklet No. 26. Ottawa: The Canadian Historical Society.

Denis, C. (1997). *We are not you: First Nations and Canadian modernity*. Peterborough, Ont.: Broadview Press.

Dimeo, P. (2002). Colonial bodies, colonial sport. "Martial" Punjabis, "effeminate" Bengalis and the development of Indian football. *International Journal of the History of Sport*, 19, 72–90.

Jones, R.L. (2002). The black experience within English semiprofessional soccer. *Journal of Sport and Social Issues*, 26, 47–65.

Paraschak, V. (1999). Doing race, doing gender: First Nations, "sport," and gender relations. In P. White & K. Young (Eds.), *Sport and gender in Canada*. Don Mills, Ont.: Oxford University Press, 153–169.

Paraschak, V. (1997). Variations in race relations: Sporting events for Native peoples in Canada. *Sociology of Sport Journal*, 14, 1–21.

Paraschak, V. (1996). Racialized spaces: Cultural regulation, Aboriginal agency and powwows. *Avante*, 2, 7–18.

Spence, C. (1999). *The skin I'm in: Racism, sports and education*. Halifax: Fernwood.

Tirone, S. (1999–2000). Racism, indifference, and the leisure experience of South Asian Canadian teens. *Leisure/Loisir*, 24, 89–114.

Wilson, B. (1999). "Cool pose" incorporated: The marketing of black masculinity in Canadian NBA coverage. In P. White & K. Young (Eds.), *Sport and gender in Canada*. Don Mills, Ont.: Oxford University Press, 232–253.

Web Links

Aboriginal Sport Circle
http://www.aboriginalsportcircle.ca
The federally funded national organization overseeing Aboriginal sport in Canada.

Ancient Future
http://www.ancient-future.com/index.html
New cross-cultural music and dance.

Canadian Charter of Rights and Freedoms
http://laws.justice.gc.ca/en/charter/
Contains the entire text of the Canadian Charter of Rights and Freedoms.

Field Hockey
http://www.fieldhockey.com/
Contains information about the game of field hockey, popular with men and women in many countries outside the United States and Canada.

Lotus Sports Club
http://www.lotussports.com/
Dragon boat racing clubs in western Canada.

Multicultural History Society
http://citd.scar.utoronto.ca/MHSO/conferenceinfo.htm
Information about multiculturalism in Ontario.

The Weekly Voice
http://www.weeklyvoice.com/
A weekly newspaper featuring the news of the Indo-Canadian community.

9

The Economics of Sport

Marc Lavoie and Dave Whitson

PAUL CHIASSON/CP PICTURE ARCHIVE

Former federal Finance Minister Paul Martin and David Dodge, governor of the Bank of Canada, pose with a replica of the new Canadian $5 bill during an unveiling ceremony in Montreal in 2002.

> We can conclude: First, locational attributes, certain league rules, and team success are important elements determining attendance. Second, the major elements in creating locational market power and so increasing the chances of franchise survival, are population and location in Canada.... Finally, the one pervasive element in the empirical analysis is the significance of a Canadian location. [This variable] is simultaneously a proxy for Canadian sporting culture and a talisman for franchise survival.... Everyone recognizes that in Canada, "Hockey is King".
>
> J.C.H Jones and D.G. Ferguson, "Location and Survival in the National Hockey League"

The 1998 quote that opens the chapter, put in perspective, well summarizes the current problems of Canadian major league hockey. Jones (1969) was the first Canadian scholar to tackle the "economics of sport" when he published an article on the National Hockey League (NHL) in the leading *Canadian Journal of Economics*. This highly experienced scholar was thus arguing, less than 15 years ago, that if the National Hockey League ever got into financial trouble, only teams located in the United States would run into difficulties, not those located in Canada. It took only seven years for this prediction to turn out to be mistaken, when the Québec Nordiques left for Denver and became the Colorado Avalanche in 1995. They were followed the next year by the Winnipeg Jets, who moved south to Phoenix.

The ongoing story of the 1990s in Canadian professional sport has been about financial losses, the need for renovated or brand-new facilities, and franchise departures. Early in the next decade, the outlook appears even bleaker: the year 2001 saw the NBA Vancouver Grizzlies depart for Memphis after only five years in the league, while in baseball the Montreal Expos were on the verge of being disbanded or displaced after the 2002 season. In the land where hockey is king, finally, some predict that only the Toronto Maple Leafs are safe and that even the fabled Montreal Canadiens could be transferred to the United States.

Since the early 1990s, Canada's sports pages have been filled with articles dealing with the business of sport. In the past, sports reporters and columnists were primarily concerned with players' performances, statistics, team gossip, and human interest stories. Occasionally, there would be some mention of an athlete playing the option year of his contract. Today, good sports journalists need to understand the economics of professional sports *as a business*. If they are to explain to their readers the intricacies of trades and the manager's likely motivations, reporters must have knowledge of team budgets, the length and structure of individual players' contracts, and the collective agreement.

In short, the days of sport's innocence—when the story was about players' dreams, historic rivalries, and record-breaking accomplishments—are gone. Sport at the professional level is now very much a business. At one level, this has always been the case (see Gruneau & Whitson, 1993, for a fuller development of this argument). Today, however, the money at stake has multiplied exponentially, so that understanding struggles over money has become essential to understanding how the sports themselves are changing, and why Canada's place is at risk.

This chapter is built on one agenda: to explain the changing economics of North American professional sports and the effects of these changes on the fortunes of Canadian teams in the "major leagues" since the 1990s. Because most of the academic research on the economics of sports, both at the theoretical level and in data gathering, actually deals with the economics of *team* sports, namely the four North American major sports—baseball, basketball, football, and hockey—major league professional team sport will be the focus of the chapter. As a result, minor leagues (such as the Canadian Football League), minor pro sports (such as North American soccer), and amateur sports will be left on the sidelines. Finally, we will devote more space to the economics of NHL hockey, since the NHL has been such an important part of Canadian popular culture since the 1930s. However, developments in other "major" leagues—the National Basketball Association (NBA), the National Football League (NFL), and Major League Baseball (MLB)—will also be considered.

The discussion that follows begins by examining the dramatic growth of the money to be made in professional sports and looking at the remarkable evolution of salaries, revenues, and franchise values since the 1950s. It then proceeds to examine questions of competitive disparity: roughly, whether teams in "small markets" can afford to be competitive on the field. Finally, we will look at the particular challenges faced by Canadian-based teams and briefly consider some of the questions of public policy that are raised when Canadian teams request tax relief or other forms of public subsidy.

SALARY EVOLUTION

The most visible, and perhaps controversial, change in the world of professional team sports is the evolution of players' salaries. This is depicted for all four major sports, from 1950 onwards, in Table 9.1. The data are presented in current American dollars, even for the NHL, since virtually all salaries there are now paid in American dollars. Several features are noticeable. First, it should be noted that salary explosions in the various leagues do not necessarily occur in step. This implies that both external and internal factors—where internal means internal to the particular league or the sport—explain the evolution of salaries. In hockey, for instance, it is said that the move of Wayne Gretzky to Los Angeles in 1988, and the contract that he obtained there, which doubled his salary, as well as the $3-million contract that Eric Lindros obtained as a rookie in 1992, were key internal factors in triggering salary inflation in the 1990s. So, too, was the decision of hockey players to make their salaries public information in the summer of 1989. External factors, conversely, refer to factors—such as television, and changes in the legal status of professional athletes—that have led to extraordinary increases in salaries in *all* team sports. Several such factors are discussed briefly below.

Inflation

Over the last 10 years, the average salary in all four major leagues has at least tripled in size. Over a 50-year period, moreover, the salaries of hockey players have been multiplied by a factor of 300, no less! Now, of course, part of this increase is attributable to generalized price inflation. As an approximation, the level of the consumer price index (CPI) has incurred a (slightly more than) tenfold multiple in the United States (and in Canada) over the last 50 years, as a result of continuous price inflation. This implies that the *real* salaries of hockey players have been multiplied by a factor of 30 over that span of time.

Yet if we compare the average salary of a hockey player with that of an ordinary employee in a Canadian firm, we can see that something more than inflation is going on here. Lavoie (1997, p. 190) has shown that in the 1950s, the salary of the average NHL hockey player was only 2.5 times the salary of the average Canadian employee. NHL hockey players, despite their hero status, had a lifestyle that was not that different, financially, from that of the average hockey fan. Before the arrival of the rival World Hockey Association (WHA) in 1972, this ratio moved up gradually to 4.5, but with the competition for players provided by the WHA, the ratio reached 8.5 by 1979. In the 1980s, with the WHA dissolved and some of its teams merged into the NHL, this ratio oscillated between 8 and 10 while team owners took advantage of their regained monopoly status—being the sole supplier of major league hockey. However, starting with the 1990–91 season, salaries have almost continuously skyrocketed. The 2001–02 average salary of NHL hockey players, which

TABLE 9.1 Average Salaries of Players, MLB, NBA, NFL, NHL, 1950–2000, in Current American Dollars, with Ratios with Respect to Hockey Salaries

	Baseball		Basketball		Football		Hockey
Year	Salary $	Ratio	Salary $	Ratio	Salary $	Ratio	Salary $
1949–51	13 300	2.66			8000	1.6	5000
1956–57	14 500	1.81			9200	1.15	8000
1967	19 000	0.95	20 000	1	25 000	1.2	20 000
1970	29 000	1.16	40 000	1.6	34 500	1.38	25 000
1972	34 000	0.92	90 000	2.43	35 000	0.95	37 000
1975	46 000	0.62			42 000	0.57	74 000
1976	51 500		140 000				86000
1977	76 000	0.84	143 000	1.58	55 300	0.61	90 000
1979	113 000	1.12	173 000	1.71			101 000
1980	143 000	1.3	190 000	1.73	69 000	0.63	110 000
1981	185 000	1.68	218 000	1.98			110 000
1982	242 000	2.01	246 000	2.05	90 500	0.75	120 000
1983	289 000	2.31	275 000	2.2	112 000	0.9	125 000
1984	330 000	2.46	340 000	2.54	158 000	1.18	134 000
1985	371 000	2.61	380 000	2.67	190 000	1.34	142 000
1986	412 000	2.74	440 000	2.84	203 000	1.31	155 000
1987	412 000	2.56	510 000	2.96	230 000	1.34	172 000
1988	440 000	2.44			250 000	1.32	180 000
1989	500 000	2.52			320 000	1.61	198 000
1990	600 000	2.43	824 000	3.33	365 000	1.47	247 500
1991	850 000	2.7	1 156 000	3.68	425 000	1.34	314 000
1992	1 028 000	2.46			492 000	1.19	417 000
1993	1 076 000	1.98	1 250 000	2.3	683 000	1.26	543 000
1994	1 168 000	1.71	1 500 000	2.2	636 000	0.94	680 000
1995	1 110 000	1.46	1 600 000	2.1	714 000	0.94	760 000
1996	1 120 000	1.29	2 200 000	2.54	795 000	0.92	866 000
1997	1 336 000	1.15	2 160 000	1.85	725000	0.63	1 160 000
1998	1 398 000	1.05	2 400 000	1.79	1 137 000	0.84	1 339 000
1999	1 568 000	1.08	2 947 000	2.02	1 081 000	0.72	1 456 000
2000	1 895 000	1.28	3 241 000	2.18	1 169 000	0.79	1 484 000
2001	2 139 000	1.27	3 484 000	2.06			1 688 000

The 2.66 ratio in the first row shown under Baseball indicates that in 1950, baseball players earned salaries that were 2.66 times greater than that of hockey players.

Source: Updated from Marc Lavoie (1997). *Avantage numérique: L'argent et la Ligue nationale de hockey*. Hull: Vents d'Ouest, 186.

exceeds $2.7 million Cdn., is now nearly 80 times that of the average Canadian employee (about $35 000). This was achieved, moreover, in an economic environment where the real incomes of average Canadian families barely grew at all (when taking inflation into account). Whereas minor league players hardly earn $50 000, it is true that the salary of the *median* NHL player (the 375th best-paid player among the 750 NHL players) is only about 66% of the *average* NHL salary (Lavoie 1997, p. 264), due to the megadeals secured by the talented few, and that this ratio is much lower in major league baseball. But even minimum salaries in the major leagues exceed the income of most lawyers or doctors.

Bargaining Evolution

An important part of salary evolution must be attributed to the stronger market power acquired by players and their unions since the late 1960s. Before that, talented players did not have any clue as to how much extra revenue their presence on the field or on the ice was generating. They did not know how much other players earned, and they did not have any agent to represent them at the time of signing their contract. In addition, even if they had an agent, their negotiating power would have been minimal since all players were under the reserve clause.

The reserve clause, a contractual restriction on player mobility that was common to all North American team sports until the late 1960s (until 1975 in baseball), allowed a team to unilaterally renew a player's contract for an extra year, under the same conditions as the previous contract, if the player refused to sign his new contract. Since the reserve clause was also contained in the new contract, professional teams understood the clause to imply that they had perpetual rights over a player, once he had signed his first professional contract. An unhappy player had no choice.

The courts eventually judged the reserve clause to be an unwarranted restriction on labour mobility. Players could play a year without a contract and then offer their services to another team in the league; alternatively, they could jump to some other rival league, when these existed briefly in the 1960s and 1970s (e.g., the American Football League [AFL] and the WHA). This forced professional leagues to enter into bargaining agreements with the unions representing the players. The new bargaining agreements have since incorporated clauses that still restrict the movements of younger players. However, such restrictions are considered legal since they have been freely negotiated by the bargaining representative of the players. In addition, these collective agreements include counter-powers, such as salary arbitration for players who lack freedom of movement. The larger point here, one that is common to all four sports, is that the more favourable conditions under which players can negotiate their salaries with owners help to explain why salaries have grown faster than team revenues.

TEAM REVENUE EVOLUTION

The large increases in salaries experienced since the 1970s would never have been possible without the large increases in revenues that professional sport teams have been able to generate. While the public generally believes that ticket prices are increased because of the high player salaries that have been granted by team owners and their managers, economists argue that salary increases are ultimately based on the larger revenues that the hired players are expected to generate.

Ticket Price Increases

Between 1977 and 2001, ticket prices to major league professional events have increased between 7% and 8% *per year* on the average, for each of the four major sports in North America (ticket prices are drawn from Lavoie [1997, p. 118] and from information released by *Team Marketing Report*). When we realize that the consumer price index in the United States has climbed at an average annual rate of only 4.5% over that period, it is clear there has been a real increase in the willingness of fans to attend baseball, basketball, football, and hockey games featuring the best players in the world. During that period, except for baseball, there has also been a large increase in the number of teams in each league and in the number of seats in the various sports venues. Thus there is no doubt that there has been an extraordinary increase in the demand for top-level professional team sport in North America.

It is true, at the same time, though, that team revenues have not grown as fast as salaries, neither over the last 20 years, nor in the more recent past. As can be computed from Table 9.1, salaries between 1977 and 2001 have grown faster than ticket prices, at a rate of 12% to 14% per year for the salaries of all major sports. Over the more recent period from 1994 to 2001, the annual rate of increase in hockey salaries has been 13%, while hockey ticket prices rose only at a rate of 5.5% per year. By contrast, basketball, football, and baseball ticket prices all increased by about 8% per year in that time; basketball salaries rose at an annual rate of 12%, those of football at a 10% rate, and those of baseball at a rate of 8.5%.

Increases in Non-Gate Revenues

It is important to understand that professional sports teams have increasingly tapped into additional sources of revenues beyond gate receipts. Since the 1960s, the most important of these have come from television. In the early years of sports television, most of this money came from contracts between the leagues and national broadcast networks: in the United States, ABC, NBC, CBS; in Canada, the CBC and CTV networks. Over the years, competition between the networks for the most popular sports "properties" (e.g., Monday night NFL football) and later, more competition from cable networks (such as ESPN and TSN, and in French Canada RDS) drove the revenues the major leagues could realize from network television steadily upwards. However, the long upward trend in media revenues for sport is now levelling off, as the major networks are starting to disengage themselves from regular-season games, letting pay television take over (see Bellamy 1998 for a fuller discussion). Pay television allows some teams, especially those where there is cross-ownership between the team and local cable interests, to extract additional funds out of the fanatic sports viewer.

Finally, it is important to appreciate how many ancillary revenue streams have become important to the success of professional sports franchises. One of the most obvious of these comes from selling naming rights to the venue; in this trend, facilities are named for corporate sponsors—the Bell Centre (in lieu of the Molson Centre), the Air Canada Centre, the Corel Centre, General Motors Place, the Pepsi Centre—at a cost of a few million dollars per year. Teams have also sought to maximize revenue from in-venue advertising, especially that which can be sold for higher rates because it can be seen on television screens. Thus, hockey arenas are now ringed by advertisements around the rink boards, and corporate logos are embedded in the ice itself; all sports venues now include electronic advertising boards. Another important and growing revenue stream comes from the sale of licensed merchandise—jerseys, shirts, caps, cups, and other souvenirs bearing the team logo. In addition, many teams now play in brand-new or entirely renovated venues and obtain a large share of the additional revenues arising from the sale of seat licences, the leasing of luxury boxes or seats, food and drink sales, and parking fees, even when entertainment other than that of their own team is taking place.

Stagnating or Falling Profits

Still, despite the growth of revenues outlined here—and over the last 10 years, revenues have more than tripled in basketball, tripled in hockey, nearly tripled in football, and doubled in baseball—it remains the case that player salaries are absorbing an ever-growing portion of total revenues. This can be seen in Table 9.2, which compares the financial situation of the average baseball and football teams for the 1990 and 2000 seasons, and that of the average basketball and hockey teams for the 1989–1990 and 1999–2000 seasons. Although the share absorbed by players' salaries gained only 10 percentage points in football, it gained 20 percentage points in baseball and basketball, and 30 percentage points in hockey! In addition, the *absolute* amount of profits made by the average major league team has stagnated or fallen during this period, except for football, while the *share* and the *rate* of profit are on a clear falling trend in all four major league sports.

TABLE 9.2 Evolution of Various Financial Measures, MLB,NBA, NFL, NHL, 1989–2000

	Baseball		Basketball		Football		Hockey	
Season	**1990**	**2000**	**1989–1990**	**1999–2000**	**1990**	**2000**	**1989–1990**	**1999–2000**
Revenues (Millions)	$51.7	105.9	$22.5	$79.9	$46.9	$127	$20.9	$60.6
Profits (Millions)	$7.0	$4.3	$4.8	$5.6	$8.9	$14.5	$3.0	$1.9
Players' share	33.5%	52.6%	40.5%	61.5%	41.2%	51.0%	28.7%	57.0%
Profit share	13.5%	4.1%	21.3%	7.0%	18.9%	11.4%	14.3%	3.1%
Profit rate	5.8%	1.6%	7.0%	2.7%	6.7%	3.1%	6.8%	1.4%
Annual capital gain	7.75%		10.75%		12.5%		12%	

The share of profit is defined as the ratio of gross profits (gross of interest costs and depreciation) to total revenues, whereas the rate of profit is defined as the ratio of gross profits to the market value of the team, as assessed by *Financial World* and *Forbes*.

Source: Numbers obtained from various issues of *Financial World* and *Forbes*, with ratio computed by authors.

Table 9.2 clearly shows, even though the numbers provided are estimates rather than official numbers, that the players have managed to improve their position considerably, at the expense of team owners. What sustains the major league owners is the remarkable increase in the market value of sports franchises; this has allowed many team owners to realize substantial capital gains (only half of which are part of taxable income in Canada) when they sell their teams. Despite the fact that an increasing number of basketball, baseball, or hockey major league teams appear to be making operating losses, the rate of growth in the market values of these teams has grown at a double-digit rate, except for baseball, over the 1990s. Hence, the rate of return on pro teams is competitive, once you take into account the capital gains of the decade. Thus owning a hockey team or a football team is, on average, a money-making business.

REVENUE AND PERFORMANCE DISPARITIES

An important question in the professional sports business concerns revenue imbalances between the big-city teams and their small-market brethren, and the competitive imbalances that are alleged to follow. Certainly, there is widely shared concern that these imbalances are occurring, at least in hockey and baseball. Over the 1990s, there is evidence that teams in Edmonton, Calgary, and Montreal all lost good players as free agents to teams willing to pay them more money. Likewise, they were unable (or unwilling) to sign top free agents themselves, and none were as successful on the ice as they were in the 1980s, before the salary escalation occurred. In baseball, meanwhile, it is widely believed that teams such as New York and Atlanta have the revenues to be perennial contenders, while others such as the Expos, the Minnesota Twins, the Milwaukee Brewers, and the Kansas City Royals are doomed from opening day to be losers.

It is important to remember that management competence remains a factor in the consistent success of some small-market teams (e.g., Oakland Athletics, New Jersey Devils), and likewise the failures of some big spenders (the Texas Rangers, the New York Rangers). Similarly, it is worth remembering that the New York Yankees were even more dominant in the 1950s, before the days of big salaries and cable television revenues. Nonetheless, there is a widely held perception that the revenue gap between large-market and small-market teams is widening, and in some circles there is a fear that competitive imbalances may be the biggest problem now faced by professional sport, a problem that might threaten the profitability and survival of major league sport, if such profitability still exists.

Disparities in performance, payrolls, and revenues were explicitly tackled by a so-called Blue Ribbon Panel on baseball economics, set up by Commissioner Bud Selig. The committee gave its report in July 2000. Although the panel was concerned only with baseball, its main conclusions probably reflect the concerns of fans and sports journalists in all major sports. Hence it is worth reproducing in full these conclusions, since they could as well apply to hockey and other sports.

> (a) *Large and growing revenue disparities exist and are causing problems of competitive imbalance.*
>
> (b) *These problems have become substantially worse during the five complete seasons since the strike-shortened season of 1994 and seem likely to remain severe unless Major League Baseball (MLB) undertakes remedial actions proportional to the problem.*
>
> (c) *The limited revenue sharing and payroll tax that were approved as part of MLB's Collective Bargaining Agreement with the Major League Baseball Players Association (MLBPA) have produced neither the intended moderating of payroll disparities nor improved competitive balance. Some low-revenue clubs, believing the amount of their proceeds from revenue sharing insufficient to enable them to become competitive, used these proceeds to become modestly profitable.*
>
> (d) *In a majority of MLB markets, the cost to clubs of trying to be competitive is causing escalation of ticket and concession prices, jeopardizing MLB's traditional position as the affordable family spectator sport* (Levin et al., 2000, p. 1).

The last statement is indisputably true. As mentioned in an early section, prices in all sports have risen briskly, much faster than the general consumer price index. A few questions arise, however, from the other statements. First, have revenue and performance imbalances increased over the years in baseball? Second, have they increased in the other three major sports? And third, what are the remedial actions that could be taken if needed?

FINANCIAL DISPARITIES

Table 9.3 shows the evolution of one (partial) measure of financial parity. The table compares the revenues of the two richest teams in each major league sport to the revenues of its two poorest teams. The table vindicates that part of the analysis of the Blue Ribbon Panel. In the second half of the 1990s and in 2000, the ratio of the richest to the poorest has moved up from about 2.5 to about 3.3 in baseball; in other words, the revenues of the two richest teams are now more than three times the revenues of the two poorest teams, and this has happened despite the modest revenue sharing arrangements put in place in 1995. The disparity has thus grown, on the basis of this measure. Admittedly, our measure of financial disparity here is a partial one, since it does not take into account all the other clubs in between. However, a more general measure of financial imbalance, based on the well-known Gini coefficient, confirms that financial disparity in baseball has indeed risen in that time period (Fort, 2000).

TABLE 9.3 **Ratios of the Revenues of the Two Richest Teams to the Revenues of the Two Poorest Teams, MLB, NBA, NFL, NHL, 1989–2000**

	Baseball	Basketball	Football	Hockey
1989–90, 1990	2.6	3.6	1.4	1.7
1990–91, 1991	2.3	2.5	1.3	2.3
1991–92, 1992	2.2	2.7	1.2	2.8
1992–93, 1993	2.2	2.5	1.5	2.6
1993–94, 1994	2.5	2.3	1.6	3.5
1994–95, 1995	3.1	2.2	2.0	3.7
1995–96, 1996	3.0	2.6	1.6	3.3
1997–98, 1997	3.1	2.7	1.6	2.6
1998–99, 1998	3.5	3.4	1.6	2.7
1999–2000, 1999	3.7	2.7	1.7	2.3
2000–01, 2000	3.2	2.5	1.7	2.4
Avg. 1989–2000	2.85	2.70	1.56	2.72

Source: Updated from M. Lavoie, *Avantage Numerique: L'Argent et la lingue nationale de hockey*. Hull: Vents d'Ouest, 1997, p. 94, with numbers obtained from various issues of *Financial World* and *Forbes*; ratios computed by authors. No data available for 1996–97 season for the NHL and the NBA.

The situation is different in basketball, football, and hockey, as shown by Table 9.3. In NFL football, financial disparity may have risen slightly, but is still very small, thanks to the most highly developed revenue sharing agreements in professional sport. In NBA basketball, with the anomalous exception of 1998, financial disparity may actually have reduced in the 1990s compared to the 1980s. Finally in NHL hockey, financial disparity was at its highest in the mid-1990s and has been reduced since, although both the Table 9.3 ratios and the more general Gini ratios (not shown here) demonstrate that financial disparity is much larger now than it used to be in the late 1980s.

Performance Disparities

But what about competitive imbalance? A statistical measure, called the coefficient of variation, has been designed to measure such imbalance. It is based on the actual disparity in performance compared to what one would probabilistically expect if all teams were of equal strength (because of random events, these teams would not all end up with a .500 field performance, unless they played an infinite amount of games). Based on this measure, have performance disparities on the field increased? Except for basketball, they have not. In NHL hockey and in NFL football, performance disparities in the 1990s are similar to what they used to be in the previous decades. In baseball, disparities are actually much lower than they were in the previous decades (Fort, 2000, table 3; Lavoie, 1997, p. 97).

How, then, can we explain the concerns of fans and league officials alike about revenue and performance imbalances? In the case of team owners, they were little concerned with this issue as long as they were able to make a profit by exploiting the players. However, now that the players are well organized in collective bargaining units, financial imbalance becomes an issue for small-market team owners who cannot increase their television and ancillary revenues to the levels reached in large metropolitan markets. Fans and the sports media now have a greater awareness of the financial conditions faced by pro teams. Because so much information is available about payrolls, fans realize that high payrolls are generally conducive to successful performance.

Statistical measures of correlation between payroll and performance, as shown in Table 9.4, support this belief. Correlation ratios can move from -1 to +1. A positive ratio near unity would indicate that increases in payroll are nearly always associated with increases in performance; the closer to zero that positive correlation ratio, the more feeble the positive relationship; a correlation ratio of zero would show that there is no relationship whatsoever between payroll and performance; a negative correlation ratio would indicate that low payrolls are associated more often than not with high performance.

Except for football, where negative correlation sometimes occurs, Table 9.4 shows there is a noticeable positive correlation in major league sport between the relative size of a team payroll and its winning percentage. While no changing pattern seems to be observable for hockey and basketball, the positive correlation between larger payrolls and better performance in baseball seems to be rising through the 1990s. This justifies the concerns that led to the creation of the Blue Ribbon Panel, as well as its second conclusion. Now that data on team payrolls are readily available, moreover, fans are aware of the implications of financial imbalance for competitive imbalance.

TABLE 9.4 Correlation Between Payrolls and Winning Percentages, MLB, NBA, NFL, NHL

	Baseball	Basketball	Football	Hockey
1989–90, 1990	.178	.721	.373	-.064
1990–91, 1991	.277	.327	.093	.314
1991–92, 1992	.154	.424	.370	.526
1992–93, 1993	.463	.235	.429	.610
1993–94, 1994	.450	.357	-.286	.550
1994–95, 1995	.446	.441	.066	.300
1995–96, 1996	.615	.415	-.122	.464
1996–97, 1997	.688	.311		.341
1997–98, 1998		.482		.338
1998–99, 1999		.386		.237
1999–2000				.499
2000–2001				.471
AVG	.409	.410	.139	.400

The higher the positive correlation number the tighter the positive association between payroll and winning performance.

Source: Data provided by Chris Dlugozima, student at the State University of New York at Stony Brook (reprinted with permission), with more recent NHL data obtained from Andrew S. Zimbalist (2002), Competitive balance in sports leagues: An introduction, *Journal of Sports Economics*, 116.

THE WOES OF CANADIAN TEAMS

In Canada, there has been a particular interest in all these schemes because of the apparently fragile condition of several of our remaining NHL franchises. Most Canadian cities, with the exception of Toronto and Montreal, which are respectively ranked approximately the 10th and the 15th biggest cities in non-Latin North America, are small-market metropolitan areas. Vancouver ranks 26th, while the next Canadian city, Ottawa, barely makes the top 50. All Canadian cities, except Toronto, have experienced the departure or the threat of departure of a major league franchise.

Professional sport in Canada has been hit hard in the 1990s for essentially five reasons. First, the Canadian dollar has taken a plunge compared to the American dollar (as have most other foreign currencies). The Canadian dollar, which was trading at par with the American dollar in the early 1970s, fell to about 62 cents at the beginning of 2002. Players' salaries are now all contracted in American dollars, and most of the travelling costs are also in American dollars, but most team revenues remain in Canadian dollars, imposing a significant burden on Canadian franchises.

In addition, the strict anti-inflation policy imposed by the Bank of Canada led to an unusually long period of recession and stagnation in the early 1990s, the effects of which were still felt in the late 1990s. This meant that the purchasing power of the average Canadian has barely grown during this period. By contrast, in the United States, there has been some growth in purchasing power, accompanied by an extraordinarily long and rapid growth in stock market prices. This, plus a general redistribution of income from the middle class to the wealthier classes, has generated a substantial increase in the size of the potential core audience to expensive major league sport.

A third important factor in the small-market Canadian equation has to do with the size and involvement of the local corporate sector. A most important revenue source in the new economy of pro sports is corporate seating: the luxury boxes and "club" seats that are now a feature of sports venues built in the last 15 years. This explains why older facilities, or even recently built venues such as the Calgary Saddledome, have been replaced or refurbished to include luxury boxes and club seats. However, this means that the amount and kind of wealth in a city, as well as the extent of corporate civic pride, have become more important to team revenues than the number of die-hard hockey fans.

Fourth, as was pointed out earlier, a whole new wave of American corporations and individuals have decided to invest in team ownership, many willing to offer long-term mega-contracts to star players. These are contracts that small-market teams—even those based in the United States—cannot afford. Smaller Canadian teams, indeed any teams with hard budget constraints, cannot compete, as was the case of the Montreal teams in the late 1990s. Indeed, the fact that, in 2000, no Canadian or Québecois investors were willing to purchase the Molson Centre and the Montreal Canadiens franchise (both once highly profitable ventures) shows just how much the economics of professional sports have changed in recent years.

That Canadian owners, outside of the Toronto Maple Leafs, struggle to compete financially in the new economics of professional sports can be shown with the help of Table 9.5. The table shows the year-by-year evolution of operating profits of Canadian franchises, in millions of dollars. The picture that arises here, perhaps surprisingly, is that Canadian franchises in the 1990s did not do any worse than their small-market American counterparts, despite the fall in the Canadian dollar. Thus, if the Canadian dollar could recover somewhat, if the Canadian economy could improve relative to that of the United States, and if Canadian teams outside Toronto can achieve better television revenues (either from greater local cable exposure, from greater sharing of national network revenues, or both), it seems entirely possible that our current major league franchises could remain viable.

There are exceptions to this verdict, however. Besides the Montreal Expos, who are on their way out, the Vancouver Canucks appear to be in severe danger. Their current loss column resembles that of the Jets' and Grizzlies' franchises before they were transferred to the United States. It should be noted, finally, that these figures, representing gross profits (before tax, interest, and depreciation payments) offer a more positive picture than the one presented by team owners when they are petitioning Canadian governments, at all levels, for financial assistance.

TABLE 9.5 Evolution of the Gross Profits of the Canadian NHL, NBA, and MLB Franchises, 1989–2000, in Millions of American Dollars

Hockey	**1989–1990**	**1990–1991**	**1991–1992**	**1992–1993**	**1993–1994**	**1994–1995***	**1995–1996**	**1997–1998**	**1998–1999**	**1999–2000**	**2000–2001**	**AVG**
Calgary	3.2	4.7	2.9	2.5	-0.3	2.7	7.8	0.6	0.7	-2.1	2.3	2.3
Edmonton	3.7	3.2	1.1	-2.3	-0.9	2.7	-0.1	2.3	2.7	3.6	2.5	1.7
Montreal	4.9	6.9	5.5	4.9	6.6	-2.3	-0.4	8.3	5.8	12.7	12.2	5.9
Ottawa				4.5	2.8	-2.6	0.1	1.2	1.4	-2.1	-4.5	0.5
Quebec	0	0.3	3.3	2.7	1.2	2.6						1.7
Toronto	3.4	6.4	8.6	10.2	7.1	3.5	3.4	6.8	2.5	17.5	15.4	7.7
Vancouver	0.9	-0.8	0.4	0.8	1.4	0.9	-0.3	-10.4	-13.7	-11.3	-3.0	-3.2
Winnipeg	-0.4	-1.5	-2.5	-2.6	-3.6	-3.2	-11.7					-3.7
Basketball									**			
Toronto							14.4	1.6	-8.0	1.2	5.1	2.8
Vancouver							7.1	1.3	-12.4	-8.5	-13.3	-5.1
Baseball	**1990**	**1991**	**1992**	**1993**	**1994*****	**1995**	**1996**	**1997**	**1998**	**1999**	**2000**	**AVG**
Montreal	6.4	-4.2	11.8	12.4	-3.8	7.1	6.2	-3.7	5.6	1.9	-8.1	2.9
Toronto	13.9	26.3	-1.3	1.3	1.4	-1.6	14.5	-20.5	-9.4	-2.8	-5.9	1.4

*NHL lockout in 1994–95 reduced season from 84 to 48 games.

**NBA lockout in 1998–99 reduced season from 82 to 50 games.

***MLB player strike in 1994 cut off season by one month and a half, as well as the series.

Source: Data taken from various issues of *Financial World* and *Forbes*.

THE ROLE OF THE PUBLIC SECTOR

Economic Impact Studies

This brings us to the role of the public sector in the economic viability of Canadian professional sports teams. Most Canadians are now aware that the strategy favoured by owners, in trying to save a franchise afflicted by financial woes, is to ask for public financing. Whenever franchise owners threaten to leave a city, they ask some well-known accounting firm to produce an economic impact study, accompanied with enthusiastic statements about city pride, the business opportunities induced by the presence of a major league franchise, and the continent-wide tourist attraction brought about by the new state-of-the-art venue.

The consensus among academic sports economists, however, is that these commissioned studies are systematically biased in their clients' interests. They routinely exaggerate the economic impact of professional sports, in part because they use the gross impact of the franchise activity rather than the much smaller net impact (typically 10 to 15 times smaller than the gross). Besides its psychological impact, the departure of a major league franchise can have only a small impact on a community. In Canada, statistics collected for the Mills committee (see below) showed that professional sport represents at best 0.06% of overall economic activity. Thus a sports team is a much less important player in the typical urban economy than many much lower profile enterprises, in both the public and private sectors. In any of the Canadian cities that have major league teams, team spending (including payroll) would be significantly smaller than that of local universities and hospitals, while cities like Vancouver and Ottawa (let alone Toronto and Montreal) would have many private businesses with many more employees and much larger budgets.

Some studies even suggest that the net economic impact of pro sport franchises could be negative (Coates & Humphreys, forthcoming). This occurs when consumers reduce their other local expenditures in order to buy season tickets (the so-called substitution effect), and when the income that has been earned locally and spent by local residents on pro sports "leaks" out of the community. Leakage occurs when players' multimillion-dollar salaries are not spent in the local economy; and with salaries easily averaging over a million dollars and many players maintaining their primary homes somewhere other than the cities they play in, this is not uncommon. All of this reinforces the conclusion that the economic impact of pro teams, as calculated by consulting firms, is highly exaggerated (see Whitson, Harvey, & Lavoie, 2001, and Levine, 2000, for a fuller treatment).

Public Funding for Private Venues

In fact, these commissioned studies convince few people today, beyond civic boosters and sports fans who want to believe in them. However, as we shall shortly see, claims that major league sports teams make major contributions to the civic economy are a familiar part of campaigns to get political approval for public subsidies. These campaigns have been so successful in the United States that a substantial part of the construction costs of sports venues over the course of the 1990s was financed by public funds. Looking at data provided by Keating (1999), it turns out that 52 major sports venues were constructed or refurbished in the United States in the 1990s, at a cost of nearly $9 billion. Taxpayers financed nearly 64% of these construction costs, which amounts to over $5.5 billion. The figures for already approved facilities to be built between 2001 and 2004 yield a similar 62% (Rappaport & Wilkerson, 2001, p. 57).

By comparison, in Canada, only 8% of sports venue construction costs in the 1990s were financed by taxpayers (numbers would change considerably if the 1989 Toronto SkyDome was to be taken into account, since $325 million out of its $625-million cost was financed ultimately by taxpayers [Whelan & Rosentraub, 1997]). Team owners of Canadian franchises often complain about the relatively high Canadian tax burden, but the single most important advantage that American franchises enjoy is that local governments heavily subsidize their venues. This means that one of the major costs of doing business in sports—the cost of building new facilities and the debt costs normally associated with this—is borne by the public sector in the United States, a rather paradoxical fact in the land of capitalism and free enterprise.

Considering that there are about 110 American franchises in major league sport, the construction costs financed by public funds represent a subsidy of about $50 million per franchise over the 1990s. There is thus some basis for claiming that public funding of new sports venues by U.S. governments (state and local) has contributed to salary inflation and to the possible financial decline of Canadian franchises. Many experts now believe that a necessary condition of financial success in professional sports, except for a few exceptional franchises located in metropolitan centres like New York or Los Angeles, lies in getting a highly subsidized venue and/or a deal giving most of the revenue streams to the team. Financially successful teams, including some in small markets, play in recently built venues that are full of luxury boxes and opportunities for advertising revenues. These can be either owned by the team owners—but built largely at public expense—and carrying little or no property tax or they can be state-of-the-art municipal venues—made available at below-market rents—with profitable management contracts that enable the team owners to accumulate lucrative revenues from advertising, catering, and other events.

In these circumstances, Canadian team owners complain, and with some justification, that they are not operating on a "level playing field" with their American-based competitors, and they have lobbied every level of Canadian government (local, provincial, and federal) for financial assistance. Moreover, pressed by distressed fans and threatening owners, federal and provincial governments have considered intervening on the professional sports scene over the last few years. In 1998, the Quebec government offered to make interest payments on a $100-million loan to help build a new stadium for the Expos on downtown land that was to be given by the federal government. In 1999, the Ontario government created a new property tax category that allowed municipalities to lower property taxes on sports venues; in turn, the Regional Municipality of Ottawa-Carleton made use of this new category to diminish the Corel Centre property tax by nearly 90%. In 2001, just before the sale of the Montreal Canadiens, the city of Montreal cut in half the property tax assessment of the Molson Centre. In Alberta, in 2002, the provincial government established a sports lottery and introduced an income tax on visiting players (which may soon be adopted by other provinces hosting an NHL team), both measures being designed to raise funds earmarked to help out the hockey teams of Calgary and Edmonton. Meanwhile in both cities the teams play in arenas built (and recently refurbished) with public money, under terms that give many different kinds of revenue-generating opportunities to the teams. Finally, the federal government sponsors NHL teams by purchasing publicity space in arenas or game programs.

The Mills Report and the Manley Proposals

Despite active lobbying by Canadian NHL team owners, though, the federal government has not yet done much beyond permitting cities (notably Edmonton and Calgary) to spend federal infrastructure money allotted to them on the upgrading of professional sports facilities. In particular, they have resisted offering direct subsidies and they have also resisted changes to tax regulations that would amount to indirect subsidies to professional sports. The government set up a subcommittee of the House of Commons, the so-called Mills Committee, to investigate the economic situation of sport in Canada, both amateur and professional. The committee submitted its report in November 1998 and in it argued that

Canadian teams in the major leagues needed at least temporary relief if they were to survive (Mills Report, 1998). None of the Mills recommendations were implemented.

During the following summer, team owners of Canadian NHL franchises continued to meet with Industry Canada representatives, seeking to convince them of their urgent financial needs. Finally, the then Industry minister, John Manley, announced that the federal government was prepared to offer temporary assistance to each of the six Canadian NHL teams. As most Canadian hockey fans will be aware, less than three days later, after an unprecedented public outcry that had provincial politicians in Alberta backing away from their earlier support, the Manley proposal was withdrawn (see Whitson et al., 2001).

CONCLUSIONS

Where does this leave Canada's major league teams? First, it can be suggested that most of the economic trends that have created difficulties for Canada's small-market teams appear likely to continue. As far as factors internal to the sports industries are concerned, salary growth shows little sign of abating. The money that teams based in centres with populous television hinterlands and large numbers of corporate headquarters are in a position to make from these sources is always going to be a lot more than it is in Canadian cities other than Toronto, and possibly Montreal. Only the possibility of generalized revenue sharing, as in the NFL, seems to be a real solution.

If we turn to factors external to the sports industries, there is perhaps more room for optimism, but no certainties. If the Canadian dollar were to strengthen in relation to its U.S. counterpart, this could help Canadian teams substantially. Likewise, if the Canadian corporate economy were to improve—to such an extent that more Canadian corporations could afford luxury seating, and more Canadian individuals could afford the prices of major league sport on a regular basis—this would undoubtedly improve the outlook for most of the Canadian-based teams.

If we look at the prospects for relief from the public sector, direct subsidies by the federal government now seem to be out of the question. However, the steps taken by Montreal and Ottawa (and by the province of Ontario) to reduce the property tax burdens of the Canadiens and the Senators, respectively, can be read as positive signs by supporters of the industry, as can steps to establish sports lotteries and to tax visiting players. Moreover, the fact that, four years after the urgent launching of the Mills committee, no further NHL team has moved south perhaps implies that the financial situation of Canadian franchises may not be as bad as the industry makes out, or at least no worse than that of their American small-market counterparts. This opinion is reinforced by financial data released by Rod Bryden and his Ottawa Senators that indicate that, thanks to the newly obtained property tax reduction and with proper revenue-sharing arrangements with the Corel Centre, the Senators would be a break-even operation before Stanley Cup playoffs. Whenever the team makes the playoffs, therefore, the business can be profitable.

Today, many Canadians are disenchanted with NHL hockey because they see players' salaries as being out of touch with their own reality. As a result, Canadians want to know what the full costs of subsidizing professional hockey (or any other sport) are likely to be, and many more Canadians than might have been the case in the 1960s or 1970s are prepared to say that other things—health care, the arts, education, even sport at the community level—are more important priorities. Questions like these are political and ultimately are questions of values and human priorities; although economics can help us understand the likely consequences of different courses of action, it cannot tell us where we want to go and what we want to do.

Critical Thinking Questions

1. What are the pros and cons of subsidizing or granting tax breaks to NHL teams in Canada?

2. Imagine that you are an advisor to the mayor of a large Canadian city. Draw up the pros and cons of subsidizing the construction of a new venue to retain a major league team.

3. It was suggested by the Mills Committee that major league athletes playing in Canada ought to receive a tax credit to harmonize their income tax rates with those that they would have paid in the United States. What do you think of the merits and the ethics of this proposal?

4. It was also proposed by the Mills Committee to grant a tax credit to cover the costs encountered by the parents of kids involved in amateur sport. What do you think of such a proposal, in light of the fact that recreational sport brings large health benefits, and in light of the fact that parents of kids taking art or music lessons also can encounter large costs?

5. Corporations or self-employed workers who purchase opera or hockey game tickets can use 50% of the cost of these tickets to reduce their taxable income. In the case of NHL hockey, it is estimated that this federal tax expenditure amounts to more than $20 million per year. Should such tax deductions be sustained?

6. What do you think NHL team owners should be looking for when bargaining for the next collective agreement if they wish to improve their financial situation? If they want to improve competitive balance in the NHL?

7. Imagine you are a portfolio advisor. Would you advise a wealthy professional to invest in units of a limited partnership designed to purchase an existing Canadian NHL franchise? Why or why not?

8. Major league hockey players earned, on average, $2.7 million in 2001–02, and hence earned about 55 times what high school teachers did. Discuss whether you believe this to be fair. Discuss the advantages and drawbacks of an economic system that leads to such discrepancies.

Suggested Readings

Cagan, J., & de Mause, N. (1998). *Field of schemes: How the great stadium swindle turns public money into private profit*. Monroe, Me.: Common Courage Press.

Downward, P., & Dawson, A. (2000). *The economics of professional team sports*. London: Routledge.

Leeds, M., & von Allmen, P. (2002). *The economics of sports*. Boston: Addison-Wesley.

Noll, R., & Zimbalist, A. (1997). *Sports, jobs and taxes: The economic impact of sports teams and stadiums*. Washington, D.C.: Brookings Institution.

Quirk, J., & Fort, R.D. (1992). *Pay dirt: The business of professional team sports*. Princeton: Princeton University Press.

Rosentraub, M. S. (1997). *Major League losers: The real cost of sport and who is paying for it*. New York: Basic Books.

Staudohar, P.D. (1996). *Playing for dollars: Labor relations and the sports business*. Ithaca, N.Y.: ILR Press.

Web Links

The Economics of Sports
http://wps.aw.com/aw_leedsvonal_econsports_1/
A site set up by the authors of the first undergraduate textbook on the economics of sports, with quizzes and several other links to economics of sports Web sites.

Forbes Magazine
http://www.forbes.com
The archives contains the financial assessment of all pro teams in all four North American major leagues, going back a few years, continuing the work of the defunct *Financial World* magazine. To get all the information, you need to register, but it is free.

The Heartland Institute
http://www.heartland.org/
Site of a right-wing organization that features articles opposing government subsidies to pro sports organizations, and reports some hearings on this topic or topics such as the legitimacy of franchise moves as discussed at Senate hearings.

HockeyZonePlus
www.http://hockeyzoneplus.com
Bilingual site run by François Coulombe and devoted to hockey. It contains a large business section on hockey, including a large historical databank on the salaries of all NHL players over the last 10 years.

Joel Maxcy's Sports Economics Page
http://snycorva.cortland.edu/~maxcy/jmsportspages.html
The site of a teacher of sports economics; has sports economists on the Web, testimonies, data and information sources, official league sites, sports news, and sports business news.

The National Hockey League Players' Association
http://www.nhlpa.com
Provides the latest salaries of all NHL players, as well as their year-by-year statistics.

Patricia's Web Site
http://www.dfw.net/~patricia/
Contains the most complete databanks on basketball.

10

Sport and Mass Media

Scott G. Martyn

Defenceman Ed Jovanovski (R) leads the charge off the bench as Canada celebrates defeating the United States 5–2 to win the gold medal in men's ice hockey at the Salt Lake 2002 Olympic Winter Games in Salt Lake City, February 24, 2002. It was Canada's first Olympic men's ice hockey gold medal in 50 years.

Television won't be able to hold on to any market it captures after the first six months. People will soon get tired of staring at a plywood box every night.

Darryl F. Zanuck, President, 20th Century Fox, 1946

INTRODUCTION

Despite the prognostications of Darryl Zanuck and others within the print and broadcast industry, the audiences captured by television in the sphere of sport are both astronomical and startling. In Canada, for example, the weekly ratings share for the first week of the 1998 Winter Games in Nagano for Canadian Broadcasting Corporation (CBC) and Radio-Canada was an amazing 28.2% and 35.2% respectively, and for the second week an equally amazing 22.2% and 30.5%. CBC's average audience each minute ranged from 850 000 daytime viewers to 1.8 million prime-time viewers. Even more impressive was the fact that an average 1.3 million Canadians stayed with CBC's coverage of the Winter Games until 2:00 a.m. Similarly, near record audiences were obtained by Radio-Canada approaching 250 000, 800 000, and 225 000 respectively. Specific events, such as Elvis Stojko's silver-medal performance in figure skating (2.9 million viewers on CBC) and the opening ceremonies (1.2 million viewers on Radio-Canada), easily outdistanced the daily averages (Canadian Broadcasting Corporation [CBC], 1998, p. 40). More recently, the men's ice hockey gold-medal victory over the United States at the 2002 Winter Games in Salt Lake City, Utah, recorded an all-time Canadian broadcast record of 8.6 million viewers (International Olympic Committee [IOC], 2002, p. 9).

As Canada's national broadcaster, "CBC has a mandate to contribute to Canadians' shared national consciousness by celebrating this country's cultural and regional diversity and achievement in every field" (CBC, 1998, p. 40). In responding to this mandate, CBC/Radio-Canada and NetStar, owner of the sport specialty channels TSN and RDS, have secured the rights for the Olympic Games until 2008, with post-2008 broadcast rights negotiations beginning in 2003. According to CBC, the public–private sector partnership, a first for Olympic television coverage in Canada, will help address the $160 million U.S. required for the broadcast rights of these Games. The International Olympic Committee (IOC), having only recently adopted the long-term broadcast rights strategy, has benefited from these broadcast agreements. From 1984 until 2008, the IOC has concluded broadcast agreements worth more than $10 billion U.S. However, the economic relationship between television and the modern Olympic movement has not been without its critics. Responding to the most persistent criticism that the Olympic Games have become too deeply imbedded in commercial ventures, Jacques Rogge (2002), president of the IOC, stated: "Without the support of the business community, without its technology, expertise, people, services, products, telecommunication, its financing—the Olympic Games could not and cannot happen."

What Rogge has endeavoured to described is the complex "triangular" relationship that has emerged between sport, sponsors, and television (Boyle & Haynes, 2000, pp. 46–66). Indeed, a symbiotic connection has developed in recent years that has come to dominate the economic structure of sport in the world today. National and international sports governing bodies, sponsors, and the mass media have become intertwined in an alliance that has shaped the production and development of sport in Canada and throughout the world. The boundaries between these institutions, according to David Rowe (1999, pp. 12–13), have blurred to the point of near invisibility, becoming so mutually indispensable that one is almost unthinkable without the other. Some organizations, such as the IOC, publicly acknowledged and, to a certain extent, embraced the symbiotic connection between sport and media. Yet past IOC president Juan Antonio Samaranch argues that the nature of his organization's long-lasting and increasingly intense courtship with the media has evolved beyond that which could be defined as a simple alliance:

> *In all their forms, the media, in other words the written and photographic press, radio and television broadcasters, form an integral part of the Olympic movement and belong, in the fullest sense of the term, to the Olympic Family.* (International Olympic Committee, 1990, p. 39)

Given such public expressions, it is little wonder that the alliance between sport and the media is often described as "the happiest of marriages, with both institutions becoming mutually dependent in an increasingly extensive and expensive exchange of exposure and rights fees for sport in return for compelling content and audience capture for the media" (Rowe, 1999, pp. 565–82).

Although the existence of sport does not depend solely on the exposure provided by the mass media and from the fees paid for the broadcast rights to their events, the success of sport as a form of commercial entertainment does. The mass media profit from this liaison by capturing an increased share of the available market, which, more often than not, remains extremely loyal readers, listeners, and viewers. Such loyalty is exemplified in the record audiences achieved year after year by CBC's "Hockey Night in Canada" double-headers, the network's most-watched programs. During the 1999–2000 season, an average of 1.3 million Canadian viewers watched the first game and almost 700 000 the second. In addition to providing live coverage of the events, the media enhance the visual production with sports commentary, further connecting the sport's "producer" to its audience. This live-broadcast sports commentary, with its flamboyant terminology and melodramatic narratives, is "a potentially powerful instrument for the symbolic unification and denigration of nations at moments of high sporting excitement" (Rowe, 1999, p. 119). Although print media sport texts have greater flexibility in the modes of writing, they devote much time and space to statistics, injury reports, trade rumours, strategy, and "insider" gossip. Despite its after-the-fact impact, it is these written words that enhance what cannot be or have not been seen and set the stage for what is to be expected in upcoming contests. If the media corporations perform their "producer" role properly, they provide advertisers the opportunity to deliver their message directly to huge audiences that would be difficult, if not altogether impossible, to reach otherwise. The resulting ratings increase enhances the corporation's ability to negotiate top dollar for commercial time on sport broadcasts and for advertisements in print media across all its year-round productions. Furthermore, the secondary effect of audience exposure to other media texts produced by the same corporation ensures a competitive advantage in the media industry. Thus, "there is great symbolic and economic value to be gained . . . from controlling the production and distribution of symbols" such as those constructed by mediated sport (Rowe, 1999, p. 72).

While each member of this "triangular" alliance has collaborated to maximize its return on investment, it also assumes the risks associated with such a cooperative relationship. The primary responsibility of presenting desirable sports events rests with the national and international sports governing bodies. This is done by constructing "highly attractive marketing vehicles for the promoters of a variety of global products, as well as offering promotional opportunities to the host city" (Whitson, 1998, p. 57). However, the danger of such an arrangement for the sports governing bodies emerges when a sufficient number of consumers become disillusioned with the product being promoted. Sport scandals like those involving the disqualification of Canadian sprinter Ben Johnson at the 1988 Seoul Olympics after testing positive for steroids, or the more recent bribery and corruption scandal that surrounded the bidding process for Olympic Games, breached the "fair play" values we, as media consumers, assign to sport. In the case of the bribery and corruption scandal, the events called into question the general history of commercial and financial affairs pertinent to staging Olympic Games, thus jeopardizing the continued viability of this sophisticated sport–media relationship. The resulting firestorm in the media, according to Canadian IOC member and chairman of the special investigative ad hoc commission that reviewed the allegations, Richard Pound (2000, p. 1), was far beyond the ability of the organization to cope.

One need not appreciate sport to realize that "its world has content that is more compelling to many than other artifacts and responsibilities of daily living" (Wenner, 1998, p. xiii). A brief glance at a daily newspaper or local news broadcast reveals the extent to which the mass media regularly devote substantial segments of their productions to sport. Sport, as both a social institution and as a medium of communication, has become a conduit for the transmission of images, symbols, and meanings that are central to our society. The purpose of this chapter is to explain the relationship between sport and the media. First, "mass media" will be defined and identified as a subset of mass communications. Next, the relationship between television, sport, and sponsorship will be explored, further demonstrating the complex triangular relationship described earlier. Third, a brief case study of a media sports scandal will be investigated, illustrating the extent to which the political economy of media sport extends. Finally, sport and the "new media" will be discussed.

DEFINING THE MASS MEDIA

The mass media, including newspapers and magazines, film, books, radio, television, advertising, cable, music recordings, and the Internet, are the creations of specialized social groups living in contemporary societies. They form part, but not all, of what has been defined as mass communication, which, in turn, is an element of the broader definition of communication. In an effort to better explain the meaning and the relationship between the various components that are collectively defined as communications, Lorimer and McNulty (1996) compiled the examples in Table 10.1.

In reviewing the various categories provided in Table 10.1, the reader should not consider mass and public communications to be independent of each other, but rather as "organizationally different phenomena" (Lorimer & McNulty, 1996, p. 36). Mass communications are distinguishable from public communications due, in part, to the system's restriction placed on how messages are produced, disseminated, and negotiated by society. In the case of sport, mass communications assist in the administration of power by ensuring that those few who control the message not only select which sports and events will be covered, but also decide what will be emphasized in the coverage. Mass communications, and specifically mass media, have a major impact on the meanings and values assigned to sporting events, while at the same time trivializing or ignoring others.

As a subset of mass communication, the mass media, according to Denis McQuail, influence our experience through publication, or the transforming of private systems of knowing into public systems and creating new biases of collective thought. It is considered a major

TABLE 10.1 Communication

Mass Communication	Public Communications
architecture	face-to-face
rituals	messengers
the arts	
material production	
education	
Mass Media	**Public Media**
newspapers	post office
magazines	telephone
books	telegraph
radio	Internet (discussion groups)
television	
advertising	
cable	
music recording	
Internet (e.g., Web sites)	
Converged Mass/Public Communications/Media	
direct mail marketing	
computerized telemarketing	
video-on-demand	
individualized information services e.g., banking	

Source: Rowland M. Lorimer and Jean McNulty. (1996). "Mass Communications, the Mass Media, Public Communications, and Modern Society," in *Mass Communication in Canada* (3rd ed.). Toronto: Oxford University Press, p. 36.

cultivator, exposing the public to selective views of society on nearly every aspect of life that shapes their beliefs and values (McQuail, 1994). Following the writings of McQuail, Lorimer and McNulty (1996, p. 40) have identified the following components of mass media:

1. *a distinct set of activities* (creating media content)
2. *involving particular technological configurations* (television, radio, videotex, newspapers, books)
3. associated with *formally constituted institutions* or media outlets (systems, stations, publications)
4. acting according to *certain laws, rules, and understandings* (professional codes and practices, audience and societal expectations and habits)
5. carried out by *persons occupying certain roles* (owners, regulators, producers, distributors, advertisers, audience members)
6. which, together, convey *information, entertainment, images, and symbols*
7. to the *mass audience.*

This seven-part definition, with each of its major elements identified in italics, demonstrates how media sports texts are constructed, or even deconstructed, in a continuous process involving the representation of a distinct set of activities by media organizations. In so doing, it outlines how the meanings and ideologies they generate have come to define our perspectives on the world.

TELEVISION, SPORT, AND SPONSORSHIP: THE PERFECT UNION

> *Sport in Canada rarely generates its own change, but tends to be shaped by other forces in the society. Until more Canadians become concerned about the effects of unregulated commercialism upon other aspects of Canadian society, it is unlikely they will ever be concerned about the effects of commercialism in sport.* (Kidd, 1970, p. 272)

Despite the proliferation of sport talk radio, sport magazines, and more recently sport Web sites, no single force has played a more central role in shaping our contemporary view of sport than television and its institutionalized values system. All previously existing forms of mass media, including books, newspapers and magazines, films, and radio, were challenged by the sports-television "revolution" of the late 1960s and early 1970s. Television was the pre-eminent mass medium of the last half of the 20th century and is certainly poised to remain a central component of mass communications for the foreseeable future. Experiments with television started in the early 1920s in both Europe and the United States. Having made rapid advancements in the technology at a number of centres throughout the world, pioneering German scientists successfully transmitted the first live television images of the Opening Ceremonies of the Games of the Eleventh Olympiad in 1936 to receiving screens in viewing halls located within a two-mile radius of the stadium. At different times during the Games, four competition venues, including the Olympic Stadium and the swimming facility, housed television equipment. During 138 hours of coverage, a total of 162 228 people watched the transmitted blurred images of athletes performing (Barney, 1993, p. 17). Yet despite the success experienced in Berlin, television was considered only an extension of the stadium, rather than an important medium in its own right.

Notwithstanding the early success with television, broadcasting was halted in Britain and United States with the onset of World War II. However, when work on the commercial application of television resumed following the cessation of hostilities, progress came quickly. Twenty-four stations were licensed in the United States in 1946 and over one hundred by 1948. By August 1949, an estimated 2 million Americans owned television sets; that number jumped to 13 million by June 1951. In Canada, despite the lack of a Canadian television station, an estimated 3600 television sets were owned in 1949 by those able to afford the costly units and geographically positioned to receive signals from American broadcasters. After three years of hurried labour by CBC's Board of Governors, television officially came to Canada on September 6, 1952, when CBFT in Montreal began telecasting, and, two days later, CBLT in Toronto.

Sport, more specifically hockey, emerged as a key element in the programming activities of Canada's new broadcaster. Although the early experiments with television focused on the Maple Leaf Gardens in Toronto, the first National Hockey League (NHL) game to be televised on CBC was actually a game in Montreal on October 11, 1952, three weeks before Toronto's television debut. The debut saw Imperial Oil purchase the television rights for that first season at just $100 per Maple Leafs game, as team owner Conn Smythe wanted to make sure that hockey was as appealing on television as it was on radio before asking for an appropriate fee. The following season, Imperial Oil purchased the rights to the games for $150 000 a year in a three-year contract. By the early 1960s, after Stafford Smythe had bought out his father's controlling stock in the Gardens, the rights sold for $9 million over six years, or approximately $21 000 per game.

The new medium developed rapidly, and its growth brought new ownership to the expanding media industry. At the same time, many private companies in Canada that already owned and operated newspaper or radio outlets were among those granted television licences on the condition that their stations operate as CBC affiliates. By 1960 there were forty-seven stations in Canada, nine wholly owned CBC stations, and thirty-eight privately owned CBC affiliates. Each of the stations was linked to the others by a coast-to-coast microwave relay system that enabled everyone but those living in the most remote areas of Canada to receive a Canadian television station. In less than a decade, three-quarters of all Canadian households possessed a television set. With the quality of telecasts steadily improving, watching television soon became the number one in-house leisure activity of Canadians.

Despite these accomplishments, many Canadians were dissatisfied with the CBC's dominant position as the country's sole broadcaster. In 1958, responding, in part, to the growing dissatisfaction of a system that saw the private broadcasters regulated by the CBC, the Conservative government of John Diefenbaker announced it would allow competitor stations. By 1960, under the independent regulatory authority of the Board of Broadcast Governors (BBG) established two years earlier, eight privately owned "second" television stations were licensed in Canada's largest municipal centres. Shortly after, on October 1, 1961, these stations formed Canada's second television network, CTV, thus providing an alternative to the programming offered by CBC stations. In 1963 CTV established its own microwave relay system linking its affiliates from coast to coast.

Regardless of the Conservative government's intentions, the statute bringing these changes into effect did not clearly specify the relationship of authority between the CBC and the BBG. Given the confusion, and unwilling to relinquish its control over Canada's private broadcasters, the "CBC tried to continue its operations just as it had done in the past" (Lorimer & McNulty, 1996, p. 181). However, under the 1968 Broadcasting Act a new agency, the Canadian Radio and Television Commission (CRTC), was given full regulatory authority over all aspects of the Canadian broadcasting system, including the CBC networks and stations. The name was changed to the Canadian Radio-television and Telecommunications Commission in 1976, when telecommunications was added to the commission's list of responsibilities. Today, the CRTC's responsibilities continue under the update Act of 1991, and the Telecommunications Act of 1993.

In their struggle to compete, television broadcasters used sport as an important component of their weekly programming mix. Historically, sports programming proved to be inexpensive, popular, and easy to schedule. In the Canadian context, sport also helped to satisfy the network's government-stipulated mandate to ensure that they conformed to Canadian content requirements.

First introduced by the BBG in 1959, Canadian content requirements have risen from 45% of broadcast hours to be devoted to programs of Canadian origin, to the present-day regulations requiring 60% Canadian content and 50% in prime time for conventional private stations. Although somewhat restricting, the definition of "Canadian" has been generously defined to include any program produced by a licensee, all productions made in Canada, and broadcasts of events taking place outside Canada in which Canadians were participating, such as NHL hockey. It also includes events that are deemed to be of special interest to Canadians, including sporting events such as the World Series.

The CBC, in an effort to achieve its Canadian content goals, began securing the rights for, and televising, international sporting events such as the 1972 Canada–Russia Summit Series, the Commonwealth and Olympic Games, as well as those games played by professional sport teams headquartered in Canada. The fees that these and other sport organizations received from television, although initially small, have in recent years mushroomed with the increased competition and complexity in the television marketplace. The television rights paid for the Olympic Games in the United States, for example, have increased exponentially for almost every Olympiad since 1960, as shown in Table 10.2.

TABLE 10.2 United States Olympic Television Rights

Games	Country	Broadcaster	Amount
1960	Rome	USA CBS	$394 940
1964	Tokyo	USA NBC	$1 500 000
1968	Mexico	USA ABC	$4 500 000
1972	Munich	USA ABC	$13 500 000
1976	Montreal	USA ABC	$25 000 000
1980	Moscow	USA NBC	$85 000 000
1984	Los Angeles	USA ABC	$225 000 000
1988	Seoul	USA NBC	$300 000 000
1992	Barcelona	USA NBC	$401 000 000
1996	Atlanta	USA NBC	$456 000 000
2000	Sydney	USA NBC	$715 000 000
2004	Athens	USA NBC	$793 000 000
2008	Beijing	USA NBC	$894 000 000

Referring back to the triangular relationship described earlier in this chapter, the resulting dependency that emerged between the sport governing bodies and the astronomical revenues garnered from television has ensured that sport will "go to any lengths to accommodate television" (Boyle & Haynes, 2000, p. 49).

As television assumed a different, more dominant role in the mediation of sport, it was no longer willing to simply televise the event. Seeking to package sport into a pattern that ensured the maximum exposure and revenue, sport governing bodies were often lobbied to make rule changes or alterations to meet the ongoing needs of the broadcaster. Networks sought to dictate when, where, and in what form sport could take place. Yet, despite the demands of television, the relationship is symbiotic, as the partners need each other to maintain and extend their influence.

Continued changes in the television and advertising industries enhanced the spectacle and value of sport as programming. With the rise of sponsored programming, the relationship between sport, sponsors, and television evolved beyond the relatively simple sponsorship of sporting events to one that now includes the sponsorship of the network productions themselves. Commercial sponsors are increasingly negotiating with not only the sport governing bodies, but also the television corporations who control the broadcast rights. Thus, as David Rowe has previously argued, the boundaries that defined sport, sponsors, and television have blurred to the point of near invisibility and have become so mutually indispensable that one is now unthinkable without the other.

MEDIA SPORTS SCANDAL: A CASE STUDY

It is worthwhile to look briefly at media sport scandals, because "they reveal how the political economy of media sport extends beyond the production, distribution and consumption of sports reports and live television" (Rowe, 1999, p. 91). In speculating about the social consequences of scandals, Cambridge social theorist John B. Thompson states they have "a corrosive impact on the forms of trust which underpin social relations and institutions" (Thompson, 1997, p. 59). Although the most contemporary media sports scandal to envelop the IOC burst onto the stage of public awareness in late November 1998, it is important to note that it did not occur during the pursuit of sport. A Salt Lake City newspaper reporter alleged that officials of the committee charged with the responsibility of securing the 2002 Winter Olympic Games committed serious improprieties. The original allegation focused on the "gift" of a college scholarship for an IOC member's daughter in exchange for his vote to help secure the Games for Salt Lake City.

Unable to contain the crisis within those organizations that made up the Olympic Family, the circle of alleged corruption in the media widened beyond simply the Salt Lake City bid committee and certain IOC members. Representatives of the United States Olympic Committee (USOC) soon came under fire for their roles in the corruption scenario, as did officials of the bid committee for Sydney's successful quest to host the 2000 Games. A severe public outcry arose as the unfolding story captured world media attention for some three months. Unable to cope with the unprecedented media attention in any meaningful way, Olympic organizations implicated in the scandal scrambled to form commissions to investigate the facts and pinpoint wrongdoing. With the possibility that a violation of federal laws had occurred, the United States Justice Department directed the FBI to launch an investigation. Much finger pointing ensued. The USOC's investigative commission, created by its president, Bill Hybl, and chaired by former U.S. senator George Mitchell, publicly denounced the IOC as a closed, unaccountable, and ethically culpable body perpetuating a compromising gift-giving and -receiving culture. Well before the USOC's action, the IOC formed its own investigative commission headed by Richard Pound. By the time Pound's commission submitted its report, four IOC members had resigned, six were expelled, ten received severe warnings, and Cameroon's René Essomba, whose name was linked to the very first disclosures of alleged corruption, had died.

Many of those commenting in the print media, backed by large segments of the population, called for the immediate resignation of Juan Antonio Samaranch. Less reactionary, but deeply disturbed by the events precipitated by the Salt Lake City disclosures, Olympic-related groups offered a litany of recommendations for change, a sweeping majority of which aimed squarely at alterations in the structure of the IOC and its manner of doing business. Recognizing that the crush of media attention, if left unchecked, might well put the existence of the IOC at risk, the organization struggled to regain its credibility by publicly acknowledging the problem was serious, apologizing for its part in the "problem," and pledging to bring about reforms in the wake of the Salt Lake City disclosures. Scores of meetings, studies and debates, written depositions from sports groups, and input from detached, independent individuals, of which Henry Kissinger was perhaps the most noted, culminated in numerous changes to the Olympic Charter. Some 50 reform measures were adopted, including a new ethics commission, and a drastic change in the IOC terms of membership. Beginning with the selection of the 2006 Winter Olympic Games host city, the IOC banned visits by individual IOC members to candidate cities bidding for the right to host the great international sports festival. Instead, a special IOC Commission, at IOC expense, now visits host city candidates.

Punctuated by the fiery comments of some members of the U.S. Congress, no post-scandal investigation response was more virulent than that recorded in the United States. This reflected the fact that the first and, ultimately, most flagrant examples of bribery and corruption involved an American city. The United States was the only country in the world to demand the IOC president's appearance before a federal government investigative committee.

Throughout the spring and summer of 1999, the U.S. Congress tried several times without success to get Samaranch to appear before one of its subcommittees for questioning on issues related to the Salt Lake City disclosures. Samaranch delayed a Washington visit until the IOC announced its reform measures. By early December this had been accomplished. The time was right to travel to Washington. And, a mid-December visit, in many ways, might be lost among the public issues that captured the attention of the mass media at the time. A focus on Y2K worries, presidential candidates, upcoming primaries, and Hillary Clinton's touted run for a Senate seat diminished media interest in Samaranch's visit to the American capital.

Juan Antonio Samaranch is not a man who is relaxed and confident in front of the media, particularly when the discourse is carried out completely in English. Spanish and Catalan are his "first" languages; French, his "second." Appearing before an aroused Congressional subcommittee with an agenda to lower the IOC's influence in the United States and raise the profile of the USOC posed an intimidating challenge for the IOC president. There was simply too much at stake for Samaranch to continue to ignore Congress—the modern Olympic movement would continue to rely on financial support from corporations with headquarters in the United States.

On Wednesday, December 15, speaking and being spoken to in Spanish through an interpreter (a condition of his appearance), Samaranch appeared before members of the House Committee of Commerce–Subcommittee on Oversights and Investigations. The gallery was packed with spectators; a formidable collection of national and international media representatives wielded cameras, pencils, laptop computers, and tape recorders. Seven congressmen formed the "hearing panel," chaired by Representative Fred Upton from Michigan. They sat behind a long table adorned with a battery of microphones. Facing them sat a sombre Juan Antonio Samaranch, flanked on either side by a translator, one to translate questions addressed to him into Spanish, the other to translate his answers into English ("Capitol Hill," 1999). To begin the proceedings, Samaranch was sworn in; then he read a carefully crafted opening statement that he delivered in English. Subsequently, the committee opened its questioning. Chairman Upton fired the first salvo, declaring that they were "here because the Olympic Games are too important to allow a culture of corruption to be whitewashed and perpetuated by a paper called reforms" ("In the Hot Seat," 1999). One after the other, the charges flew across the committee room: the IOC reforms were simply an exercise in "window-dressing . . . a whitewash"; the newly created IOC ethics panel "lacks teeth"; anti-corruption rules won't even apply "to the IOC president or his successor" ("Samaranch unruffled," 1999).

Samaranch sat unperturbed, resolute in his conviction that the IOC had met the challenges imposed and reformed its house. In the end, after six hours of testimony (two hours by Samaranch), the subcommittee vowed close monitoring of the IOC's pledge to change and threatened to "implement legislation that would ban American companies from financially supporting the Olympics" if officials failed to follow through ("IOC's Samaranch Weathers Storm," 1999). With the subcommittee's final admonition, the real motivation behind Congress's desire to confront Samaranch in the nation's capital had surfaced. U.S. government officials appeared less concerned with the Salt Lake City scandal and more interested in the political leverage and media coverage that the scandal afforded them. Each fragment of every report, scrap of commentary, photograph, and video image of Samaranch during testimony, and all other elements of sports discourse that were produced in both visual and verbal languages, carried with them a kind of political message.

Major American newspaper accounts of the hearing judged Samaranch's performance before the committee as generally effective. If Samaranch had been only moderately persuasive in defusing the subcommittee's charges, it was the testimony of three important American allies that decisively took the political wind out of Upton's sails. Testifying on behalf of the IOC were Henry Kissinger, former U.S. secretary of state; Howard Baker, former U.S. senator from Tennessee; and former White House chief of staff, Kenneth Duberstein. Kissinger told the committee that the IOC had "come as close to achieving [reforms] as possible, replacing corrupt members with enthusiastic athletes" ("In the Hot Seat," 1999). Baker pleaded for the lawmakers "to be patient . . . Samaranch is well meaning . . . fully dedicated to reform" ("Samaranch Sparkles," 1999). Duberstein announced that "Samaranch is living reform every day" ("Samaranch Sparkles," 1999). Following the questioning and answering, a weary but relieved Samaranch and his colleagues retired from the proceedings, confident that IOC reforms, given a chance to work, would satisfy Congressional USOC "protectionists."

Finally, there has been much speculation about the impact of the recent Olympic scandal on the state of Olympic marketing programs, television and sponsor relationships, and overall support for the various Olympic organizing committees. Recent opinion polls conducted to gauge the public's support for Olympic sponsors and interest in the Olympic Games broadcasts indicate that the Olympic crisis described above did not adversely affect the perception of the Olympic Games (IOC, 1999, p. 2). Nevertheless, the IOC has been proactive in its attempts to limit the damage caused by the scandal to the Olympic family. The addition of Hill & Knowlton, an international public relations firm with offices in 34 countries, to its team of lawyers and marketing experts is indicative of the IOC's new position within the ever-expanding marketplace of international sport. The modern Olympic movement today is quite different from what it was in 1980, and perhaps the scandal outlined above was a negative consequence of the IOC's global "celebrity" status. Whatever the origins of the scandal, it is clear that all who underestimate the political economic weight of the media sports cultural complex do so at their own peril. We must each acknowledge that, as Richard Pound has noted, "no political accommodation, whether in sport or politics in general, can occur without making choices, and each choice has its own set of consequences" (IOC, 1999, p. 3).

SPORT AND THE NEW MEDIA

With the rapid advancements in communications technologies, it is easy to forget that technological changes have been a constant feature of the historical development of the media sports cultural complex. Advancements in photography (1830s), the typewriter (1860s), transatlantic cable (1866), telephone (1876), motion pictures (1894), wireless telegraphy (1895), magnetic tape recording (1899), radio (1906), and television (1923) have each played a significant role in the development of mediated sport. As we move into an increasingly international arena, new media technologies are expanding "the possibilities of cultural production into areas normally associated with consumption, enabling fans to produce their own custom-made texts out of the 'raw' material supplied" (Rowe, 1999, p. 168). Consequently, new media are positioned to extend the passive experience of the sports media consumer beyond that previously offered by merging the traditional roles of spectator and participant.

The expanding multimedia marketplace, which includes terrestrial broadcasting, cable television, satellite broadcasting, cable multipoint multi-channel distribution service (MMDS), open video systems (OVS), and emerging video and audio media via the Internet, is of enormous relevance to the mass media, given their traditional roles as major information carriers. CBC, for example, recently sought to consolidate its leadership position on the Internet in Canada by ensuring the coordinated development of the corporation's Internet products—media contents, database information, software, etc.—for the entire country. CBC Web sites have received repeated recognition for their effectiveness and the interest they have stimulated among audiences both at home and abroad. The main CBC Web site (www.cbc.ca), for example, now receives more than 3.5 million page views each week.

In addition to projects developed within CBC, public–private sector partnerships, such as those previously discussed, have made it possible to create sites associated with various special events. One such endeavour was CBC coverage made available on the World Wide Web (WWW) of the Nagano Olympic Winter Games produced in partnership with Sympatico and companies belonging to the Stentor group. By accessing this site, users were able to obtain accurate, and in some cases real-time, information about the various Olympic events. The initiative met with great success, making CBC the most trusted and most used online reference on the Olympics in Canada. Furthermore, a record number of visits were made to the CBC Olympic sites, making them the most frequently visited sites in Canada.

Additional partnerships, such as those with Avant-Go and Bell Mobility, have allowed users to download CBC content onto their hand-held organizers or to receive daily updates on their cell phones. Using various Internet and data technologies, CBC Radio and CBC Newsworld have extended the availability of content by providing on-demand access to their hourly newscasts in Real Audio and Real Video formats. Other partnerships, such as those with chapters.ca and cdplus.com, allow users to search out various retail products while simultaneously providing CBC with an opportunity to deliver relevant product information available on cbc.ca to an extended audience.

The inclusive nature of Internet communication technologies has not only enabled the mass media to extend their delivery of sport, but also has provided an opportunity for computer-equipped sport fans to communicate with each other through a number of online discussion forums and produce relatively inexpensively their own Web sites. Despite these advances in communication technologies, true convergence of traditional broadcast media forms and WWW operations has yet to be achieved in the public domain.

There is another Internet—already operational—where the minimum connection speed is almost 3000 times faster than a dial-up modem. On average, users receive connections up to one hundred times faster than home users experience with a broadband connection. It is a network so swift and so powerful that its advocates are claiming it has already changed the way we will interact with the Internet in the future. This new Internet, called Internet2, is under development in over 190 universities and research laboratories across the globe. Although its usage is limited to the research and education communities, its benefits could spill over into the mainstream in only a few years. Various media corporations, as well as companies such as McDonald's, Johnson & Johnson, and Ford, are keenly watching developments on the new network. The fast-food chain has already shown interest in the tele-immersion experiments run on Internet2, envisioning tele-immersion cubicles in its restaurants so those away from home could have dinner with their family.

With the increased bandwidth capabilities of Internet2, the development and implementation of software applications that enable such things as the broadcasting of high-definition television (HDTV) over the Internet have already become a reality. Multicasting, or broadcasting from one server to many recipients with one data stream, could enable a single Web server site to supply thousands of users with a continuous, uninterrupted feed. These developments create new possibilities not only for those involved in the distribution of media, but also for those who produce its content. In general, the discoveries made on Internet2 are poised to speed up the technological and corporate convergence of the "traditional" mass media.

In the meantime, various sports governing bodies, sponsors, and television networks have invested heavily in developing their own sport Web sites to bolster their regular television output; at the same time, the boundaries between these three entities are blurred by their promotion of one another on their Web sites. This relationship is further muddied by the recent ownership positions taken in a number of professional sport franchises by key figures in the high-tech media industry. Not surprisingly, the true convergence of the "traditional" media forms, if not already achieved, should be anticipated with the introduction of the next Internet.

CONCLUSIONS: SPORT, MEDIA, AND CULTURAL POWER

Whoever controls the media—the images—controls the culture.

—Allen Ginsberg, poet and author

Sport has played a critical role in the globalization process, regularly providing audiences from different cultures, languages, religions, and political ideologies with some of the largest global spectacles of our time. The Olympic Games, the World Cup of soccer, and the Super Bowl are among those sporting events that repeatedly attract audiences in excess of 100 million. With the continued proliferation of specialty sport newspapers and magazines, sport talk radio, sport channels, and sport Web sites, the media have become increasingly interlinked with these and other sport spectacles. In contemporary society, the mass media are the primary vehicle through which sports texts are produced and disseminated.

To establish a framework for the analysis of the relationship between sport and the media, this chapter has provided the reader with a theoretical outline of the triangular relationship that has emerged between sport, sponsors, and television. It then set out the components of mass media, identifying them as a subset of mass communication. The mass media were defined as a distinct set of activities, involving particular technological configurations, associated with formally constituted institutions or media outlets, acting according to certain laws, rules, and understandings, carried out by persons occupying certain roles, which together convey information, entertainment, images, and symbols to mass audiences.

Next, the relationship between television, sport, and sponsorship was explored, amplifying how the mass media have functioned within the wider political, economic, and cultural contours of society. In an effort to reveal the extent to which the political economy of media sport extends beyond the production, distribution, and consumption of mediated sports, this chapter included a case study of a recent media sports scandal. Finally, I have closed this chapter with a brief discussion of sport and the new media, revealing that technological change has been a constant feature of the media sports cultural complex, and how it is positioned to merge the traditional media forms, as well as those roles played by spectator and participant.

The capacity of each student of sport "to decode media sports texts and to detect the forms of ideological deployment of sport in the media is, irrespective of cultural taste, a crucial skill" (Rowe, 1999, p. 8). Given the position occupied by the mass media in today's society, along with the significant impact the media have on the meanings and values assigned to sporting events, it is also essential that we understand the relationship between sport and the media. With the ability to interpret mediated sport texts, students of sport are able to embark on a journey that will illuminate the process by which media sports are presented, created, and assigned various meanings within the wider political, economic, and cultural contours of our society.

Critical Thinking Questions

1. Why are media corporations prepared to spend huge sums of money on securing the television rights to sporting events?

2. Has the integration of sports and media into a combined totality moved sports away from the classical values of fair play and toward commercialization and profit? Are the two mutually exclusive?

3. How do the powerful allegiances being forged between television and sponsors present a challenge to those bodies that have traditionally run sport at either a national or international level?

4. Considering the rapid development of new media technologies, will the increasing capacity for international communications stifle Canadian cultural production or will it expand its possibilities?

Suggested Readings

Boyle, R., & Haynes, R. (2000). *Power play: Sport, the media and popular culture*. Harlow, England: Pearson Education Limited.

Gruneau, R., & Whitson, D. (1993). *Hockey Night in Canada: Sport, identities, and cultural politics*. Toronto: Garamond Press.

Lorimer, R., & McNulty, J. (1996). *Mass communication in Canada* (3rd ed.). Toronto: Oxford University Press.

McLuhan, M., & Fiore, Q. (2001). *The medium is the massage: An inventory of effects*. Corte Madera, Calif.: Gingko Press Inc.

McQuail, D. (1994). *Mass communication theory: An introduction* (3rd ed.). Thousand Oaks, Calif.: Sage.

Rowe, D. (1999). *Sport, culture and the media*. Buckingham, England: Open University Press.

Wenner, L. A. (Ed.). (1989). *Media, sport, and society*. Newbury Park, Calif.: Sage.

Wenner, L. A. (Ed.). (1998). *MediaSport*. London: Routledge.

Web Links

The Canadian Association of Journalists (CAJ)
http://www.eagle.ca/caj/
A Web site established by the CAJ containing a directory of Canadian journalists, an on-line archive of *Media Magazine*, and Internet resources for those interested in various aspects of journalism.

Canadian Newspaper Association (CNA)
http://www.cna-acj.ca/
A site for the people who publish and work for newspapers in Canada, as well as those who read newspapers, including an online resource of Canadian newspapers and media sources.

Canadian Radio-television and Telecommunications Commission (CRTC)
http://www.crtc.gc.ca/eng/welcome.htm
A Web site providing information about the history of Canada's broadcasting and telecommunication systems, as well as the relevant documents and speeches involving the Canadian agency responsible for regulating the system.

Ipsos-Reid Corporation
http://www.angusreid.com/
A Web site devoted to the collection and analysis of marketing data, providing both the public and private sector with insight into the thoughts, feelings, and intentions of people throughout the world.

Journal of Mass Media Ethics
http://jmme.byu.edu/
A Web site devoted to explorations of ethics problems and issues in the various fields of mass communication.

Media Awareness Network
http://www.media-awareness.ca/eng/
A Web site that provides resources for media education across the curriculum, focusing primarily on K - 12, while providing the user with information and "food for thought" on the evolving media culture.

Nielsen Media Research
http://www.nielsenmedia.com/
This Web site primarily provides information about the media measurement services available at Nielsen Media Research and the various means used to collect the data. Audience estimates for broadcast and cable networks, nationally distributed syndicated programs, and satellite distributors for various populations are made available on the Web site.

Scholarly Sport Sites
http://www.ucalgary.ca/library/ssportsite/
A subject directory that brings together Web sites that will assist the serious sports researcher on a broad range of topics.

11

Canadian Sport and Politics

Hart Cantelon

PAUL CHIASSON/CP PICTURE ARCHIVES

Prime Minister Jean Chrétien and then Quebec premier, Lucien Bouchard, hold up Montreal Canadiens' jerseys during a banquet in tribute to Maurice "Rocket" Richard, Montreal 1999.

Exaggerated nationalism is one of the greatest dangers of our society. We must confess that this phenomenon is also manifested in the Olympic Movement. Against this attitude a definite standpoint must be taken. Olympic Games must, conforming to the Olympic Rules, always be a festival of peace, a chivalrous competition between athletes and never between countries. Emphasizing national interests on the field of sports will be a deterioration of the Games, as it leads to excesses and makes it difficult to maintain the amateur definition.

Avery Brundage, Confidential circular letter to IOC members, 1957

INTRODUCTION

Avery Brundage was the president of the International Olympic Committee from 1952 to 1972. It was he, after the assassination of Israeli athletes at the 1972 Munich Olympic Games, who uttered the infamous words, "The Games must go on." For Brundage, political events, however tragic, should not interfere with his beloved Olympics. Sport and politics did not mix. At Munich the IOC president was seen as an anachronism in the world of international sport. How much more so, 30 years later?

The presence at Barcelona in 1992 of the American "Dream Team" made up of National Basketball Association professionals arguably sunk forever the notion of Olympic competition strictly for amateurs. Boycotts in 1980 (Moscow) and 1984 (Los Angeles) demonstrated how entrenched were the connections between Olympic competition and the sporting ambassadors who represent the nation state. As for excesses, the late Nick Auf der Maur (1976) once noted that the $1.4-billion Canadian price tag for the 1976 Montreal Olympics should be contrasted with the construction costs of St. Lawrence Seaway ($1.23 billion Canadian in 1975 dollars) and the TransCanada gas pipeline ($970 million Canadian in 1975 dollars). In fact, the only truth left to the Brundage pronouncement is the fact that the Olympic Games have gone on, albeit in a form that would dismay the former IOC president. The contemporary Olympics might be characterized as an explicitly politicized sporting movement. And the Canadian nation-state is an active participant in this high-profile international sports arena, sending both its professional sports entertainers (NHL hockey players) and state-supported national team members to Winter and Summer Games.

But it is not only the Olympic Games that interests the contemporary nation-state. Sport participation at all levels, from the entrance-level programs for youngsters to the high-performance international competition has become part of government-funded initiatives. "Sport matters," as British prime minister Tony Blair tersely states it (Department for Culture, Media and Sport, 2000, p. 2).

There are many ways in which one might address the relationship of sport and politics. One could suggest how sport has always been political. One could demonstrate the "dark side" of the relationships through undue interference, such as in sports boycotts. One could compare nation-states whose presence in sport is minimal with those that see sport as an integral part of national life. One might describe the nationalist fervour that uses sport as a demonstrative platform, such as has occurred in the United States after the attack on the New York City World Trade Center. One might engage in a content analysis of a series of policy documents to show the changing presence of the state in sport. Yes, there are many ways in which sport and politics might be addressed. My intention in this chapter is to articulate theoretically some fundamental concepts that relate to sport and politics. This articulation can be introduced with a series of questions:

- What is the state?
- What interventionist role in issues of social welfare does government play, as the administrative wing of the state?
- What is public policy and what role does it play in the creation of state policy toward sport?

- How is a national sports policy implemented and what are the consequences, positive and negative?

The chapter, therefore, is structured along themes suggested respectively by each of these questions.

THEORY OF THE STATE

It would be presumptuous to suggest that in a few short pages one could outline fully what is meant by the state.[1] Despite its complexity, it is important to understand the deeper meaning suggested by such entities as "the Canadian State." Richard Gruneau has argued that as a starting point, one might "define *the state* as that complex of institutions which politically embodies the values and interests of the people of any given society" (1982, p.3).

Implicit in Gruneau's definition is a notion of *homogeneity*, that is, there are nationally accepted values and interests among the citizens. On some levels this is true. Canadians generally accept the importance of interpersonal values such as politeness, honesty, reliability, friendliness, and a concern for others. Most believe in a distribution of resources so that underprivileged Canadians have adequate income and access to medical care. And if Canadians watch televised sport, they are likely to tune into ice hockey broadcasts (Bibby, 1995). But to suggest that this is all that needs to be said about the state would be incorrect. (And Gruneau is cognizant of this as well.) For this definition does not reflect the tensions that exist in deciding the distribution of state resources and the directions that state policy might take.

This insight raises questions of power: who decides how and why resources are to be distributed as they are and who will receive more or less of said resources. The German sociologist Max Weber saw *power* as the possibility of implementing individual or group intentions despite opposition from others (1978, p. 942). But since no one individual or group has absolute control of power or absolute lack of power, the complexity deepens. In any policy implementation or government directive, there could be conflict between elected political representatives, non-elected civil servants, or interests outside of the government administration. Thus, it must also be kept in mind that it is very difficult to determine what is meant exactly by such phrases as "in the national interest" or "on behalf of the citizens."

But it leads to even greater complexity for there are those who, while acknowledging that power is distributed unequally, maintain that the various "interest groups" found in any contemporary nation have equal opportunity to influence state policies. This theoretical position, popular in North America, is called *pluralism* and assumes that in Canada and the United States everyone, either personally or through affiliation to some group, has access to power; further, no one group can have too much power to influence state policies. Ralph Miliband has provided an excellent summation of this position.

> In these societies, citizens enjoy universal suffrage, free and regular elections, representative institutions, effective citizen rights, including the right of free speech, association and opposition; and both individuals and groups take ample advantage of these rights, under the protection of the law, an independent judiciary and a free political culture. (Miliband, 1973, p. 4)

The result, according to the pluralist position, is that no state government can ignore the wishes and demands of effective interest group lobbying and when all is said and done, "the national interests" of citizens will be met.

As persuasive as the pluralist argument might appear, there are difficulties with it, so say the Marxist theorists. Interest-group pluralism must and does take place within a particular **mode of production**, i.e., the socioeconomic basis of the society in question. With the collapse of the Soviet Union and its eastern bloc satellite states, the dominant mode of production of the globalizing world is that of market capitalism. Hence, the Marxist theorists argue, regardless of the diversity of lobby efforts, all have their origin within the capitalist mode of production. In the last instance, therefore, the long-term interests of capital always have primacy.

This is an important observation, for despite differences in culture, history or traditions, all nation-states now operate under the auspices of global capitalism. Those that do so "freely" are deemed to be democratic and "modern." Those few like Cuba that maintain a planned socialist mode of production are shunned and labelled oppressive and totalitarian. The Third World nations if they "modernize," i.e., introduce the market economy, will too enjoy the privileges of their First World cousins. What characterizes this pervasive mode of production is a highly industrialized level of economic activity that operates primarily under private ownership. The importance of this observation for sport policy will be made shortly. But there is one further aspect of state theory that first needs to be made.

This is the question of the boundaries of the state and might be introduced with the now-famous statement uttered by then-prime minister Pierre Trudeau: "The state has no business in the bedrooms of the nation" (Collier, 1997, p. 47). If state intervention is not welcome in the homes of citizens, are there other aspects of personal everyday life in which the state should not intervene? Implicit in this question is the notion that there must be at least one other realm of the nation that is not governed by state authorities. This is called **civil society**, that is the area of life that appears in what is known as "the public sphere," the volunteer activity an individual might spend in sports organizations, charitable associations, schools, religious institutions, trade unions, social movements, and the like. Consequently, the social world that any person is born into might be diagrammed as

in which the individual both acts and is acted upon by both civil and state society.

Just as there are debates about the distribution of power in the nation-state, so too there are debates concerning the degree to which civil society is autonomous from state influence. Pluralists would argue that the clearly defined parameters of the state structure negate any undue interference on the part of the latter. But for Marxist scholars like Antonio Gramsci, much of civil society is integrated into the state structure.

In the analysis of Italian society under the fascist government of Benito Mussolini, Gramsci was struck with the allegiance that the organized working classes and agricultural sector paid to Mussolini when it was clearly in their interest to resist his political policies.

Gramsci believed this allegiance rested in an important observation that Karl Marx noted in *The German Ideology*. It is worth quoting verbatim:

> *The ideas of the ruling class are in every epoch the ruling ideas: i.e., the class which is the ruling material force of the society, is at the same time its ruling intellectual force. The class which has the means of material production at its disposal, consequently also controls the means of mental production so that the ideas of those who lack the means of mental production are on the whole subject to it.* (Marx & Engels, 1976, p. 67)

From this observation, Gramsci fleshed out his theoretical concept of **hegemony**. It is the legitimation of a particular way of viewing the world that may or may not be in the interests of all who hold such a view. Hegemony is most powerful when it operates in those areas of life that at first glance appear to be outside state influence, that is civil society. Thus Gramsci argued that the structure and ideology of schooling, of sports, of the trade union movement, of religious and volunteer organizations were such that the capitalist world order would be maintained. Consent was manufactured for both those who gain considerable privilege from such a worldview and for those who would be disadvantaged by it.

This is a difficult concept to understand and it is wise to provide an example of how it operates. In my introductory classes in the sociology of sport, I introduce students to hegemony by asking the entire class to stand. I then ask all students who cannot skate to sit down. The remaining standing group are to think back to their first experience in learning to skate. I can embellish the image by having them recall the ice, indoors or out, the temperature, who they were with, etc. But my primary goal is to have them think about the skates they were wearing. All students whose skates were black are to sit down. Almost all the remaining standing students will be female, and many of the students in the class think I must be some kind of magician. But there is no magic here; it is hegemony, for structured into our common-sense notions of sport are issues of gender. Females by and large "should" learn to skate in white skates, boys in black skates. Today with the growing popularity of ice hockey among women, fewer women will be standing in my classroom exercise. But it is telling just how sustaining is the connection between skate colour and gender when there is no correlation whatsoever with learning the skill of skating.

What is both fascinating and troubling about Gramsci's hegemony is that it operates almost entirely without coercion. Individuals "freely" choose to legitimate ideas and values that may not be in their long-term interest. And for those who espouse this intervention of the state interests into civil society, there will be profound implications because of the state policies that are put in place and which are legitimated through the democratic process.

At this point, I wish to close the discussion on the state with the challenge that good citizenship requires the individual to think about the debates on the state. A final summary by Gordon Marshall is appropriate here:

> *Any definition of the state has to recognize its complexity. Its boundaries are not clearly defined and* [are] *constantly changing. It is the site of internal conflicts not only between different organizations but also within organizations. There is no single state interest but rather, various interests within different parts of the state. These interests are neither solely state-centred nor wholly society-centred but develop instead through bargaining between different groups in civil society and different state actors.* (1994, p. 508)

THE ROLE OF GOVERNMENT

The most visible aspect of state society, and one that many people assume "is" the state, is the administrative arm, the different levels of government. Since it is government that is directly responsible for issues of public policy formation and their delivery, it is important to outline the role that elected officials play in this matter.

Earlier I noted that the pluralist notion of the state seems to make perfect sense because of such things as the rights of citizens to freedom of assembly, freedom of speech, and universal suffrage. We generally speak about these rights as part and parcel of democratic societies. But here again, there is a good deal more complexity than at first appears, for as C.B. Macpherson noted years ago, "democracy has become an ambiguous thing, with different meanings...even opposite meanings...for different peoples" (1965, p. 2).

In a series of four talks that were first presented on CBC Radio as part of the Massey Lectures, Professor Macpherson outlined some observations about democracy that are important to keep in mind. First, "our" liberal democracy is only one of several representations of what is known as democracy. Second, liberal democracy is fundamentally a system of power, that is, people are governed such that they may be made to do things they would not otherwise choose to do, and to refrain from doing things they might like to do. Third, and this ties in with the Marxist concept of the state, liberal democracy has a history linked to a particular economic system. Those nation-states with a capitalist market mode of production are the only ones to also espouse a liberal democratic ideology. The fourth important observation that Macpherson makes is that within liberal democratic states, the notion of liberalism preceded that of democracy. **Democracy** originally meant rule by the common people and as such was to be feared by the superior social classes. **Liberalism**, on the other hand, meant "that both the society as a whole and the system of government were organized on a principle of freedom of choice" (Macpherson, 1965, p. 6). And as Macpherson notes, "In its fully developed form, when most individuals offered their labour on the market to those who possessed accumulated capital on which they could employ other people's labour, it is known as the **capitalist market economy**" (1965, p. 7). It was well after the liberal market state was up and running, that questions of democratic rights and liberties were addressed. One such important liberty was the **right of association**, the right to associate with whom one wished, either in political parties or organizations that might bring pressure on elected and non-elected state authorities. Hence, the final observation that Macpherson makes is the basis of the pluralist notion of the state.

Notwithstanding, the Marxist concept of the state gains strength because of Macpherson's observations. Political decisions are in the last instance made within the dictates of the marketplace. Ralph Miliband makes its consequences nakedly clear.

> [C]apitalist regimes have mainly been governed by men [sic] who have either genuinely believed in the virtues of capitalism, or who, whatever their reservations as to this or that aspect of it, have accepted it as far superior to any possible alternative economic and social system, and who have therefore made it their prime business to defend it. (Miliband, 1973, p. 65)

The importance of this observation cannot be overemphasized. Regardless of which political party might be the elected government in Canada, the United States, or Australia (the three nations used as case studies in this text), one can predict that they will work within the capitalist market economy. In short, there is no question of a revolutionary manifesto from any political party as the political platform in liberal democratic societies. However, it does mean that where differences occur between political parties, such differences are found generally in the area of *social welfare policies*. Gary Teeple has defined such polices in the following manner:

> *... social policies, programs, standards, and regulations in order to ... provide for, answer, or accommodate certain social needs for which the capitalist mode of production in itself has no solution or makes no provision.* (Teeple, 1995, p.15)

Put another way, because of the inequalities that can and do occur within the capitalist market economy, and in order to address potential dissent and unrest, the state has an obligation to provide for all citizens, and for certain disadvantaged groups, those provisions that only can be provided on a collective basis.

It is in the area of social welfare policies that one can first see the explicit state presence in sport. Generally such debates take place as a response to the philosophical question concerning the "right" of the state to intervene into what has historically been considered civil society. If one considers play as utterly devoid of any work-like characteristic, as incompatible with its opposite, then politically, one is not likely to consider organized play (sport) as a bone fide area of social welfare. If, on the other hand, the oppositional aspects of work and play are blurred, as they were in the former Soviet Union,[2] one is more likely to see social welfare policies concerning sport.

Within this philosophical debate, political parties may choose to include sport as a legitimate aspect of social welfare (*provision*). But it should also be kept in mind that the state, through government *regulation*, has historically intervened into the realm of play (see Goodman, 1979; Kidd, 1996; Metcalfe, 1978). To mention two examples of intervention through regulation, consider the following. Carey Goodman carefully documents the fundamental transformation that Jewish parenting patterns and the concept of "playground" had to undergo when municipal ordinances prohibited children from playing in the New York City streets in front of their parents' businesses. Bruce Kidd notes how the Canadian state "contributed to the developing practice and meaning of sports, primarily through regulation of leisure" (1996, p. 19). Countless other examples could be cited. Simply put, it is futile to argue that sport and politics have at one time been separate. As I have already noted, liberal democracy is a form of power in which the behaviour of citizens can be regulated. But the question that I wish to raise immediately is the question of provision, how and why do governments come to see *play* (in its most general definition as a continuum from spontaneous leisure pursuits to organized competitive sport) as a legitimate benefactor of social welfare policy?

STATE INTERVENTION INTO SPORT AS SOCIAL WELFARE PROVISION

Canada, Australia, and the United States have much in common when it comes to the historical legacy of sport. All were former British colonies and despite the revolutionary fracture that represented American–British relations, like the Canadians and Australians, the Americans owe much of their sporting pursuits and ethos to Britain. While competition was important, it was to take place within the bounds set up by the Victorian notion of "the gentlemanly amateur." The image of this sporting gentleman presumed sport was the social birthright of middle-class men and their exclusive pleasure garden.

Such an austere position reigned supreme in most sporting circles until after World War II. The quotation by Avery Brundage that began this chapter is echoed by the long-standing conservatism of Canadian politicians. Sport is part of civil society and, like Trudeau's pronouncements about the state and the nation's bedrooms, was an area of everyday life that should be state-free. The parliamentary debates about Canadian participation at the 1936 Berlin Olympic Games included the retort from Prime Minister King, "It is doubtful that anyone participating in the Olympic Games is a representative of the Government of this country" (Canada, 1936, p. 159). Such an attitude prevailed even after World War II "by the Liberal Health Minister, Paul Martin, who bore the responsibility for the National Physical Fitness program" (Kidd, 1980, p. 2). And yet by the 1970s, Canada had its first minister of sport, Iona Campagnolo, who would unabashedly declare, "Sport is now recognized as a legitimate Canadian cultural activity, not just the concern of a few sweaty athletes" (Gray, 1979, p.13). What accounts for this rather rapid "about face" on the part of the Canadian polity?

I would argue that a very plausible answer lies in the highly pragmatic concept of sport that came to define the activity in the Soviet Union after the 1917 Revolution (see Cantelon, 1981). Sport was no private pleasure garden for elitist men but the work-like profession of those with athletic ability, male and female alike. World records were to be surpassed continually by these athletic workers.

This philosophy marked the future direction of the international high-performance sport program and, with the Soviet entrance into the 1952 Helsinki Olympic Games, transformed utterly the gentlemanly ethos of sporting competition. In the USSR, sports organizations and their athletes had definite goals to achieve, both at home and as established foreign-policy objectives. The Soviet worker-athlete came to epitomize excellence in sport. And this sporting transformation had a lasting impact on the Canadian notion of non-state provision of sport.

As a long-time member of the international sports fraternity, Canada needed to do something about its declining fortunes in competition, particularly its regular losses in ice hockey after 1952, to the USSR. By September 1961, Bill C-131, An Act to Encourage Fitness and Amateur Sport, was passed unanimously in the House of Commons. As Macintosh et al. carefully document, the Bill was particularly meant as a sporting transfusion to halt "the country's sagging reputation in Olympic and World Cup hockey" (1987, p. 11).

Three important observations can be made about this watershed document. First, Bill C-131 represents the explicit entry of the Canadian government into the provision domain of sporting intervention. As Prime Minister John Diefenbaker declared during the debates leading up to the passage of the Bill:

> *There are tremendous dividends in national pride from some degree of success in athletics. The uncommitted countries of the world are now using these athletic contests as measurements of the strength and power of the nations participating.* (Canada, 1960, p. 39)

Second, it is telling that this Bill was passed unanimously. Just as no political party in a liberal democratic state is likely to ever conceive of a revolutionary political platform, so too it is unlikely that any party will have a dramatically different policy toward sport from its political opponents.[3] Sport may now have explicit political purposes to serve, but unlike other aspects of partisan politics, the purposes fall under the rubric of any and all party platforms. Bill C-131 escorted in the legitimacy of sport as part of the government's social welfare policy directives. Finally, international sport at the height of the Cold War, John Diefenbaker's veiled comments notwithstanding, was "war without weapons" (Goodhart & Chataway, 1968; Orwell, 1958). A victory over the Soviet Union was more than a sporting win; it was a victory for the capitalist world over its arch enemy, state communism.

By 2002, the state presence in Canadian sport was an accepted aspect of the social world. Whereas in 1936 Mackenzie King could categorically state that international athletes did not represent the nation, the contemporary national-team athlete is given financial assistance through Sport Canada's Athletic Assistance Program (AAP) to explicitly represent Canada as a role model, national hero, and messenger for national unity and pride (Sport Canada, 2002). The provision aspects of this state presence are implemented through the mechanism of public policy formation. Our attention can now focus on this mechanism.

THE MECHANISM OF PUBLIC POLICY FORMATION[4]

Once the officials of any nation-state make the decision that sport is an important avenue of intervention, policies are normally put in place to reflect the role that sport is to play. As already noted, under the auspices of regulation, what is lawful and orderly behaviour is often reflected in the area of sport. So too, particularly after the invention of nuclear weapons of mass destruction, international sports competition was seen as a reasonable and pragmatic alternative to war. Some nation-states legitimate their intervention for military or state security reasons, the "fit to fight" mentality. Others emphasize the importance of promoting national motivational programs such as the Canadian ParticipAction, or the Australian "Life Be In It" schemes to encourage a healthy lifestyle. Regardless of the underlying causes of state involvement, invariably intervention comes about through the mechanism of public policy formation.

Les Pal (1992) has argued that the citizens in any nation-state have some common-sense notion of what the government is doing with reference to the latter's policies. As such, **policy** is a general guide of how the state, for example, decides questions of distribution of resources. Pal goes on to define **public policy** "as a course of action or inaction chosen by public authorities to address a given problem or interrelated set of problems" (1992, p. 2). It is clear from the discussion above that the Canadian government chose to intervene in the civil realm of sport in response to the declining fortunes of Canadian athletes in international competition, particularly hockey.

Any issue (and in our case, specifically sport-related) can achieve public agenda status if the issue is seen as a "public problem." Obviously to achieve the notoriety implicit in the notion of a public problem, there have to be persons and/or groups who champion the issue as such. These persons can be external to the government and represent the pluralist notion of "interest groups" or lobbyists who seek to influence the government on a particular issue of public importance. Thus, **lobbying** can be defined as an organized form of persuasion, whose aim is to advocate for a particular issue or point of view aimed at those who are directly or indirectly responsible for making decisions (e.g., politicians) that will affect the outcome of the lobbyists' efforts.

In the lead-up to the passage of Bill C-131, for example, lobbyists came from a wide spectrum of Canadian society. But issues can become part of the public agenda from within the government as well. In fact, whether there is external lobbying or internal actions of government officials, in the end, it is necessary for the politicians to ensure that programs are put in place to deliver the policy objectives.

THE ADMINISTRATION OF CANADIAN SPORT AND ITS CONSEQUENCES

The political figure who arguably put in place the administrative apparatus of the Canadian government policy on sport was the Honourable John Munro, then-minister of National Health and Welfare. On January 18, 1969, the minister stood before delegates of the Canadian Amateur Sports Federation and spelled out his (and the government's) vision of sport. Gone was the rhetoric that denied any relationship between sport and politics. Instead were representations of sport as culture, of sport as a legacy of Greek civilization, and the pronouncement that "a sound mind in a sound body" was enduring. The Canadian government would take its rightful place in the provision of sport for important political reasons. It would promote national unity, always tenuous in a country as geographically expansive as Canada and with two official language groups (French and English). It would heighten the international stature of the nation, through its athletes, as social historian Bruce Kidd describes them, "sweat-suited philanthropists" (Kidd, 1988). Excellence in sport was to be pursued on two levels: sporting victories in international competition and greater involvement of Canadians in participatory programs. Munro declared that the government had "a moral duty to assist" (1969, p. 3) the volunteer sports organizations in the development of athletic talent in the country. Finally, the minister grounded the provisions in the ideology of liberal democracy. Canada would not be like the Soviet Union with its blatant ideology of communism. Our athletes would not be "performing animals in a gilded cage, or wards of the state who are retained solely for their capacity to win" (p. 4). In a classic sleight of hand, Munro dismisses Soviet-style provision with the admonition that state-supported Canadian athletes would develop in the true spirit of Olympism. But as the Dubin Commission would later reveal, such pronouncements were mere hollow rhetoric (Dubin, 1990). Nonetheless, with Munro's speech, the Canadian government steadily and relentlessly became the dominant player in Canadian non-professional sport.

It is beyond the scope of this chapter to address this development in detail. Rather, the following table will highlight the steady interventionist activity of the Canadian state into sport.

In the various government documents and task forces commissioned throughout the years there is a consistency to the rhetoric that is used to justify the role that the state plays in Canadian sport. Continually one reads:

- *The volunteer is the backbone of Canadian sport.*

This remains true, and to its credit, the state through organizations such as the Coaching Association of Canada has introduced and delivered an internationally recognized coaching program, the National Coaching Certification Program (NCCP), which deals with both the technical and theoretical aspects of coaching. Most volunteer sports organizations encourage (sometimes demand) that their coaches and administrators become NCCP-certified. The downside of the certification process is that it implicitly suggests that there is one correct

TABLE 11.1

DOCUMENT	DATE	RELEVANCE
Report of the Task Force on Sport for Canadians	1969	Politicians, athletes, and sports officials tour the country seeking a commitment to a visible state presence in Canadian sport
Munro speech to Canadian amateur sports federation	1969	Set in motion the organization strategy of state provision in sport
Sport Canada, Recreation Canada	1971	The embryo of the Canadian sports system is described in detail
Toward a national policy on amateur sport: a working paper	1977	Iona Campagnolo, Minister of State, Fitness and Amateur Sport, traverses the country seeking feedback as to what should be the Canadian sport policy.
Toward a National Policy on Fitness and Recreation	1979	A discussion paper that complemented its companion document, national policy on amateur sport
Partners in Pursuit of Excellence: A National Policy on Amateur Sport	1979	Iona Campagnolo's "White Paper on Sport," the detailed plan of state intervention in Canadian sport
A Challenge to the Nation: Fitness and Amateur Sport in the 80s	1981	Gerald A. Regan, Minister Responsible for Fitness and Amateur Sport, outlines his agenda for the Canadian sports system
Toward 2000: Building Canada's Sport System	1988	Appraisal of the Canadian sport system since its inception in the 1970s
Amateur Sport: Future Challenges	1990	A follow-up report of the 1988 document that also included information forthcoming from the Dubin Commission
Sport: The Way Ahead	1992	A comprehensive document that spelled out the future direction of Canadian sport
Report of the Core Sport Commissioner (The Best Report)	1994	J.C. Best, Core Sport Commissioner, outlines the gradual government withdrawal of universal support of Canadian sport and how support will be objectively measured
Sport in Canada: Leadership, Partnership and Accountability. Everybody's Business (The Mills Report)	1998	Chair Dennis Mills further clarifies the area of government support and more explicitly outlines the desired partnership of state and private-sector involvement
Towards a Canadian Sport Policy: Report on The National Summit on Sport	2001	Minister Denis Coderre brings delegates from all avenues of sport to Ottawa to discuss the future direction of Canadian sport policy

way to coach or administer sport, which leads to what Peter Berger et al. call "technological consciousness" (1974).

- *It is assumed that the Canadian public is willing to pay for its sports participation at least up to a certain level of athletic expertise.*

The 1977 *Toward a National Policy on Amateur Sport* noted, "As a generalization it is apparent that most parents in Canada seem committed to paying most of the individual costs of their children's participation in sports, at least until the intensity and time demands of the sport require unusual spending..." (Campagnolo, p. 9). Conveniently, this logic fits perfectly with the authority-terrain that the federal government has staked out for itself in the sport delivery system. It also echoes the Marxist argument that state policy is embedded in the mode of production. Individual choice and private disposable income form the basis upon which most Canadians wish their sport system to be organized, i.e., two ramparts of the liberal market economy.

- *The federal government's initiatives in sport will take place only with national and international calibre athletes.*

With this narrow window of responsibility, the federal government maintains the separation of provincial and federal jurisdictions as determined by the British North America Act. The federal government "may" assist the provinces in the delivery of programs below national or international calibre, but generally leave this to provincial initiatives. This in itself causes problems and reflects other areas of tension between the provinces. For example, in its first incarnation, the Canada Games was meant to provide capital grants for the construction of sports facilities throughout the country. Participation was to fuel interest in sport, and the coming together of young men and women from the diverse provinces and territories was seen as a catalyst for the national unity goals of the Liberal government of Pierre Trudeau (Canada, 1969). All well and good, except the "have" provinces of Ontario, Quebec, and British Columbia (and sometimes Alberta) saw the Games as their national Olympics, their athletes as ambassadors of the province. In short, the competitions were there to be won. And so by 1975, the goal of the Canada Games changed dramatically. They were "to provide a national development competition of high calibre for a maximum number of athletes from all provinces and territories" (Canada Games Council, 1975, p. 2). Such a policy severely disadvantages some provinces and territories.

- *Non-professional sport in Canada is to be organized in a highly specific way.*

This statement is reflective of the organizational characteristics of the government's civil service. There are accountability standards and short-term and long-term planning objectives, and the structure generally suggests an administration whose goals are maximum efficiency and productivity. In fact, the metaphor first uttered by John Munro has been repeated continually since he first stated it. The organizational structure of Sport Canada, Munro commented, was "designed to move the administration of sport off the kitchen tables and into a more professional and efficient atmosphere" (Munro, 1971, p. 2). In theory, this structural change is not necessarily odious. However, in practice it had a profound negative impact upon those volunteers who were unfamiliar with governmental accounting procedures

(*Globe and Mail*, 1978, p. C1). In many cases it drove from sports administration the volunteers who were not interested in paid employment and who did not have the time or inclination to gain the expertise necessary to work within the government bureaucracy (see Macintosh & Whitson, 1990). The "professional bureaucrat" was recruited to fill the vacuum left by the retreating volunteers. Countless research (see for example, Beamish, 1975; Hall, Cullen, & Slack, 1990; Hollands & Gruneau, 1979; Macintosh & Whitson, 1990) has documented the systemic class- and gender-based discrimination of the Canadian sport organizations, with the transformation from volunteer to bureaucratic professional administration.

- *The government has the dual responsibility to deliver "sport for all" and "high-performance sport."*

I will not go into any great detail here, but the evidence would suggest that the Canadian government's strategy has continually privileged high performance at the expense of sport for all. The creation of the Coaching Association of Canada, the development of the NCCP program, the performance goals of the Canada Games, the Athlete Assistance Program, and the withdrawal in 2002 of support for ParticipAction, all suggest that high performance rules the day. And in the government insistence on the objective calculation of accountability and efficiency, it is far easier to count medals won and records set than it is to ascertain who is hiking in national parks, paddling on rivers, or playing pick-up hockey on outdoor ponds and rinks.

- *The government provision of sport insists upon cooperative initiatives: individual citizen, national sports federation, government and the private sector.*

While the importance of any of the agents may increase or decrease over time, the combination remains constant. Never was the administrative arm of the state to monopolize. From the outset it was acknowledged that the federal government was essential to "coordinate existing programs to meet national goals and international challenges." But it was also noted "Canadian sport, if it was to flourish, must receive additional help from business as well" (Campagnolo, 1979b, p. 9).

With the dismantling of the welfare state and the championing of neo-conservative economic policy, the more recent policy papers have steadily stressed the necessity of the private sector and individual Canadians to take a more active role in the nation's sport. Thus, the Mills Report (Canada, 1998) notes the "benefits" that accrue when clothing companies like Roots Canada outfit national team members. Previously, the *Report of the Core Sport Commissioner* (Best, 1994) put in motion a program in which not all sports would receive federal government funding. Such initiatives remind one of the tenuous relationship between sport as a bone fide agency worthy of public policy concern and the shaky foundation of sport as social welfare policy.

- *With government provision policies, the state assumes ultimate authority over sport.*

The steady influx of tax dollars into non-professional sport since 1969 meant that athletes and their sports federations became increasingly dependent on government funding. By 1981 the Regan report (*A Challenge to the Nation*) estimated that the government was bankrolling 90% of the costs of non-professional Canadian sport. The implications of such dependency are obvious. Sport Canada has considerable influence in determining the competitions in which athletes will compete; or in the case of the 1980 Moscow Olympic Games, those competitions that would be boycotted (see Cantelon, 1984). The authority of national coaches and their training regimes took precedence over local community coaches. Even the equipment used and uniforms worn were decided by the state with its sponsorship agreements with private-sector firms. At the same time, when the government changes its funding policies, as it did dramatically in 1994, the dependency of athletes and sports federations suffers greatly. Some in the sports community see such consequences as acceptable; for others they represent the unwelcome presence of the state within the civil society of sport (see Canada, 2001). But one thing is clear, once state provision for sport becomes a reality, it is almost impossible to remove its presence. This is no more evident than Sport Canada's Athlete Assistance Program (AAP); it is worthwhile to take a brief historical look at this government initiative.

SPORT CANADA'S ATHLETE ASSISTANCE PROGRAM

While the 1969 *Task Force on Sports* document ushered in state provision in Canadian sport, it was not until 1981 that the AAP was set in place "to provide identified athletes with direct financial assistance" (Minister Responsible for Fitness and Amateur Sport, 1982, p. 1). Figures 11.1 and 11.2 graphically illustrate the expansion of the AAP program and the number of athletes who receive financial support from it (Canadian Heritage, 2002).

FIGURE 11.1

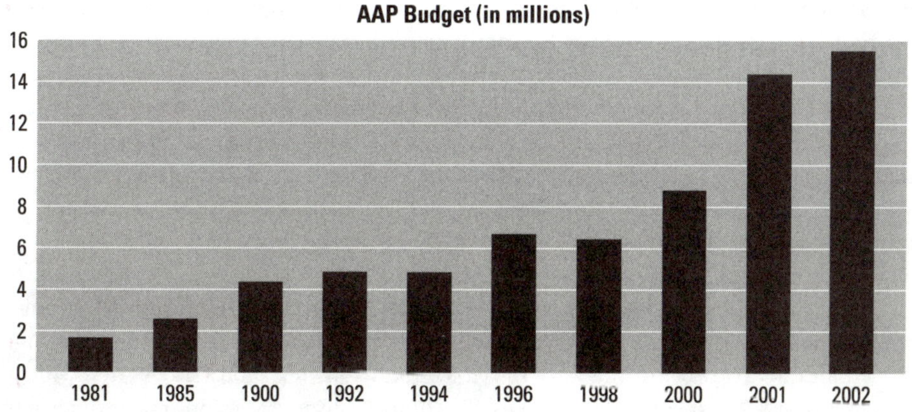

Athlete Assistance Program Annual Budget

And just as the government documents all express a rhetoric that justifies the state presence in sport, so too does the *AAP Handbook* carefully articulate the responsibilities of Sport Canada, the NSOs, and individual athletes (Sport Canada, 2002). A careful reading of the handbook regulations suggests that it would be almost impossible for any Canadian athlete to work outside the framework of the AAP, even if this was considered a feasible option. And for its part, "Sport Canada reserves the right to cancel or reduce the amount of funding if Parliament changes the funding levels" (p. 2-1). In essence, the AAP has resulted in the creation of an athletic wing of the federal civil service, albeit without many of the welfare benefits of the civil service (see Beamish & Boroway, 1988; Kidd & Eberts, 1982).

FIGURE 11.2

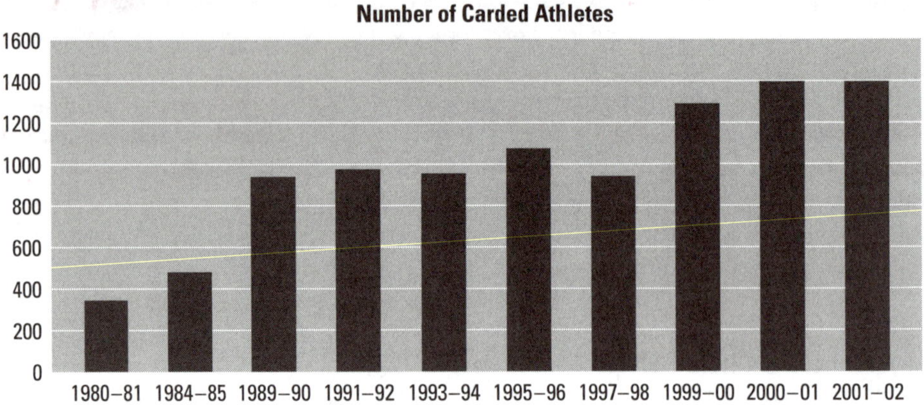

Source: Canadian Heritage (2002). Sport Canada: the Athlete Assistance Program—AAP Data. www.canadianheritage.gc.ca/Sportcanada/SC.

CONCLUSIONS

The history of the Canadian state demonstrates the regulatory and provisional aspects of public policy towards sport. This chapter has concentrated on issues of provision. State involvement has provided facilities and programs that probably would not exist without such policies. Rural and small-town Canada has sports facilities that otherwise would have been unaffordable. Canadian sport policy has quite rightly demanded that national sports organizations develop and deliver programs that reflect other progressive policies of the government: gender equity in programming, coach athlete ethics guidelines, sexual harassment policies, access to materials and programs in the two officials languages, programming for mentally and physically challenged Canadians, etc. And for those non-professional athletes who are pursuing excellence, there are top-level national training sites, state-of-the art training programs and coaching, international-level competitions, and financial support to augment personal income.

But there are other consequences of the state presence in sport. Public provision comes from tax dollars and as the cost overrun to the Montreal Olympic Games, and the protests (Bread not Circuses) against the Toronto bid for the 1996 and 2008 Games attests, many citizens resent this expenditure (see Lenskyj, 2000). State intervention into civil society means that individual citizens lose some freedom to do things as they would choose to do. The demands for NCCP program certification may have, for example, forced some long-time coaches out of sport; those who have neither the time nor inclination to obtain the necessary certification. The individual might be unable to access public facilities or to use them exactly as he or she might like. Considerable tension surrounds the issue of construction of facilities paid for by tax dollars and the primary tenants of such facilities, normally high-performance professional teams. And public provision brings with it a professional management administration and ethos, which is but one way in which sport might be managed.

At a deeper level, it must be remembered that social welfare policies are embedded in the liberal democratic view of the state. With its endorsement of the market economy and private ownership, constant political debates take place as to what should or should not be provided for citizens. State provision of sport in many ways acts as a barometer for economic cycles of prosperity or recession/depression. With prosperity comes lobbying for greater state involvement; with recession less. And always there will be those who believe that public provision should be minimal, with the marketplace and individual entrepreneurial initiatives being the provider.

At the outset I noted that there are many ways in which one might address the relationship of sport and politics. This chapter has tried to show the theoretical relationship that exists between concepts like the state, government, public policy, and policy implementation. As such, it has presented material and arguments that underlie those approaches that one might otherwise choose to pursue the sport–politics relationship. It should be clear that it is impossible to speak of sport devoid of politics for sport has a ubiquitous presence in all nation-states. It should also be clear that state intervention in sport can vacillate between minimal regulatory activity to a maximum provisional presence. Finally, it should be evident that the rudimentary theoretical material presented can be applied to a particular nation-state, be it Canada, the United States, or Australia.

Endnotes

1. Much of this discussion comes from several sources, including Collier, 1997; Gruneau, 1982; Marshall, 1994; Miliband, 1973; Offe, 1990; Teeple, 1995.

2. I have most fully considered this in my discussion of the Soviet categories of worker athletes and athletic workers in the paper "Stakhanovism and its influence on the development of Soviet international sport." *Proceedings: Fourth Canadian Symposium on the History of Sport and Physical Education*. University of British Columbia, Vancouver, 1979.

3. For example, even the latest of Canadian government policy documents, the Mills Report, included a representational parliamentary membership.

4. The arguments presented in this section principally come from Johnson, 1978; and Pal, 1992.

Critical Thinking Questions

1. Why is it important to understand something about the theory of the state in order to appreciate the sport/politics relationships?

2. What connections need to be made between the concepts of public policy, social welfare reform, and government intervention into sport?

3. What are the most important reasons that governments intervene in sporting matters on a provisional basis?

4. What is it about the Canadian system of government that makes its government intervention into sport somewhat different than other nation-states?

5. What are the advantages of having sport seen as a legitimate public policy concern that might not be addressed by a private-sector–organized sport system?

6. Access the Heritage Canada Web site at www.canadianheritage.gc.ca/. Follow the links to Sport Canada and its Athlete Assistance Program. Why does the author state that it would be almost impossible for a Canadian high-performance athlete to operate outside the AAP program, even if he or she wished to do so?

Suggested Readings

Arnaud, P., & Riordan, J. (1998). *Sport and international politics.* New York: E & FN Spon.

Canada. (1969). *Report on the task force on sports for Canadians.* Ottawa: The Queen's Printer.

Canada. (1988). *Toward 2000: Building Canada's sport system—the report of the taskforce on national sport policy.* Ottawa: Government of Canada Fitness and Amateur Sport.

Canada. (1992). *Sport: The way ahead.* Minister's Task Force on Federal Sport Policy. Ottawa: Minister of Supply and Services Canada.

Canada. (1998). *Sport in Canada: Leadership, partnership and accountability—everybody's business.* Standing Committee on Canadian Heritage, Sub-committee on the Study of Sport in Canada. Ottawa: Public Works and Government Services Canada-Publishing.

Canada. (2001). *Towards a Canadian sport policy: Report on the national summit on sport.* Ottawa: The Government of Canada.

Collier, K. (1997). *After the welfare state.* Vancouver: New Star Books.

Hill, C. (1996). *Olympic politics.* New York: St. Martin's Press.

Macintosh, D., Bedecki, T., & Franks, C.E.S. (1987). *Sport and politics in Canada: Federal government involvement since 1961.* Kingston, Ont.: McGill-Queen's Press.

Macintosh, D., & Whitson, D. (1990). *The game planners: Transforming Canada's sport system.* Montreal & Kingston: McGill-Queen's University Press.

Miliband, R. (1973). *The state in capitalist society: The analysis of the western system of power.* London: Quartet Books.

Riordan, J., & Krüger, A. (1999). *The international politics of sport in the twentieth century.* New York: E & FN Spon.

Teeple, G. (1995). *Globalization and the decline of social reform.* Toronto: Garamond Press.

Web Links

The *Atlantic* Online
http://www.theatlantic.com
Scholarly essays dealing with sport in contemporary society, including political issues.

British Studies
http://elt.britcoun.org.pl/s_index.htm
Issues specific to sport and politics in the United Kingdom.

The Government of Canada

http://www.gc.ca

Follow the links to Fitness & Amateur Sport and/or Sport Canada to see latest policy issues from the federal government.

Sport Information Resource Centre (SIRC)

http://www.soirtquest.com/

Issues and developments concerning Canadian sport federations.

References for Sport and Politics

http://www.sp.uconn.edu/~yian/frl/45polit.htm

Andrew Yiannakis maintains the Web site for the North American Society for Sport Sociology. This link outlines important references for sport and government.

Arts & Letters Daily

http://www.aldaily.com/

Excellent site managed by a retired New Zealand academic that highlights the best editorials from around the world, often concerning sport and politics.

12

Sport and Religion

Christopher Stevenson

FRANK GUNN/CP PICTURE ARCHIVE

Members of the Hamilton Tiger-Cats and the Montreal Alouettes huddle for a prayer on the field after a CFL East division semifinal game in Hamilton in 2001.

The Lord delighteth in a pair of sturdy legs.

Leslie Stephen (Maitland, *The Life and Letters of Leslie Stephen*)

This chapter is titled "Sport and Religion," but more properly this should read "Sport and Christianity," because it is *Christianity* and its relationship with sport that will be our specific focus. The reason for concentrating on Christianity rather than on Islam, Judaism, or Buddhism is that it has been Christian beliefs and values that have had such a powerful influence on the development of societies in Europe and North America. And more particularly these Christian beliefs and values have had an enormous influence on the development of sport in these societies. The values that are enshrined in modern European and North American legal systems, political systems, and social structures—the foundations upon which these societies have developed—were specifically derived from Christianity. And so the kind of society that Canadians developed from the 17th century onward was built on Christian ideals and ideas.

No one can doubt that other faith traditions were also present during the development of modern societies and modern sport, but these faith traditions—whether Native spirituality in North America or rabbinical Judaism in Europe—were rather marginal factors in the development of modern societies and modern sport. The ideas and ideals of rabbinical Judaism, for example, had little impact on the ways in which European societies developed through the 17th, 18th, and 19th centuries. Similarly, the values and beliefs of the Aboriginal peoples of North America had little influence on the ways in which North American societies developed. The reason is simple—these faith traditions were those of very much marginalized groups within these societies who had very limited access to any form of social power. Christians, on the other hand, predominated in these societies and held firmly onto the levers of power, and so their values, ideals, and ideas of Christianity became the foundations of these modern societies.

The organization of this chapter is as follows. First, we will look at the evidence that sport and religion have had a long history of interrelationships. Second, we will focus very specifically on the defining influence that one particular strand of Protestant Christianity—"Muscular Christianity"—has had on the development of "modern sport." Finally, we will examine some of the contemporary issues surrounding the relationship between Christianity and elite, competitive sport.

SPORT AND RELIGION IN EARLY SOCIETIES AND CULTURES

It is important to appreciate that sport and games have long been associated with religion. Indeed, in many societies, sport, games, and religion have been closely intertwined and interdependent. Allen Guttmann (1978) has emphasized this point. He suggests that there is "plentiful evidence" that most early or historical societies "incorporated running, jumping, throwing, wrestling, and even ball playing in their religious rituals and ceremonies" (p. 16). He points us back to Ancient Greece and explains that the various sporting festivals or games, such as the Olympic, the Pythian, the Isthmian, and the Nemean games, were indeed "sacred festivals, [and] integral aspects of the religious life" (p. 21) of the Greek culture of the time. Guttmann quotes Ludwig Deubner as saying: "The Olympic games were sacred games, staged in a sacred space and at a sacred festival; they were a religious act in honour of the deity. Those who took part did so in order to serve the god and the prizes which they won came from the god.... The Olympic games had their roots in religion" (p. 21).

And if we consider the various indigenous cultures in the Americas as another example, here, too, we find considerable evidence of the use of games in and as religious rituals and ceremonies. Stewart Culin, an early American anthropologist, wrote about the games of the Plain Indian culture, which were played "usually at fixed seasons as the accompaniment of certain festivals or religious rites" (Guttmann, 1978, p. 17). Culin went on to suggest that, "in general, games appear to be played ceremonially, as pleasing to the gods, with the object of securing fertility, causing rain, giving and prolonging life, expelling demons, or curing sickness." Similarly, Guttmann points us to the relay races of the Jicarilla Apaches of the U.S. Southwest, the "lograces" of the Timbira Indians of Brazil, and the ball games of the Maya and Aztecs—all of which, as far as we can discern, were intimately related to their religious practices and ceremonies.

SPORT, GAMES, AND THE EARLY CHRISTIAN CHURCH

But what of the early Christian societies—what was their attitude toward such games and contests? It seems quite clear that the general attitude of the early Christian church toward games, physical contests, and recreational pastimes was largely negative. By late in the 4th century CE, when the Roman Empire had became officially Christian, the church was so strongly opposed to such mass spectator spectacles as the Roman Games that they were officially abolished in 393 CE (Barney, 1996). Not only were the Games viewed as decadent, they were also seen as cruel and barbaric with their emphasis on such spectacles as fights between wild beasts as well as gladiatorial fights to the death.

This was partly the double legacy of the teachings of St. Paul and St. Augustine. St. Paul's attitude toward the body, or the "flesh" in his terminology, was that flesh corrupts—thus, while one's "spirit" might be true to God's teachings and wants to put these into practice, it is the "flesh" that corrupts these pure desires and causes us to turn away from God and toward perversions and evil (Galatians, 5: 16–26). St. Augustine also had a strongly negative attitude toward "the body" and anything associated with it—sexuality, gluttony, drunkenness, and so on. This attitude derived, so he tells us, from his own experiences as a young man when he enjoyed all sorts of bodily pleasures. Augustine eventually turned away from such things, repented of them, and then condemned them vigorously in his writings and his teachings (*Confessions*). The influence of both of these "saints" was powerful in the early church (even, indeed, into the modern era) and resulted in a fundamental Christian attitude of suspicion toward anything to do with the body.

And so from the early church, and for nearly 1900 years thereafter, the Christian attitude toward games and sport has been one of distrust. It has been the soul that has had the highest value, the highest priority, with the body and its physical passions and desires very much treated as a hindrance to true spirituality. Some strands of Christianity have even promoted the mortification of the flesh—deliberate mutilations, or deliberately ignoring disease or injury—as a means of overcoming bodily passions and becoming more in tune with the mind of God. It has only been when "use" or "need" could be argued that the church has given its approval to games and physical contests and recreations. Let us look at a particular example of this in the case of the Puritans.

THE PURITANS

The Puritans were a group of Christians who have come to have a rather unpleasant reputation. The popular notion of Puritans is that they were against anything and everything that gave pleasure! Lord Macaulay had a famous saying, that "the Puritan hated bear-baiting, not because it gave pain to the bear, but because it gave pleasure to the spectators" (Firth, 1968, p. 142). This is rather unfortunate because, as with most stereotypes, it is largely inaccurate. Certainly, the Puritans of the 1570s to the 1640s were a people who strove to live pure, "holy," Christian lives and tried hard to focus on "purifying" themselves spiritually—hence their name, Puritan. And they certainly established rules for living in order to better achieve their spiritual goals, but these rules were primarily for themselves and not necessarily for everyone else. The objective was for each person *individually* to achieve holiness.

The popular ideas about Puritans as killjoys comes from the behaviour of some branches of Puritanism in the late 1500s and early 1600s. When the Puritans established their communities in the New World, in Massachusetts and Connecticut, and so on, they established laws for these communities in accordance with their values and beliefs. They were concerned for the sanctity of the Sabbath Day and were appalled that others would spend the day "full heathenishly, in taverning, tippling, gaming, playing and beholding of bear-baitings and stage-plays" (Guttmann, 1988, p. 26). And so when they had the power to do so, they instituted laws to govern community behaviour on Sundays. Guttmann (1988) tells us, for example, of the Act of 1644 which established "that no person or persons shall hereafter upon the Lords-Day, use, exercise, keep, maintain, or be present at any wraslings, shooting, Bowling, ringing of Bells for Pleasure or Pastime, Masque, Wake, otherwise called Feasts, Church-Ale, Dancing, Games, Sport or Pastime whatsoever" (p.27). In Massachusetts Bay in 1630, John Baker was "whipped for shooteing att fowle on the Sabbath day," (p. 27) and "Vermonters who ran, rode, jumped, or danced on Sunday were subject to ten lashes and a 40 shilling fine" (p. 28). It is on such evidence that some historians have come to the conclusion that "the Puritans saw their mission to erase all sport and play from men's lives" (Brailsford, 1969, p.141).

However, a closer look at the writings of the Puritans suggests that their attitudes to physical activity were not entirely negative. They certainly recognized that people needed recreation from their labours—but it had to be *a purposeful and godly recreation*. The key here, therefore, is that if recreational activities can be claimed to be "useful," such as rest or recreation, then they are acceptable. Guttmann (1988) provides us with evidence of this approach by Puritan thinkers from the 17th century; thus, Perkins, in 1614, believed that "rest from labour with the refreshing of bodie and mind, is necessary" (p.30). Elton, in 1625, agreed: "There are such movings of the body as bee honest and delightfull exercise of the minde, and serve to the refreshing of the body and minde, as Shooting, Tennis-playing, Stoolball-playing, Wrestling, Running, and such like" (p. 30). And in 1726, Cotton Mather declared:

> *We would not be misunderstood ... that a due Pursuit of Religion is inconsistent with all manner of Diversion: No, we suppose there are Diversions undoubtedly innocent, yea profitable and of use,* to fit us for Service, by enlivening and fortifying our frail Nature, Invigorating the Animal Spirits, and Brightening the Mind, *when tired with close Application to Business. (Wagner, 1976, p. 144; emphasis added)*

What was implied in these pronouncements was that the purpose for participating in such activities *must be* a useful one; that, according to Richard Baxter, "the *end* to which you really intend in using it, must be to fit you for your *service to God*" (Guttmann, 1988, p. 31; emphasis in original). Usefulness, then, was a legitimate rationale for justifying the playing of games and sport—even for the Puritans! But usefulness within limits; there was to be no playing on the Sabbath, and complete avoidance of any association with cruelty, and no gambling, no drinking, and no idleness or wastefulness.

RELIGION AND THE DEVELOPMENT OF MODERN SPORT

But surely these cultures of the past and their fusion of religion and games have little relevance to today's modern sport. Not so! In fact, modern sports might not exist—at least in their current form and in their current dominance—if it had not been for the influence of a particular set of ideas contained in Protestant Christianity: "Muscular Christianity."

What I am suggesting is that there was a historical moment, a window of opportunity, when the possibility of the development of "modern sport" occurred. I do not mean the very day or the very hour when this happened; rather there was a period of time—not very long, but long enough, a decade or so—when significant influences came into alignment creating the possibility that the "modern" forms of sport could evolve. This historical moment was obviously somewhat different for different sports, but by and large many of the beginnings of modern sports occurred sometime between the 1830s and the 1880s.

A number of scholars have argued that in order for traditional folk games to be changed into the beginnings of modern sports, society needed to see itself and the natural world around it differently; that is, it had to take on "modern" attitudes and values, based on a secular, rational, and scientific worldview (see Guttmann, 1978, pp. 80–89). But there also needed to be a change in the reasons *why* people played these games and sports, and this reason (in the new scientific, rational world order) had to be that of *usefulness*. Sports could be permitted, even accepted, if they were seen as *useful*.

In order to appreciate the great importance of what happened in the development of modern sport, it is important to understand the huge transformation between the early 1800s and the 1880s in the ways in which sports and games were played. Traditional folk games and sporting recreations were wild and unruly affairs, minimally organized and played irregularly, often once or twice a year and mostly associated with local festivals and country fairs, and characterized by much drunkenness, gambling, and violent behaviour. For example, the result of a 16th-century "football" game was that "much harme was done, some in the great thronge falling into a trance, some having their bodies bruised and crushed; some their arms, heades or legges broken, and some otherwise maimed or in peril of their lives" (Dunning & Sheard, 1979, pp. 23–24).

Each community had its own version of these games, with rules and customs peculiar to itself, to which there was much local loyalty. There could be any number of participants playing at one time, there was nothing consistent about the size of playing surface or the types of balls or sticks or goals that could be used, there were different ways in which players could score, and "goals" could be situated in different places on and around the playing area. For example, many different types of early forms of stick and ball games were played on ice in Europe and in North America through the 1700s and into the early 1800s—games called shinney, ricket, and hurling—well before any one game called "hockey" emerged to be the dominant form of the sport (see Gruneau & Whitson, 1993). All of this rich diversity meant that inter-community competition was a rarity, partly because of the daunting logistics of travel to another community, either by foot or by horseback, and because it meant playing by someone else's rules and customs.

Yet out of this chaotic mix of many different ways of playing football, hockey, baseball, and all sorts of other games, the modern form of sport emerged; that is, a way of playing these games evolved that was qualitatively and quantitatively different from the old, traditional ways of playing. Allen Guttmann (1978) has argued that modern sports have a particular set of characteristics; thus (1) participation in these sports is not limited to only certain social groups or classes, (2) sports skills, techniques, and training methods become highly specialized and "scientific" in nature, (3) the playing and training systems that are used in these sports are highly efficient and focused, (4) sports' organizational structures are bureaucratic in nature, (5) the highly sophisticated and complex measurement of performance is a central feature of the competition, and (6) records are kept. So, out of the irregular, crude, idiosyncratic, traditional sports, a new efficient, standardized, rationalized, "modern" type of sport evolved.

Guttmann (1978; 1988) argues that this development of "modern" sport was but one part of the changes that were taking place in western societies from the 17th century onwards. There was a growing acceptance of a secular and scientific world-view that was associated with new forms of rationality and the concomitant development of industrial economies and bureaucracies, and above all with an emphasis on "achievement." These ideas influenced all aspects of social life, including the types of activities with which one filled one's recreational, non-working time. And so the evolution of modern sport out of its roots in traditional folk games was the result of the slow development of this "modern," rational, and scientific world-view.

But the final piece of the puzzle had to be the justification that sports were *useful*. It is here that Christianity, in the guise of a particular logic called "Muscular Christianity," played a critical role. There had always been considerable resistance from the social elite groups in society to the traditional games played by the lower classes; they saw them as depraved and depraving, as a waste of time, and associated with gambling, drinking, riotous behaviour, and physical violence. So, somehow, these negative attitudes toward sport had to change in order for modern sport to become socially accepted and, indeed, encouraged. What was essential was to frame these emerging sports in such a way that the old negative connotations were dispensed with and new, positive, "modern" rationales adopted—and the watchword was "usefulness."

Muscular Christianity provided that rationale at a particularly crucial moment in the development of modern sport. During the 1850s in England, two writers, Thomas Hughes and Charles Kingsley, both active Christians, wrote a number of novels and essays in which they promoted the ideas and values that came to be known as Muscular Christianity. This was a Christianity that was robust and active, in which honesty, openness, strength of character, and a dedication to one's country were celebrated as the highest of virtues. The Muscular Christian, it was said, "has hold of the old chivalrous and Christian belief, that a man's body is given to him to be trained and brought into subjection, and then used for the protection of the weak, the advancement of all righteous causes, and the subduing of the earth which God has given to the children of men" (Hughes, 1861, p.83). And—surprise!—this was a Christianity whose virtues could be demonstrated par excellence in sports! In books like *Tom Brown's Schooldays*, Thomas Hughes promoted the idea that strength of character, piety, and manliness were learned on the sports field. For, according to Charles Kingsley, "Games conduce not merely to physical, but to moral health; that in the playing-fields boys acquire virtues which no books can give them; not merely daring and endurance, but, better still, temper, self-restraint, fairness, honour, unenvious approbation of another's success and all that 'give and take' of life which stand a man in such good stead when he goes forth into the world" (Haley, 1978, p.119).

Muscular Christianity, then, provided an argument that said that sports are useful because they contribute to building up the participant's morality, character, manliness, piety, and patriotism. Through playing the new forms of "modern" sport, character is built—and not just any "character" but the most desirable of Christian characters. As one of Tom Brown's teachers says about the game of cricket, "the discipline and reliance on one another which it teaches is so valuable.... It merges the individual into the eleven; he doesn't play so that he may win, but that his side may" (Hughes, 1994, p. 349).

It was this collection of ideas that provided the last piece of the puzzle in setting the stage for the development of modern sports. Muscular Christianity provided the most positive function possible for the playing of sport—and it quickly caught on. Sport soon became an accepted feature of school life, played by the students, guided by the teachers, and praised for their character-transforming qualities by the headmasters. Schools throughout England, and then throughout the British Empire and into North America, used the arguments of Muscular Christianity to justify the introduction of sports into schools. It became commonplace for teachers to be hired according to their abilities in sport, rather than their command of their academic subject matter. By the 1880s the "games ethic" was supreme throughout the English-speaking world, and schools in North America—and particularly those private boarding schools designed to educate the sons of the elites—had introduced sports into the recreational times of their students. Schools such as Upper Canada College in Ontario (established in 1829) and Rothesay Collegiate School in New Brunswick (established in 1891) are striking examples of schools in which sports were (and still are!) promoted as building the desirable character in the sons (and more recently, the daughters) of the leading families in the Dominion.

This belief that games and sports could positively influence a participant's character, converting him into a person of morality, self-discipline, and with an obedient nature, was also seized upon as a solution to the increasingly difficult social problems of the growing towns and cities in both Europe and North America. These cities, growing in population because of huge migrations in from rural areas and increasing immigration from all parts of Europe and beyond, were faced with serious social problems—overcrowded urban spaces, and the rapidly growing prevalence of drunkenness, gambling, and various riotous behaviours. Civic leaders tried a variety of reform measures and municipal ordinances to deal with these problems, to little or no avail. What they needed was some way to divert the new urban working classes away from their dissolute and destructive activities and to turn them toward alternative, socially and morally improving activities. And Muscular Christianity, as linked with sport, seemed to fill the bill with its emphasis on morality and other Christian virtues. In many cities, civic leaders took the new "modern" forms of sport and promoted them in the organizations that were working with the urban working-class populations. The YMCAs, for example, soon began to use sports in addition to their traditional activities of bible studies and meetings, both as a means of attracting young men into their buildings and as a means of moulding their characters. Whether or not sport was successful as a means of urban social control, society's enthusiasm for sport nevertheless grew by leaps and bounds.

Muscular Christianity, therefore, played a critical role in the development of modern sport—the role of providing the acceptable justifications for participating in sport. Without these justifications, it is conceivable that the modern forms of sport that were just beginning to emerge might not have been accepted by the schools of the time, nor by the influential civic leaders, opinion makers, and reformers of the time. The probability is that our current social reality would be something quite different, and possibly sports—in the forms that we know them today and with the meanings we attribute to them today—would also be quite different.

What is also significant about Muscular Christianity is that its central ideas and beliefs still remain with us *today*. The idea that "sports build character" comes directly from Muscular Christianity; the idea that somehow those who play sports well also have moral characters that are beyond reproach comes from Muscular Christianity; the idea that sports can be used to train qualities of leadership, obedience to authority, and self-discipline comes from Muscular Christianity; the idea that sports provide an ideal training ground in masculinity—that sport, and particularly extreme contact sport, transforms young boys into men—comes from Muscular Christianity; the idea of sacrificing oneself for the success of one's team, one's school, or one's country comes from Muscular Christianity. All these ideas still have currency today in justifying the presence of sport in a variety of today's social settings, including schools, colleges and universities, management training courses, juvenile delinquency programs, and inner-city projects.

CONTEMPORARY TOPICS

Let us now turn to the present day and look at some of the contemporary issues surrounding sport and Christianity. We will look at a number of topics, beginning, first, with superstition and sport; second, we will look at some issues concerning the contemporary interaction between these two, apparently quite contradictory, value systems—elite, competitive sport, and Christianity; and finally, we will examine some of the critiques of evangelical Christianity's use of sport as part of its marketing techniques for evangelistic crusades and events.

Superstition and Sport

Sport, in many ways, is a hot-bed of superstition. Players, coaches, fans, all have their own particular "lucky" charms and "lucky" rituals, which they believe or at least hope contribute to a positive outcome for their team in the game. But what do we know about these superstitions, and why do people have them and use them?

Most people have some experience of superstitions: "A black cat crossing your path brings bad luck," but "A four-leaf clover brings good luck." Newspaper reports often provide examples of the many (often bizarre) superstitions that are rampant in the world of sports, including always eating the same meal before a game, always performing the same pre-game routines, always wearing the same clothes that they wore when they last won a game, never stepping on the lines on the field, and so on. Some athletes carry around talismans—the "lucky" T-shirt, the "lucky" sneakers, the "lucky" stuffed bear, the "lucky" coin, and many others. Jack McCallum (1992) has described the superstitions of Bill Parcells when he was head coach of the NFL New York Giants. Parcells, he said, "doesn't want any of his players or staff to precede him into the locker room, and he always wants to see the same players—Phil Simms, Brad Benson and Chris Godfrey—before he sees anyone else. He'll never pick up a penny that has tails facing up" (p. 204).

Mari Womack (1992) has analyzed some of these rituals and talismans and has identified a number of different types. First of all, there are the "*day-of-game*" rituals. Womack quotes a professional hockey player as saying, "When you win you try not to change anything. Nothing. You do everything exactly the same as you did the whole day of your win" (p. 196). But when a ritual "fails"—that is, the team or the athlete loses a game—then the rituals are changed as the athlete searches for a new pattern of behaviour that will "ensure" a win. Then there are the "*pregame*" rituals. These are rituals associated with getting ready for the game: getting the equipment together, getting dressed, being prepared by the medical staff, and so on. For example, says Womack, "some hockey players dress the entire left side of their bodies first—socks, skates, kneepads, etc.—before dressing the right side" (p. 197). The third category of rituals are the "*activity-specific*" rituals. Womack (1992) describes the actions of Al Hrabosky when he was a pitcher for the Kansas City Royals.

> *Before an important pitch, Hrabosky turns his back on the batter and stalks toward second base. He stares into center field.... Hrabosky then goosesteps back to the mound and glares at the batter. He swings his left foot back and forth across the pitching rubber, takes off his hat with his left hand and wipes across his head with his right forearm. He jerks his head up and down, and from side to side. Finally he pitches.* (p. 191)

And finally there are the "*rites of protection.*" These are actions and rituals performed in order to control "vague, undefined, and potentially threatening events or situations" (Womack, 1992, p. 198). Such situations in sport range from those potentially causing injury to those causing the team or the individual to lose the game. Players hide talismans such as medallions, crosses, or "lucky" charms in their uniforms or even in their shoes. Other players wear the same equipment they've worn since their college or junior days; Wayne Gretzky, for example, was renowned for the "old" style of hockey helmet he always wore. And some players prefer to work with particular teammates; Steve Carleton, when he pitched for the St. Louis Cardinals, always insisted that Tim McCarver played as his catcher—no one else.

But why do the athletes use these rituals and how do they believe they work? A classic explanation was offered by the anthropologist Bronislaw Malinowski (1927): that ritual is used to allay anxiety and to inspire confidence. Malcolm B. Hamilton (1995) suggested that superstition is always related to some definite outcome the individual wishes to achieve, and that the practitioners see them as a set of behaviours that are merely the means to an expected end. That is, ritual behaviours are, in essence, attempts to explain, understand, and control reality.

Professing Christians and the Dilemma of the Ethic of Competitive Sport

Christianity and the Sport Ethic It is common these days to have elite athletes openly and enthusiastically confess their Christian faith. But many scholars and theologians have argued that there is a serious contradiction between the value system (the ethic) of elite sport and that of Christianity. Hoffman (1992) points out that Christianity promotes "an ethic that places a premium on the Christian distinctives of submitting ends to means, product to process, quantity to quality, caring for self to caring for others" (p. 122). The ethos of sport, on the other hand, emphasizes "the use of strength, speed, and power to push human limits and aggressively dominate opponents in the quest of victories and championships" (Coakley, 2001, p. 94). Hoffmann asks the question: "Can the mind of Christ co-exist with the killer instinct?"

Stevenson (1991, 1997) investigated these issues by means of in-depth, biographical interviews with a number of elite athletes, all professing Christians, associated with the Athletes-in-Action Christian organization, and currently or recently a member of a national team, a professional team, or a college team. These athletes were committed to their sport and clearly valued the experiences and rewards associated with it. But they had also experienced significant problems in trying to live by the normative values of the competitive sport culture. They saw these normative values as being the following:

1. The Importance of Winning
   As athletes they knew that they were expected to strive to win at all costs, to be willing to do anything to achieve success—even to put up with playing with pain and injury. However, they struggled with this—was winning *really* this important? Was it *really* worth all this stress and the significant possibility of serious, even permanent, injuries?

2. The Importance of Social Status
   They understood and appreciated that success in sport brings popularity and status, and they had enjoyed these additional rewards. Yet at the same time, they questioned an ethic that continually asked, "What have you done for us today?" They questioned the need to be continually "paying the price" in dedication, obedience, loyalty, and sacrifice of self in a sport system that jettisoned the worn-out and unworthy without a moment's thought or regret.

3. Relationships with Coach and Team
   They realized that contemporary sports were predicated on a hierarchical authority structure, with the coach at the pinnacle of power and obedience as the proper response of all those under him or her. But they struggled with some of the consequences of this power hierarchy and the expectations of blind obedience, especially in situations when their own self-interest conflicted with that of the team. They realized that they were supposed to be pleased when a teammate scored a last-minute goal or made a fantastic save, but what if that player was playing in their position?

4. Relationship with Opponents
   They understood the need to get "psyched up" to play another team or to compete in an event. But they struggled with the apparent need to see their opponents as "the enemy" who "should be intimidated, punished and defeated" (p. 490).

5. Expectations of Others
   They appreciated the attention that being an elite athlete brought with it, but they had some difficulties with the expectations that others had of them as "athletes"—the expectations of how they were supposed to behave, the possibilities of now being thought "stuck-up" to "too good for old friends," and so on. They struggled with trying to juggle all these conflicting expectations.

As a consequence of these difficulties with the ethic of competitive sport, some athletes experienced crises; they spoke of the stress they felt, the injuries they suffered, the strained relationships with other non-athletic friends, the difficulties with their schoolwork, and so on. Some of these problems became so severe that the athletes sometimes withdrew from their sports for a while. And some were able to return only into a lesser competitive environment. Others spoke of their need to search for some deeper meaning in their sports involvement. The sport experience was supposed to make them feel good, successful, and fulfilled—yet they reported feeling only emptiness, unhappiness, and struggle—was this all there was?

Living as a Christian and as an Athlete If these are the consequences of the clash between the ethic of elite, competitive sport and the values of Christianity, how do professing Christian athletes survive? How do they reconcile the contradictions sufficiently to allow them to continue to compete and yet also feel that they are living out their faith? Stevenson (1991, 1997) examined these questions by asking probing questions of the same elite athletes, and in addition, Dunn and Stevenson (1998) also asked similar questions of non-elite, church-league hockey players, once more by means of in-depth interviews.

Among elite and non-elite athletes, there was one group who dealt with the contradiction between value systems of their faith and of their sports by simply either ignoring it, or by compartmentalizing their sport and their faith. Some athletes said that when they were at church they were "Christian," but in hockey, they were hockey players and "left their Christianity in the locker room." Others admitted that since they really did not know how to integrate their faith into the rest of their lives, it really was not much of a problem. Another group of elite and non-elite athletes were more pragmatic; they accepted the dominance of the sport ethic when they were playing their sport—aggression, dominance, "it's all part of the game," they said—but within that context, they tried to play the games as "Christianly" as possible, trying to obey the rules of the game, not to foul unnecessarily, not to deliberately hurt an opponent, and so on. Some took an approach to their game in which they played "for Christ" and tried to give Him 100% of their effort, strength, and will. Ironically, this meant that they now tried to win even more avidly—only this time "for Christ"! One of their rationales was that with success came the chance to evangelize—people will listen to winners, so winning would give them a chance to speak to others about their faith.

The final group of elite and non-elite athletes were those who were seriously committed to living out their Christian faith in all aspects of their lives, including in their sports. These athletes had considerable difficulties in accommodating their Christian values with the expectations of their sports, whether elite or non-elite. So they tried to put their sports "into perspective" and tried not to let their athletic goals and priorities take over their lives. Most of these athletes reported that they eventually had to withdraw from their sports, at least at the elite levels. They struggled with these decisions, but felt that it was the only way they could remain true to their beliefs.

Critiques of Evangelical Christianity's Use of Sport

One of the more obvious, contemporary examples of the relationship between sport and Christianity is the highly visible use of sport and sport figures by evangelical Christian organizations (such as Athletes-in-Action, Sports Ambassadors, and Sports Outreach America) as a means of attracting audiences to their cause and their message. It is the marketing of evangelical Christianity through the medium of sport—Brian Aitken (1993) calls it "the selling of Jesus." As Oral Roberts once commented, "Sports are becoming the Number One interest of people in America. For us to be relevant we had to gain the attention of millions of people in a way they would understand" (Coakley, 2001, p.470). Such organizations often use high-profile, professional sports "stars" as the headliners in their campaigns, the "honey" to attract the clientele that the organizers desire. These sports figures are introduced with great fanfare and often give a short talk about their own journeys as sports heroes and as Christians, after which the event is then given over to the evangelists proper, and the sports stars stay around to autograph baseballs or photographs or even bibles.

Tony Ladd and James Mathisen (1999) have argued that this use of sport heroes in evangelism corresponds to American evangelical Christianity's discovery of marketing techniques as means of reaching the non-evangelical masses. Ladd and Mathisen, along with others (for example, Flake, 1992), have characterized this use of sport as a return to, or a revitalization of, Muscular Christianity. But if one looks at this phenomenon more closely, it seems clear that there is little about this contemporary use of sport as a marketing tool that is reminiscent of the original tenets of Muscular Christianity and its desire to build an exemplary Christian character.

In fact, there has been some substantial criticism of this use of sport and sport heroes as tools of evangelism by such Christian organizations. Brian Aitken (1993) and Shirl Hoffman (1992), for example, have each offered a number of such criticisms. Aitken first speaks of the tendency (as he sees it) of such organizations to be opportunistic toward their "star" recruits from the world of sport; he is critical of the way they use them during their periods of popularity, but seem to discard them once their public profile becomes diminished. He also argues that there is little in the way of pastoral care in the mission of such organizations. Although people, including athletes, often come to the evangelistic events seeking practical help with life problems, the sports organizations, in Aitken's view, offer them very limited resources—and these tend to be almost exclusively religious remedies, based on a deep-seated belief that faith heals all ills.

Both Hoffman and Aitken are concerned about the sometimes implicit, sometimes explicit, ideological messages conveyed in the evangelical Christian literature and preaching. Aitken is critical of the fundamentalist ideology that the organizations tend to embrace—an acceptance of Old Testament morality, conservative politics, and a belief in the "traditional family"—which tends to glorify the "American way of life" and its emphasis on success, conspicuous consumption, obedience to authority, the nuclear family, and right-wing politics. At the same time, Hoffman is concerned about evangelical organizations' deliberately ignoring social issues, such as racism, gender discrimination, violence and brutality, and especially these social issues in the sport context. A number of moral and ethical issues arise in elite, competitive sport that need to be faced and about which judgments need to be reached. But, Hoffman says, "when sport is harnessed to the evangelistic enterprise, evangelicals become as much endorsers of the myths reinforced by popular sport as they do of the Christian gospel" (1992, p. 121) and thus have as much a stake in confirming the "goodness" of sport, and ignoring the "problems," as the sports promoters themselves.

Aitken, Hoffman, and other writers have also been critical of an approach to competition endorsed by evangelicals called variously "Total Release Performance" or "Praise Performance." The idea is that your performance is an act of love to God, so you should always put everything that you have into it—your effort, attention, strength, determination—everything, 100% ! In this way, so the evangelical Christian argument goes, you are expressing to God your gratitude for everything He has done for you. As one of the athletes in Stevenson's (1991) research explained,

> *No longer was I competing to make my place on the team or for my scholarship or for my coach or even for myself, but I was competing for Christ, and Christ was the only one in the stands.... And so the only way I could fail in Christ was if I didn't try my best.... So from that perspective it helped because I knew that I was giving my best, and that was 100% of what I had, and so that was good enough.* (p. 251)

This all sounds rather positive and laudable, but as Aitken points out, one of the implications of such an approach is that any instance of losing must mean that the athlete was in fact *not* giving 100%, not trying as hard as he or she could, not obeying the coach as he or she should. Another implication is that in this way almost anything can become sanctified—if you are using your talents to the best of your ability, "for God," then that's all you have to be concerned about. Even hitting an opponent as hard as you can becomes an act of worship and so is approved. "I'm going to hit you guys with all the love I have in me," said Rich Saul, a professional football player (Hoffman, 1992, p. 118). Clearly, this makes little sense. There must be some prior, moral, Christian evaluation of the appropriate "fit" of the activity itself. But it seems that evangelical Christian organizations that use sport and sport figures would rather turn a blind eye to the problems and contradictions inherent in elite, competitive sport—where, as Hoffman (1992) points out, "aggression is vented, old scores are settled, number one taken care of, [and] where the discourteous act looms" (p. 114).

CONCLUSIONS

So what have we learned? We now have an appreciation of just how complex the relationship has been between religion, on the one hand, and sport, games, and physical recreations, on the other hand. We can see how the close integration of religion and games in earlier cultures gave way in early Christianity to a fundamental distrust of anything to do with the physical body—a distrust that could be modified only by reference to an argument of the "usefulness" of certain forms of physical activity; an approach we see in the case of the Puritans and their attitudes toward sports, games, and physical pastimes. This rationale of "usefulness" was seen as particularly appropriate for the application of the ideas of Muscular Christianity to the playing of sport. Sport, it was argued, is an excellent arena in which a desirable Christian and manly character could be both demonstrated *and* developed. Sport, then, was justified as a superb means of "building character" and so was able to thrive and develop in late 19th- and early 20th-century society. As Bishop William T. Manning declared in 1925, "Clean, wholesome, well-regulated sport is a most powerful agency for true and upright living.... True sport and true religion should be in the closest touch and sympathy.... A well played game of polo or of football is in its own way as pleasing to God as a beautiful service of worship in the Cathedral" (Willis & Wettan, 1977, p. 196).

The contemporary relationship between sport and Christianity also appears to be predicated on the theme of "usefulness." The current use of sport and sports heroes by evangelical Christian organizations is based on the attractiveness of both to those segments of the population that the organizations are trying to draw to their meetings and rallies—primarily, young men! However, as we have seen, this relationship is fraught with problems of contradictory values, of the lack of pastoral care toward these athletes, and of the turning-of-a-blind-eye by these organizations to some of the on-going problematic practices in elite, competitive sport.

What does the future hold for this relationship? Will evangelical Christianity continue to find it "useful" to use sport and sports heroes in their campaigns, or will the excesses of high-profile, mass-spectator, commercialized sport eventually prove too much even for these most pragmatic of organizations? Will elite athletes continue to find such apparent succour and comfort in their faiths that they will continue to express it publicly, or will the realities of the inherent contradictions between the values and beliefs of Christianity and those of elite sport eventually prove too much for even the most committed of athletes? And will the value of "usefulness" continue to be the supreme justification in evangelical Christianity that it currently appears to be, or will some other rationale—say, the rationale of "grace," "the fundamental Christian doctrine which teaches that humankind was secured by God in an act of unmerited favour" (Hoffman, 1992, p. 122), or a rationale of "the divine spark called play ... [the] celebration of humanity's status in the divine order" (Hoffman, 1992, p. 122)? Only time will tell.

Critical Thinking Questions

1. Religion was at the core of the Olympic Games in Ancient Greece. Discuss the role that religion plays in the Modern Olympic Games, considering all aspects of the games from the Opening Ceremonies to the Closing Ceremonies.

2. Discuss the extent to which the attitudes of the Puritans (in all their complexity) toward games and physical recreations are still represented in the attitudes toward sports and games of contemporary leaders in church, school, and city.

3. Can sport itself be a "religion"? Discuss the issues surrounding this controversy and identify the set of arguments that makes most sense to you.

4. Describe examples of the use of talismans and ritual behaviours in church ceremonies and in sports. Discuss the similarities and differences between these uses of talismans and ritual behaviours, and compare their purposes in each social setting.

5. How easy is it to live up to your beliefs and ideals in highly stressful and competitive situations? Discuss this issue and provide examples from your own experiences in such social situations and in particular those involving competitive sport.

6. Choose a sport (such as golf, football, swimming, hockey) or choose a level of sport (such as intramurals, high school, local recreational league, national championships) and try to identify which ideas from Muscular Christianity are still present or identifiable in this sport or level of sport.

7. Some writers have offered criticisms of the use of sport and high-profile sports stars by evangelical Christian organizations. Choose a Christian sports organization and discuss its use of sport and sports stars in its evangelical missions and events.

Suggested Readings

Dunn, R., & Stevenson, C.L. (1998). The paradox of the church hockey league. *International Review for the Sociology of Sport*, 33, 131–41.

Guttmann, A. (1978). *From ritual to record: The nature of modern sports*. New York: Columbia University Press.

Higgs, R.J. (1995). *God in the stadium: Sports and religion in America*. Lexington, Ky.: University of Kentucky Press.

Hoffman, S.J. (1992). *Sport and religion*. Champaign, Ill.: Human Kinetics.

Ladd, T., & Mathisen, J. A. (1999). *Muscular Christianity: Evangelical Protestants and the development of American sport*. Grand Rapids, Mich.: Baker Books.

Stevenson, C.L. (1991). The Christian-athlete: An interactionist-developmental analysis. *Sociology of Sport Journal*, 8, 362–79.

Stevenson, C.L. (1997). Christian athletes and the culture of elite sport: Dilemmas and solutions. *Sociology of Sport Journal*, 14, 241–62.

Web Links

Athletics in Action
http://www.athletesinaction.org
Contains information about the mission of AIA, the events they host, and their programs.

The Fellowship of Christian Athletes
http://www.fca.org
Contains information about the FCA organization, resources that are available, and information specific to students and to adults.

Hockey Ministries International
http://www.gospelcom.net/hmi/
Contains general information about HMI and a list of the camps its offers.

Motor Racing Outreach
http://www.gospelcom.net/mro/
Provides a variety of links, gift ideas, as well as the teams and drivers involved in this ministry.

The National Christian College Athletic Association
http://www.thenccaa.org
Contains general information about NCCAA events, mission and outreach, and member institutions.

Sports Ambassadors
http://www.gospelcom.net/oci/sa/sports.htm
Overview of the Sports Ambassadors organization and its activities.

The Young Men's Christian Association
http://www.ymca.net
Outlines the history of the YMCA, its mission, its programs, and its local offices.

13

Current Trends and the Future of Sport

Dwight Zakus

STEVE MASON/PHOTODISC

The beginning and future of sport–children and parents involved.

Time present and time past
Are both perhaps present in time future,
And time future contained in time past.

T.S. Eliot, "Burnt Norton," *Four Quartets*

"It's déjà vu all over again."
"The future ain't what it used to be."

Yogi Berra, former New York Yankee baseball player and manager

Prediction of the future is the stuff of many social actors-soothsayers, fortunetellers, statisticians, and futurologists. Previous chapters presented material that indicates the ways in which humans construct their social settings and then act within those structures. Many issues arise concerning the specific social conditions that people find themselves in and those they inherit from previous generations. We have, however, volition in how we as social actors construct our lives and how we establish social conditions that will be part of future generations of Canadians. Nothing in the past is totally deterministic; we are not totally confined in our future by current or past social actions or conditions.

The scholars whose work was studied in previous chapters are not predicting the future through the materials they present. Yet one might see much in their work to make sense of today and tomorrow in what they write. Remember that today's events (social processes) are part of history once they occur. And history is the record of change in human social activities and structures.

Many would argue that the past is important to understanding the future. This is a yes and no statement. Yes, history is important to understand the future, but not completely so. On the other hand, an old adage claims that to not heed the past leaves one or society to repeat the past and the difficulties. So where Canadians are currently, based on where they have come from, does not provide the whole picture; however, we can make some sense of the future based on current trends.

This chapter will begin by discussing approaches to change. Then a discussion of current trends in sport will be presented. Here we will look at some data that point to future directions. In the third section, we discuss several structural changes and what these hold for future scenarios for sport. A summary completes this chapter.

PREDICTIONS AND ACTIONS ON AND IN THE FUTURE

How then does change occur and what do humans do to change? Whichever model of change one identifies as that holding most salience for their lives, it is based on particular assumptions (see Malloy, Ross, & Zakus, 2000). Three models are discussed in this section. Each should be understood on its own and any judgments made with the premise that each has its strengths and weaknesses. Students are urged to consider each process on its own and to explore their own assumptions and values for each model with regard to the future of sport.

An Evolutionary View of Change

Many people understand change as an evolutionary process. That change follows a pattern of increasing size and complexity over time. Here, current and past trends are identified and extended cognitively or statistically into the future. Change will occur within the context of the current situation in some iterative process.

This pattern is primarily conservative. That is, what is and what are seen as appropriate should be maintained in the future. Sport as it is currently structured and operated is the model to continue. When change is necessary, it is often a reactive rather than a proactive process. To deal with change, "more" is needed. More money, more people, more or larger organizations, more marketing, more effectiveness, or more state intervention is seen as necessary. The issue is not with the current context and operation of sport, but with greater demands on and in sport.

People operating from this perspective will actually resist change. They wish to *conserve* what is and will do so actively. This is a central way in which change is dealt with. For example, the discussions in Chapter 7 on gender issues in sport indicated how men have traditionally defined and operated sport and seek to continue to do so. Here the values, roles, and traditions in sport are espoused and the historic power enjoyed by men in sport is promoted as the way in which sport should continue.

Any change made is often done in response to legislation, political correctness, or tokenism rather than in a meaningful way. The expression "If it ain't broke, don't fix it" is espoused and indicates a gradual change within the context of the current structure, pattern, or operation of sport. The use of rational techniques such as statistical extrapolation is also employed in this context of change.

A Reformist View of Change

In western history many changes have been a response to the need for reform. Reformist approaches seek to improve the current state of human life, most often within the current context and power structures. For example, the church has led many such changes. The other key institution has been the state. In both cases, some problematic or structural issue arose. The issue meant that current structures and operations required attention to bring the situation back into line. Here are elements of the conservative approach, only with a distinction in that some major or structural change within that context is required (e.g., the Protestant Reformation within the Christian church).

Following Canada's poor results in the 1976 Montreal Olympics, it was recognized that Canada's sport structure needed reforming. This included a new approach to funding athletes to prepare for major international competitions and how the sports were governed and managed (see Macintosh & Whitson, 1990). The nature of sport was not questioned. The nature of the circumstances in which sport operated was questioned. What resulted was more of a reformation of the current sport-governing model and not of the nature of the traditional model of sport governance. However, as reform was instituted, many further changes followed, many that were major structural and operational ones.

A second major example of this type of change resulted from the Ben Johnson disqualification during the 1988 Seoul Olympic Games. The resultant Dubin Inquiry led to many reforms within the current sport structure, but not to a wholesale change in that structure.

As a result of this inquiry, global issues with doping in sport received greater attention, and reactions within Canadian sport led to many institutional changes. Canada set in place organizations to test, educate, and control the use of doping substances and practices. These changes led to Canada being acknowledged as a leader in this area and were partially responsible for the World Anti-Doping Agency (WADA) being headquartered in Montreal.

In both of these examples, the principles of equality and democracy were affronted. The playing field was not level and it was believed that it must somehow be made more equal. It did not matter that athletes of the former eastern bloc nations were state employees and therefore were funded, nor that they were systematically using doping techniques to enhance their performance (which, under the practices at that time, were indifferently dealt with). Those struggling to remain amateurs (unpaid labour) and those choosing not to dope were competing in an unequal context. New social practices and structures were needed within the world of sport to reduce or ideally eliminate these inequalities.

A Radical View of Change

The most strident approach to change is identified as the radical approach. Here the fundamental understanding of sport, its structure, power relations, and operations are questioned. Not only are they questioned but they are seen as being in need of wide-ranging fundamental change. That is, current definitions and structures of sport are problematic and are not fulfilling the values and goals they purport, so change is demanded.

At the heart of this approach is that the social and economic basis of society results in many inequalities. Most often these inequalities relate to capitalism and the resultant class-based society. The social matters identified in all the preceding chapters indicate this focus. Issues of power differences, market operations, and tacit inequality are central within this type of social structure. Change proposed within this approach demands a fundamental change of society, a breaking down of the inequalities inherent in capitalism.

Obviously such a change involves an unlikely scenario. What then is possible? A first response has been made by the state to attempt to rectify the inequalities. Welfare state programs (see Chapters 3, 4, 9, and 11) are one response, but not a radical one. Second, individual social action through protest and lobbying are indicated. In Canada, women's groups pushed change through in both general and sport-specific legislation by more radical means such as pressure groups (lobbying government) and open protest activities (large public demonstrations and marches).

In the end, however, both of these actions led to reformist change, not the radical change they would indicate. This points to the concept of hegemony and to the maintenance of a wider status quo.

CURRENT TRENDS

One way in which we use the past to indicate what might happen in the future is to use historical data and extrapolate possible future trends. This is quite a common way for various people to determine what might happen in the future. For example, stock markets and government departments use techniques based on past statistical information to evaluate what prices, economic activity, or other social conditions might be and how they might be addressed.

Another way in which the past is used is to look for patterns. Often in human history, patterns have repeated themselves (with some obvious inherent differences). Again, this is not to say that history *will* repeat itself, but certainly that similar circumstances might lead to similar future events. What does this indicate for sport?

Several demographic characteristics can provide information on what the future of Canadian sport might be. This includes population growth and aging; immigration as a percentage of population; degree of urbanization; and sport participation rates. Each of these is discussed in the following sections.

Population Growth and Aging

Canada is an aging country with a low birth rate. Population growth has been approximately 1% per annum between 1996 and 2001, and the population is projected to increase by less than 1% to 2006 (Statistics Canada, 2002, accessed 20/01/02). Added to this is the fact that Canada is also an aging nation and seeks immigrants to continue to grow (see below). With regard to sport, we ask which sports will continue to have participants and will produce national and international calibre athletes. Likewise, how much will certain sport spectator markets grow or be maintained?

The "baby-boomer" post–World War II age group is seen as a key indicator of several social issues into the early 21st century. The bulge of people born between 1946 and 1965, a 19-year cohort of the population, overrepresents how the total population is affected. As this cohort matures and the size of population that will support their retirement, health needs, and workforce inputs is disproportionately smaller, several economic and social issues will accrue. In 2001 the baby boomers were aged 36 to 55 years. According to 2001 population projections, this age group totals approximately 32% of the total population and will remain around that level until 2006, when the first part of the cohort reaches retirement age.

Sport Canada (1998) reported that 38.3% of the 55-plus age group felt that age was a factor in their non-participation in sport. A further 23.6% reported that health and injury kept them from sport (these figures for females only are 40% and 24% respectively). With female life expectancy higher than that of males, who are the primary participants in sport, the likely figure for female non-participation will increase. The above two factors, added to pressures such as lower household disposable income, increasing costs of sport equipment, registration, and membership fees, limited leisure time, and the availability of numerous other competing leisure activities (e.g., video games, home computers, Internet access) point to significant economic impacts on sport, sport participation, and the management of sport in the future (Sport Canada, 1998, pp. 60–62). Sport Canada also reports the 55-plus age group has the lowest indirect involvement in sport as well.

Immigration

Immigration to Canada will remain a significant factor in the makeup of the country in the future. Immigration was a significant feature of the settling of Canada, and it remains a key to Canada's population growth. Since 1986 immigration to Canada contributed to 48 to 51% of Canada's population growth (Boyd & Vickers, 2000, p. 4). In the 1996 census, immigrants made up 17% of the population (Boyd & Vickers, 2000, p. 9). Throughout the 1980s, immigrants increasingly came from places other than the United States, the United Kingdom, and Europe, and in 1996 people from places other than those more traditional sources made up 48% of all immigrants (Boyd & Vickers, 2000, p. 9).

With an increasing proportion of the population not being of Anglo-American, European, or Canadian origins, what will the effect be on sport in Canada? Will these new people follow the traditional sports of Canada? What sports do they bring with them? What are the implications on sport facilities and state subsidies as a result of this shift? Are the newcomers sport spectators and for which sports? Will they become socialized as Canadians and support western sport as participants and spectators?

These questions point to changes that will influence the future of Canadian sport. Many immigrants will come to live more as Canadians than as they did in their home country and will participate actively and as spectators in Canadian sport. It is difficult to determine how many immigrants will come to cheer for Canadian athletes in major international competitions or who and how many will be representative athletes for Canada. Further, their influences in the social construction of sport indicate that change will occur as they bring with them their backgrounds in the structure and operation of sport, providing a rich mosaic of new sport interests.

Urbanization

In 1931, 54% of the population lived in urban centres; that percentage rose to 70% in 1961 and 78% in 1996 (Statistics Canada, January 2, 2002, p. 4). Most of this population is located along the U.S. border. These statistics have implications for sport in the provision of teams, leagues, and facilities in both urban and rural settings. In rural settings there are fewer children, youths, and adults to populate teams and therefore leagues for competition. To have separate teams and leagues for boys and girls or single community teams and leagues is increasingly difficult to bring about. The contraction of the hinterland has had a considerable effect on sport. Many villages and towns have disappeared from the map. As they disappear, so too do the school playing fields, the local arena, and other recreational facilities. This then becomes a "catch-22" situation as there are no or few facilities to allow sport participation with too few participants to warrant demand and too few taxpayers to fund the facilities (see Gruneau & Whitson, 1993, pp. 205–10).

Conversely, increased urban populations and new suburbs put pressures on the provision of teams, leagues, coaches, and managers for sport. These increasing populations also put greater demands on parks, pools, arenas, stadiums, tracks, and other sport facilities in urban settings. Both aspects, the human and matériel, put pressure on local and provincial state provision of sport. Add to this the demands for large publicly funded stadium and arena facilities for professional or elite sport, and the result is further pressure on the state (at all levels in this case). However, this claim is not supported by a 1998 Sport Canada document, which indicates that "the unavailability of sport facilities and programs ranked last among the reasons for non-participation" in sport (Sport Canada, 1998, p. 57), which suggests that current provision is not a problem.

Nonetheless, urbanization is a double-edged sword in Canadian sport, for the state has to balance financial and political pressures to ensure that Canadians are continually able to access sport. Local, provincial, and national sport organizations also are under pressure to find and train athletes, coaches, managers, and administrators for both rural and urban sport. These factors provide major challenges for those in government and sport.

Sport Demographics

To understand the statistical trends in sport, two documents must be examined. The first is the above-mentioned Sport Canada (1998) document (and its earlier 1994 Highlights), which identifies trends for the 15-plus age groups. The second is Kremarik's (2000) summary of sport trends for 5- to 14-year-olds derived from the 1998 General Social Survey (GSS). Between the two we can make observations about the total Canadian population at this time (2002).

Both documents define sport participation to include those who engage in a particular sport at least once a week, but does not include activities for recreation (e.g., walking, aquafitness, bicycling, body building, hiking, jogging, skateboarding) that might be defined as sport by some people. The data presented here are therefore limited as the separation between sport as recreation (schoolyard softball) and sport in an organized league (a formal community softball league) is questionable. It does raise, however, the question of whether sport participation can be studied and understood only in the context of formal (usually adult-organized) teams and leagues.

Kremarik (2000) noted that 2.2 million children aged 5 to 14 (54% of this age range) participated in some form of sport in 1998. Further, nearly half of this total participated in more than one sport. He also indicated that soccer (31%), swimming (24%), hockey (24%), baseball (22%), and basketball (13%) were the top five of ten sports this age group actively participated in (Kremarik, 2000, p. 21). While this article does not have as much data as the Sport Canada publication, it does provide insight as to why 5- to 14-year-olds are involved in sport.

Kremarik (2000) did further statistical analysis of the GSS data to understand the degree to which parental involvement in sport and family income affect sport participation among this group. His findings confirm that children from families where at least one parent is active in a sport or is a volunteer in sport (coach, manager, administrator, etc.) are more likely to participate in sport. There is some evidence here to support socialization theory. This is important for the future of sport as it indicates that participants, support for particular sports, and volunteers to support the whole sport system are being generated.

As noted in Chapter 1, socialization in and via sport is significant. Think back on your own involvement and history in sport, reflecting particularly on the socialization aspect. This also raises a number of interesting questions. What will new immigrants bring to Canadian sport and will their children be socialized in and through sport—and if so, how? Will traditional Canadian sports continue or will new sports rise to prominence? How well will volunteerism work under these conditions? More simply put, how will future generations of Canadian children and youth become participants and future volunteers in sport?

Another key variable indicating sport participation in this age group was family income. Analysis by Kremarik (2000, pp. 22–23) found participation rates in sport of 79.3% for children in households with incomes of $80 000 and over, 62.5% in homes with incomes of $40 000 to $80 000, and 49.4% in homes with incomes of less than $40 000. These figures are higher than those reported for the correlation between sport participation and family income for youths 15 years and up (Sport Canada, 1998, p. 21). Children and youths from sport-active two-parent households with over $80 000 of family income were 12 times more likely to be in sport than those in a home with an inactive parent and family income of less than $20 000 (Kremarik, 2000, p. 23). Finally, Kremarik (2000) stated that this "suggests that income is a barrier for children from households in lower income groups" (p. 22, citing results from Offord, Lipman, & Duku, 1998). Again, the current structure of Canadian society and of sport in our society contains inequalities that are detrimental to wider participation and the overall development of individuals and the society.

If we look at the Sport Canada data for 1992 and 1998 for those 15 years and older, we find that participation rates have fallen, gender differences are expanding, and the influence of age in that gap is notable (see Table 13.1). Similar results were found in each GSS for the influence on sport participation of income, level of education attainment, labour force participation, and mother tongue (note that the 1998 report also provides information on competitions on teams and in leagues that indicate future trends). An interesting difference between the two surveys was seen in the most popular sport. In the 1992 summary, the sports with most participants were hockey, baseball, volleyball, golf, and bowling. By 1998 the order had changed to golf, hockey, baseball, swimming, and basketball. The fact that participation rates for hockey were not the highest is interesting. Whether this is a shift in interest or a result of age demographics posits an interesting research topic for the future and for claims indicated in the next section.

TABLE 13.1 Active Sport Participation of Canadians, 15+ Years Old

	1992		1998		
	000s	**% (M:F%)**	**000s**	**% (M:F%)**	**Net change**
Total	9594	45.1	8309	34.2	-10.9
Males	5454	52.3	5140	43.1	-9.2
Females	4141	38.1	3169	25.7	-12.4
15–18	1185	76.8 (80:64)	1121	68.2 (80:55)	-8.6
19–24	1375	61.3	1235	51.1 (63:39)	-10.2
25–34	2483	52.8	1781	38.6 (48:29)	-14.2
35–54	3196	43.0	2937	31.4 (39.5:23)	-11.6
55 and over	1355	25.3 (28:22)	1234	19.8 (25:15)	-5.5

Source: Adapted from Sport Canada, 1998, pp. 12, 13.

Another variable of interest for the future of sport in the Sport Canada (1998) report concerns participation rates in essentially volunteer positions in coaching, administration, and officiating (see Table 13.2a, b—note: this table also indicates spectator rates for amateur sport). Within these figures several points are notable.

First, the number of female coaches has risen by 300% between 1992 and 1998, while the number of 15- to 18-year-olds coaching has doubled. These are strong positive signs for the future of sport in Canada. Level of education and income held constant over the two surveys with the number of indirect contributions rising with higher education and income levels.

TABLE 13.2A Indirect Involvement in Sport, Comparison of 1992 and 1998

	1992	1998
Administration/Helper	9.2	7.0
Referee	2.6	3.9
Coach	3.9	7.1
Spectator	23.9	31.5

Source: Adapted from Sport Canada, 1998, p. 39.

Spectatorship at amateur sport events is an interesting variable. The change between 1992 and 1998 was 8%. Of this, 55% of spectators were aged 15 to 18 years old and a further 36% were aged 19 to 24 years old. What one can surmise from these figures is that peer group and young parents are more highly involved than those in the older age categories are. As nearly 31% of the total population is involved in amateur sport, one can argue that socialization is occurring and future sport participants and spectators are being developed. This rate must be juxtaposed with that for elite and professional and entertainment sport. Clearly there will be overlaps between the two, but a comparison of live audience participation would be interesting.

TABLE 13.2B Direct and Indirect Involvement in Sport, 1998 Figures

	Thousands	%	Thousands	%	Thousands	%
Population aged 15 and over	24 260		11 937		12 323	
Regularly participate in sport	8 309	34.2	5 140	43.1	3 169	25.7
Through a club or organization	4 599	19.0	2 238	19.6	2 261	18.3
Competition and/or tournament	2 992	12.3	2 076	17.4	916	7.4
Coach	1 729	7.1	962	8.1	766	6.2
Referee/official/umpire	937	3.9	537	4.5	399	3.2
Administrator/helper	1 706	7.0	842	7.1	864	7.0
Spectator at amateur sport competition	7 651	31.5	4 040	33.8	3 611	29.3

Source: Based on data from the Statistics Canada General Social Survey, 1998.

STRUCTURAL CHANGES AND THE FUTURE OF CANADIAN SPORT

This section will look at the larger or macro level of social structure to point to different future issues in Canadian sport. There are many issues, as previous chapters have exhibited. In this chapter, only a few, but not necessarily the key, structural topics are addressed. Readers are directed to Chapter 2 in the Malloy, Ross, and Zakus (2000) book for a further reading of the possible topics. The few topics presented here simply attempt to raise issues about the future and the possible outcomes of those topics.

Sport is seen as a central feature of modern society, but it must also be understood as a cultural element as well. That is, while embracing a set of socially constructed activities and structures, sport must also be understood in relation to the cultural elements that complete its place in those social activities and structures. Sport is a system of symbols and signs that define it beyond the definitions usually employed. Most often sport is seen as a subcultural element of the general (i.e., Canadian) culture that embraces a series of its own subcultural elements (i.e., within each type of sport, within sport teams and clubs, and within different sport organizations). Following the discussion of sport as a cultural element, we will focus on a few aspects of the underlying capitalist nature and operation of our society. Much that was presented in previous chapters makes note of this fact. The nature of capitalism and the future of sport are inextricably intertwined, for the market base of our society is in a dialectical relationship with the cultural structures arising from that base.

Sport as a Cultural Element

With the implementation of the 1995 North American Free Trade Agreement (NAFTA), the question of Canadian sovereignty took on greater importance. Canada has always struggled to maintain a separate identity in its relationship first with Britain and now the United States, both culturally and economically. As a colonial or dependent state, Canada has had to define and protect its identity as a unique and separate nation. What, then, is this identity? Are we what former prime minister Brian Mulroney claimed: a nation that is culturally defined by hockey?

As noted in Chapter 11, the state claimed sport to be a central, important feature of how Canadians see and understand themselves. To further emphasize this, in 1994 the federal government passed an act to recognize ice hockey (winter) and lacrosse (summer) as Canada's national sports (National Sports of Canada Act, Chapter N-16.7). These, of course, are symbolic elements of what partially defines Canada's cultural identity.

Culture has many definitions; however, language, common understandings, identifiable ways of living, symbols that point to a common identity (e.g., flag, anthem, currency, buildings, historic sites), and ways of thinking are often seen as the key elements (see Chapter 1 in Gruneau & Whitson, 1993, for a discussion of this concept). If one thinks about what it is that makes being Canadian unique, one begins to make sense of culture. Culture is an important element of any society and is often protected by legislation and government bureaus.

FIGURE 13.1

Aislin/*Montreal Gazette*

In the above section, we noted that hockey does not now have the largest participant base, pointing out a unique cultural contradiction. Many arguments would arise over the place of hockey in defining "Canadianness" (see Kidd, 1970, and Metcalfe, 1987, for a wider discussion of this topic). For example, the 1972 Canada–U.S.S.R. hockey series illustrates an absolute high of Canadian sport achievement. The dramatic late goal by Canada's Paul Henderson gave Canadians cause to celebrate both being Canadian and Canada being the world power in hockey. Many of your parents and grandparents will remember fondly the pride and excitement in this moment.

For some time, Canada enjoyed supremacy in a series of Canada Cup victories. This position, however, has declined. Recent defeats in world, junior, and women's competitions, and pre-2002 Olympic Winter Games (OWG), have eroded Canada's position in world hockey and now threaten part of Canadian cultural identity. This naturally leads to the question of how relevant hockey is to all Canadians and how culturally reduced Canadians feel when defeated in various world hockey competitions (cf. Jackson, 1994) or, conversely, ecstatic when a Canadian athlete wins a gold medal in half-pipe snowboarding.

In recent OWG Canada finished ninth in 1992, seventh in 1994, fourth in 1998, and fourth in 2002 in the medal standings. Yet the national mood appeared low as the men's hockey team finished second in 1992, fourth in 1994, and second in 1998. In Canada, the "home of hockey," anything less than a gold medal in men's ice hockey adversely affects the national mood. The gold-medal win by the men's team in the 2002 OWG led to euphoric celebrations throughout Canada, seemingly overriding achievements by other Canadian athletes (including the women's ice hockey gold-medal win over the United States). Sunday

February 24, 2002, will be as revered as is the day Paul Henderson scored the series-winning goal in 1972. Both events reclaimed Canada's position as the best nation in world ice hockey, however suspect that claim might be in reality.

The degree to which sport generally or a sport specifically contributes to Canadian identity is open to debate. There does seem to be some degree to which this correlation makes intuitive sense. Just as many Canadians can remember where they were when Canada defeated the U.S.S.R. in 1972, many also remember Ben Johnson's 100-metre race in the 1988 Seoul Olympics as an identifying moment. This later moment had less of the euphoria, and the sad outcome has had a long-term effect on the Canadian psyche. For good or bad, sport has come to occupy a central position in Canadian identity.

Canada's national and international teams have come to represent more than their own performances. Their successes and failures influence Canadians to different degrees. One does not have to be a fan or sport aficionado to revel in outcomes of local, regional, national, or international teams. Spontaneous crowd outbursts, flag waving, and euphoric cheering by the general population are an expression of nationalistic joy that is easily witnessed. As both fans and non-fans exhibit this behaviour, they are saying something important about being Canadian. For example, the public outburst over Jamie Salé and David Pelletier's pairs figure skating silver medal, which was upgraded to gold after a judging scandal was revealed, at the Salt Lake City 2002 OWG gives some indication of how widely sport raises national feelings.

While Canadians might not be identified with hockey as profoundly as in the past, sport is certainly a key element of our culture. But we can observe the tensions between traditional sports and newer sport forms. Will future generations of Canadians only cheer for our mogul and aerial skiers, half-pipe and slalom snowboarders, or eXtreme-games athletes? Or will they continue to show support for our curlers, gymnasts, fencers, and wrestlers? Will the Canadian state and the IOC continue with traditional sports or focus on those sports that are more commercially viable? It is likely that if Canadian athletes show strongly in the newer sports, attention, funding, and inclusion of the newer sport forms will follow.

Government Involvement in Sport

The Canadian state, at all levels, provides economic and structural support for what are identified as merit goods and public goods in the sport sector (Berrett, Slack, & Whitson, 1993). A merit good results when citizens feel great pride over an athlete's Olympic or World gold-medal win, where the basis for that athlete's success results from a state-developed and -funded sport program. A public good in sport occurs when a major sport facility or games festival is funded in part by the state (e.g., the facilities for and the holding of the 1988 Calgary Winter Olympic Games). Under current economic circumstances, the question of how much longer this funding continues arises.

The complexity of the funding structure and the rise of managerialism and economic rationalism in the 1980s indicate that the state is struggling to be all things to all sports. With diminishing funds and more sports seeking recognition and support, those not achieving international success and, at the same time, large participant bases will not likely continue to receive government funding.

Perhaps a larger issue for state sport bodies is their success in international competitions and the number of participants at the lower levels of its structure. Canada's success at the Olympic Games and Olympic Winter Games has been of varying levels (see Table 13.3 for the medal counts). The question whether this is an adequate return for the level of funding provided will continue. While Canada's sport system is one of the best in the world, the development of athletic talent might not match the inputs.

An analysis of the talent identification and development programs at the national, provincial, and territory levels, as well as their overall coherence, would be necessary to substantiate this claim. However, the results from major competitions indicate these systems are problematic (see also Chapters 3, 4, and 11). On the other hand, and looking at the figures in the second section of this chapter, the question of how the sport governing bodies can attract more participants and develop successful world class athletes (future outputs) becomes central.

TABLE 13.3 Olympic Results—Summer and Winter Games

	Gold Medals	**Silver Medals**	**Bronze Medals**
Pre-1969 Task Force			
1908	3	3	9
1912	3	2	3
1920 (OG/OWG totals)*	2/1	3/0	3/0
1924	0/1	3/0	1/0
1928	4/1	4/0	7/0
1932	2/1	5/1	8/5
1936	1/1	3/0	5/0
1948	0/2	1/0	2/1
1952	1/1	2/0	0/1
1956	2/0	1/1	3/2
1960	0/2	1/1	0/1
1964	1/1	2/0	0/0
1968	1/1	3/1	1/1
Post 1969 Task Force			
1972	0/0	2/1	3/0
1976	0/1	2/1	3/0
1980**	0/0	0/1	0/1
1984**	10/2	18/1	16/1
1988 (19 & 13 on medal table)***	3/0	2/2	5/3
1992 (11 & 9 on medal table)	7/2	4/3	7/2
1994 (OWG only) (3rd)	3	6	4
1996 (OG only) (21st)	3	11	8
1998 (OWG only) (4th)	6	5	4
2000 (OG only) (27th)	3	3	8
2002 (OWG only) (4th)	6	3	8

*OG-Olympic Games (Summer); OWG-Winter Olympic Games

**Boycotts occurred in each of these Olympic Games.

***Numbers in parentheses indicate Canada's position in the overall medal table for the OG and OWG.

Source: Zakus, 1988, p. 150 and IOC Web page.

New Technologies and Sport

The issues concerning drug use in sport are well known. Clearly more must be done if there is a true desire to rid sport of performance-enhancing substances and practices. As mentioned above, Montreal is now host to the World Anti-Doping Agency, which is chaired by a Canadian, Richard Pound. Sport and drug-related issues are not a recent topic. As John Hoberman (1992) and Terry Todd (1987) have noted, this issue has a long history in sport and will likely be with us for some time. It appears that new failures and scandals do not overly surprise many people.

An issue in sport that will have more dramatic consequences is related to new genetic knowledge and future practices. The Human Genome Project to map the human DNA sequence is leading to a number of medical advances. Other genetic research has led to cloning; it will not be long before in vitro fertilization "designer babies" are born. The genetic factors sought in these babies could potentially be those necessary to produce top sport performers (Cole, 1994). Featherstone (1991, cited in Cole, 1994) noted

> *the potential consequences here for, to take an example, sport are tremendous. Not only is there the capacity to enhance performance and repair, or replace body parts to produce cyberbodies. There is also the potential to genetically design optimum types of bodies best suited for particular sports.* (p. 22)

Clearly, a debate over this type of human performance manipulation will soon be forthcoming in the world of sport. It is more a question of when rather than if we will see cyborgs (human-like robots with digitally controlled prostheses) in sport.

The above focuses directly on the human body. Certainly new knowledge about the science and techniques of training are enhancing athletic ability. Technology, however, has also rapidly advanced in the area of sport equipment and facilities. For example, golf club and ball development has reached a point where the length of the course, or the ability to extend the length of the course, is outstripped by golfers' ability to hit the ball great distances. The question of whether it is the equipment or the athlete leading to new records becomes central. Expensive ballparks, stadiums, and arenas are quickly outdated as new building materials, techniques, and designs evolve. Many new sport facilities have short lives, costing governments considerable amounts in public infrastructure investment.

Both human and matériel technological developments will give rise to numerous future debates. The question of what this means to the average person on the street must be raised. Does it matter that some people seek to dope or to pay huge amounts for designer babies? Will the contest be between genetic or pharmaceutical corporations to decide which has the best product to replace the competition of sport? Will humans enjoy watching these genetically constructed "athletes" and cyborgs over "normal" humans? How much of this is science fiction and how much the future of sport?

This debate raises fundamental issues about the human and social nature of sport. Clearly this will be an important issue at the top end of sport production, but is not likely to be as significant for the average active sportsperson. Other than being consumers for new clothes, shoes, and other sporting goods, most of us will continue in sport the same way people have for years. Here again it must be stated that much of the focus on sport tends to the upper, elite, professional, entertainment levels. For many of us this discussion is fascinating but not the reality of sport as we encounter it throughout life.

The Future of Canadian Sport in the Global Context

To predict the future of Canadian sport is fraught with difficulty. The predictions will likely be based on incorrect assumptions, leaving the prognosis faulty. Should this, however, deter us from trying to make sense of that future? Sport in Canada is part of the broader, global structure of sport. To understand Canadian sport, we must look at and make sense of sport in the larger social context (Maguire, 1999). Much has been written lately about globalization and the place of sport in this expanded world. In this section we will look at some of these assumptions and attempt to indicate what might happen to Canadian sport.

Canadian society is generally based on a liberal-democratic, capitalist structure. Canada is part of the global capitalist structure. Sport, which is a central feature of Canadian society, has to be understood within this context.

Sport, as with any other area of society, is affected by the changes inherent in capitalism. As discussed in previous chapters, sport has to generate products and services through production and build markets for consumption to sell those goods and services to realize the extra value they contain. Capital must expand by realizing the extra value through favourable market exchange if the economic system is to remain viable. Sport and its nexus with several other industries (e.g., tourism, events, media) point to the ways in which capital investment has grown.

For example, professional sport franchises continue to be part of larger media and entertainment complexes. As Harvey, Law, and Cantelon (2001) note, over 31% of the total professional sport franchises in North America are part of media and entertainment corporations. Here vertical and horizontal integration of different forms of capital (corporations) are merged. Each element of the new, larger integrated organization contributes value to that overall corporate operation.

What does this mean for Canada and Canadians? What does this mean for Canadian cities attempting to become "world class" (see Whitson & Macintosh, 1993)? With the move of the Québec Nordiques to Denver in 1995 and the Winnipeg Jets to Phoenix in 1996, we witnessed the move of Canadian teams to larger population centres in the U.S. Sunbelt—that is, to larger markets, both live and television.

Will this be a scenario to be repeated with, for example, the Calgary Flames and Edmonton Oilers? With salaries escalating and being set in U.S. dollars, with small market reaches and with other limitations on their operations, Canadian teams face this question constantly. This assumes that hockey teams in Vancouver and Montreal (already owned by U.S. interests) and Toronto will retain their NHL franchises because they operate in larger markets. This assumption, however, might not save these franchises. Vancouver lost its NBA team, the Grizzlies, to Memphis in 2001 and Montreal's MLB team, the Expos, is one of two baseball franchises set for contraction of MLB in 2002 or 2003. The four most recent NHL expansion franchises were located in U.S. cities. Finally, it is nearly a decade since a Canadian NHL franchise won the Stanley Cup.

Canadian top-level professional sport is on the edge of chaos. *Globe and Mail* columnist James Christie's 2001 top sport losses included "Joe Fan" in the number one position (Christie, accessed 24/12/01). Will Canadians have only U.S.–based major league teams to cheer for in the future?

With the CFL continuing to experience variable support and ongoing crises, lacrosse and soccer failing to maintain professional leagues, and market conditions unable to support major league franchises, it is likely that Canada will continue as a hinterland or dependent source of athletes and fans. Certainly a large number of Canadian towns and cities are capable of supporting professional, semi-professional, and development-level franchises.

Perhaps a key example of this is major junior hockey. The Canadian Hockey League (CHL) and its three divisions (Western, Ontario, Quebec) continue to provide the majority of new players for the NHL and its farm teams (Canadian Hockey League, accessed 1/23/02), although this is at a falling rate. Of the 65 CHL franchises, 61 are in eight provinces (and four in northwest U.S. cities). This trio of leagues is seen globally as a key pathway to being drafted into the NHL. Not only are Canadian youths seeking places on these teams, but European and U.S. players also migrate to compete in the CHL.

Because of the strength of the CHL and with viable minor league farm teams in other Canadian cities (e.g., Winnipeg, Saint John, St. John's, Halifax, Hamilton), professional hockey will continue to exist. The CFL will continue as a culturally unique sport in localized markets. Baseball will continue to locate development-level franchises in various-sized Canadian cities. Figure skating will continue to enjoy a following although it is clearly within the media and entertainment complex (e.g., International Management Group's Ice Capades). The Canadian Professional Golf Association (CPGA) will continue to hold its tournament season; however, it will struggle for recognition of its Open and other regular events by the USPGA.

Canada is part of the North American market economy, but it cannot compete with the major U.S. media and entertainment corporations for audiences and revenues. Its population continues to be roughly a tenth that of the U.S. Its dollar remains at less than par with the U.S. dollar. As Canada remains a dependent state within the North America system, it will remain in a secondary position in sport production and consumption. However, this is not a negative or bad situation. Bigger is not necessarily better. Whether Canada will retain all or some of its remaining major professional sport leagues is open to debate. If we look back to the 1950s we see that Canada had only two major professional sport franchises, the Toronto Maple Leafs and the Montreal Canadiens. For the moment, Canada has eight major league franchises—five in hockey, two in baseball, and one in basketball. Are Canadians and Canadian sport any better or worse off at this time? It can be argued there is considerable currency in smaller, localized professional sport franchises and leagues.

Smaller franchises and leagues compete in markets comparable to their size. That is, they do not have to compete globally for markets, revenues, and media exposure to exist. In identity building, smaller localized franchises have many positive impacts. The first is in community building. Second is in rivalry with other local, similar franchises. The third is in the effect on local production and consumption patterns. Sport can continue to fulfil its social and cultural role within the local environment.

This notion of local leagues holds importance with regard to spectatorship in another way. More and more major league sport is that of corporate sponsors or of packaged seating that is beyond the reach of most of the middle and working classes to afford. Increasingly, television will allow sport fans to actively participate in "live" events. Even this form of participation is being segmented into packages of channels for sport fans. For example, hockey fans are able to buy a package of games, much as they would have bought a package of games in the arena. Again this is not necessarily a bad thing. People can still watch "live" the sport of their choice through traditional (e.g., television) and newer (e.g., the Internet [see Chapter 10] and digital interactive television) technologies. Further, this might add to the number of fans for live local amateur sport and local leagues.

CONCLUSIONS

As radical change is not likely on the broader level, can radical change occur in smaller ways? Even this is not likely, as conservative forces are able to control the sport agenda. Although sport is mooted to be a social practice that has emancipating and egalitarian potential, those pushing for radical change are not able to mount the necessary resistance and resources. The Olympic movement, with Olympism as its guiding philosophy, is regarded as the epitome of sport. Its games support and promote elite sport, which draws the agenda and resources away from a truly egalitarian structure for sport. Radical sport movements linked historically to workers' movements illustrate this radical type of sport structure; then again, this restructuring remains unrealized (remember that many of these movements were based in societies attempting to operate on socialist principles).

Within most liberal-democratic capitalist states, the future of change is firmly in the control of conservatives and reformists. With sport linked to many values and higher ideals, it seems both ironic and sad that the current situation does not permit these values full expression in the way sport is understood, structured, and provided.

As change is a constant in life we must expect and be ready to deal with it. Clearly a proactive stance is better than a reactive one. Nor can we hope that serendipity will operate. For we wish as humans to make changes that are seen as better and not simply to react to situations that are often imposed on us. We have, in other words, the ability to be volitional. We can work within the current structure of sport or we can become involved in oppositional groups (e.g., the Bread not Circuses coalition in Toronto). Or we can create new futures for sport, through new sport types (e.g., snowboarding, eXtreme sports) or new structures for sport (e.g., eXtreme Games) (Rinehart, 1998).

While for many people sport is a central feature of their lives, it is not a necessary condition, merely a sufficient one. Those studying sport and how sport operates at all levels must realize that the individual problems we encounter will not necessarily be resolved at the structural level or become a structural issue. However, using our imaginations and implementing ideas can make new futures for sport.

A previous text on Canadian sport (Hall, Slack, Smith, & Whitson, 1992) followed the premise of sociologist C. Wright Mills that it is

> *necessary for anyone who wishes to understand the changing nature of sport or any other significant feature of social life to relate the personal troubles of individuals' lived experience to the public issues of social structure.* (p. 236)

For some, sport is a given fact of their life, for others an unobtainable desire. Canada has a vast sport system, but it does not provide opportunities for all or wider success through athletic achievement or simply through opportunities to participate (e.g., the disabled, economically disadvantaged). Why this is so and how it can be changed relate to individual challenges to the assumptions about sport and its enjoyment as a basic social right.

Challenging one's own assumptions of what sport is, how it is structured, its cultural position, the social opportunities it might or should provide, and how it should operate are key to the future of Canadian sport. It is not something or someone out there that determines or is responsible for that future. As indicated in several places throughout this text, each individual has volition and the ability to identify and work toward change.

It is possible to understand this type of change by looking at available statistics and making estimations of the future (toward a conservative change). Others might look at social structures and seek to change the power relations in and resultant from those structures (toward a reform in the structure). Again, others might take a more active role and seek to break down the structures that inhibit, exclude, or operate unequally (through a more radical action). While we collectively struggle to identify who we are as a person, a people, and a nation, sport provides unique and important ideas and outcomes for this activity.

On a daily basis sport provides a basis of social discourse and a daily activity for many of us. While we might not all be directly active in sport, we will likely connect through the mediation of sport. Whatever our involvement, we must critically reflect and morally act to improve our own and others' involvement and enjoyment of sport. That is, we must use critical thinking to follow Mills's (1959) promise.

Critical Thinking Questions

1. Look up the latest data from the StatsCan Web site regarding involvement in sport (comparable to Table 13.2). What do they show? How have sport and sport activity changed (if that is so)? What are the reasons, in your estimation, for these changes? What might happen from the current date to the next data collection?

2. What features of Canadian sport could contribute to maintaining a unique and separate country and culture?

3. How do the figures in Table 13.1 indicate how the various levels of government might ensure the continuation of sport? What special features of sport would be part of that future?

4. Would cyborg sport be marketable? Why? How?

5. In the discussion of structural issues and the future of sport, certain aspects of sport provision were not included (e.g., for disabled people, First Nations people, economically disadvantaged people). Identify the current state of sport for these groups and how we might address the structural issues you have noted.

6. On a piece of paper draw a line down the middle of the page. On the left side list the arguments for future bids by Canadian cities to host Olympic or Olympic Winter Games. On the right side list the negative aspects of such a bid. What action(s) might be taken to decide whether to bid for these games?

7. Debate the idea that hockey is Canada's unique cultural characteristic.

8. In the future, will current new sport forms (e.g., skateboarding, snowboarding, aerial and mogul skiing, mountain-bike trick riding) be attractive to participants, con-

sumers, the media, and the organizers of major games? Or will more traditional sports retain their position?

9. Complete a poll of 20 to 30 students asking them what sports they participate in, what sports they watch live or on television, and which sports they would want to see in the Olympics. Compare the figures you obtain with those presented in the second section of this chapter, those found on television, and those in the Olympic Games and Winter Olympic Games programs. What do the results of this informal poll indicate?

Suggested Readings

Gruneau, R., & Whitson, D. (1993). *Hockey Night in Canada: Sport, identities and cultural politics.* Toronto: Garamond Press.

Macintosh, D., & Whitson, D. (1990). *The game planners: Transforming Canada's sport system.* Montreal & Kingston: McGill-Queen's University Press.

Maguire, J. (1999). *Global sport: Identities, societies, civilizations.* Cambridge: Polity Press.

Wright Mills, C. (1959). *The sociological imagination.* New York: Free Press.

Web Links

The Amateur Athletic Federation of Los Angeles
http://www.aafla.org
A library funded by some of the Los Angeles 1984 Games windfall. A major library and electronic collection of Olympic and sport materials.

Canadian Olympic Committee
http://www.coa.ca
Current and historical information on Canada at the Olympics. Links to other sport and Olympic sites.

The International Olympic Committee
http://www.olympic.org
The site of the "grandparent" of all sport organizations. Has several internal links to different parts of the IOC and links to other elements of the Olympic family. Future games sites are also linked through this site.

Sport Canada
http://www.pch.gc.ca/sportcanada/
Covers the development of sport nationally. Includes links to all national sport governing bodies and other national and international sport sites.

Statistics Canada Web site
http://www.statscan.ca
Contains a number of pages and links with recent studies on the nature of Canada, Canadians, and how they live their lives.

References

Aboriginal Sports/Recreation Association of B.C. (1995). Media Release on the 1997 North American Indigenous Games planned for Victoria, B.C., October.

Adams, A. (1993, January 20). Youngsters leaving hockey at an earlier age, study shows. *The Evening Telegram* (St. John's, Nfld.).

Adler, P., & Adler, P. (1991). *Backboards and blackboards: College athletes and role engulfment*. New York: Columbia University Press.

Aitken, B.W.W. (1993). The emergence of born-again sport. In *Religion and sport* (ed. Prebish, C.). Westport, Conn.: Greenwood Press.

Albom, M. (2000, July 16). Parents often drop ball in youth sports. *Detroit Free Press*.

Allison, M.T. (1988). Breaking boundaries and barriers: Future directions in cross-cultural research. *Leisure Sciences*, 10, 247–59.

American College of Sports Medicine (ACSM). (1994). Position stand: Exercise of patients with coronary heart disease. *Medicine and Science in Sports and Exercise*, 26, i–v.

American Psychiatric Association. (2000). *Diagnostic and statistical manual of mental disorders—* DSM-IV-TR (4th ed., Text Revision). Washington, D.C.: American Psychiatric Press.

Anderson, D., Broom, E., Pooley, J., Rhodes, E., Robertson, D., & Schrodt, B. (1989). *Foundations of Canadian physical education, recreation, and sport studies*. Dubuque, Iowa: Wm. C. Brown.

Anshel, M.H. (1997). *Sport psychology: From theory to practice*. Scottsdale, Ariz.: Gorsuch Scarisbrick.

Armstrong-Doherty, A. (1995). Athletic directors' perceptions of environmental control over interuniversity athletics. *Sociology of Sport Journal*, 12, 75–95.

Association of Universities and Colleges of Canada. (1966). *Physical education and athletics in Canadian universities and colleges*. Ottawa: Canadian Association of Health, Physical Education, and Recreation.

Atkinson, M. (2000). Brother, can you spare a seat? Developing recipes of knowledge in the ticket scalping subculture. *Sociology of Sport Journal*, 17, 151–70.

Atkinson, M. (2002). Fifty million viewers can't be wrong: Professional wrestling, sports entertainment, and mimesis. *Sociology of Sport Journal*, 19, 47–66.

Atlantic Universities Athletic Association. (2002). Profile/history of athletic university sport. [Online]. Available at www.athleticuniversitysport.com/history/mainpage.htm.

Auf der Maur, N. (1976). *The billion-dollar game: Jean Drapeau and the 1976 Olympics*. Toronto: James Lorimer & Company.

Augustine, St. (1961). *Confessions*. Harmondsworth, Middlesex: Penguin Books.

Baillie, P.H.F., & Danish, S.J. (1992). Understanding the career transition of athletes. *The Sport Psychologist*, 6, 77–98.

Bandura, A. (1977) *Agression: A social learning analysis*. Englewood Cliffs, N.J.: Prentice Hall.

Bandura, A., & Walters, R. (1963). *Social learning and personality development*. New York: Holt, Rinehart & Winston.

Barney, R.K. (1993) Golden egg or fools' gold? American Olympic commercialism and the IOC. In International Olympic Academy, *Proceedings: Thirty-third session of the International Olympic Academy*. Olympia, Greece: International Olympic Academy, p. 17.

Barney, R.K. (1996). Prologue: The Ancient Games. In *Historical dictionary of the modern Olympic Movement*. Westport, Conn.: Greenwood Press, pp. xxi–xxxxi.

Baumert, P.W., Henderson, J.M., & Thompson, N.J. (1998). Health risk of adolescent participants in organized sports. *Journal of Adolescent Health*, 22, 460–65.

Bausell, R., Bausell C., & Siegel, D. (1991). *The links among alcohol, drugs and crime on American college campuses: A national followup study.* Towson, Md.: Towson State University.

Beals, K.A., & Manore, M.M. (1998). Nutritional status of female athletes with subclinical eating disorders. *Journal of the American Dietetic Association*, 98, 419–26.

Beamish, R.B. (1975). *Socioeconomic and demographic characteristics of the national executives of selected amateur sports in Canada.* Working papers in the sociological study of sports and leisure. Kingston, Ont.: Sport Studies Research Group.

Beamish, R.B., & Boroway, J. (1988). *Q. What do you do for a living? A. I'm an athlete.* Kingston, Ont.: Sport Studies Research Group.

Becker, H.S. (1963). *Outsiders: Studies in the sociology of deviance.* New York: Free Press.

Beiser, M., Hou, F., Hyman, I., & Tousignant, M. (1998, October). Growing up Canadian — A study of new immigrant children. [Online]. Available at http://www.hrdc-drhc.gc.ca/stratpol/arb/publications/research/abw-98-24e.shtml.

Bellamy, R. (1998). The evolving television sports marketplace. In *MediaSport* (ed. Wenner, L.). London: Routledge, pp. 73–87.

Benedict, J. (1998). *Athletes and acquaintance rape.* Thousand Oaks, Calif.: Sage.

Berger, P., Berger, B., & Kellner, H. (1974). *The homeless mind: Modernization and consciousness.* New York: Vintage Books.

Berkowitz, L. (1969). The frustration-aggression hypothesis revisited. In *Roots of aggression* (ed. Berkowitz, L.). New York: Atherton, pp. 1–29.

Berrett, T., Slack, T., & Whitson, D. (1993). Economics and the pricing of sport and leisure. *Journal of Sport Management*, 7, 199–215.

Best, J.C. (1994). *Report of the core sport commissioner.* Ottawa: Minister of Supply and Services Canada.

Bhabha, H.K. (1994). *The location of culture.* London: Routledge.

Bialeschki, D., & Michener, S. (1994). Re-entering leisure: Transition within the role of motherhood. *Journal of Leisure Research*, 26, 57–74.

Bibby, R. (1995). *The Bibby report: Social trends Canadian style.* Toronto: Stoddart.

Birrell, S., & Richter, D. (1987). Is a diamond forever? Feminist transformations of sport. *Women's Studies International Forum*, 10, 395–410.

Blinde, E. (1989). Unequal exchange and exploitation in college sport: The case of the female athlete. *Arena Review*, 13(2), 110–23.

Blinde, E.M., & Stratta, T.M. (1992). The "sport career death" of college athletes: Involuntary and unanticipated sport retirement. *Journal of Sport Behavior*, 13, 3–20.

Booth, D., & Loy, J. (1999). Sport, status, and style. *Sport History Review*, 30, 1–26.

Borowy, J., & Little, M. (1991). *A time and space just for us.* Toronto: Central Neighbourhood House.

Bourdieu, P. (1984). *Distinction: A social critique of the judgment of taste.* Cambridge: Harvard University Press.

Boyd, M., & Vickers, M. (2000). 100 years of immigration in Canada. *Canadian Social Trends*, Autumn, 2–12.

Boyle, R., & Haynes, R. (2000). *Power play: Sport, the media and popular culture.* Harlow, England: Pearson.

Brackenbridge, C.H. (2001). *Spoilsports: Understanding and preventing sexual exploitation in sport.* London: Routledge.

Brailsford, D. (1969). *Sport and society: Elizabeth to Anne.* London: Routledge and Kegan Paul.

Brewer, B.W. (1993). Self-identity and specific vulnerability to depressed mood. *Journal of Personality*, 61, 343–64.

Brown, D. (1986). Militarism and Canadian private education: Ideal and practise, 1861–1918. *Canadian Journal of History of Sport and Physical Education*, 17, 46–59.

Brundage, A. (1957). Confidential circular letter to IOC members. Lausanne: Reference Number 104, August 28.

Bryant, J.E., & McElroy, M. (1997). *Sociological dynamics of sport and exercise*. Englewood, Colo.: Morton.

Caillois, R. (1961). *Man, play and games*. New York: The Free Press.

Campagnolo, I. (1977). *Toward a national policy on amateur sport*. A Working Paper. Ottawa: Government of Canada.

Campagnolo, I. (1979). *Partners in pursuit of excellence: A national policy on amateur sport*. Ottawa: Minister of Supply and Services Canada.

Canada. (1936). House of Commons debates, February 13.

Canada. (1960). House of Commons debates, November 21.

Canada. (1969). *Report on the task force on sports for Canadians*. Ottawa: The Queen's Printer.

Canada. (1998). *Sport in Canada: Leadership, partnership and accountability—everybody's business*. Standing Committee on Canadian Heritage, Sub-committee on the Study of Sport in Canada. Ottawa: Public Works and Government Services Canada-Publishing.

Canada. (2001). *Towards a Canadian sport policy: Report on the national summit on sport*. Ottawa: The Government of Canada.

Canada Games Council. (1975). *Canada Games handbook: An outline of policies and organizational procedures*. Ottawa: Canada Games Council.

Canadian Association for Health, Physical Education, Recreation, and Dance. (1989). *Quality daily physical education rationale handbook*. Ottawa: Government of Canada Fitness and Amateur Sport.

Canadian Broadcasting Corporation. (1998). *CBC annual report: 1997–1998*. Ottawa: Canadian Broadcasting Corporation.

Canadian Charter of Rights and Freedoms (CCRF). [Online]. Available at http://www.laurentia.com/ccrf/ccrf-prnt.html.

Canadian Fitness and Lifestyle Research Institute (CFLRI). (1999). *1999 physical activity monitor*. [Online]. Available at www.cflri.ca.

Canadian Fitness and Lifestyle Research Institute (CFLRI). (2000). *2000 physical activity monitor*. Ottawa: Canadian Fitness and Lifestyle Research Institute.

Canadian Heritage. (2002). *Sport Canada: The Athlete Assistance Program—AAP Data*. [Online]. Available at www.canadianheritage.gc.ca/Sportcanada/SC.

Canadian Hockey League. (2002). About the CHL. [Online]. Available at www.chl.ca/CHL/about.html.

Canadian Interuniversity Sport (CIS). (2000a). *CIS guideline on athletic awards*. [Online]. Available at www.cisport.ca/awards/awards_criteria.htm.

Canadian Interuniversity Sport (CIS). (2000b). *2000–2001 awards data collection*. [Online]. Available at www.cisport.ca/awards/2000_data.htm.

Canadian Interuniversity Sport (CIS). (2002). *Historical snapshot*. [Online]. Available at www.cisport.ca/about/history/htm.

Canadian Intramural Recreation Association (CIRA). (2002). *Organizational profile and overview*. [Online]. Available at www.intramurals.ca/cira/overview.html.

Canadian Teachers' Federation. (1990). *A capella: A report on the realities, concerns, expectations and barriers experienced by adolescent women in Canada*. Ottawa: Canadian Teachers' Federation.

Cantelon, H. (1981). Ideal-typical models of sport: The USSR and the Canadian adaptation. *Proceedings: National Association for Physical Education in Higher Education*. Champaign, Ill.: Human Kinetics Publishers.

Cantelon, H. (1984). The Canadian absence from the XXIInd Olympiad: Some plausible explanations. In *Sport and international understanding* (ed. Ilmarinen, M.). Berlin: Springer-Verlag.

Capitol Hill Hearing Testimony. (1999, December 15). Retrieved March 1, 2000, from Federal Document Clearing House, Inc. via Lexus-Nexus database.

Carr, C.N., Kennedy, S.R., & Dimick, K.M. (1996). Alcohol use among high school athletes. *The Prevention Researcher*, 3, 1–3.

Chad, K.E., Humbert, M.L., & Jackson, P.L. (1999). The effectiveness of the Canadian Quality Daily Physical Education Program on school physical education. *Research Quarterly for Exercise and Sport*, 70, 55–64.

Charbonneau, L. (2002, February). Universities give $2.4 million in student athlete awards. *University Affairs*, 32.

Chartrand, J.M., & Lent, R.W. (1987). Sports counseling: Enhancing the development of the student-athlete. *Journal of Counseling and Development*, 66, 164–67.

Chelladurai, P., & Danylchuk, K.E. (1984). Operative goals of intercollegiate athletics: Perceptions of athletic administrators. *Canadian Journal of Applied Sports Sciences*, 9, 33–41.

Christie, J. (2001). Past year say its share of losers. *Globe and Mail*. [Online]. Available at www.globeandmail.com.

Coakley, J.J. (2001). *Sport in society: Issues and controversies* (7th ed.). New York: McGraw-Hill.

Coates, D., & Humphreys, B.R. (forthcoming). The effect of professional sports on earnings and employment in the services and retail sectors in U.S. cities. *Regional Science and Urban Economics*.

Cole, C. (1994). Resisting the canon: Feminist cultural studies, sport, and technologies of the body. In *Women, Sport, and Culture* (eds. Cole, C., & Birrell, S.). Champaign-Urbana, Ill.: Human Kinetics.

Collier, K. (1997). *After the welfare state*. Vancouver: New Star Books.

Conley, C. (1999). The agreeable recreation of fighting. *Journal of Social History*, 33, 57–72.

Cosentino, F. (1975). A history of the concept of professionalism in Canadian sport. *Canadian Journal of History of Sport and Physical Education*, 6(2), 75–81.

Cosentino, F. (1988). Physical education in Canada. In *A history of physical education* (Cosentino, F., Dinning, M., Jones, K., & Malszecki, G.). Toronto: Captus Press, pp. 227–58.

Cosentino, F. (1998). *Afros, Aboriginals and amateur sport in pre World War One Canada*. Canada's Ethnic Group Series, Booklet No. 26. Ottawa: The Canadian Historical Society.

Costas, B. (2000). *Fair ball: A fan's case for baseball*. New York: Broadway Books.

Cox, A.E. (1985). Sport in Canada, 1868–1900. In *History of sport in Canada* (eds. Howell, R.A., & Howell, M.L.). Champaign, Ill.: Stipes Publishing Company, pp. 105–64.

Cragg, S., Cameron, C., Craig, C.L., & Russell, S. (1999, November). *Canada's children and youth: A physical activity profile*. Ottawa: Canadian Fitness and Lifestyle Research Insitute publication.

Crossett, T. (1999). Male athletes' violence against women: a critical assessment of the athletic affiliation, violence against women debate. *Quest*, 51, 244–57.

Curtis, J., & McTeer, W. (1990). Sport involvement and academic attainment in university: Two studies in the Canadian case. In *Psychology and sociology of sport: Current selected research* (Vol. 2) (eds. Vander Velden, L., & Humphrey, J.H.). New York: AMS Press, pp. 177–92.

Curtis, J., McTeer, W., & White, P. (1999). Exploring effects of school sport experiences on sport participation in later life. *Sociology of Sport Journal*, 16, 348–65.

Curtis, J.E., & Birch, J.S. (1987). Size of community of origin and recruitment to professional and Olympic hockey in North America. *Sociology of Sport Journal*, 4, 229–44.

Dagg, A., & Thompson, P. (1987). *MisEducation*. Toronto: Ontario Institute for Studies in Education Press.

Danish, S.J., & Nellen, V.C. (1997). New roles for sport psychologists: Teaching life skills through sport to at risk youth. *Quest*, 49, 100–13.

Danish, S.J., Owens, S.S., Green, S.L., & Brunelle, J.P. (1997). Building bridges for disengagement: The transition process for individuals and teams. *Journal of Applied Sport Psychology*, 9, 154–67.

Danylchuk, K. E. (1995). Academic performance of intercollegiate athletes at a Canadian university: Comparisons by gender, type of sport and affiliated faculty. *Avante*, 1, 78–93.

Davis, C. (1999). Eating disorders, physical activity, and sport: Biological, psychological, and sociological factors. In *Sport and Gender in Canada* (eds. White, P., & Young, K.). Don Mills, Ont.: Oxford University Press, pp. 85–106.

Deacon, B. (2001). Physical education curriculum review report. British Columbia Ministry of Education, Curriculum Branch, November. [Online]. Available at www.bced.gov.bc.ca/irp/reports/pereport.pdf.

Deacon, J. (1997, January 20). Darkening the hockey dream. *Maclean's*, p. 54.

Deacon, J. (2001, March 26). Rink rage. *Maclean's*, March 26, pp. 21–24.

Delattre, E. (1975). Some reflections on success and failure in competitive athletics. *Journal of the Philosophy of Sport*, 2, 133–39.

Denis, C. (1997). *We are not you: First Nations and Canadian modernity*. Peterborough, Ont.: Broadview Press.

Department for Culture, Media and Sport. (2000). *A sporting future for all*. London: Government Publishing House.

Department of National Health and Welfare. (1969). *Report of the task force on sports for Canadians*. Ottawa, Ont.: The Queen's Printer for Ontario.

Dickerson, M.G. (1984). *Compulsive gamblers*. London: Longman.

Dollard, J., Doob, L., Miller, N., Mowrer, O., & Sears, R. (1939). *Frustration and aggression*. New Haven: Yale University Press.

Donnelly, P. (1999). Who's fair game? Sport, sexual harassment, and abuse. In *Sport and Gender in Canada* (eds. White, P., & Young, K.). Toronto: Oxford University Press, pp. 107–28.

Dubin, C.L. (1990). Commission of inquiry into the use of drugs and banned practices intended to increase athletic performance. Ottawa: Minister of Supply and Services Canada.

Dunn, R., & Stevenson, C.L. (1998). The paradox of the church hockey league. *International Review for the Sociology of Sport*, 33, 131–42.

Dunning, E. (1999). *Sport matters: Sociological studies of sport, violence and civilization*. London: Routledge.

Dunning, E., & Sheard, K. (1979). *Barbarians, gentlemen, and players: A sociological study of the development of rugby football*. Oxford: Martin Robertson.

Ebaugh, H.R.F. (1988). *Becoming an ex: The process of role exit*. Chicago: University of Chicago Press.

The Economist. (1998, June 6). Superhuman heroes, p. 10.

Eitzen, D.S. (1996). Classism in sport: The powerless bear the burden. *Journal of Sport & Social Issues*, 20, 95–105.

Eitzen, D.S., & Sage, G.H. (2003). *Sociology of North American sport* (7th ed.). Toronto: McGraw-Hill.

Elias, N., & Dunning, E. (1986). *The quest for excitement: Sport and leisure in the civilizing process*. Oxford: B. Blackwell.

Ewing, B.T. (1998). High school athletes and marijuana use. *Journal of Drug Education*, 28, 147–58.

Fejgin, N. (1994). Participation in high-school competitive sports: A subversion of school mission or contribution to academic goals? *Sociology of Sport Journal*, 11, 211–30.

Figler, S.K., & Whitaker, G. (1991). *Sport and play in American life*. Dubuque, Iowa: Wm. C. Brown.

Firth, C.E. (1968). *Macaulay's history of England*. Volume 1. New York: AMS Press.

Fischler, S. (1991). *Bad boys: The legends of hockey's toughest, meanest, most-feared players*. Whitby: McGraw-Hill Ryerson.

Fisher, S.F., & Wise, D. (1974). *Canada's sporting heroes: Their lives and times*. Don Mills, Ont.: General Publishing Company Limited, p. 24.

Flake, C. (1992). The spirit of winning: Sport and the total man. In *Sport and religion* (ed. Hoffman, S.J.). Champaign, Ill.: Human Kinetics, pp. 161–76.

Floyd, M. F. (1998). Getting beyond marginality and ethnicity: The challenge for race and ethnic studies in leisure research. *Journal of Leisure Research*, 30, 3–22.

Fort, R. (2000). Revenue disparity and competitive balance in Major League Baseball. Statement for the Senate Subcommittee on Antitrust, November 17.

Fraleigh, W. (1982). Why the good foul is not good. *Journal of Physical Education, Recreation, and Dance*, 52, 41–42.

Freysinger, V. J. (1995). The dialectics of leisure and development for women and men in midlife: An interpretive study. *Journal of Leisure Research*, 27, 61–84.

Frideres, J.S. (1988). Racism. *The Canadian encyclopedia* (2nd ed., vol. III). Edmonton: Hurtig Publishers, 1816.

Ganley, T., & Sherman, C. (2000, February). Exercise and children's health. *Physician and Sportsmedicine* 28(2). [Online]. Available at www.physicianandsportsmedicine.com.

Gear, J.L. (1973). Factors influencing the development of government sponsored physical fitness programmes in Canada from 1850 to 1972. *Canadian Journal of History of Sport and Physical Education*, 4(12), 1–25.

Gibbons, S. L., & Van Gyn, G. H. (1996). It's more complex than coed vs. non coed: The British Columbia project on gender equitable coed physical education. *CAHPERD Journal*, 62, 4–10.

Gibbons, S. L., Wharf-Higgins, J., Gaul, C. A., & Van Gyn, G. H. (1999). Listening to female students in high school physical education. *Avante*, 5, 1–20.

Gibbons, S.L., Van Gyn, G.H., Wharf-Higgins, J., & Gaul, C.A. (2000). Girls' participation in physical education. *CAHPERD Journal*, 66, 26–32.

Glaser, D. (1974). The classification of offenses and offenders. In *Handbook of Criminology* (ed. Glaser, D.). Chicago: Rand McNally, pp. 45–84.

Glazer, N. (1970). Ethnic groups in America: From national culture to ideology. *Minority responses* (ed. Kurokawa, M.). New York: Random House, pp. 74–86.

Globe and Mail. (1978, August 5). Boxing almost took a knockout blow from Sport Canada with bad management, bad luck and misunderstanding, p. C1.

Gomme, I.M. (1998). *The shadow line: Deviance and crime in Canada* (2nd ed.). Toronto: Harcourt Brace Canada.

Goodhart, P., & Chataway, C. (1968). *War without weapons: The rise of mass sport in the twentieth century and its effect on men and nations*. London: W.H. Allen.

Goodman, C. (1979). *Choosing sides: Playground and street life on the Lower East Side*. New York: Schocker Books.

Gould, D. (1984). Psychosocial development and children's sport. In *Motor development during childhood and adolescence* (ed. Thomas, J.R.). Minneapolis, Minn.: Burgess, pp. 212–36.

Gramann, J.H., & Allison, M.T. (1999). Ethnicity, race and leisure. In *Leisure studies: Prospects for the twenty-first century* (eds. Jackson, E.L., & Burton, T.L.). State College, Pa.: Venture Publishing, pp. 283–97.

Grant, C., & Darley, F. (1993). Reaffirming the coach-athlete relationship: A response from intercollegiate athletics. *The Counseling Psychologist*, 21, 441–44.

Gray, C. (1979, February 10). A day in the life of Iona Campagnolo. *Weekend Magazine*.

Greenberg, J.S., & Pargman, D. (1986). *Physical fitness: A wellness approach*. Englewood Cliffs, N.J.: Prentice-Hall Inc.

Greendorfer, S.L., & Blinde, E.M. (1985). Retirement from intercollegiate sport: Theoretical and empirical consideration. *Sociology of Sport Journal*, 2, 101–10.

Greendorfer, S.L., & Lewko, J. (1978). The role of family members in sport socialization of children. *Research Quarterly*, 49, 146–52.

Grove, J.R., Lavallee, D., & Gordon, S. (1997). Coping with retirement from sport: The influence of athletic identity. *Journal of Applied Sport Psychology*, 9, 191–203.

Gruneau, R. (1982). Sport and the debate on the state. In *Sport, culture, and the modern state* (eds. Cantelon, H., & Gruneau, R.). Toronto: University of Toronto Press, pp. 2–38.

Gruneau, R. (1988). Modernization or hegemony: Two views on sport and social development. In *Not just a game: Essays in Canadian sport sociology* (eds. Harvey, J., & Cantelon, H.). Ottawa: University of Ottawa Press, pp. 9–32.

Gruneau, R., & Whitson, D. (1993). *Hockey Night in Canada: Sport, identities and cultural politics*. Toronto: Garamond Press.

Guilianotti, R. (1999). *Football: A sociology of the global game*. Cambridge, England: Polity Press.

Guttmann, A. (1978). *From ritual to record: The nature of modern sports*. New York: Columbia University Press.

Guttmann, A. (1988). *A whole new ball game: An interpretation of American sports*. Chapel Hill, N.C.: University of North Carolina Press.

Hagan, J. (1991). *The disreputable pleasures: Crime and deviance in Canada* (3rd ed.). Toronto: McGraw-Hill Ryerson.

Haines, B. (1999). *CIAU comparative study 1998–1999*. Ottawa: Canadian Intercollegiate Athletics Union.

Haley, B. (1978). *The healthy body and Victorian culture*. Cambridge, Mass.: Harvard University Press.

Hall, A.M., Cullen, D., & Slack, T. (1990). The gender structure of national sport organizations. *Sport Canada occasional papers*, 2(1), December. Ottawa: Government of Canada, Fitness and Amateur Sport.

Hall, A., Slack, T., Smith, G., & Whitson, D. (1991). *Sport in Canadian society*. Toronto: McClelland & Stewart.

Hamilton, M.B. (1995). *The sociology of religion: Theoretical and comparative perspectives*. London: Routledge.

Hardman, K., & Marshall, J. (2000). The state and status of physical education in schools in international context. *European Physical Education Review*, 6, 203–29.

Harvey, J. (2000). What's in a game? In *Taking sport seriously* (ed. Donnelly, P.). Toronto: Thompson Educational Publishing, Inc.

Harvey, J., Law, A., & Cantelon, M. (2001). North American professional team sport franchises ownership patterns and global entertainment conglomerates. *Sociology of Sport Journal*, 18, 435–57.

Hoberman, J. (1992). *Mortal engines: The science of performance and the dehumanization of sport*. New York: Free Press.

Hoffman, S.J. (1992). *Sport and religion*. Champaign, Ill.: Human Kinetics.

Holland, A., & Andre, T. (1994). Athletic participation and the social status of adolescent males and females. *Youth & Society*, 25, 388–407.

Hollands, R., & Gruneau, R.S. (1979). Social class and voluntary action in the administration of Canadian amateur sport. *Working papers in the sociological study of sports and leisure 2*. Kingston, Ont.: Sport Studies Research Group.

Hollingshead, K. (1998). Tourism, hybridity, and ambiguity: The relevance of Bhabha's "third space" cultures. *Journal of Leisure Research*, 30, 121–56.

Holmes, J., & Silverman, E. (1992). *We're here, listen to us*. Ottawa: Canadian Advisory Council on the Status of Women.

Hoover, N.C. (1999). *National survey: Initiation rites and athletics for NCAA sports teams*. [Online]. Available at www.alfred.edu/news/html/hazing_study_99.html.

Hoover, N.C., & Pollard, N.J. (2000). *Initiation rites in American high schools: A national survey*. [Online]. Available at www.alfred.edu/new/html/hazing_study.html.

Howell, C. (2001). *Blood, sweat and cheers: Sport and the making of modern Canada*. Toronto: University of Toronto Press.

Howell, N., & Howell, M.L. (1969). *Sports and games in Canadian life: 1700 to the present*. Toronto: Macmillan of Canada.

Howell, R.A., & Howell, M.L. (1985). Developments prior to 1800. In *History of sport in Canada* (eds. Howell, R.A., & Howell, M.L.). Champaign, Ill.: Stipes Publishing Company Limited, pp. 1–45.

Hughes, R., & Coakley, J. (1991). Positive deviance among athletes: The implications of overconformity to the sport ethic. *Sociology of Sport Journal*, 8, 307–25.

Hughes, T. (1861). *Tom Brown at Oxford*. London: Macmillan.

Hughes, T. (1994). *Tom Brown's Schooldays*. London: Penguin Books.

Humbert. M.L. (1995). On the sidelines: The experiences of young women in physical education classes. *Avante*, 1, 58–77.

Humbert, M. L., & Chad, K. E. (1998). Determining barriers to implementing quality daily physical education. *Journal of the International Council for Health, Physical Education, Recreation, Sport, and Dance*, 34, 12–17.

Hums, M. A., MacLean, J., Richman, J. M., & Pastore, D. L. (1994). Influences on women's intercollegiate sport in the United States and Canada. *Journal of the International Council for Health, Physical Education, Recreation, Sport, and Dance*, 31, 34–37.

Hunter, P.L., & Whitson, D.J. (1992). Women's leisure in a resource industry town: Problems and issues. *Loisir et société/Society and Leisure*, 15, 223–43.

Inglis, S. (1991). Influence in and around interuniversity athletics. *Journal of Sport Management*, 5, 18–33.

International Olympic Committee. (1990). *Media Guide*. Lausanne, Switzerland: International Olympic Committee.

International Olympic Committee. (1999). *Marketing Matters*, 15. Lausanne, Switzerland: International Olympic Committee.

International Olympic Committee. (2002). *Global Television Report: Salt Lake 2002 Olympic Winter Games*. Lausanne, Switzerland: International Olympic Committee.

In the hot seat: Samaranch defends Olympic reforms in House grilling. (1999, December 16). *The Salt Lake Tribune*. Retrieved March 1, 2000, from Lexus-Nexus database.

IOC's Samaranch weathers storm on Capitol Hill. (1999, December 16). *Japan Economic Newswire*. Retrieved March 1, 2000, from Lexus-Nexus database.

Isajiw, W.W., Sev'er, A., & Driedger, L. (1993). Ethnic identity and social mobility: A test of the "drawback model." *Canadian Journal of Sociology*, 18, 177–96.

Iso-Ahola, S. (1999). Motivational foundations of leisure. In *Leisure studies: prospects for the twenty-first century* (eds. Jackson, E.L., & Burton, T.L.). State College, Pa.: Venture Publishing.

Iso-Ahola, S.E., & Crowley, E.D. (1991). Adolescent substance abuse and leisure boredom. *Journal of Leisure Research*, 23, 260–71.

Issari, P.L., & Coombs, R.H. (1998). Women, drug use, and drug testing: The case of the intercollegiate athlete. *Journal of Sport and Social Issues*, 22, 153–69.

Jackson, E.L., Crawford, D.W., & Godbey, G. (1993). Negotiating leisure constraints. *Leisure Sciences*, 15, 1–11.

Jackson, R. (1986). The effect of international sport on Canadian interuniversity athletics. In *The role of interuniversity athletics: A Canadian perspective* (ed. Taylor, A.W.). Ottawa, Ont.: Sports Dynamic, pp. 39–42.

Jackson, S.J. (1994). Gretzky, crisis, and Canadian identity in 1998: Rearticulating the Americanization of culture debate. *Sociology of Sport Journal*, 11, 248–446.

James, C.E. (1995). Negotiating school through sports: African Canadian youth strive for academic success. *Avante*, 1, 20–36.

Jobling, I.F. (1970). *Sport in nineteenth century Canada: The effects of technological changes on its development*. Unpublished doctoral dissertation, University of Alberta, Edmonton.

Johnson, A. (1978). Political economy of sport. *American Behavioral Scientist*, 21, 318–42.

Johnson, J. (2000). *Sport hazing experiences in the context of anti-hazing policies: The case of two southern Ontario universities*. Unpublished master's thesis, University of Toronto, Toronto.

Jones, J.C.H. (1969). The economics of the National Hockey League. *Canadian Journal of Economics*, 2, 1–20.

Jones, J.C.H., & Ferguson, D.G. (1988). Location and survival in the National Hockey League. *Journal of Industrial Economics*, 36, 443–57.

The Journal of Addiction and Mental Health. (1999). The Internet provides gambling opportunities—and solutions. 2(5), November/December.

Joyce, K.M. (1979). Public opinion and the politics of gambling. *Journal of Social Issues*, 35, 144–65.

Kahl, J. (1959). *The American class structure*. New York: Rinehart.

Katz, J. (1988). *Seductions of crime: Moral and sensual attractions of doing evil*. New York: Basic Books.

Keating, R.J. (1999). Sports pork: The costly relationship between major league sports and government. *Policy Analysis*, 339, 1–33.

Kelly, J.R. (ed.). (1993). *Activity and aging*. Newbury Park, Calif.: Sage.

Kendall, D., Murray, J.L., & Linden, R. (2000). *Sociology in our times*. Scarborough, Ont.: Nelson Thomson Learning.

Kenyon, G.S. (1969). Sport involvement: A conceptual go and some consequences thereof. In *Aspects of contemporary sport sociology* (ed. Kenyon, G.S.). Chicago: The Athletic Institute.

Kenyon, G., & McPherson, B. (1973). Becoming involved in physical activity and sport: A process of socialization. In *Physical activity: Human growth and development* (ed. Rarick, G.L.). New York: Academic Press.

Kerr, G. (1996). The role of sport in preparing youth for adulthood. In *Youth in transition: Perspectives on research and policy* (eds. Galway, B., & Hudson, J.). Toronto: Thompson Educational Publishing.

Kerr, G., & Dacyshyn, A. (2000). The retirement experiences of elite, female gymnasts. *Journal of Applied Sport Psychology*, 12, 115–33.

Keyes, M. (1989a). Government involvement in fitness and amateur sport. In *A concise history of sport in Canada* (Morrow, D., Keyes, M., Simpson, W., Cosentino, F., & Lappage, R.). Toronto: Oxford University Press, pp. 325–43.

Keyes, M. (1989b). Sport and technological change. In *A concise history of sport in Canada* (Morrow, D., Keyes, M., Simpson, W., Cosentino, F., & Lappage, R.). Toronto: Oxford University Press, pp. 256–86.

Keyes, M. (1989c). Women and sport. In *A concise history of sport in Canada* (Morrow, D.,

Keyes, M., Simpson, W., Cosentino, F., & Lappage, R.). Toronto: Oxford University Press, pp. 230–55.

Kidd, B. (1970). Canada's "national" sport. In *Close the 49th Parallel etc: The Americanization of Canada* (ed. Lumsden, I.). Toronto: University of Toronto Press, pp. 257–74.

Kidd, B. (1980). *Sport and the Canadian state.* Draft paper presented at the 1980 National Association for P.E. in Higher Education conference, June 5–8.

Kidd, B. (1983). In defence of Tom Longboat. *Canadian Journal of History of Sport,* 14, 34–63.

Kidd, B. (1988). The elite athlete. In *Not just a game: Essays in Canadian sport sociology* (eds. Harvey, J., & Cantelon, H.). Ottawa: University of Ottawa Press.

Kidd, B. (1996). *The struggle for Canadian sport.* Toronto: University of Toronto Press.

Kidd, B. (1999). The economic case for physical education. *CAHPERD Journal,* 65, 4–10.

Kidd, B., & Eberts, M. (1982). *Athlete's rights in Canada.* Toronto: Ministry of Tourism and Recreation.

Koukouris, K. (1994). Constructed case studies: Athletes' perspectives of disengaging from organized competitive sport. *Sociology of Sport Journal,* 11, 114–39.

Kremarik, M. (2000, Autumn). A family affair: Children's participation in sports. *Canadian Social Trends,* 20–24.

Ladd, T., & Mathisen, J.A. (1999). *Muscular Christianity: Evangelical Protestants and the development of American sport.* Grand Rapids, Mich.: Baker Books.

Landers, D., & Landers, D. (1978). Socialization via interscholastic athletics: Its effects on delinquency. *Sociology of Education,* 51, 299–303.

Landis, J.R. (1983). *Sociology: Concepts and characteristics.* Belmont, Calif.: Wadsworth.

Lapchick, R.E. (2000). Crime and athletes: New racial stereotypes. *Society,* 37, 14–20.

Lappage, R.S. (1974). *Selected sports and Canadian society.* Unpublished doctoral dissertation, University of Alberta, Edmonton.

Lappage, R.S. (1977). Sport as an expression of western and maritime discontent in Canada between the wars. *Canadian Journal of History of Sport and Physical Education,* 8(1), 50–71.

Lappage, R.S. (1978). British Columbia's contribution to the dominion-provincial youth training program through the provincial-recreation program. *Canadian Journal of History of Sport and Physical Education,* 9(1), 86–92.

Lappage, R.S. (1988). The Kenora Thistles' Stanley Cup trail. *Canadian Journal of History of Sport,* 19(2), 79–100.

Lathrop, A.H., & Murray, N. (1998). A discipline under siege: Who took the physical out of education? *Avante,* 4, 92–100.

Lavoie, M. (1989). Stacking, performance differentials, and salary discrimination in professional ice hockey: A survey of evidence. *Sociology of Sport Journal,* 6, 17–35.

Lavoie, M. (1997). *Avantage numérique: L'argent et la Ligue nationale de hockey.* Hull: Vents d'Ouest.

Lavoie, M. (2003). The entry draft in the National Hockey League: Discrimination, style of play, and team location. *American Journal of Economics and Sociology,* 62.

LeClair, J. (1992). *Winners and losers: Sport and physical activity in the '90s.* Toronto: Thompson Educational Publishing, Inc.

Lenskyj, H. (1988). *Women, sport and physical activity: Research and bibliography.* Ottawa: Minister of State Fitness and Amateur Sport.

Lenskyj, H. (1992a). Unsafe at home base: Women's experiences of sexual harassment in university sport and physical education. *Women in Sport and Physical Activity Journal,* 1(1), 19–34.

Lenskyj, H. (1992b). Sexual harassment: Female athletes' experiences and coaches' responsibilities. *Sports Science Periodical on Research and Technology in Sport,* 12(6), 1–6.

Lenskyj, H. (1993). Running risks: Compulsive exercise and eating disorders. In *Consuming Passions: Feminist counselling approaches to weight preoccupation and eating disorders* (eds. Brown, C., & Jasper, K.). Toronto: Second Story Press, pp. 91–108.

Lenskyj, H. (1994a). Sexuality and femininity in sport contexts: Issues and alternatives. *Journal of Sport and Social Issues*, 18, 356–76.

Lenskyj, H. (1994b). Girl friendly sport and female values. *Women in Sport and Physical Activity Journal*, 3(1), 35–46.

Lenskyj, H. (1997). No fear? Lesbians in sport and physical education. *Women in Sport and Physical Activity Journal*, 6(2), 7–22.

Lenskyj, H. (2000). *Inside the Olympic industry: Power, politics, and activism*. Albany, N.Y.: State University of New York Press.

Leonard, W.M., II (1996). The odds of transiting from one level of sport participant to another. *Sociology of Sport Journal*, 13, 288–99.

Leonard, W.M., II (1998). *A sociological perspective of sport* (3rd ed.). Boston, Me.: Allyn and Bacon.

Levin, R.C., Mitchell, G.J., Volcker, P.A., & Will, G.F. (2000, July). *The report of the independent members of the Commissioner's Blue Ribbon Panel on baseball economics*.

Levine, M.V. (2000). The impact of downtown sports stadiums on urban economies: A comparison of Baltimore and Montreal. *Avante*, 6, 33–51.

Li, P.S. (1990). Race and ethnicity. In *Race and ethnic relations in Canada* (ed. Li, P.S.). Toronto: Oxford University Press, pp. 3–17.

Limbert, J., Crawford, S. M., & McCargar, L. J. (1994). Estimates of the prevalence of obesity in Canadian children. *Obesity Research*, 2, 321–27.

Lindsay, P.L. (1970). The impact of the military garrisons on the development of sport in British North America. *Canadian Journal of History of Sport and Physical Education*, 1, 33–44.

Lindsay, P.L. (1985). The pioneer years prior to confederation. In *History of sport in Canada* (eds. Howell, R.A., & Howell, M.L.). Champaign, Ill.: Stipes Publishing Company, pp. 46–104.

Longley, N. (2000). The underrepresentation of French Canadians on English Canadian NHL teams. *Journal of Sports Economics*, 1, 236–56.

Lorenz, K. (1966). *On aggression*. New York: Harcourt, Brace, & Jovanovich.

Lorimer, R., & McNulty, J. (1996). *Mass communication in Canada* (3rd ed.). Toronto: Oxford University Press.

Luke, M.D. (2000). Physical and health education curriculum: Cross-Canada perspectives. *CAHPERD Journal*, 66, 4–12.

Lumpkin, A., Stoll, S. K., & Beller, J.M. (1994). *Sport ethics: Applications for fair play*. St. Louis, Mo.: Mosby-Year Book, Inc.

Lüschen, G. (2000). Doping in sport as deviant behavior and its social control. In *Handbook of sports studies* (eds. Coakley, J., & Dunning, E.). London: Sage, pp. 461–76.

MacDougall, C., Cooke, R., Owen, N., Willson, K., & Bauman, A. (1997). Relating physical activity to health status, social connections and community facilities. *Australian and New Zealand Journal of Public Health*, 21, 631–37.

Macintosh, D. (1985). Sport and the wider goals of government. *CAHPER Journal*, 51, 23–26.

Macintosh, D. (1990). Interschool sport programs in Canada. *CAHPER Journal*, 56, 36–40.

Macintosh, D., Bedecki, T., & Franks, C.E.S. (1987). *Sport and politics in Canada: Federal government involvement since 1961*. Montreal & Kingston: McGill-Queen's University Press.

Macintosh, D., & Whitson, D. (1990). *The game planners: Transforming Canada's sport system*. Montreal & Kingston: McGill-Queen's University Press.

Macpherson, C.B. (1965). *The real world of democracy*. Toronto: Hunter Rose Company.

Maguire, J. (1999). *Global sport: Identities, societies, civilizations*. Cambridge: Polity Press.

Maitland, F. W. (1906). *The life and letters of Leslie Stephen*. London: Duckworth and Co.

Majors, R. (1990). Cool pose: Black masculinity and sports. In *Sport, men, and the gender order: Critical feminist perspectives* (eds. Messner, M., & Sabo, D.). Champaign, Ill.: Human Kinetics Press, pp. 109–14.

Malinowski, B. (1927). *Coral gardens and their magic*. London: Routledge and Kegan Paul.

Malloy, D.C., Ross, S., & Zakus, D.H. (2000). *Sport ethics: Concepts and cases in sport and recreation*. Toronto: Thompson Educational Publishing, Inc.

Mandigo, J.L. (2001). *The globalisation of the Active Schools concept* [10 pages]. [Online]. Available at www.ophea.net/farticles.cfm.

Mannell, R.C. (1999). Leisure experience and satisfaction. In *Leisure studies: Prospects for the twenty-first century* (eds. Jackson, E.L., & Burton, T.L.). State College, Pa.: Venture Publishing.

Marcia, J.E. (1993). The ego identity status approach to ego identity. In *Ego identity: A handbook for psychosocial research* (eds. Marcia, J.E., Waterman, A.S., Matteson, D.R., Archer, S.L., & Orlofsky, J.L.). New York: Springer-Verlag, pp. 3–21.

Marcotte, G. (1997). The future of physical education: A time for commitment. *CAHPERD Journal*, 63, 9–11.

Marshall, G. (ed.). (1994). *The concise Oxford dictionary of sociology*. Oxford: Oxford University Press.

Martens, F.L. (1985). Academic achievement of intercollegiate athletes in physical education at the University of Victoria. *CAHPER Journal*, 51, 14–22.

Martindale, D. (1962). *Social life and cultural change*. New York: D. Van Nostrand.

Marx, K., & Engels, F. (1976). *The German ideology*. Moscow: Progress Publishers.

Mathews, A.W. (1974). *Athletics in Canadian Universities*. Ottawa: The Association of Universities and Colleges in Canada.

McCallum, J. (1992). Green cars, black cats and lady luck. In *Sport and religion* (ed. Hoffman, S.J.). Champaign, Ill.: Human Kinetics, pp. 203–11.

McElroy, M. (1983). Parent-child relations and orientations toward sport. *Sex roles: A Journal of Research*, 9, 997–1004.

McGowan, E., & Rail, G. (1996). Up the creek without a paddle: Canadian women sprint racing canoeists' retirement from international sport. *Avante*, 2, 118–36.

McNeal, R. (1995). Extracurricular activities and high-school dropouts. *Sociology of Education*, 68, 62–81.

McQuail, D. (1994). *Mass communication theory: An introduction* (3rd ed.). Thousand Oaks, Calif.: Sage.

McTeer, W., & Curtis, J. (1999). Intercollegiate sport involvement and academic achievement: A follow-up study. *Avante*, 5, 39–55.

Melnick, M., Sabo, D., & Vanfossen, B. (1992a). Educational effects of interscholastic athletic participation on African-American and Hispanic youth. *Adolescence*, 27, 295–308.

Melnick, M., Sabo, D., & Vanfossen, B. (1992b). Educational effects of interscholastic athletic participation on social, educational, and career mobility of Hispanic girls and boys. *International Review for Sociology of Sport*, 27, 57–75.

Messner, M. (1990). When bodies are weapons: Masculinity and violence in sport. *International Review for the Sociology of Sport*, 25, 203–18.

Metcalfe, A. (1978). Working class physical recreation in Montreal, 1860–1895. *Working papers in the sociological study of sports and leisure*. Kingston, Ont.: Sport Studies Research Group.

Metcalfe, A. (1987). *Canada learns to play: The emergence of organized sport, 1807–1914*. Toronto: McClelland and Stewart Limited.

Miliband, R. (1973). *The state in capitalist society: The analysis of the western system of power*. London: Quartet Books.

Miller, P.S., & Johnson, J. (1998). *Handbook on orientation and transition for students at the University of Toronto*. Toronto: Faculty of Physical Education and Health, University of Toronto.

Miller, P.S., & Kerr, G.A. (2002). The athletic, academic and social experiences of intercollegiate student-athletes. *Journal of Sport Behavior*, 25, 346–67.

Miller, P.S., & Kerr, G.A. (in press). The role of experimentation of intercollegiate student-athletes. *The Sport Psychologist*.

Mills, C. Wright. (1959). *The Sociological Imagination*. New York: Free Press.

Mills, D. (1998). Sport in Canada: Everybody's business. Standing Committee on Canadian Heritage, Subcommittee on the Study of Sport in Canada.

Mills Report (1998). *Sport in Canada: Leadership, partnership and accountability*. Ottawa: Sub-Committee on the Study of Sport in Canada, Government of Canada.

Minister Responsible for Fitness and Amateur Sport. (1982). *Draft document: Guide to the Athlete Assistance Program*. Published by authority of the Minister.

Ministry of Education. (2001). *Report of the Minister's Advisory Group on the provision of co-instructional activities*. Ottawa: The Queen's Printer for Ontario.

Miracle, A.W., Jr., & Rees, C.R. (1994). *Lessons of the locker room: The myth of school sports*. Amherst, N.Y.: Prometheus Books.

Morgan, C. (1995). In search of the phantom misnamed honour: Duelling in Upper Canada. *The Canadian Historical Review*, 76, 529–62.

Moriarty, D., & Moriarty, M. (1986). Sport/fitness programs and sociocultural influences in eating disorders. *CAHPER Journal*, 53(4), 4–9.

Moriarty, D., & Holman-Prpich, M. (1987). Canadian interuniversity athletics: A model and method for analyzing conflict and change. *Journal of Sport Management*, 1, 57–73.

Morrow, D. (1987). Sweetheart sport: Barbara Ann Scott and the post World War II image of the female athlete in Canada. *Canadian Journal of History of Sport*, 18(1), 36–54.

Morrow, D. (1989). Montreal: The cradle of organized sport. In *A concise history of sport in Canada* (Morrow, D., Keyes, M., Simpson, W., Cosentino, F., & Lappage, R.). Toronto: Oxford University Press, pp. 1–22.

Morrow, D., Keyes, M., Simpson, W., Cosentino, F., & Lappage, R. (1989). *A concise history of sport in Canada*. Toronto: Oxford University Press.

Mullick, R. (2002, February). CFL legends. The official site of the Canadian Football League, [Online]. Available at www.cfl.ca/CFLLegends/home.html.

Munro, J. (1969). Speech prepared for delivery to the Canadian Amateur Sports Federation. Ottawa: Skyline Hotel, January 18.

Munro, J. (1971). *Sport Canada Recreation Canada*. Presented to the National Advisory Council on Fitness and Amateur Sport. May 7.

Murphy, G.M., Petitpas, A.J., & Brewer, B.W. (1996). Identity foreclosure, athletic identity, and career maturity in intercollegiate athletes. *The Sport Psychologist*, 10, 239–46.

Murphy, P., Williams, J., & Dunning, E. (1990). *Football on trial: Spectator violence and development in the world of football*. London: Routledge.

Nack, W., & Yaeger, D. (1999, September 13). Who's coaching your kid? The frightening truth about child molestation in youth sports. *Sports Illustrated*, 39–53.

National Coaching Certification Program, Coaching Theory I Manual. (1988). Gloucester, Ont.: Coaching Association of Canada.

Naughton, J. (1996). Alcohol abuse by athletes poses big problems for colleges. *Chronicle of Higher Education*, 43, A47–A48.

Nelson, M.B. (1991). *Are we winning yet? How women are changing sports and sports are changing women*. New York: Random House.

Nelson, M.B. (1994). *The stronger women get, the more men love football: Sexism and the American culture of sports*. New York: Harcourt Brace.

Nixon, H. L., & Frey, J.H. (1996). *A sociology of sport*. Belmont, Calif.: Wadsworth.

Offe, C. (1990). *Contradictions of the welfare state*. J. Keane, ed. Cambridge: The MIT Press.

Offord, D., Lipman, E., & Duku, E. (1998). *Sports, the arts, and community programs: Rates and correlates of participation*. Ottawa: Human Resources Development.

Okihiro, N. R. (1984). Extracurricular participation, educational destinies and early job outcomes. In *Sport and the sociological imagination* (eds. Theberge, N., & Donnelly, P.). Fort Worth, Tex.: Texas Christian University Press, pp. 334–49.

Ontario University Athletics (OUA) (2001). The Constitution and By-Laws Ontario University Athletics in the Canadian Interuniversity Athletic Union.

Ontario University Athletics (OUA) (2002). *OUA history*. [Online]. Available at www.oua.org/html/other_pages/other_pages/members_information/history.html

Orwell, G. (1958). The sporting spirit. In *George Orwell: Selected writings* (ed. Bott, G.). London: Heinemann Educational Books, Ltd.

Ouellet, J. G. (1986). The role of athletics in a Quebec university. In *The role of interuniversity athletics: A Canadian perspective* (ed. Taylor, A.W.). Ottawa: Sports Dynamic, pp. 29–32.

Pal, L. (1992). *Public policy analysis: An introduction*. (2nd ed.). Scarborough: Nelson Canada.

Pan, D.W., & Baker, J.A. (1998). Perceptual mapping of banned substances in athletics: Gender- and sport-defined differences. *Journal of Sport and Social Issues*, 22, 170–82.

Paraschak, V. (1997). Variations in race relations: Sporting events for Native peoples in Canada. *Sociology of Sport Journal*, 14, 1–21.

Pearson, R.E., & Petitpas, A. (1990). Transitions of athletes: Developmental and preventive perspectives. *Journal of Counseling and Development*, 69, 7–10.

Pearton, R. (1986). Violence in sport and the special case of soccer hooliganism in the United Kingdom. In *Sport and Social Theory* (eds. Rees, R., & Miracle, A.). Champaign, Ill.: Human Kinetics, pp. 67–84.

Pedlar, A. (1996). Community development: What does it mean for recreation and leisure. *Journal of Applied Recreation Research*, 21, 5–23.

People for Education, (2001). *The 2001 tracking report*. [Online]. Available at www.peoplefor education.com.

Physical activity promotion and school physical education. (1999, September). *Research Digest*, 3. [Online]. Available at www.fitness.gov.

Pound, R. W. (2000). What Happens When It Goes Wrong?: Notes on the IOC's Trial Under Fire, 1998–1999. In *Bridging three centuries: Intellectual crossroads and the modern Olympic movement* (eds. Wamsley, K.B., et al.). London, Ont.: International Centre for Olympic Studies, The University of Western Ontario.

Pronger, B. (1993, January 25). Push 'em back. *University of Toronto Bulletin*, 20.

Psycho-physiological contributions of physical activity and sports for girls. (1998, March). *Research Digest*, 3. Available at www.fitness.gov.

Rappaport, J., & Wilkerson, C. (2001). What are the benefits of hosting a major league sports franchise? *Economic Review of the Federal Reserve Bank of Kansas City*, 55–86.

Rayner, M. (1998, July 16). CIAU faces split over scholarships. *Western News*.

Regan, G.A. (1981). *A challenge to the nation: Fitness and amateur sport in the 80's*. Ottawa: Minister of Supply and Services Canada.

Reid, D.G. (1995). *Work and leisure in the 21st century: From production to citizenship.* Toronto: Wall and Emerson, Inc.

Rice, C., & Russell, V. (1995). EmBodying equity. *Our Schools Our Selves*, September, 14–36; December, 32–54.

Rinehart, R. E. (1998). *Players all: Performances in contemporary sport*. Bloomington, Ind.: Indiana University Press.

Robinson, L. (1998). *Crossing the line: Sexual harassment and abuse in Canada's national sport.* Toronto: McClelland and Stewart.

Rogge, J. (2002). Olympic Marketing Structure. Lausanne, Switzerland: International Olympic Committee. [Online]. Available at http://www.olympic.org/uk/organisation/facts/introduction/.

Rojek, C. (2000). *Leisure and culture.* New York: Palgrave.

Rowe, D. (1999). *Sport, culture and the media.* Buckingham, England: Open University Press.

Sabo, D., Melnick, M., & Vanfossen, B. (1993). High school athletic participation and postsecondary educational and occupational mobility: A focus on race and gender. *Sociology of Sport Journal*, 10, 44–56.

Sage, G.H. (1990). *Power and ideology in American sport* (2nd ed.). Champaign, Ill.: Human Kinetics.

Sage, G.H. (1997). Physical education, sociology, and sociology of sport: Points of intersection. *Sociology of Sport Journal*, 14, 317–39.

Samaranch sparkles in Washington. (1999, December 16). *Los Angeles Times*. Retrieved March 1, 2000, Lexus-Nexus database.

Samaranch unruffled by charges in Congress. (1999, December 16). *The Globe and Mail.*

Schaefler, C., & Kaduson, H. (1994). *The quotable play therapist*. Northvale, N.J.: Jason Aronson Inc.

Scheff, T.J. (1984). *Being mentally ill: A sociological theory* (2nd ed.). New York: Aldine.

Schlossberg, N. (1981). A model for analyzing human adaptation to transition. *The Counseling Psychologist*, 9, 2–18.

Schneider, V. E. (1997). Interuniversity athletics: Separation from physical education. *Avante*, 3, 88–97.

Schor, J.B. (1992). *The overworked American: The unexpected decline of leisure.* New York: Basic Books.

Schrodt, B. (1983). Changes in the governance of amateur sport in Canada. *Canadian Journal of History of Sport*, 14(1), 1–20.

Schwartz, M. (2000). Alberta's Ever Active Schools program. *Runner*, 38, 6–7.

Scott, R. (1987). *Jackie Robinson: Baseball great.* New York: Chelsea House Publishers.

Semotiuk, D.M. (1986). Internal factors affecting elite sport in Canadian universities. In *The role of interuniversity athletics: A Canadian perspective* (ed. Taylor, A.W.). Ottawa: Sports Dynamic, pp. 59–76.

Shaw, S.M. (1992). Dereifying family leisure: An examination of women's and men's everyday experiences and perceptions of family time. *Leisure Sciences*, 14, 271–86.

Shaw, S.M. (1997). Controversies and contradictions in family leisure: An analysis of conflicting paradigms. *Journal of Leisure Research*, 29, 98–112.

Shilling, C. (1993). *The body and social theory.* London: Sage.

Siedentop, D. (1994). *Introduction to physical education, fitness and sport* (2nd ed.). Mountain View, Calif.: Mayfield.

Sinclair, D.A., & Orlick, T. (1995). Positive transitions from high-performance sport. *The Sport Psychologist*, 7, 138–50.

Smith, M.D. (1983). *Violence and sport.* Toronto: Butterworths.

Spence, C. (1999). *The skin I'm in: Racism, sports and education.* Halifax: Fernwood.

Spence, J., Mandigo, J., Poon, P., & Mummery, W. (2001). A survey of physical education enrolment at the secondary level in Alberta. *Avante*, 7, 97–106.

Spence, J.C., & Gauvin, L. (1996). Drug and alcohol use by Canadian athletes. *Journal of Drug Education*, 26, 275–87.

Sport Canada. (1994). Sport Participation in Canada by Statistics Canada for Sport Canada—1994 [1992 Report Highlights]. Ottawa: Sport Canada. [Online]. Available at http://www.pch.gc.ca/progs/sc/pubs/status_e.cfm.

Sport Canada. (1998). *Sport Participation in Canada: 1998 Report*. Report prepared by Statistics Canada for Sport Canada. Ottawa: Minister of Public Works and Government Services Canada.

Sport Canada. (2002). *Sport Canada: Athlete Assistance Program Policies, Procedures and Guidelines.*: [Online]. Available at www.canadianheritage.gc.ca/Sportcanada/SC.

Spreitzer, E. (1994). Does participation in interscholastic athletics affect adult development? A longitudinal analysis of an 18–24 age cohort. *Youth & Society*, 25, 368–87.

Statistics Canada. (1994). Sport Participation in Canada: Highlights. [Online]. Available at http://www.pch.gc.ca/Sportcanada/sc_e/statU.S.html.

Statistics Canada. (1994–95). National health survey.

Statistics Canada. (1998). General social survey.

Statistics Canada. (2002a). Canadian Statistics: Population. [Online]. Available at http://www.statcan.ca/english/Pgdb/popula.htm#pop/.

Statistics Canada. (2002b). Population by ethnic origin, 1996 Census. [Online]. Available at http://www.statcan.ca/english/Pgdb/People/Population/demo28a.htm.

Stebbins, R.A. (1993). *Canadian football: The view from the helmet*. Toronto: Canadian Scholars Press.

Stebbins, R.A. (1996). *Tolerable differences: Living with deviance* (2nd ed.). Toronto: McGraw-Hill Ryerson.

Stephens, T., & Craig, C. (1990). *The well-being of Canadians*. Ottawa: CFLRI.

Stevenson, C.L. (1991). The Christian-athlete: An interactionist-developmental analysis. *Sociology of Sport Journal*, 8, 362–79.

Stevenson, C.L. (1997). Christian athletes and the culture of elite sport: Dilemmas and solutions. *Sociology of Sport Journal*, 14, 241–62.

Stodolska, M., & Jackson, E.L. (1998). Discrimination in leisure and work experienced by a white ethnic minority group. *Journal of Leisure Research*, 30, 23–46.

Stuck, M.F. (1988). Beliefs and behaviors—sport and clean living. *Arena Review*, 12, May 113–24.

Summerfield, L. (1990). Promoting physical activity and exercise among children. ERIC Clearinghouse on Teaching and Teacher Education ED328556.

Swain, D.A. (1991). Withdrawal from Sports and Schlossberg's model of transitions. *Sociology of Sport Journal*, 8 152–60.

Taylor, A.W. (1986). The role of interuniversity athletics: A Canadian perspective. Ottawa: Sports Dynamic.

Team Marketing Report. (1998). *A guide to inside the ownership of professional sports teams*. Chicago: TMR.

Teeple, G. (1995). *Globalization and the decline of social reform*. Toronto: Garamond Press.

The Sports Network (TSN). (1991). *Hockey, a white man's game?*

Thelin, J.R. (1994). *Games colleges play: Scandal and reform in intercollegiate athletics*. Baltimore: Johns Hopkins Press.

Thompson, J.B. (1997). *Media scandals: Morality and desire in the popular culture marketplace*. New York: Columbia University Press.

Tirone, S. (1999–2000). Racism, indifference, and the leisure experience of South Asian Canadian teens. *Leisure/Loisir*, 24, 89–114.

Tirone, S., & Pedlar, A. (2000). Understanding the leisure experiences of a minority ethnic group: South Asian teens and young adults in Canada. *Loisir et société/Society and Leisure* 23, 145–69.

Tirone, S. C., & Shaw, S.M. (1997). At the center of their lives: Indo Canadian women, their families and leisure. *Journal of Leisure Research*, 29, 225–44.

Todd, T. (1987). Anabolic steroids: The gremlins of sport. *Journal of Sport History*, 14, 87–107.

Tremaine Drahota, J.A., & Eitzen, D.S. (1995). The role exit of professional athletes. *Sociology of Sport Journal*, 15, 263–78.

Tremblay, M.S., Inman, J.W., & Willms, J.D. (2000). The relationship between physical activity, self-esteem, and academic achievement in 12-year-old children. *Pediatric Exercise Science*, 12, 312–23.

Tricker, R., & Connolly, D. (1997). Drugs and the college athlete: An analysis of the attitudes of student athletes at risk. *Journal of Drug Education*, 27, 105–19.

Vertinsky, P., Batth, I., & Naidu, M. (1996). Racism in motion: Physical activity and the Indo-Canadian female. *Avante*, 2(3), 1–23.

Wagner, P. (1976). Puritan attitudes towards physical recreation in 17th century New England. *Journal of Sport History*, 3, 139–51.

Walker, M.B. (1992). *The psychology of gambling*. New York: Pergamon.

Wamsley, K.B. (1999). The public importance of men and the importance of public men: Sport and masculinities in nineteenth century Canada. In *Sport and Gender in Canada* (eds. White, P., & Young, K.). New York: Oxford University Press, pp. 24–39.

Wamsley, K.B., &. Kossuth, R. (2001). Fighting it out in nineteenth century Upper Canada/Canada West: Masculinities and physical challenges in the tavern. *Journal of Sport History*, 27, 405–30.

Wamsley, K.B., & Whitson, D. (1998). Celebrating violent masculinities: The boxing death of Luther McCarty. *Journal of Sport History*, 25, 419–31.

Warshaw, R. (1988). *I never called it rape*. New York: Harper and Row.

Washburn, R. (1978). Black under-participation in wildland recreation: Alternative explanations. *Leisure Sciences*, 1, 175–89.

Wearing, B. (1998). *Leisure and feminist theory*. London: Sage.

Webb, W.M., Nasco, S.A., Riley, S., & Headrick, B. (1998). Athletic identity and reactions to retirement from sports. *Journal of Sport Behavior*, 21, 338–62.

Weber, M. (1978). *Economy and society: An outline of interpretative sociology*. In two volumes. G. Roth & C. Wittich, eds. Berkeley, Calif.: University of California Press.

Wechsler, H., et al. (1997). Binge drinking, tobacco, and illicit drug use and involvement in college athletics. *Journal of American College Health*, 45, 195–200.

Welk, G.J. (1999). The youth physical activity promotion model: A conceptual bridge between theory and practice. *Quest*, 5, 5–23.

Wells, C. (1996, March). Physical activity and women's health. *Research Digest* 2, [Online]. Available at www.fitness.gov.

Wenner, L.A., ed. (1998). *MediaSport*. London: Routledge.

West, C., & Zimmerman, D. (1991). Doing gender. In *The social construction of gender* (eds. Lorber, J., & Farrell, S.). London: Sage, pp. 13–37.

West, J.T. (1973). Physical fitness, sport and the federal government 1909 to 1954.

Canadian Journal of History of Sport and Physical Education, 4(2), 26–42.

Whelan, R., & Rosentraub, M.S. (1997). Sports and economic development north of the border: Baseball subsidies with a Canadian flavor and a French accent. In *Major League losers* (ed. Rosentraub, S.). New York: Basic Books, pp. 321–76.

White, P., & Young, K., eds. (1999). *Sport and gender in Canada*. Don Mills, Ont.: Oxford University Press.

White, P.G., & Curtis, J.E. (1990). Participation in competitive sport among anglophones and francophones in Canada: Testing competing hypotheses. *International Review for the Sociology of Sport*, 25, 125–42.

Whitson, D. (1998). Circuits of promotion: Media, marketing and the globalization of sport. In MediaSport (ed., Wenner, L.A.). London: Routledge.

Whitson, D., & Macintosh, D. (1993). Becoming a world-class city: Hallmark events and sport franchises in the growth strategies of western Canadian cities. *Sociology of Sport Journal*, 10, 221–40.

Whitson, D., Harvey, J., & Lavoie, M. (2001). The Mills report, the Manley subsidy proposals, and the business of the major-league sport. *Canadian Public Administration*, 43, 127–56.

Wickberg, E.B. (1988). Chinese. *The Canadian Encyclopedia* (2nd ed., vol. I). Edmonton: Hurtig Publishers, 415–17.

Willis, J. D., & Wettan, R. G. (1977). Religion in sport in America: The case for the sports bay in the Cathedral Church of St. John the Divine. *Journal of Sports History*, 4, 189–207.

Wilson, B. (1999). "Cool pose" incorporated: The marketing of black masculinity in Canadian NBA coverage. In *Sport and gender in Canada* (eds. White, P., & Young, K.). Don Mills, Ont.: Oxford University Press, pp. 232–53.

Winick, C. (1991). A paradigm to clarify the life cycle of changing attitudes toward deviant behavior. In *Perspectives on deviance: Dominance, degradation and denigration* (eds. Kelly, R.J., & MacNamara, D.E.J.). Cincinnati, Ohio: Anderson, pp. 1–14.

Womack, M. (1992). Why athletes need ritual: A study of magic among professional athletes. In *Sport and religion* (ed. Hoffman, S.J.). Champaign, Ill.: Human Kinetics, pp. 191–202.

Wuest, D. A., & Bucher, C.A. (1995). *Foundations of physical education and sport* (12th ed.). St. Louis, Mo.: Mosby.

Yates, A., Shisslak, C., & Crago, M. (1994). Overcommitment to sport: Is there a relationship to the eating disorders? *Clinical Journal of Sport Medicine*, 4, 39–46.

Young, K. (1991). Sport and collective violence. *Exercise and Sport Science Review*, 19, 539–87.

Young, K. (1993). Violence, risk, and liability in male sports culture. *Sociology of Sport Journal*, 10, 373–96.

Young, K., & Wamsley, K.B. (1996). State complicity in sports assault and the gender order in twentieth century Canada: Preliminary observations. *Avante*, 2, 51–69.

Young, K., & White, P. (1995). Sport, physical danger and injury: The experiences of elite women athletes. *Journal of Sport and Social Issues*, 19, 45–61.

Young, K., White, P., & McTeer, W. (1994). Body talk: Male athletes reflect on sport, injury, and pain. *Sociology of Sport Journal*, 11, 175–94.

Zakus, D.H. (1988). A preliminary examination of the dialectical change in "modern" sport and of the intervention of the Canadian state in sport between 1968 and 1988. Unpublished doctoral dissertation, University of Alberta.

Zimbalist, A. (2002). Competitive balance in sports leagues: An introduction. *Journal of Sports Economics*, 3, 111–21.

Index